William Houston

Documents illustrative of the Canadian Constitution

William Houston

Documents illustrative of the Canadian Constitution

ISBN/EAN: 9783337207380

Printed in Europe, USA, Canada, Australia, Japan

Cover: Foto ©Suzi / pixelio.de

More available books at **www.hansebooks.com**

DOCUMENTS

ILLUSTRATIVE OF THE

CANADIAN CONSTITUTION.

EDITED WITH

NOTES AND APPENDIXES.

BY

WILLIAM HOUSTON, M.A.,

LIBRARIAN TO THE ONTARIO LEGISLATURE.

TORONTO:
CARSWELL & CO., LAW PUBLISHERS.
1891.

PRINTED BY
THOS. MOORE & CO., LAW PRINTERS
22 & 24 ADELAIDE ST. EAST
TORONTO.

PREFACE.

THIS volume is the result of an attempt to bring together in a single collection the documents which contain the constitution of the Dominion of Canada and illustrate its historical development. A much larger number of documents might legitimately have been included under this description, but the line had to be drawn somewhere, and I have chosen to draw it between those that are of international and imperial origin on the one hand, and those that have resulted from the exercise of colonial autonomy on the other. Any apparent violations of this principle of classification have been dictated by considerations of convenience which are too obvious to call for specific mention. Many documents that are either not imperial or not constitutional have been added in the form of appendixes to the text. It is hoped that they will prove to be not the least useful part of the collection.

Where the material to choose from is abundant and the space is limited there will always be differences of opinion as to what should properly be included. While I have received much valuable advice on this point from eminent statesmen and publicists, I feel bound to say, in justice alike to them and myself, that the plan of the work is essentially my own. My belief that the true line of development of the Canadian constitution takes us back, not to the French *regime* in Canada, but to the colonial governments of what is now the United States is sufficient to account for the absence of all French documents, except the articles of capitulation of Quebec and Montreal. If space had permitted I would gladly have inserted as appendixes some of the constitutional documents of the British colonies; I have been forced to content myself with the United States constitution, on which, as regards federal form, our own is avowedly modelled.

I have made no attempt to interpret the documents here collected. Mine was the humbler but infinitely more useful task, to see that the texts were as correct as possible, and to give in the form of notes such historical information and references as would tend to lighten the labours of the student without supplying him with ready-made opinions. Alike in selection and annotation I have had primarily in view the needs of students of political and legal science in universities and law schools, and the chief aim of the collection—to give them a chance to think for themselves—would have been defeated if I had impertinently undertaken to think for them and give them the results.

Gratitude for valuable aid and counsel requires that I should mention the names of those who have been specially helpful to me. Easily first must be placed Dr. Bourinot, Mr. Douglas Brymner, and Mr. William Kingsford, each of whom has in his own way usefully illustrated Canadian history. To Thomas Hodgins, Q.C., Æmilius Irving, Q.C., and Hon. David Mills, Q.C., I am indebted for hints which lessened greatly the labor of research. To Mr. Francis Parkman of Boston, and Mr. Justin Winsor of Harvard University, my thanks are due for prompt responses to requests for information on historically doubtful points. Mr. James Bain of the Toronto free library, Mr. J. P. Macdonnell of the Ontario Civil Service, Mr. David Boyle of the Canadian Institute, J. M. McEvoy, B.A. of the University of Toronto, and A. F. Chamberlain, M.A., of Clarke University, have all taken a warm personal interest in the progress of the work and rendered practical and valuable assistance in its preparation.

WM. HOUSTON.

Toronto, March 31st, 1891.

TABLE OF CONTENTS.

	PAGE.
INTRODUCTION	VII
CHRONOLOGICAL INDEX	XVIII
TREATY OF UTRECHT, 1713	3
REPRESENTATIVE INSTITUTIONS IN THE MARITIME PROVINCES	7
Nova Scotia—	
1. Settlement of Halifax	7
2. Commission to Governor Cornwallis	9
3. Letter from Governor Lawrence to Lords of Trade	16
4. Letter from Lords of Trade to Governor Lawrence	17
5. Opinion of Crown Law Officers	17
6. Constitution of Legislative Assembly	18
7. Letter from Lords of Trade to Governor Lawrence	21
Prince Edward Island—	
Commission to Governor Paterson	21
New Brunswick—	
Commission to Governor Carleton	22
CAPITULATION OF QUEBEC	26
CAPITULATION OF MONTREAL	32
TREATY OF PARIS, 1763	61
ROYAL PROCLAMATION, 1763	67
COMMISSION TO GOVERNOR MURRAY	74
LORD MANSFIELD'S JUDGMENT IN CAMPBELL v. HALL	79
QUEBEC ACT, 1774	90
Quebec Revenue Act, 1774	97
Quebec Revenue Act, 1775	102
Colonial Tax Repeal Act, 1778	104
Canadian Revenue Control Act	106
CONSTITUTIONAL ACT, 1791	112
Constitutional Act Amendment Act, 1830	134
Constitutional Act Suspension Act, 1838	136
Indemnity Act, 1838	140
Suspension Act Amendment Act, 1839	142
UNION ACT, 1840	149
Union Act Amendment Act, 1848 (use of French language)	175
Union Act Amendment Act, 1854 (Elective Legislative Council)	177
Union Act Amendment Act, 1859 (Speaker of " ")	180
CONFEDERATION ACT (British North America Act, 1867)	186
(British North America Act, 1871)	225
(Parliament of Canada Act, 1875)	227
(British North America Act, 1886)	229
COLONIAL HABEAS CORPUS ACT, 1862	240
COLONIAL LAWS VALIDITY ACT, 1865	241

TABLE OF CONTENTS.

	PAGE.
GOVERNOR-GENERALS' COMMISSIONS AND ROYAL INSTRUCTIONS	245
Commission to Lord Monck	245
Instructions to Lord Monck	248
Letters Patent Constituting the office of Governor-General	253
Instructions to Governors	256
Commission to Lord Lorne	258
TREATIES RELATING TO CANADA	265
Treaty of Ryswick, 1697	265
Treaty of Utrecht, 1713	3
Treaty of Aix-la-Chappelle, 1748	265
Treaty of Paris, 1763	61
Treaty of Versailles, 1783	266
Treaty of Paris, 1783	267
CANADIAN BOUNDARIES	271
Boundaries of Nova Scotia	271
Boundaries of New Brunswick	272
Boundaries of Quebec and Ontario	273
Boundaries of Manitoba	277
Boundaries of British Columbia	278
Boundaries of the North-West Territories	279
Boundaries of the Dominion of Canada	280
EXTRADITION	282
Jay Treaty, London, 1794	282
Ashburton Treaty, Washington, 1842	283
FISHERIES	284
1. *Stipulations with France*	284
Treaty of Utrecht, 1713	3
Treaty of Paris, 1763	61
Treaty of Versailles, 1783	266, 284
Treaty of Paris, 1814	285
2. *Stipulations with United States*	285
Treaty of Paris, 1783	268
Convention of London, 1818	285
Treaty of Washington, 1854	286
Treaty of Washington, 1871	287
3. *Stipulations with Russia*	288
ENGLISH LAW INTRODUCED INTO UPPER CANADA	290
TRIAL BY JURY INTRODUCED INTO UPPER CANADA	292
RESPONSIBLE GOVERNMENT	293
Lord Durham's report, 1839	293
Russell's Despatches, 1839	299
Legislative Assembly resolutions, 1841	303
QUEBEC CONFERENCE RESOLUTIONS, 1864	305
CONSTITUTION OF THE UNITED STATES OF AMERICA	317
GENERAL INDEX	334

INTRODUCTION.

THE purpose of this introduction is to explain briefly the author's views on the teaching of history in general and of Canadian constitutional history in particular. They may be summed up in the statement that while *ex cathedra* lectures are an antiquated and ineffective method of dealing with any subject in the class-room, they are particularly out of place in the academic treatment of history. It is of course important that the student should have a wide acquaintance with historical facts, and that he should have well-defined opinions as to the general principles that underlie and explain them ; but in so far as the educative value of the subject is concerned, the manner in which he acquires his knowledge and arrives at his opinions is of far greater importance than the knowledge and the opinions themselves. Facts that are simply memorized and principles that are simply appropriated, whether from text books read or lectures heard, count for little in real education ; facts that are discovered by patient research and principles that are reasoned out from the facts, serve a really useful educative purpose.

History is one of the inductive sciences, and it should be dealt with on the inductive method. The student should be required to collect facts for himself by the investigation of such sources as may be available, instead of learning them by rote from treatises or lectures, and he should be encouraged and required to form and express his own opinions, instead of adopting those formulated for his instruction by the historian or the lecturer. His collection of historical facts will undoubtedly be meagre and his opinions will probably be wrong, but this is no more than can with the most perfect truth be said of every one who either writes a text-book or delivers a lecture. The difference is one of degree only, and fortunately the question of more or less is of little consequence educationally, provided that the student's acquaintance with the subject is the result of his own honest endeavor to get at the truth, not of his asssimilation of the opinions of other people. The degree of culture that results from the academical use of history is determined, not by the fact that knowledge of a certain kind has been acquired, but by the fact that knowledge of some kind has been acquired in a certain way.

The truth of these statements will become more evident if it be borne in mind that the mass of historical facts is a shifting quicksand. Every now and then some new writer—a Gardiner, a Freeman, or a Stubbs—re-explores the old familiar ground, unearths a number of facts that cannot be rejected or ignored, and erects on the enlarged basis a modified inductive superstructure. It would be absurd to suppose that the last word on the subjects of which they treat has been said even by them. History is not only, from the pedagogical point of view at least, a science but it is one of the most progressive of the sciences, and any method of academical treatment that does not put the student in possession of a method of investigation, and at the same time tend to free him from prejudices and preconceptions, is worse than useless for purposes of culture.

Fortunately some progress has been made in this direction by the introduction of the "seminary method" into universities and colleges, and history has benefitted more from the change than almost any other subject. In all progressive American institutions the seminary is rapidly superseding the lecture, and the latter retains a foothold only in places which do not come under this description. In a very short time such academical performances as "lectures," in the sense of formal *ex cathedra* deliverances of professorial opinions will be unknown, and the consummation of the change cannot take place too soon. In the lecture-room the teacher works after a fashion, and the students are supposed to absorb the erudition that has been carefully stored up and is now poured forth for their benefit;

in the seminary the student works under the direction of the teacher, who saves him time in his search for facts but carefully abstains from any attempt to control his reason. It is easy to understand the nature of the change effected in the academical atmosphere by the substitution of the seminary for the lecture method. The result is nothing less than the substitution of intellectual life for intellectual death. It has been so wherever the change has taken place; it will be so everywhere else when the change does take place.

The great merit of the seminary is that it facilitates the use of the inductive method, which the lecture system absolutely precludes. Induction is a species of reasoning, and the lecturer cannot teach by reasoning for his students and telling them his conclusions. They must do their own reasoning, draw their own inferences, discover their own principles, establish their own laws. They may do this erroneously, but they must do it if they are to derive any intellectual training from the academical use of history, and especially of political history. Mere soundness of opinion is fortunately of less importance, where no one can be absolutely and indisputably right, than are open-mindedness, freedom from prejudice, and the habit of closely observing phenomena and reasoning from them.

"History is past politics and politics present history," says Mr. Freeman, and this is but another way of saying that past and present states of political society throw light upon each other. Usually history is taught as if the past served in this respect the more important purpose of the two. The student is asked to begin at the beginning and come down through a series of more or less arbitrarily selected events and institutions until he makes the acquaintance of the state of society which is his own environment, if indeed he is allowed to come so near. It is easy to see how such a view of historical method should have been universally acted upon at a time when method claimed little attention and received less; it is difficult to understand why it is still generally practised at a time when the study of methods is occupying the attention of the foremost intellects of the day. It is perhaps too much to expect the present generation of professorial lecturers on history and politics to abandon the only method they know anything about, but it will not be incumbent on their successors to submit to conventional and traditional limitations.

The true method of teaching history, as of teaching other subjects that lend themselves to inductive treatment, is to pass from the known to the unknown, to start from the here and now and travel backward and outward until the entire ground has been covered. The student should begin with the history and the institutions of his own time and his own country, and his knowledge of these will enable him to understand the history and the institutions of other times and of other lands. All valuable knowledge is comparative. One never knows anything thoroughly until he has compared or contrasted it with something else. His progress in real culture is conditioned on a never ending process of differentiation of things that are similar to each other, and of assimilation of things that are different from each other. If the study of the past is helpful to the comprehension of the present much more is the study of the present helpful to the comprehension of the past. The reason is obvious. It is extremely difficult to form a clear or useful conception of what is distant either in time or in place; it is comparatively easy to form a clear conception of what is within the range of every day experience. It would be unreasonable to expect such a conception as a student can form of the Roman comitia to be helpful to him in comprehending the nature of an American town meeting, or such a conception as he can form of an Old English witenagemot to aid him in understanding the functions of a modern parliament; but to comprehend clearly the nature of a town meeting or a parliament will aid him in getting a useful conception of the comitia or witenagemot, and he can make a study of both town meeting and parliament in actual operation.

This view of method in relation to history is especially true of constitutional history, which is substantially a digest of human experience in the development of governmental machinery. It is more limited and more definite than general history, and is, both in its own nature and in the methods applicable to its acamedical use, closely akin to legal science. No subject in a university curriculum is better suited for inductive treatment than constitutional history, and therefore no subject, apart altogether from its intrinsic interest in relation to the advancement of civilization, is more valuable as an educative instrument. The line of causation is usually discernible with a minimum of uncertainty as to the correctness of the results arrived at, and the number of phenomena to be observed, analyzed, and classified as a basis of induction are for the most part not open to reasonable dispute as matters of fact.

To a greater or less extent in every country the history of the constitution is to be traced by means of documents, the correct interpretation of which is, in relation to the subject and for other reasons, a matter of the greatest importance. Usually the student is deprived of the valuable training afforded by the practice of hermeneutics, because he is expected to learn the meaning of a document either from a text-book writer's gloss or from a lecturer's interpretation. That both writer and lecturer may be wrong in their opinions is the least regrettable feature of this system, because, fortunately, neither gloss nor interpretation is likely to be long remembered after the examination in preparation for which they have been "crammed" by the student; infinitely more mischievous is the waste of time and opportunity which might have been utilized in enabling him to master a method that would have made him ever afterwards independent of text-books and lecturers by placing him on a par with both. If their opinions are right he should be put in possession not of them but of the way to arrive at them by his own unaided efforts; if they are wrong he has at least a chance of avoiding some errors which he must on the ordinary plan imbibe, if it be but for a time. The same remarks apply *mutatis mutandis* to the generalization of constitutional principles from those events that come under the name of precedents. Acquaintance with certain facts must be made by reference to narratives, but their relation to each other as antecedents and consequents, if not as causes and effects, must be established by an exercise of reason. The reasoning in this case must be the student's own if he is to benefit educationally by the time given to the subject, and he must reason from consequent to antecedent, if a premium is not to be put on the mere exercise of memory.

It is interesting to note that in some respects the constitutional history of Canada is better adapted for academical use than the constitutional history of either England or the United States, which is equivalent to saying that it surpasses in that respect the constitutional history of any other country wheresoever. The constitutional history of the United States is too largely a written history; that of England is too largely an unwritten one. In the one country precedent counts for too little in the interest of speculation; in the other it counts for too much in the interest of definiteness. The history of the Canadian constitution involves a great deal of documentary interpretation, but it involves also a great deal of generalization from recorded instances. The constitution at present bears a strong resemblance in form to that of the United States, and it would have been surprising if it had not done so, in view of the fact that it was avowedly modelled upon it; but it bears an equally strong, though less easily discerned, similarity in its mode of operation to that of England, through the adoption from the latter of the constitutional device known as "responsible government." For purposes of inductive treatment, therefore, it possesses most of the merits of each, being at the same time comparatively free from the defects of either, while the colonial position of Canada is from the academical point of view an advantage rather than otherwise. At every stage of Canadian history the ultimate political sovereignty has been, as it now is, vested in the British Parliament, and constitutional complications, at once caused and resolved by the gradual tendency towards colonial autonomy, impart to the subject an interest that is quite unique in the whole range of comparative constitutional history.

A similarly unique interest attaches to the study of jurisprudence and of international law in connection with Canadian history. In the Province of Quebec ever since the passage of the Quebec Act in 1774 French law has been the recognized rule of decision in all matters of controversy relating to property and civil rights, and the codification of French law in Quebec followed its codification in France. On the other hand the common law of England is the rule of decision in all the other Canadian Provinces, and therefore it is quite possible for a Canadian student to take up the study of either the common or the civil law as a living system without going beyond the boundaries of his own country, and to study them inductively in comparison or contrast with each other. As the State of Louisiana has a civil code, while all the other States of the Union have the common law, the student in the United States has a similar privilege, but in a less convenient field. Canada as a quasi-autonomous country enjoys quasi international relations, and is saddled with quasi international responsibilities, but of formal relation or formal responsibility she has none. She is allowed a real voice in the making of treaties with the United States, and is permitted and expected to supplement them with legislation when legislation is necessary; but on the other hand her representatives in international negotiations are formally appointed by the British Government, and if the Canadian Parliament were to refuse the necessary confirmatory legislation the British Parliament could in any case, and probably would in some cases, enact it.

It is unnecessary to describe at any length the manner in which the following documents may be most advantageously used. All that need be attempted is to lay down a few general propositions, in the application of which there will be room for an infinite variety of pedagogical devices. No two teachers will ever deal with them in precisely the same way; no progressive teacher will ever deal with them in precisely the same way with successive classes. These general propositions, with the reasons on which they are founded, may be thus briefly stated:—

1. The first document taken up should be the British North America Act of 1867, which is the present constitution of Canada. It should be studied with a view to ascertaining its

textual meaning, determining its legal validity, and comprehending its political working. It is a matter of minor importance in what order these various lines of inquiry are prosecuted, but the order here stated is not without certain obvious advantages. The Act abounds in technical terms, and failure to catch their precise meaning must needs leave an obscure impression of the import of the statute as a whole. As examples of terms that stand in need of elucidation may be cited such expressions as "Privy Council," "Executive Council," "privileges" and "immunities" of Parliament, "seised," "freehold," "free and common soccage," "franc-alleu," "in roture," "allegiance," "Royal assent," "disallow," "royalties." To appreciate clearly the force of these and analogous expressions is not all that is necessary to the comprehension of the text, but it is at least a good first step towards it. The legal validity of the document is due to the fact that it is the Act of a sovereign Parliament, but it is an Act that embodies a compact between the federating Provinces. Its legal effect must be determined by judicial decisions, but in the reasoning on which those decisions are based some account must be taken of the intentions of the parties to the federation. Already a long line of judicial findings has laid the foundation of an interesting and important constitutional jurisprudence for Canada. The political working of the constitution is a wide subject, but one that cannot be evaded. All who know anything about it can understand that the student of the mere letter, however thorough and expert, may go out into public or professional life loaded up with the most absurd misconceptions. Nothing is said in the British North America Act, for instance, about the responsibility of the Governor-General's cabinet, or of its solidarity, and yet these are among its most important features. Not much is said, except what is now misleading, as to the manner of electing the House of Commons. The financial relations of the Provinces to the Dominion have been extensively changed since the Act was passed. The fiscal system has been modified, either slightly or radically, over and over again. These are only a few of the matters which come under the head of "political working," but they will serve to give some idea of the comprehensiveness of the phrase. In connection with both the textual meaning and the political working of the Act the commissions and instructions issued to the Governor-General should be read, indeed must be read, in order to get a clear idea of either the one or the other, and closely connected with the subject of the legal validity of the constitution is the Act of 1865, which states the grounds on which the validity or invalidity of colonial legislation must be determined. It is needless to say that the Imperial Acts of 1871, 1875, and 1886, supplementary to the Act of 1867, must now be read with it, just as if they were part of its text.

2. The British North America Act should be compared or contrasted with other constitutional documents, to which it is more or less closely related either formally or historically. Pre-eminent among these is, of course, the constitution of the United States. The analytical comparison between them, should, without being too minute in detail, be so carefully made as to enable the student to grasp the essential differences between the constitutions of the two countries, not merely as a matter of textual interpretation but also in their respective political operations. These differences have been frequently and accurately described, but they must none the less be thought out by each generation of students for themselves; and this can be done only as the result of a careful analytical comparison. The " Quebec Resolutions " of 1864, which embody the agreement originally entered into by the various parties to the Canadian Confederation, should receive a certain amount of attention in this connection. More important, however, are the Imperial enactments which chronologically precede the British North America Act of 1867, and each of which was in turn the Canadian Constitution—the Union Act of 1840, the Constitutional Act of 1791, the Quebec Act of 1774, and the Royal Proclamation of 1763. These have a relation to the present constitution that is not merely historical; the nature of that relation can be ascertained only by the comparative method, and the comparison should be made by each student for himself.

In the last analysis some part of what he should discover may escape him, but he ought not on that account to be deprived of the chance to try what he can do.

3. These constitutional documents should be taken up in the inverse chronological order. The comparison should be one of consequent with antecedent for the purpose of ascertaining the causal relation between them. It is easy to dogmatise in history by alleging that a certain condition precedent is sufficient to account for a certain other condition which succeeds it, the cause being studied before the effect; the safer and better way is to acquaint oneself with the condition that is the effect, and then proceed to search for some previous condition that will suffice to explain it. The former course puts a premium on dogmatism and memorization; the latter encourages reasoning and research. It is needless to say that these documents should be studied in their relation to each other, as well as their relation to the British North America Act. They are the milestones of constitutional progress, and the nature of the intervals between them must be clearly made out by him who would read them aright.

4. The documents which precede the Royal Proclamation are all constitutionally important—the Treaty of Paris as containing the precise definition of the concessions made by the British to the French Government when Canada passed finally under British dominion; the Articles of Capitulation as the chronological background of the treaty stipulations; and the documents relating to the establishment of parliamentary government in Nova Scotia, Prince Edward Island, and New Brunswick, whose representative institutions have enjoyed a continuous existence ever since.

5. Finally the class work should be done on the seminary plan. Anything of the nature of a lecture is hopelessly out of place. That nondescript kind of intercourse between teacher and taught which is connoted by the term "socratic method" is the ideal to be attained. The teacher, as conductor of the seminary exercises, should be nothing more than the first amongst equals. The relationship between him and his students

should be such as would obtain among a band of searchers after truth, each of the others having as good a right as he has to believe and maintain that he has discovered it. Written exercises should form a constant feature of class work, and these exercises should in turn become subjects of class discussion. Only by frequent applications of the test of committing views to paper can the rate or the character of the progress made be accurately ascertained. The assumption that a single written examination at the end of a course is a fair or useful criterion of a student's attainments is as untenable as the assumption that mere accumulations of knowledge, without any reference to the manner in which it has been acquired, have any real educational value. The single terminal examination has outlived whatever usefulness it ever had, and it must shortly follow, if it does not precede, the *ex cathedra* lecture into academical oblivion.

CHRONOLOGICAL TABLE.

	1492.	First voyage of Columbus.
	1497.	Cabot discovered Newfoundland.
First voyage of Jacques Cartier....	1534.	
Second voyage of Jacques Cartier..	1535.	
Third voyage of Jacques Cartier...	1541.	
	1542.	De Soto discovers the Mississippi.
	1564.	French Settlement in Florida.
Gilbert in Newfoundland..........	1583.	
	1584.	Raleigh's first voyage (Virginia).
	1606.	London and Plymouth charter.
	1607.	Jamestown (Virginia), founded.
Quebec founded by De Champlain..	1608.	
Fourth voyage of De Champlain...	1610.	Discovery of Hudson River.
Fifth voyage of De Champlain ...	1611.	Discovery of Hudson Bay.
Sixth voyage of De Champlain, and ascent of the Ottawa..........	1613.	
	1614.	New Amsterdam founded.
De Champlain at the Georgian Bay	1615.	
	1619.	First Legislative Assembly in America (Virginia).
Tenth voyage of De Champlain...	1620.	Landing of "Pilgrims" at Cape Cod and at Plymouth.
Nova Scotia granted to Sir William Alexander by James I.........	1621.	Dutch West India Company.
	1623.	New Hampshire settled.
"One Hundred Associates,".......	1627.	
Quebec taken by Sir David Kirke..	1629.	Massachusetts charter.
	1630.	First General Court of Massachusetts.
Canada and Acadia restored to France by the Treaty of St. Germain-en-Laye	1632.	Maryland granted to Calvert.
Twelfth voyage of De Champlain (first "Governor" of Canada)..	1633.	
Death of De Champlain..........	1635.	First Assembly of Maryland.
De Montmagny Governor	1636.	Roger Williams in Providence.
	1636.	Harvard College founded.
	1639.	First written Constitution in America adopted by Connecticut, and first General Court of the Province.

* The events recorded in the left hand column belong to the history of what is now British America; those in the right hand column belong for the most part to the history of what is now the United States.

CHRONOLOGICAL TABLE.

Settlement of Montreal	1642.	Charter granted to Rhode Island.
	1643.	New England Confederacy.
D'Ailleboust, Governor of Canada.	1648.	Treaty of Westphalia.
De Lauson, Governor	1651.	
	1652.	Maine annexed to Massachusetts,
D'Argenson, Governor	1658.	Indian war at Esopus.
Bishop Laval at Quebec	1659.	Quakers hanged in Boston.
D'Avangour, Governor	1660.	Berkeley Governor of Virginia.
Colbert, Prime Minister of France.	1661.	
	1662.	Charter granted to Connecticut.
"Sovereign Council" established with De Mesy as Governor of "New France."	1663.	Rhode Island charter.
Seminary of St. Sulpice acquire Montreal	1663.	
De Tracy Viceroy, and De Courcelles Governor	1664.	New York taken by the British.
West India Company granted Monopoly of Canadian Trade	1664.	Connecticut and New Haven united.
Iroquois country invaded	1666.	
Bay of Quinte Seminary Mission	1668.	First Assembly of New Jersey.
	1669.	First Assembly of North Carolina.
Hudson Bay Company chartered	1670.	Charleston (S. C.) founded.
De Frontenac Governor	1672.	
	1673.	Mississippi discovered by Joliet and Marquette.
Laval Bishop of Quebec	1674.	First Assembly of South Carolina.
De la Salle visits France	1674.	New Netherlands (New York), New Jersey and Delaware ceded to Britain by Holland.
Reduction of tithe to one-twentysixth	1679.	First Assembly of New Hampshire.
Indian Council at Montreal	1680.	De la Salle on the Illinois.
	1682.	Penn founds Pennsylvania.
De la Barre Governor	1682.	De la Salle descends the Mississippi.
	1682.	First Assembly of Pennsylvania.
	1684.	The Mississippi Company established.
De Denonville Governor.	1685.	
Hudson Bay Forts taken	1686.	Andros Governor of Massachusetts.
Departure of Bishop Laval	1688.	N. York annexed to N. England.
Massacre of Lachine	1689.	William III. King of Britain.
De Frontenac Governor	1689.	Andros expelled from Massachusetts.
Quebec attacked by Phips	1690.	N. Hampshire annexed to Massachusetts.
	1697.	Treaty of Ryswick.
Death of De Frontenac	1698.	
De Calieres Governor	1699.	Penn visits America.
Indian Treaty of Peace (Montreal).	1701.	New charter for Pennsylvania.
	1702.	War of Spanish succession.
De Vaudreuil Governor	1703.	
"Superior Council" created	1703.	
Capture of Port Royal (Annapolis).	1710.	Hunter Governor of New York.
Expedition of Walker and Hill against Quebec	1711.	
	1712.	Crozat's Mississippi Charter.
	1713.	Treaty of Utrecht.
Nicholson Governor of Acadia	1714.	George I. King of Great Britain.
Death of Louis XIV	1715.	

CHRONOLOGICAL TABLE.

Phillips Governor of Acadia	1717.	Law's Mississippi Charter.	
	1718.	New Orleans founded.	
Louisburg fortified	1720.	Burnet Governor of New York.	
	1722.	Fort Oswego built by Burnet.	
Armstrong Governor of Acadia	1723.	Paper money in Pennsylvania.	
Fort Niagara rebuilt	1725.		
De Beauharnois Governor of Canada.	1726.		
	1727.	George II. King of Great Britain.	
Newfoundland a British Province	1728.		
	1731.	Crown Point occupied by the French.	
	1732.	Louisiana made a Royal Province.	
	1733.	Georgia Settled.	
Iron forges at Three Rivers	1737.		
Verandrye ascends the Red River.	1738.	N. Jersey separated from N. York.	
Mascarene Governor of Acadia	1740.		
Louisburg captured	1745.		
De la Galissonniere Governor of Canada	1747.		
De la Jonquiere Governor Canada.	1748.	Treaty of Aix-la-Chapelle.	
Halifax founded	1749.	Slaves admitted to Georgia.	
Cornwallis Governor of Acadia	1749.		
Fort Rouillé built at Toronto	1749.	De Celoron's Ohio Expedition.	
Hopson Governor of Acadia	1752.		
Duquesne Governor of Canada	1752.		
Lawrence Governor of Acadia	1753.	Osborn Governor of New York.	
	1754.	First Assembly of Georgia.	
	1754.	Interprovincial Congress at Albany	
Expatriation of the Acadians	1755.	Braddock's Expedition to Fort du Quesne.	
De Vaudreuil Governor of Canada.	1755.	Dieskau defeated at Fort George.	
First Assembly of Nova Scotia	1758.	Abercrombie defeated at Fort Ticonderoga.	
Quebec taken by Wolfe	1759.	Niagara taken by Johnston.	
Montreal taken by Amherst	1760.	George III., King of Great Britain.	
Province of Quebec created	1763.	Treaty of Paris.	
Murray, first Governor of Quebec.	1763.		
	1765.	The Stamp Act passed.	
Carleton Governor of Quebec	1766.	Repeal of the Stamp Act.	
Prince Edward Island made a Province	1769.	Pontiac killed.	
	1769.	Colonial Tax Act passed.	
First Assembly of Prince Edward Island	**1773.**	Destruction of tea at Boston.	
Lord Mansfield's Judgment	1774.	Boston Port closed.	
The Quebec Act passed	**1774.**	First Revolutionary Congress, (Philadelphia.)	
Montgomery and Arnold invade Canada	1775.	Battle of Lexington.	
	1776.	Declaration of Independence.	
	1778.	Articles of Confederation.	
Haldimand Governor of Quebec	1778.	Colonial Tax Act repealed.	
Immigration of U. E. Loyalists	1783.	Treaties of Paris and Versailles.	
New Brunswick made a Province	1784.		
Lord Dorchester Governor of Quebec	1786.	Cotton introduced into Georgia.	
	1787.	Constitution of the United States.	
	1789.	George Washington, President.	
Constitutional Act passed	**1791.**		
First Parliaments of Upper and Lower Canada	1792.	Washington made the capital.	

CHRONOLOGICAL TABLE.

		1794.	The Jay Treaty (London.)
Prescott Governor of Canada		1796.	Washington's retirement.
Second Parliament of Upper Canada (York)		1797.	John Adams, President.
		1801.	Thomas Jefferson, President.
Selkirk's Colony in Prince Edward Island		1803.	Louisiana ceded by France.
Craig Governor of Canada		1806.	Lewis and Clark reach the Pacifi
		1809.	James Madison, President.
Prevost Governor of Canada		1811.	
Selkirk's settlers at Red River		1812.	War declared against Britain.
		1814.	Treaty of Ghent.
Sherbrooke Governor of Canada		1816.	
		1817.	James Monroe, President.
Richmond Governor of Canada		1818.	Convention of London.
		1819.	Florida purchased from Spain.
Dalhousie Governor of Canada		1820.	Maine admitted as a State.
Cape Breton annexed to Nova Scotia		1820.	Missouri compromise.
		1825.	John Quincy Adams, President.
Canada Company formed		1826.	
		1829.	Andrew Jackson, President.
Aylmer Governor of Canada		1830.	First railway in United States.
Revenue Control Act		1831.	
First Assembly in Newfoundland		1832.	
Gosford Governor of Canada		1835.	
		1837.	Victoria Queen of Britain.
Rebellion in Canada		1837.	Martin Van Buren, President.
Lower Canadian Constitution Suspended		1838.	
Durham Governor of British America		1838.	
Sydenham Governor of the Canadas		1839.	
Union Act		**1840.**	
Sydenham Governor of Canada		1841.	William H. Harrison, President.
First Parliament of Canada		1841.	John Tyler, President.
Responsible Government introduced		1842.	
Bagot Governor of Canada		1842.	Ashburton Treaty (Washington.)
Metcalfe Governor of Canada		1843.	
Great fire in Quebec City		1845.	James Knox Polk, President.
Elgin Governor of Canada		1846.	War with Mexico.
		1848.	Treaty with Mexico.
Rebellion losses agitation		1849.	Zachary Taylor, President.
		1850.	Willard Filmore, President.
		1850.	Fugitive Slave Bill.
Gavazzi Riots in Montreal		1853.	Franklin Pierce, President.
Clergy Reserves secularized		1854.	Reciprocity Treaty (Washington.)
Feudal Tenure abolished		1854.	Kansas-Nebraska Bill passed.
Head Governor of Canada		1855.	Kansas riots.
		1857.	James Buchanan, President.
		1857.	"Dred Scott" case.
Canadian Federation mooted		1859.	Harper's Ferry uprising.
The Anderson (fugitive slave) case.		1860.	
Monck Governor of Canada		1861.	War of Secession begun.
		1861.	Abraham Lincoln, President.
Self-Governing Colonies made responsible for their own defence.		1862.	The *Alabama* sails from Liverpool.
Colonial Habeas Corpus Act		1862.	
Quebec Conference		1864.	

Colonial Laws Validity Act	1865.	Andrew Johnson, President.
Fenian Raids	1866.	
Confederation Act	**1867.**	
Lisgar Governor of Canada	1868.	
North-West Territories acquired	1869.	Ulysses S. Grant, President.
Province of Manitoba created	1870.	
British Columbia added to Canada	1871.	Treaty of Washington.
Dufferin Governor of Canada	1872.	
	1877.	Rutherford B. Hayes, President.
Lorne Governor of Canada	1878.	
Canadian Pacific Railway Company organized	1881.	James A Garfield, President.
	1881.	Chester A. Arthur, President.
Lansdowne Governor of Canada	1883.	
North-West Rebellion suppressed	1885.	Grover Cleveland, President.
Stanley Governor of Canada	1888.	
	1889.	Benjamin Harrison, President.

ERRATA.

Page 25, Note 28— For " Appendix M " read " Appendix B, p. 272."

Page 89, Note 13— For " Case of Ireland against England " read " Case of Ireland's being bound by Acts of Parliament in England stated."

Page 183, Note 15— For " pp. 175-176 below " read " pp. 175-176 above."

Pages 235-236— Note 50 should be Note 44, and the numbering of the intermediate notes should be changed so that 44 becomes 45; 45 becomes 46; 46 becomes 47; 47 becomes 48; 48 becomes 49; and 49 becomes 50.

EXTRACTS FROM THE TREATY OF UTRECHT,[1] 1713.

The Treaty of Peace and Friendship between the Most Serene and Most Potent Princess Anne, by the Grace of God, Queen of Great Britain, France, and Ireland, and the Most Serene and Most Potent Prince Lewis the XIVth, the Most Serene and Most Potent Christian King, concluded at Utrecht, the $\frac{31}{1}$ day of $\frac{March,}{April,}$ 1713.[2]

I. That there be an universal peace, and true and sincere friendship, between the most Serene and most Potent Princess Anne, Queen of Great Britain, and the most Serene and most Potent Prince Lewis the XIVth, the most Christian King, and their heirs and successors, as also the kingdoms, states, and subjects of both, as well without as within Europe; . . . . . .

X. The said most Christian King shall restore to the kingdom and Queen of Great Britain, to be possessed in full right for ever, the bay and streights of Hudson,[5] together with all lands, seas, sea-coasts, rivers, and places situate in the said bay and streights, and what belong thereunto, no tracts of land being excepted, which are at present possessed by the subjects of France. All which, as well as any buildings there made, in the condition they now are, and likewise all fortresses there erected, either before or since the French seized the same, shall, within six months from the ratification of the present treaty, or sooner if possible, be well and truly delivered to the British subjects, having commission from the Queen of Great Britain to demand and receive the same, entire and undiminished, together with all the cannon and cannon-ball which are therein, as also with a quantity of powder, if it be there found, in proportion to the cannon-ball, and with the other provision of war usually belonging to cannon. It is, however, provided, that it may be entirely free for the company of Quebec, and all other subjects of the most Christian King whatsoever, to go by land or by sea, whithersoever they please, out of the lands of the said bay, together with all their goods, merchandizes, arms, and effects, of what nature and condition soever, except such things as are above reserved in this article. But it is agreed on both sides, to determine within a year, by commissaries to be forthwith named by each party, the limits which are to be fixed between the said Bay of Hudson and the places appertaining to the French;[4] which limits both the British and French subjects shall be wholly forbid to pass over, or thereby to go to each other by sea or by land. The same commissaries shall also have orders to describe and settle, in like manner, the boundaries between the other British and French colonies in those parts.

XI. The above-mentioned most Christian King shall take care that satisfaction be given, according to the rule of justice and equity, to the English company trading to the Bay of Hudson, for all damages and spoil done to their colonies, ships, persons, and goods, by the hostile incursions and depredations of the French, in time of peace, an estimate being made thereof by commissaries to be named at the requisition of each party. The same commissaries shall moreover inquire as well into the complaints of the British subjects concerning ships taken by the French in time of peace, as also concerning the damages sustained last year in the island called Montserat, and others, as into those things of which the French subjects complain, relating to the capitulation in the island of Nevis, and Castle of Gambia, also to French ships, if perchance any such have been taken by British subjects in time of peace; and in like manner into all disputes of this kind, which shall be found to have arisen between both nations; and due justice shall be done on both sides without delay.

XII. The most Christian King shall take care to have delivered to the Queen of Great Britain, on the same day that the ratification of this treaty shall be exchanged, solemn and authentic letters or instruments, by virtue of which it shall appear that the island of St. Christopher's is to be possessed alone hereafter by British subjects, likewise all Nova Scotia or Acadie, with its ancient boundaries,[5] as also the city of Port Royal, now called Annapolis Royal, and all other things in those parts which depend on the said lands and islands, together with the dominion, propriety, and possession of the said islands, lands, and places, and all right whatsoever, by treaties or by any other way obtained, which the most Christian King, the Crown of France, or any the subjects thereof, have hitherto had to the said islands, lands, and places, and the inhabitants of the same, are yielded and made over to the Queen of Great Britain, and to her Crown, for ever, as the most Christian King doth at present yield and make over all the particulars above said[6]; and that in such ample manner and form that the subjects of the most Christian King shall hereafter be excluded from all kind of fishing in the said seas, bays, and other places, on the coasts of Nova Scotia, that is to say on those which lie towards the east, within 30 leagues, beginning from the island commonly called Sable, inclusively, and thence stretching along toward the south-west.

XIII. The island called Newfoundland, with the adjacent islands, shall from this time forward belong of right wholly to Britain; and to that end the town and fortress of Placentia, and whatever other places in the said island are in the possession of the French, shall be yielded and given up, within seven months from the exchange of the ratifications of this treaty, or sooner, if possible, by the most Christian King, to those who have a commission from the Queen of Great Britain for that purpose. Nor shall the most Christian King, his heirs and successors, or any of their subjects, at any time hereafter, lay claim to any right to the said island and islands, or to any part of it or them. Moreover, it shall not be lawful for the subjects of France to fortify any place in the said island of Newfoundland, or to erect any buildings there, besides stages made of boards, and huts necessary and useful for drying of fish; or to resort to the said island, beyond the time necessary for fishing and drying of fish. But it shall be allowed to the subjects of France to catch fish, and to dry them on land, in that part only, and in no other besides that, of the said island of Newfoundland, which stretches from the place called Cape Bonavista to the northern point of the said island, and from thence running down by the western side, reaches as far as the place called Point Riche.[7] But the island called Cape Breton, as also all others, both in the mouth of the river of St. Lawrence and in the gulf of the same name, shall hereafter belong of right to the French, and the most Christian King shall have all manner of liberty to fortify any place or places there.[8]

XIV. It is expressly provided that in all the said places and colonies to be yielded and restored by the most Christian King, in pursuance of this treaty, the subjects of the said King may have liberty to remove themselves within a year to any other place, as they shall think fit, together with all their moveable effects. But those who are willing to remain there, and to be subject to the kingdom of Great Britain, are to enjoy the free exercise of their religion according to the usage of the Church of Rome, as far as the laws of Great Britain do allow the same.[9]

XV. The subjects of France inhabiting Canada, and others, shall hereafter give no hindrance or molestation to the five nations or cantons of Indians, subject to the Dominion of Great Britain, nor to the other natives of America, who are friends to the same. In like manner the subjects of Great Britain shall behave themselves peaceably towards the Americans who are subjects or friends to France; and on both sides they shall enjoy full liberty of going and coming on account of trade. As also the natives of those countries shall, with the same liberty, resort as they please to the British and French colonists, for promoting trade on the one side and the other, without any molestation or hindrance, either on the part of the British subjects or of the French. But it is to be exactly and distinctly settled by commissaries, who are, and who ought to be accounted the subjects and friends of Britain or of France.

NOTES TO THE TREATY OF UTRECHT.

1 The text is reprinted from the "Collection of Treaties between Great Britain and other powers," published by George Chalmers at London in 1790. In that collection the Treaty of Utrecht is, according to the compiler, "printed from the copy which was published by authority in 1713."

2 The two dates here given are according to the Old Style and the New Style; the latter had been adopted by France in 1582, and it was not adopted in England till 1751.

3 For the Charter of the Hudson Bay Company see Ontario Sessional Papers, vol. xi, No. 31.

4 The boundary was never determined by the commissaries appointed under the Treaty of Utrecht (Ont. Sess. Papers, vol. xi. No. 31, p. 136 p.), and it remained unsettled until Canada became a British Province. There was then no pressing reason for defining it, and it remained undetermined until it was defined by the Imperial Act of 1889, 52 & 53 Vict. cap 28, which settled the northern boundary of Ontario.

5 These ancient boundaries are thus given by Murdoch in his "History of Nova Scotia or Acadia": "Acadia was then bounded on the north by the Gulf of St. Lawrence, on the east by the Atlantic, on the south by the river Kennebec, and on the west by the Province of Canada, its northwesternmost boundary being in Gaspe Bay." Thus defined, Acadia included the present Provinces of Nova Scotia and New Brunswick, and part of the State of Maine. The St. Croix river is named as the boundary, instead of the Kennebec, in the Commission to Walter Paterson, the first Governor of Prince Edward Island, in 1769, and this definition is repeated in the Commission to Thomas Carleton, the first Governor of New Brunswick, in 1784. (See Dominion of Canada Sessional Papers, vol. xvi. No. 70.) For an account of disputes between the French of Acadia and the British Colonists of New England over the district between these two rivers, see Kingsford's "History of Canada," Murdoch's "History of Nova Scotia," and the volume of "Selections" mentioned in Note 6.

6 Governor Philipps was instructed, in 1720, to appoint Commissioners to confer with Commissioners appointed by the Governor of Canada as to the boundaries of Acadia. This was never done, and for correspondence on the subject see "Selections from the Public Documents of the Province of Nova Scotia," Halifax, 1869. Gov. Philipps' instructions are given in the Dom. Sess. Papers, Vol. xvi, No. 70.

7 Compare the provisions of this treaty respecting fishing privileges with those reserved to France in the Treaty of Paris, 1763. See also the provisions in the Treaty of Versailles, 1783, relating to the same franchises; and the provisions of the Treaty of Paris, 1783, the Treaty of Ghent, 1814, the Convention of 1818, and the Treaty of Washington, 1871, dealing with the claims of the United States to the Canadian fisheries. For these documents see Appendix A.

8 This right was exercised in the case of Louisburg, which was made the centre of French operations in Acadia. Cape Breton was finally ceded to Great Britain by the Treaty of Paris, 1763.

9 Compare the concessions made in the articles of capitulation of Montreal, 1760; in the Treaty of Paris, 1763; in the Quebec Act, 1774; and in the Constitutional Act, 1791.

REPRESENTATIVE ASSEMBLIES IN THE MARITIME PROVINCES.[1]

Nova Scotia.[2]

---

1. *The Introduction of British Settlement and of Civil Government.*[3]

WHITEHALL, 7th March, 1749.

A proposal having been presented unto His Majesty for the establishing a civil government in the Province of Nova Scotia, in North America, as also for the better peopling and settling the said Province, and extending and improving the fishery thereof, by granting lands within the same, and giving other encouragement to such of the officers and private men lately dismissed His Majesty's land and sea service, as shall be willing to settle in said Province. And His Majesty having signed his royal approbation of the report of the said proposals, the Right Honourable the Lords Commissioners for Trade and Plantations,[4] do by His Majesty's commands give notice[5] that proper encouragement will be given to such of the officers and private men lately dismissed[6] His Majesty's Land and Sea Service as are willing to accept of grants of land, and to settle with or without families in Nova Scotia. That fifty acres of land will be granted in fee simple to every private soldier or seaman, free from the payment of any quit rents or taxes for the term of ten years, at the expiration whereof no person to pay more than one shilling per annum for every fifty acres so granted.

That a grant of ten acres, over and above the fifty, will be made to each private soldier or seaman having a family, for every person including women and children of which his family shall consist, and from the grants made to them on the like conditions as their families shall increase, or in proportion to their abilities to cultivate the same.

That eighty acres on like conditions will be granted to every officer under the rank of Ensign in the land service, and that of Lieutenant in the sea service, and to such as have families fifteen acres over and above the said eighty acres for every person of which their families shall consist.

That two hundred acres on like conditions will be granted to every Ensign, three hundred to every Lieutenant, four hundred to every Captain, and six hundred to every officer above the rank of Captain.

And to such of the above mentioned officers, as have families, a further grant of thirty acres will be made over and above their respective quotas for every person of which their families shall consist.[7]

That the lands will be parcelled out to the settlers as soon as possible after their arrival, and a civil government established, whereby they will enjoy all the liberties, privileges, and immunities enjoyed by His Majesty's subjects in any other of the Colonies and Plantations in America, under His Majesty's government, and proper measures will also be taken for their security and protection.

That all such as are willing to accept of the above proposals shall, with their families, be subsisted during the passage, also for the space of twelve months after their arrival.

That they shall be furnished with arms and ammunition as far as will be judged necessary for their defence, with a proper quantity of materials and utensils for husbandry, clearing and cultivating the lands, erecting habitations, carrying on the fishery, and such other purposes as shall be deemed necessary for their support.

That all such persons as are desirous of engaging in the above settlement, do transmit by letter, or personally give in their names, signifying in what regiment or company, or on board what ship they last served, and if they have families they intend to carry with them, distinguishing the age and quality of such person to any of the following officers appointed to receive and enter the same in the books open for that purpose, viz:—John Pownell,[a] Esq., Solicitor and Clerk of the Repts. of the Lords Comrs. of Trade and Plantations, at their office at Whitehall; John Russell, Esq., Comr. of His Majesty's Navy at Portsmouth; Philip Vanburgh, Esq., Comr. of His Majesty's Navy at Plymouth.

And the proper notice will be given of the said Books being closed, as soon as the intended number shall be completed, or at least on the 7th day of April.

It is proposed that the transports shall be ready to receive such persons on board on the 10th April, and be ready to sail on the 20th, and that timely notice will be given of the place or places to which such persons are to repair in order to embark.

That for the benefit of the settlement, the same conditions which are proposed to private soldiers and seamen shall likewise be granted to Carpenters, Shipwrights, Smiths, Masons, Joiners, Brickmakers, Bricklayers, and all other artificers necessary in building or husbandry, not being private soldiers or seamen.

That the same conditions as are proposed to those who have served in the capacity of Ensign shall extend to all Surgeons, whether they have been in His Majesty's service or not, upon their producing proper certificates of their being duly qualified.

By order of the Right Hon. the Lords Comrs. of Trade and Plantations.

THOMAS HILL,
Secretary.

2. *Commission of Governor Cornwallis,*⁹ *1749.*

GEORGE THE SECOND, by the Grace of God of Great Britain, France and Ireland, King, Defender of the Faith, etc. To our trusty and well-beloved, the Honorable EDWARD CORNWALLIS, Esquire, Greeting. Whereas we did by our letters patent under our Great Seal of Great Britain, bearing date at Westminster the eleventh day of September in the second year of our reign, constitute and appoint Richard Philipp's,¹¹ Esquire, our Captain General and Governor in Chief, in and over our Province of Nova Scotia or Acadie¹² in America, with all the rights, members and appurtenances whatsoever thereunto belonging, for and during our will and pleasure; as by the said recited letters patent, relation being thereunto had, may more fully and at large appear.

Now know you that we have revoked and determined, and by these presents do revoke and determine the said recited letters patent, and every clause, article and thing therein contained; and further know you that we reposing special trust and confidence in the prudence, courage, and loyalty of you, the said Edward Cornwallis, of our special grace, certain knowledge and meer motion, have thought fit to constitute and appoint you, the said Edward Cornwallis, to be our Captain General, & Governor in Chief in and over our Province of Nova Scotia or Acadie in America, with all the rights, members, and appurtenances whatsoever thereunto belonging, and we do hereby require and command you to do and execute all things in due manner that shall belong unto your said command and the trust we have reposed in you according to the several powers and authorities granted or appointed you by this present Commission and the instructions herewith given you, or by such further powers, instructions and authorities as shall at any time hereafter be granted or appointed you under our signet and sign manuel, or by our order in our privy Council, and according to such reasonable laws and statutes as hereafter shall be made or agreed upon by you with the advice and consent of our Council and the Assembly of our said Province, under your government hereafter to be appointed in such manner and form as is hereafter expressed.

And for the better administration of justice, and the management of the public affairs of our said Province, we hereby give and grant unto you, the said Edward Cornwallis, full power and authority to chuse, nominate, and appoint such fitting and discreet persons as you shall either find there or carry along with you not exceeding the number of Twelve, to be of our Council[12] in our said Province. As also to nominate and appoint by warrant under your hand and seal all such other officers and ministers as you shall judge proper and necessary for our service and the good of the people whom we shall settle in our said Province until our further will and pleasure shall be known.

And our will and pleasure is, that you the said Edward Cornwallis, (after the publication of these our letters patent) do take the Oaths appointed to be taken by an Act[13] passed in the first year of his late Majesty's, our Royal father's reign, entitled " An Act for the further security of His Majesty's Person and Government and the succession of the Crown in the Heirs of the late Princess Sophia, being Protestants, and for extinguishing the hopes of the pretended Prince of Wales and his open and secret abettors." As also that you make and subscribe the Declaration mentioned in an Act[14] of Parliament made in the twenty-fifth year of the reign of King Charles the Second, entitled " An Act for preventing danger which may happen from Popish Recusants." And likewise that you take the usual Oath for the due execution of the office and trust of our Captain General & Governor in Chief of our said Province, for the due and impartial administration of justice; and further that you take the oath required to be taken by Governors of Plantations to do their utmost that the several laws relating to Trade and the Plantations be observed. All which said oaths and declaration our Council in our said province, or any five of the members thereof, have hereby full power and authority and are required to tender and administer unto you and in your absence to our Lieutenant Governor, if there be any upon the place, all which being duly performed you shall administer unto each of the members of our said Council, as also to our Lieutenant Governor, if there be any such upon the place, the said oaths mentioned in the said Act entitled " An Act for the further security of His Majesty's Person and Government and the succession of the Crown in the Heirs of the late Princess Sophia, being Protestants, and for extinguishing the hopes of the pretended Prince of Wales and his open and secret abettors ;" as also to cause them to make and subscribe the afore-mentioned declaration and to administer to them the oath for the due execution of their places and trusts.

And we do hereby give & grant unto you full power and authority to suspend any of the members of our said Council to be appointed by you as aforesaid from sitting, voting, and assisting therein if you shall find just cause for so doing.

And if it shall at any time happen that by the death, departure out of our said Province, suspension of any of our said Councilors, or otherwise, there shall be a vacancy in our said Council (any five whereof we do hereby appoint to be a quorum), our will and pleasure is that you signify the same unto us by the first opportunity that we may under our signet & sign manuel constitute and appoint others in their stead.

But that our affairs at that distance may not suffer for want of a due number of Councilors, if ever it shall happen that there shall be less than nine of them residing in our said Province, we hereby give and grant unto you the said Edward Cornwallis full power and authority to chuse as many persons out of the principal freeholders inhabitants thereof as will make up the full number of our said Council to be nine and no more; which persons so chosen and appointed by you shall be to all intents and purposes Councilors in our said Province until either they shall be confirmed by us, or that by the nomination of others by us under our sign manuel or signet our said Council shall have nine or more persons in it.

And we do hereby give and grant unto you full power & authority, with the advice and consent of our said Council, from time to time as need shall require, to summon and call General Assemblys of the Freeholders and Planters within your Government according to the usage of the rest of our Colonies & Plantations in America.[15]

And our will and pleasure is that the persons thereupon duly elected by the major part of the Freeholders of the respective counties and places & so returned shall before their setting take the Oaths mentioned in the Act entitled " An Act for the further security of his Majesty's Person and Government and the succession of the Crown in the Heirs of the late Princess Sophia being Protestants, and for extinguishing the hopes of the pretended Prince of Wales and his open and secret abettors," as also make and subscribe the afore-mentioned declaration (which Oaths & Declaration you shall commissionate fit persons under our Seal of Nova Scotia to tender and administer unto them,) and until the same shall be so taken and subscribed no person shall be capable of sitting tho' elected, and we do hereby declare that the persons so elected and qualified shall be called and deemed the General Assembly of that our Province of Nova Scotia.

And that you the said Edward Cornwallis with the advice and consent of our said Council and Assembly, or the major part of them respectively, shall have full power and authority to make, constitute, and ordain Laws, Statutes, & Ordinances for the Publick peace, welfare & good government of our said province and of the people and inhabitants thereof and such others as shall resort thereto, & for the benefit of us, our heirs and successors, which said Laws, Statutes, and Ordinances are not to be repugnant, but as near as may be agreeable, to the Laws and Statutes of this our Kingdom of Great Britain.[16]

Provyded that all such Laws, Statutes & Ordinances, of what nature or duration so ever be within three months or sooner after the making thereof transmitted to us under our Seal of Nova Scotia for our approbation or disallowance thereof, as also duplicates by the next conveyance.

And in case any or all of the said Laws, Statutes & Ordinances not before confirmed by us shall at any time be disallowed, and not approved & so signified by us our Heirs or Successors under our or their sign manuel & signet, or by order of our or their privy Council unto you the said Edward Cornwallis, or to the Commander in Chief of our said Province for the time being, then such and so many of the said Laws, Statutes, and Ordinances as shall be so disallowed & not approved shall from thenceforth cease, determine, & become utterly void & of none effect, anything to the contrary thereof notwithstanding.

And to the end that nothing may be passed or done by our said Council or Assembly to the prejudice of us our Heirs & Successors, we will & ordain that you the said Edward Cornwallis shall have and enjoy a negative voice in the making and passing of all Laws, Statutes & Ordinances as aforesaid.

And you shall & may likewise from time to time, as you shall judge it necessary, adjourn, prorogue & dissolve all General Assemblies as aforesaid.

And our further will and pleasure is that you shall and may keep & use the Publick Seal of our Province of Nova Scotia for sealing all things whatsoever that pass the Great Seal of our said Province under your Government.

And we do further give and grant unto you the said Edward Cornwallis full power and authority from time to time & at any time hereafter, by yourself or by any other to be authorized by you in that behalf, to administer and give the Oaths mentioned in the aforesaid Act to all and every such person or persons as you shall think fit, who shall at any time or times pass into our said Province or shall be residing or abiding there.

And we do by these presents give and grant unto you the said Edward Cornwallis full power and authority, with advice and consent of our said Council, to erect, constitute, and establish such and so many Courts of Judicature & Publick Justice within our said Province and Dominion as you and they shall think fit and necessary for the hearing & determining all causes as well Criminal as Civil according to Law and Equity, and for awarding of Execution thereupon with all reasonable and necessary powers, authorities, fees & privileges belonging thereunto, as also to appoint & commissionate fit persons in the several parts of your Government to administer the oaths mentioned in the aforesaid Act, entitled

"An Act for the further security of His Majesty's Person & Government & the Succession of the Crown in the Heirs of the late Princess Sophia being Protestants, and for extinguishing the hopes of the pretended Prince of Wales and his open and secret abettors;" as also to administer the aforesaid declaration unto such persons belonging to the said Courts as shall be obliged to take the same.

And we do hereby authorise and impower you to constitute and appoint Judges, & in cases requisite Commissioners of Oyer & Terminer, Justices of the Peace, and other necessary officers & ministers in our said Province for the better administration of Justice and putting the Laws in execution, and to administer or cause to be administered unto them such oath or oaths as are usually given for the due execution and performance of offices and places and for the clearing of truth in Judicial Causes.

And we do hereby give and grant unto you full power & authority, where you shall see cause, or shall judge any offender or offender in criminal matters or for any fines or forfeitures due unto us fit objects of our mercy, to pardon all such offenders and to remitt all such offences, fines and forfeitures, treason & willfull murder only excepted; in which cases you shall likewise have power upon extraordinary occasions to grant reprieves to the offenders untill & to the intent our Royal pleasure may be known therein.

We do by these presents authorise and empower you to collate any person or persons to any churches, chapels, or other ecclesiastical benefices within our said Province as often as any of them shall happen to be void.

And we do hereby give & grant unto you the said Edward Cornwallis. by yourself or by your captains & commanders by you to be authorised, full power and authority to levy, arm, muster, command & employ all persons whatsoever residing within our said Province, and as occasion shall serve, to march from one place to another or to embark them for the resisting & withstanding of all enemies, pirates & rebels, both at land and sea, and to transport such forces to any of our plantations in America, if necessity shall require, for the defence of the same against the invasion or attempts of any of our enemies ; and such enemies, pirates & rebels, if there shall be occasion to pursue and prosecute in or out of the limits of our said Province and plantations or any of them & (if it shall so please God) to vanquish, apprehend & take them, & being taken, according to law to put to death or keep and preserve them alive at your discretion, & to execute Martial Law in time of invasion or other times when by law it may be executed, & to do & execute all & every other thing or things which to our Captain Generals & Governor in Chief, doeth or ought of right to belong.

And we do hereby give & grant unto you full power and authority by & with the advice and consent of our said Council of Nova Scotia, to erect, raise & build in our said Province such & so many forts & platforms, castles, citys, boroughs, towns & fortifications as you by the advice aforesaid shall judge necessary, and the same or any of them to fortify and furnish with ordnance, ammunition & all sorts of arms fit and necessary for the security and defence of our said Province, and by the advice aforesaid the same again, or any of them, to demolish or dismantle as may be most convenient.'

And for as much as divers mutinies & disorders may happen by persons shipped and employed at sea during the time of war, and to the end that such as shall be shipped & employed at sea during the time of war may be better governed & ordered, we hereby give and grant unto you, the said Edward Cornwallis, full power and authority to constitute & appoint captains, lieutenants, masters of ships, & other commanders & officers, and to grant to such captains, lieutenants, masters of ships, & other commanders & officers commissions in time of war to execute the law martial according to the directions of such laws as are now in force or shall hereafter be passed in Great Britain for that purpose, and to use such proceedings, authorities, punishments and executions upon any offender or offenders who shall be mutinous, seditious, disorderly or any way unruly either at sea or during the time of their abode or residence in any of the ports, harbours or bays of our said Province, as the cause shall be found to require according to the martial law and the said directions during the time of war as aforesaid.

Provyded that nothing herein contained shall be construed to the enabling you or any by your authority to hold plea or have any jurisdiction of any offence, cause, matter or thing committed or done upon the high sea, or within any of the havens, rivers or creeks of our said Province under your government by any captain, commander, lieutenant, master, officer, seaman, soldier or person whatsoever, who shall be in our actual service & pay in or on board any of our ships of war or other vessels, acting by immediate Commission or Warrant from our Commissioners for executing the office of our High Admiral of Great Britain for the time being, under the Seal of our Admiralty, but that such captain, commander, lieutenant, master, officer, seaman, soldier, or other person so offending shall be left to be proceeded against & tryed as their offences shall require, either by Commission under our Great Seal of Great Britain, as the Statute of the 28th of Henry the Eighth directs, or by Commission from our said Commissioners for executing the office of our High Admiral, or from our High Admiral of Great Britain for the time being, according to the afore-mentioned Act for the establishing articles & orders for the regulating and better Government of His Majesty's Navies, Ships of War & Forces by Sea, and not otherwise.

Provyded nevertheless that all disorders & misdemeanors committed on shore by any captain, commander, lieutenant, master, officer, seaman, soldier or other person whatsoever belonging to any of our ships of war or other vessels acting by immediate Commission or Warrant from our said Commissioners for executing the office of High Admiral, or from our High Admiral of Great Britain for the time being under the Seal of our Admiralty, may be tried & punished according to the laws of the place where any such disorders, offences, and misdemeanors shall be committed on shore, notwithstanding such offender be in our actual service, & borne in our pay, on board any such our ships of war or other vessels acting by immediate Commission or Warrant from our said Commissioners for executing the office of High Admiral, or our High Admiral of Great Britain for the time being as aforesaid, so as he shall not receive any protection for the avoiding of justice for such offences committed on shore from any pretence of his being employed in our service at sea.

And our further will and pleasure is that all publick money raised, or which shall be raised by any Act hereafter to be made within our said Province be issued out by Warrant from you by & with the advice and consent of the Council & disposed of by you for the support of the Government, and not otherwise.

And we do likewise give & grant unto you full power and authority, by & with the advice and consent of our said Council, to settle and agree with the Inhabitants of our Province for such lands, tenements, & hereditaments as now are or hereafter shall be in our power to dispose of, and them to grant to any person or persons upon such terms and under such moderate quit rents, services, and acknowledgments to be thereupon reserved unto us as you by & with the advice aforesaid shall think fit. Which said grants are to pass & be sealed by our seal of Nova Scotia, and being entered upon record by such officer or officers as shall be appointed thereunto shall be good & effectual in law against us, our heirs and successors.

And we do hereby give you the said Edward Cornwallis full power to order and appoint fairs, marts & markets, as also such and so many ports, harbours, bays, havens and other places for convenience & security of shipping & for the better loading & unloading of goods & merchandizes, as by you with the advice & consent of the said Council shall be thought fit and necessary.

And we do hereby require & command all officers & ministers, civil & military, and all other Inhabitants of our said Province, to be obedient, aiding and assisting unto you the said Edward Cornwallis in the execution of this our commission and of the powers & authorities herein contained, and in case of your death or abscence out of our said Province to be obedient, aiding & assisting unto such person as shall be appointed by us to be our Lieutenant Governor or Commander in Chief of our said Province; to whom we do therefore by these presents give & grant all & singular the powers & authority's herein granted, to be by him executed & enjoyed during our pleasure or untill your arrival within our said Province.

And if upon your death or absence out of our said Province there be no person upon the place commissionated or appointed by us to be our Lieutenant Governor or Commander in Chief of the said Province, our will & pleasure is that the Eldest Councilor, who shall be at the time of your death or absence residing within our said Province, shall take upon him the administration of the government and execute our said Commission & Instructions and the several powers and authorities therein contained in the same manner & to all intent and purposes as either our Governor or Commander in Chief should or ought to do in case of your absence until your return, or in all cases untill our further pleasure be known herein.[17]

And we do hereby declare, ordain & appoint that you the said Edward Cornwallis shall & may hold, execute & enjoy the office & place of our Captain General & Governor in Chief in & over our said Province of Nova Scotia, with all its rights, members & appurtenances whatsoever, together with all & singular the powers and authorities hereby granted unto you for and during our will & pleasure.

In witness whereof we have caused these our letters to be made patent. Witness ourself at Westminster the sixth day of May in the twenty-second year of our reign.

By writ of Privy Seal.

[L. S.]   (Signed)   YORKE & YORKE.[18]

3. *Extract from a Letter of Governor Lawrence*[19] *to the Lords of Trade and Plantations.*

JANY. 12TH, 1755.

I acquainted your Lordships in a former Letter that Mr. Pownall had, as from your Lordships expressed to the Chief Justice some doubts about the Legislative authority of the Council.[20] I now transmit your Lordships his opinion thereon it is a case I am by no means a competent judge of but that power has hitherto passed unquestioned in this Colony, and I doubt not but your Lordships are well satisfied by both the Governors[21] that have gone home, how impossible it is in our present circumstances, to call an assembly, and what numberless inconveniences would attend the collecting a set of people such as are to be found in this Province, in that shape, until we are better prepared for it, or it is in their power to grant money towards defraying the public expense.

CHARLES LAWRENCE.

---

4. *Extract from a Letter of the Lords of Trade and Plantations to Governor Lawrence, dated*

WHITEHALL, MAY 7TH, 1755.

Immediately upon the receipt of your Letter, we took into Consideration the observations made by the Chief Justice upon the power of the Governor & Council of Nova Scotia, to pass Laws without an assembly, and as it appeared to us to be a matter of very great consequence, We transmitted those observations together with such parts of His Majesty's Commission and Instructions as related to the passing of Laws to His Majesty's Attorney & Sollicitor Genl. for their opinion upon this point, and having received their report, we herewith inclose to you a copy of it for your Guidance and Direction, and though the calling of an Assembly may in the present circumstances of the Colony be difficult and attended with some inconveniences, yet as the Attorney and Sollicitor General are of opinion that the Governor and Council have no power to enact Laws, we cannot see how the Government can be properly carried on without such an Assembly; We desire therefore you will immediately consult with his Majesty's Chief Justice in what manner an Assembly can be most properly convened, of what number of members it shall consist, how those members shall be elected, and what rules and methods of proceeding it may be necessary to prescribe for them, transmitting to us as soon as possible Your Opinion and Report thereupon, in as full and explicit a manner as possible, to the end We may lay this matter before His Majesty for His Majesty's further Directions therein.

As the Validity, however, of the Laws enacted by the Governor and Council, or the authority of those acting under them, do not appear to have been hitherto questioned, It is of the greatest consequence to the Peace and Welfare of the Province that the opinion of His Majesty's Attorney & Sollicitor General should not be made public untill an Assembly can be convened and an Indemnification passed for such Acts as have been done under Laws enacted without any proper authority.

---

5. *Opinion of the Attorney and Solicitor General.*

Pursuant to your Lordships' desire Signified to Us by Mr. Hill in his Letter of the 31st of March last, setting forth, that a doubt having arisen whether the Governor and Council of His Majesty's Province of Nova

Scotia have a Power of enacting Laws within the said Province, and Jonathan Belcher, Esq., having transmitted to your Lordships his observations thereupon inclosing to Us a Copy of the said Observations together with Copys of several clauses in the Commission and Instructions of the said Governor of that Province referred to (all which are herewith returned) and desiring our opinion, whether the said Governor and Council have or have not a Power to enact Laws for the public Peace, Welfare and good Government of the said Province and the People and the Inhabitants thereof.

We have taken the said Observations and clauses into Our Consideration and are humbly of opinion that the Governor and Council alone are not authorized by His Majesty to make Laws till there can be an Assembly.

His Majesty has ordered the Government of the Infant Colony to be pursuant to his Commission and Instructions and such further Directions as He should give under his Sign Manual or by Order in Council.

All of which is humbly submitted to Your Lordships Consideration.

April 29th, 1755.   (Signed)   WM. MURRAY.[22]
                                                              RICHD. LLOYD.

6. *Proposed Constitution of the Legislative Assembly.*

At a Council[23] holden at the Governor's House in Halifax, on Monday, the 3rd Jany., 1757.

His Excellency, the Governor, together with His Majesty's Council, having had under mature consideration the necessary and most expedient measures for carrying into Execution those parts of His Majesty's Commission and Instructions which relate to the calling General Assemblies within the Province, came to the following Resolutions thereon, viz:

That a House of Representatives of the inhabitants of this Province be the Civil Legislature thereof, in Conjunction with His Majesty's Governor or Commander in Chief for the time being, and His Majesty's Council of said Province, the first House to be Elected and Convened in the following manner, and to be stiled the General Assembly, vizt.

That there shall be Elected for the Province at large until the same shall be divided into Counties.................... 12 members.
        For the Township of Halifax .... 4 "
        For the Township of Lunenburg.......... 2 "
        For the Township of Dartmouth........ 1 "
        For the Township of Lawrence Town.... 1 "
        For the Township of Annapolis Royal.... 1 "
        For the Township of Cumberland........ 1 "

That when twenty-five Qualified Electors shall be settled at Pisiquid, Minas, Cobequid, or any other Townships which may hereafter be erected, each of the said Townships so settled, shall for their encouragement be entitled to send one Representative of the General Assembly, and shall likewise have a Right of voting in the Election of Representatives for the Province at large.

That the House shall always consist of at least sixteen members present besides the Speaker, before they enter upon Business.

That no person shall be chosen as a member of the said House, or shall have a Right of Voting in the Election of any Member of the said House, who shall be a Popish Recusant, or shall be under the Age of Twenty-One Years, or who shall not at the time of such Election, be possessed in his own Right of a Freehold Estate within the District for which he shall be Elected, or shall so vote, nor shall any Elector have more than One Vote for each Member to be chosen for the Province at large, or for any Township; and that each Freeholder present at such Election, and giving his Vote for one Member for the Province at large shall be obliged to Vote also for the other Eleven.

That respecting Freeholds which may have been conveyed by the Sheriff, by virtue of an Execution, the Right of Voting shall remain and be in the Persons from whom the same were taken in Execution, until the time of Redemption be elapsed.

That no Non-Commissioned Officer or Private Soldier in actual Service shall have a right of voting, by virtue of any Dwelling built upon Sufferance, nor any Possession of Freehold, unless the same be registered to him.

That all the Electors shall, if so required at the time of the Election, take the usual State Oaths appointed by Law, and declare and subscribe the test.

That any Voter shall at the request of any Candidate be obliged to take the following Oath,[24] which Oath, together with the State Oaths, the Returning Officer is hereby empowered to administer:

"I A. B., do swear that I am a Freeholder in the Township of   , in the Province of Nova Scotia, and have Freehold Lands or Hereditaments lying or being at   within the said Township, and that such Freehold Estate hath not been made or granted to me fraudulently on purpose to qualify me to give my vote, and that I have not received or had by myself, or any person whatsoever in Trust for me, or for my use and benefit, directly or indirectly, any sum or sums of money, office, place, or employment, gift or reward, or any promise or security for any money, office, employment or gift in order to give my vote at this Election, and that I have not before been Polled at this Election, and that the place of my abode is at   ."

That a precept be issued by His Excellency, the Governor, to the Provost Marshal or Sheriff of the Province requiring him by himself or his

Deputys to Summon the Freeholders of the Province to meet within their respective Districts, at some convenient place and time, to be by the said Provost Marshal or one of his Deputies appointed, and of which he or they shall give Twenty days Notice then and there to elect (agreeable to the Regulations hereby prescribed) such a number of Representatives, as shall in the said precept be expressed, agreeable to the preceding detail.

That on account of the present rigorous season, the precept for Convening the first Assembly be made returnable in Sixty days from the date thereof, at which time the Assembly shall meet at such place as His Excellency, the Governor, shall appoint in the Precept.

That the Provost Marshal or his Deputy shall be the returning officer of the Elections, to be held by him with the Assistance of three of the Freeholders present, to be appointed and sworn by the returning officer for that purpose, and in case a scrutiny shall be demanded, the same shall be made by them, and in case of further contest the same to be determined by the House. The Poll for each Township to be closed at the expiration of Forty-eight hours from the time of its being opened; and for the Province at large the Poll, after four days from the time of its being opened for the election, shall be sealed up by the returning officer for each Township, and transmitted to the Provost Marshal by the first opportunity, that seasonable notice may be given to the persons who shall upon examination appear to have been chosen by the greatest number of the said votes. Provided, nevertheless, that if the votes in the Township of Annapolis Royal and Cumberland for the first members of the Province at large, shall not be returned Eight days before the expiration of the time limited for returning the Precept, the Provost Marshall shall, in such case, proceed to declare who are the persons elected, from the other votes in his hands.

That the Provost Marshall or his Deputy, shall appoint for each candidate, such one person as shall be nominated to him by each candidate, to be Inspectors of the returning officer and his assistants.

That no person shall be deemed duly Elected who shall not have the vote of a majority of the Electors present.

That the names of all persons voted for, together with Names of the Voters, shall at the time of voting be publickly declared and entered on a Book kept for that purpose.

That in case of the Absence of any of the members from the Province, for the term of two months, it shall and may be lawful for the Governor, Lieutenant Governor, or Commander-in-Chief (if he shall judge it necessary) to issue his Precept for the choice of others in their stead.

That the Returning Officer shall cause the foregoing Resolution to be publicly read at the opening of each meeting for the Elections, and to govern the said meeting agreeable thereto.[25]

CHARLES LAWRENCE.

7. *Extract from Letter of Lords of Trade to Governor Lawrence.*

WHITEHALL, FEBY. 7, 1758.

We have fully considered that part of your Letter which relates to the calling an Assembly, and also the Plan for that purpose, contained in the minutes of the Council transmitted with it, and having so often and so fully repeated to you our sense and opinion of the propriety & necessity of this measure taking place, it only now remains for Us to direct its being carried into immediate execution, that His Majesty's subjects (great part of whom are alleged to have quitted the Province on account of the great discontent prevailing for want of an Assembly) may no longer be deprived of that privilege, which was promised to them by His Majesty, when the Settlement of this Colony was first undertaken, and was one of the conditions upon which they accepted the Proposals then made. We are sensible that the Execution of this measure may in the present situation of the Colony be attended with many difficulties, and possibly may in its consequences, in some respects interfere with, and probably embarrass His Majesty's service; but without regard to these Considerations, or to what may be the opinion of individuals with respect to this measure, We think it of indispensable necessity that it should be immediately carried into execution.

Prince Edward Island.[26]

Commission to Governor Paterson, 1769.

GEORGE THE THIRD, by the grace of God, of Great Britain, France, and Ireland, King, Defender of the Faith, &c. To our trusty and well-beloved WALTER PATERSON, Esquire, greeting. Whereas we did by Our Letters Patent bearing date at Westminster the Eleventh day of August, one thousand, seven hundred and sixty-six, in the sixth year of Our Reign, constitute and appoint our trusty and well-beloved William Campbell, Esquire, commonly called Lord William Campbell, to be our Captain-General and Governor-in-Chief in and over Our Province of Nova Scotia, bounded on the westward by a line drawn from Cape Sable across the entrance of the Bay of Fundy to the mouth of the River St. Croix, by the said river to its source, and by a line drawn due north from thence to the southern boundary of Our Colony of Quebec,[27] to the northward by the said boundary as far as the western extremity of the Bay des Chaleur, to the eastward by the said Bay and the Gulf of St. Lawrence to the Cape or Promontory called Cape Breton, in the Island of that name, including that Island,[28] the Island of St. John,[29] and all other Islands within six leagues of the coast, and to the southward by the Atlantic Ocean from the said Cape to Cape Sable aforesaid, including the Island of that name, and all other Islands within forty leagues of the coast, with all the rights, members, and appurtenances whatsoever thereunto belonging, for and during our will and pleasure as by the said recited Letters Patent, relation being thereunto had, may more fully at large appear. Now, know You that we have revoked and determined, and by these presents do revoke and determine, such parts and so much of the said recited Letters Patent, and every clause, article, and thing therein contained as relates to or mentions the Island of St. John. And Further Know You, that we, reposing especial trust and confidence in the prudence, courage, and loyalty of you the said Walter Paterson, of Our especial Grace, certain knowledge, and mere motion, have thought fit to constitute and appoint, and by these Presents do constitute and appoint you the said Walter Paterson to be our Captain-General and Governor-in-Chief in and over our Island of St. John, and our Territories adjacent thereto in America, and which now are, or hitherto have been dependent thereupon, and we do hereby require and command you to do and execute all things in due manner that shall belong to your said command.[20] * *

In witness whereof, We have caused these Our Letters to be made Patent: Witness Ourselves at Westminster, the fourth day of August, in the ninth year of Our Reign.

By Writ of Privy Council.

YORKE Q. YORKE.

New Brunswick.

Commission[30] *to Governor Carleton, 1784.*

GEORGE THE THIRD, by the Grace of God, of Great Britain, France and Ireland, King, Defender of the Faith, &c. To Our Trusty and Well-beloved THOMAS CARLETON, Esquire, Greeting. We, reposing especial trust and confidence in the prudence, courage, and loyalty of you, the said Thomas Carleton, of Our special grace, certain knowledge and mere motion, have thought fit to constitute and appoint you, the said Thomas Carleton, to be our Captain-General and Governor-in-Chief of our Province of New Brunswick, bounded on the westward by the mouth of the River St. Croix, by the said river to its source, and by a line drawn due north from thence to the southern boundary of Our Province of Quebec,[27] to the northward by the said boundary as far as the western extremity of the Bay des Chaleur, to the eastward by the said Bay and the Gulf of St. Lawrence to the Bay called Bay Verte, to the south by a line in the centre of the Bay of Fundy from the River St. Croix, aforesaid, to the mouth of the Musquat River, by the said river to its source, and from thence by a due east line across the isthmus into the Bay Verte to join the eastern line above described, including all islands within six leagues of the coast, with all the rights, members and appurtenances whatsoever thereunto belonging, and We do hereby require and command you to do and execute all things in due manner that shall belong to your said command.³ ¹   *   *   *   *   *

In witness whereof, We have caused these Our Letters to be made Patent: Witness Ourself, at Westminster, the sixteenth day of August, in the twenty-fourth year of Our Reign.

By Writ of Privy Seal.   YORKE.

NOTES TO REPRESENTATIVE ASSEMBLIES IN THE MARITIME PROVINCES.

1 These Assemblies were established, not by Acts of the British Parliament, but by commissions and instructions issued by the King to the Governors of Provinces. In this respect their origin was similar to that of the Assemblies of many of the British Provinces along the Atlantic coast, and different from that of the Assemblies of Upper and Lower Canada. See the Commission to Lord Cornwallis, 1749, and the Constitutional Act, 1791.

2 The papers relating to Nova Scotia are reprinted from the volume published at Halifax in 1869, entitled "Selections from the Public Documents of the Province of Nova Scotia." These selections were published in compliance with a resolution adopted by the House of Assembly in 1865, and were made from papers in the archives of Nova Scotia, Paris, and London.

3 The interval between 1713 and 1749 was occupied by conflicts with the French settlers of the district along the Bay of Fundy, and with the Indians who were allied with the French. The seat of British authority was Annapolis, and the country was under military rule. The centre of French influence and operations was Louisburg, which was taken by an expedition from New England in 1745, but was restored to France by the treaty of Aix-la-Chapelle in 1747. The project outlined in this paper was prompted by a desire to create in Nova Scotia a British settlement that would prove a real counterpoise to Cape Breton.

4 The full title of this Department of the Imperial Administration was: "The Committee of His Majesty's Privy Council appointed for the consideration of matters relating to Trade and Foreign Plantations." The First Lord Commissioner at this time was George Montague, third Earl of Halifax, whose title is perpetuated in the name of the city which resulted from the settlement project. In 1782 the so-called "Board of Trade and Plantations" was abolished by statute, and this proved the way for the creation of the modern Colonial Department under the control of one of the "Secretaries of State."

5 This notice was inserted as an advertisement in the London *Gazette* of March, 1749.

6 On account of the peace of Aix-la-Chapelle two years before.

7 See the similar grants specified in the Royal Proclamation, 1763.

8 Brother of Thomas Pownall, who in 1757 became Governor of Massachusetts, and in 1766 published in England a work of some value on "The Administration of the Colonies." The name here is misspelt.

9 The Hon. Edward Cornwallis, fifth son of the third Baron Cornwallis, and uncle of the Lord Cornwallis, who surrendered with his army at Yorktown and afterwards took a prominent part in the negotiations which resulted in the union of Great Britain and Ireland. He was Governor till 1752.

10 Philipps was appointed Governor in 1719, and again in 1728. The Commission issued in the latter year is the one here referred to. It is printed in full in the Sessional Papers of the Dominion Parliament, vol. xvi., No. 70.

11 See Note 5 to the Treaty of Utrecht.

12 There had been a Council before, but its membership was increased by this Commission. After the creation of the Assembly in 1758 it was both an Executive and a Legislative Council till 1838, when Lord Durham took steps to separate the two functions and assign them to distinct bodies. See the instructions to Lord Durham in the Dom. Sess. Papers, vol. xvi., No. 70.

13 1 George I. cap. 13.

14 25 Charles II. cap. 2.

15 For a history of the constitutional machinery of the various British Provinces in America see Bancroft's "History of the United States of America," edition of 1886. Lodge's "Short History of the English Colonies in America" is a good summary of the subject. A collection of colonial documents, including the most important charters, was published as early as 1792 in Philadelphia by Ebenezer Hazard. See also "The Federal and State Constitutions, Colonial Charters, and other Organic Laws of the United States," compiled by Ben. Perley Poore, Washington, 1877. Several of the Assemblies referred to in the text had been in active operation for more than a century before the settlement of Halifax.

16 Laws were made until 1758 by the Governor and Council without an Assembly. For specimens of their legislative work see the "Selections from the Public Documents of Nova Scotia."

17 When Governor Lawrence died, somewhat suddenly, in 1760, Chief Justice Belcher, who was at that time President of the Council, administered the Government.

18 See the signatures appended to the commission to Governor Paterson of Prince Edward Island, Governor Carleton of New Brunswick, and Governor Murray of Quebec. In Maseres' "Collection of Commissions," the commission to Sir Danvers Osborn as Governor of New York, 1754, is signed "Yorke and Yorke."

19 Governor Lawrence had been major in a regiment that formed part of the garrison of Louisburg prior to its restoration to France under the Treaty of Aix-la-Chapelle. He came to Halifax in 1749, and became first a member and afterwards the President of the Council. He succeeded to the Governorship in 1756, after having served for three years as administrator. At his instance, and under his direction the expatriation of the Acadian French took place in 1755. The papers published in the Nova Scotian "Selections" show that he complied very reluctantly with the explicit instructions of the Lords of Trade and Plantations to call an Assembly, and that he actually succeeded in postponing action for three years.

20 The "Mr. Pownall" here mentioned was John Pownall, Secretary to the Board of Trade and Plantations. The Chief Justice was Jonathan Belcher, son of Gov. Belcher, of Massachusetts. He had studied law in England, and been appointed Chief Justice in 1754. Both he and Mr. Pownall were well acquainted with the working of colonial Assemblies.

21 Cornwallis and Hopson.

22 Attorney-General Murray shortly afterwards became Lord Chief Justice Mansfield. The opinion is here given without reasons, but some light may be thrown on the latter by a perusal of Lord Mansfield's judgment in *Campbell* v. *Hall.*

23 Chief Justice Belcher had previously prepared a scheme, the leading feature of which was that all the members should be elected by the Province at large. To this feature Gov. Lawrence objected, and this constitution was the result of the ensuing compromise. The passage omitted contains simply the definition of the boundaries of the six townships named. No duration was fixed for each Assembly, and one actually continued without a dissolution from 1770 to 1785. The Lords of Trade and Plantations suggested the New Hampshire writ of summons as a model. For modifications of the proposed constitution, adopted at the instance of the "Lords," see the Nova Scotian "Selections," p. 726.

24 See similar oaths in the Quebec Act, 1774, and the Constitutional Act, 1791.

25 Gov. Lawrence, in a letter written on the 26th of December, 1758, informs the Lords of Trade and Plantations that the first Assembly had met and "passed a number of laws." He confessed that he was agreeably disappointed at the way in which it did its work.

26 The name of the island was long after this commission changed from St. John to Prince Edward, as a compliment to Edward, Duke of Kent, the father of Queen Victoria. While it was part of Nova Scotia, in 1763, it was surveyed into counties and townships, and granted in large tracts to a few proprietors, who were permitted to charge a yearly rental from settlers on their lands. This landlord system was maintained till 1873, when the Canadian Parliament agreed, as one of the conditions of the entrance of the Province into the Dominion, to extinguish the claims of the proprietors and convert the tenancies into freeholds (see Dominion Statutes, 36 Vict. chap. 40). It was at the instance of the proprietors that the island was made a separate Province in 1769.

27 See the Royal Proclamation of 1763, which created the Province of Quebec.

28 For the political status of Cape Breton see Appendix M.

29 *Mutatis mutandis* the remainder of the commission to Gov. Paterson is substantially identical in terms with the commission to Governor Cornwallis, already given at length. It requires him to take and administer the same oaths; to keep and use the "Great Seal"; to call, adjourn, prorogue, and dissolve "General Assemblies"; to establish courts and appoint judges and officers for the administration of justice; to grant pardons and reprieves; to levy troops and erect forts; to dispose of public lands; and to provide facilities for trade and navigation. The Commission will be found *in extenso* in the Dominion Sessional Papers, vol. xvi., No. 70. It is there stated that this is the only constitutional document on file amongst the records of Prince Edward Island.

30 The text of this Commission is printed at length in the Dom. Sess. Papers, vol. xvi., No. 70. It is there stated that this is the only constitutional document that can be found among the records of the Province. It is supposed that at Confederation the missing papers were transferred to England in accordance with instructions sent out to the Governor to that effect. The separation of New Brunswick from Nova Scotia, like that of Upper from Lower Canada seven years later, was due to the influx of United Empire Loyalists from the United States.

31 The remainder of the Commission is virtually identical with the Commissions to Governor Cornwallis, of Nova Scotia, and Governor Paterson, of Prince Edward Island, except that a clause is inserted transferring the custody of idiots and lunatics, and their estates, from the Imperial to the Provincial authorities.

ARTICLES DE CAPITULATION DE QUEBEC, 1759.[1]

Articles de capitulation demandés par M. de Ramzay,[2] Lieutenant pour le Roy commandant les haute et basse villes de Quebec, Ch^{er} de l' Ordre Royal & Militaire de St. Louis, à son Excellence Monsieur le Général des troupes de sa Majesté Britanique.

"The capitulation demanded on the part of the enemy, and granted by their Excellencies Admiral Saunders and General Townshend, &c., &c., &c., is in manner and form hereafter expressed."

ARTICLE PREMIER.

Mr de Ramzay demande les honneurs de la guerre pour sa garnison, & qu'elle soit ramenée à l'armée en sureté par le chemin le plus court, avec armes, bagages, six pieces de canon de fonte, deux mortiers ou obusiers, et douze coups à tirer par pièce.

"The garrison of the town, composed of land forces, marines, and sailors, shall march out with their arms[3] and baggage, drums beating, matches lighted, with two pieces of French canon, and twelve rounds for each piece; and shall be embarked as conveniently as possible, to be sent to the first port in France."

2.

Que les habitans soient conservés dans la possession de leur maisons, biens, effets et privileges.

"Granted upon their laying down their arms."

3.

Que les dits habitans ne pourront être recherchés pour avoir porté les armes à la deffense de la ville, attendu qu'ils y ont été forcés, & que les habitans des colonies des deux couronnes y servent egalement comme milices.

"Granted."

4.

Qu'il ne sera pas touché aux effets des officiers & habitans absens.

"Granted."

5.

Que les dits habitans ne seront point transferés ni tenus de quitter leurs maisons jusqu'à ce qu'un traité definitif entre S. M. T. C. et S. M. B.[4] ayt reglé leur état.

"Granted."

ARTICLES OF THE CAPITULATION OF QUEBEC, 1759.[1]

Articles of Capitulation demanded by Mr de Ramzay,[2] the King's Lieutenant, commanding the high and low towns of Quebec, Knight of the Military Order of St. Louis, to His Excellency the General of the troops of his Britannic Majesty.

La capitulation demandée d'autre part a été accordée par son Excellence Général Townshend, Brigadier des armées de sa Majesté Britanique en Amerique de la manière & aux conditions exprimées cy dessous.

1.

Mr. de Ramzay demands the honors of war for his garrison, and that it be taken back to the army in safety by the shortest route, with arms, baggage, six pieces of brass canon, two mortars or howitzers, and twelve rounds for each piece.

La garnison de la ville, composée des troupes de terre, de marinne, et matelots, sortiront de la ville avec armes[3] et bagages, tambour battant, meche allumée, avec deux pieces de canon de France et douze coups à tirer pour chaque piece, et sera embarquée le plus commodement possible pour être mise en France au premier port.

2.

That the inhabitants be preserved in the possession of their houses, goods, effects, and privileges.

Accordé, en mettant les armes bas.

3.

That the said inhabitants shall not be called to account for having borne arms in defence of the town, seeing that they have been forced to it, and that the inhabitants of the colonies of both crowns equally serve as militia.

Accordé.

4.

That the effects of absent officers and inhabitants shall not be touched.

Accordé.

5.

That the said inhabitants shall not be removed, nor forced to leave their houses until a definitive treaty between his Most Christian Majesty and his Britannic Majesty have settled their status.

Accordé.

6.

Que l'exercise de la relligion Catholique, apostolique, et romaine sera conservé ; que l'on donnera des sauvegardes aux maisons des ecclésiastiques, relligieux et relligieuses, particulierement à Mgr. l'Evêque de Quebec qui, rempli de zèle pour la relligion et de charité pour le peuple de son diocèse, desire y rester constamment, exercer librement et avec la décense que son état et les sacrés mystères de la relligion Catholique, apostolique, et romaine exigent, son authorité episcopale dans la ville de Quebec lorsqu'il jugera àpropos, jusqu'à ce que la possession du Canada ait été décidée par un traité entre S. M. T. C. et S. M. B.[5]

" The free exercise of the Roman religion is granted, likewise safeguards to all religious persons, as well as to the Bishop, who shall be at liberty to come and exercise, freely and with decency, the functions of his office, whenever he shall think proper, until the possession of Canada shall have been decided between their Britannic and most Christian Majesties."

7.

Que l'artillerie et les munitions de guerre seront remises de bonne foy, et qu'il en sera dressé un inventaire.

"Granted."

8.

Qu'il en sera usé pour les malades, blessés, Commissaire, aumoniers, medecins, chirurgiens, apoticaires, et autres personnes employés au service des hopitaux conformement au traité d'echange du 6 fevrier, 1759, convenu entre leurs M. T. C. et B.

"Granted."

9.

Qu'avant de livrer la porte et l'entrée de la ville aux troupes angloises, leur général voudra bien remettre quelques soldats pour être mis en sauve-gardes aux églises, couvents, et principales habitations.

"Granted."

10.

Qu'il sera permis au Lieutenant de Roy commandant dans la ville de Quebec d'envoyer informer M^r le Marquis de Vaudreuil,[6] Gouverneur Général, de la reddition de la place, comm' aussi que le Général pourra écrire au ministre de France pour l'en informer.

"Granted."

6.

That the exercise of the Catholic, Apostolic, and Roman religion shall be preserved; that safe-guards shall be given to the houses of the clergy, to the monasteries and the convents, especially to His Lordship the Bishop of Quebec, who, full of zeal for religion and of love for the people of his diocese, desires to remain constantly in it, to exercise freely, and with the decency which his standing and the sacred mysteries of the Catholic, Apostolic, and Roman religion requires, his episcopal authority in the town of Quebec, whenever he shall think fit, until the possession of Canada has been decided by a treaty between his most Christian Majesty and his Britannic Majesty.[5]

Libre exercise de la religion romaine, sauves gardes accordées à toutes personnes religieuses ainsi qu'à M^r l'evêque qui pourra venir exercer librement et avec decence les fonctions de son état lorsqu'il le jugera àpropos, jusqu' à ce que la possession du Canada ayt été décidée entre sa Majesté B. et S. M. T. C.

7.

That the artillery and ammunition shall be given up in good faith, and that an inventory of them shall be made out.

Accordé.

8.

That the treatment of the sick, the wounded, the commissary, the chaplains, the physicians, the surgeons, the apothecaries, and other persons employed in the hospital service shall be in accordance with the cartel of the 6th of February, 1759, arranged between their most Christian and Britannic Majesties.

Accordé.

9.

That before the surrender of the gate and of the entrance of the town to the English troops, their General will be good enough to send some soldiers to be placed as safe-guards over the churches, the convents, and the principal residences.

Accordé.

10.

That leave shall be granted to the Lieutenant of the King commanding in the town of Quebec to send to inform the Marquis de Vaudreuil,[a] Governor-General, of the surrender of the place, as also that the General shall be allowed to write to the French Minister to inform him of it.

Accordé.

11.

Que la présente capitulation sera exécutée suivant sa forme et teneur, sans qu' elle puisse être sujette à l' inexécution sous prétexte de represailles ou d' une inexécution de quelque capitulation précédente.⁷

"Granted."

Le présent traité a été fait et arreté double entre nous au camp devant Quebec, le 18ᵐᵉ Septembre, 1759.

CHAS. SAUNDERS.
GEO. TOWNSHEND.
DE RAMZAY.

Endorsed:—Capitulation of Quebec.
in Genˡ Townshend's
of Sepʳ 20th, 1759.

NOTES TO THE CAPITULATION OF QUEBEC.

1 The left hand page contains the contract of surrender, the stipulations of the French commander being in French, and the replies of the British commanders in English. The right hand page contains an English translation of the French stipulations and a French translation of the British concessions. The French text in both columns is printed from a certified copy of the original document in the "Colonial Office Papers" under the title of "America and the West Indies," vol. 88. There are verbal differences between this text and the one given in Knox's "Historical Journal of the Campaigns in North America," (vol. II, p. 87). From the latter the text in vol. O. of the "Statutes of Lower Canada" seems to have been taken, with the correction of some literal errors. The "First Series" of historical documents published by the "Literary and Historical Society of Quebec" contains two versions of these articles, one given at p. 22 of the "Evenements de la Guerre en Canada," the other as appendix No. 7 to the "Memoire du Sieur de Ramezay." Appendix No. 2 to the same "Memoire" is the draft of these articles sent by the Marquis de Vaudreuil to De Ramezay to be used in the event of the surrrender of Quebec becoming a necessity. The texts of the draft and of the version given in the "Evenements" agree verbally with the text here printed, while the one given in Appendix No. 7 to the "Memoire" agrees verbally with that given by Knox. The English translation of the French stipulations is based on the contemporary translation given by Knox, and on the translation given in the "Documents Relative to the Colonial History of the State of New York," vol. x., p. 1011. These differ from each other, and neither of them has been followed where there seemed to be room for improvement. The British conces-

11.

That the present capitulation shall be executed according to its form and tenor, without being subject to non-execution under pretext of reprisals or of the non-execution of some previous capitulation.[7]

Accordé.

The present treaty has been made and executed in duplicate between us at the camp before Quebec, this 18th of September, 1759.

CHAS. SAUNDERS.
GEO. TOWNSHEND
DE RAMZAY.

Endorsed :—Capitulation of Quebec, in Genl Townshend's of Sep^t 20th, 1759.

---

sions are printed almost identically in Knox's "Historical Journal," in the New York "Documents," and in the "Annual Register" for 1759 (p. 247). Knox's text has been here followed as he was on the spot.

[2] Knox spells the name "De Ramsay." In the "Memoire" referred to in note 1, which was written by himself, he spells it "De Ramezay." This "Memoire" was found by M. Faribault in 1852, in the Archives of the Bureau de la Marine, where to all appearance it had lain from the time when the author prepared it as a defence of himself against the charge of having too hastily surrendered Quebec after the death of Montcalm.

[3] Compare this concession with that granted by Gen. Amherst the following year. See the Capitulation of Montreal.

[4] "Sa Majeste Tres Chretienne et Sa Majeste Britannique."

[5] In the draft articles sent by the Marquis de Vaudreuil to Lieutenant de Ramzay article 6 is accompanied by the following comment: "Prouver que c'est l'interest de S. M. B. dans le cas ou le Canada luy resteroit, et qu'en Europe touttes les conquettes que font les divers souverains, ils ne changent point l'exercise de religion qu 'autant que ces conquettes leur restent."

[6] Then encamped at St. Augustin, "four leagues from Quebec." From this head quarters he wrote on the 21st of September to M. Berryer in France a brief account of the battle between Wolfe and Montcalm, and of the subsequent surrender of Quebec, which he characterized as premature and contrary to orders.

[7] The reference seems to be to the massacre of British prisoners of war, two years before, at Fort William Henry, by the Indian allies of Moncalm. See Parkman's "Montcalm and Wolfe," chapter xv.

ARTICLES DE CAPITULATION DE MONTREAL, 1760.[1]

Articles de Capitulation entre son Excellence le Général Amherst, Commandant en Chef les troupes & forces de Sa Majesté Britanique en l'Amerique Septentrionale, et son Excellence le Mis de Vaudreuil, Grand Croix de l'Ordre Royal et Militaire de St. Louis, Gouverneur et Lieutenant General pour le Roy in Canada.

Art. 1er.

Vingt-quatre heures après la signature de la présente capitulation, le Général Anglois fera prendre par les troupes de Sa Majesté Britanique possession des portes de la Ville de Montreal, et la garnison Angloise ne poura y entrer qu après l' evacuation des troupes françoises.

" The whole garrison of Montreal must lay down their arms, and shall not serve during the present war.[2] Immediately after the signing of the present capitulation, the King's troops shall take possession of the gates, and shall post the guards necessary to preserve good order in the town." [3]

Art. 2.

Les troupes et les milices, qui seront en garnison dans la ville de Montréal, en sortiront par la porte de[4]———— avec tous les honeurs de la guerre, six pièces de canon, et un mortier, qui seront chargés dans le vaisseau òu le Marquis de Vaudreuil embarquera, avec dix coups à tirer par pièce. Il en sera usé de même pour la garnison de trois rivières pour les honeurs de la guerre.

" Referred to the next Article."[5]

Art. 3.

Les troupes et milices qui seront en garnison dans le Fort de Jacques Cartier et dans l'Isle Ste Helene, & autres forts, seront traittées de même et auront les mêmes honeurs, et ces troupes se rendront à Montreal, ou aux 3 Rivières, ou à Quebec, pour y estre toutes embarquées pour le premier port de mer en France par le plus court chemin. Les troupes qui sont dans nos postes situés sur nos frontièrs, du costé de l'Accadie, au Détroit, Michilimakinac, et autre postes, jouiront des mêmes honeurs et seront traittées de même.

" All these troops are not to serve during the present war, and shall likewise lay down their arms ; the rest is granted."

ARTICLES OF THE CAPITULATION OF MONTREAL, 1760.[1]

Articles of Capitulation between their Excellencies, Major-General Amherst, Commander-in-Chief of his Britannic Majesty's troops and forces in North America, on the one part, and the Marquis de Vaudreuil, &c., Governor and Lieutenant-General for the King in Canada, on the other.

ART 1.

Twenty-four hours after the signing of the present capitulation, the English General shall cause the troops of his Britannic Majesty to take possession of the gates of the town of Montreal, and the English garrison shall not enter the place till after its evacuation by the French troops.

Toute la garnison de Montreal doit mettre bas les armes, et ne servira point pendant la présente guerre[2]; immédiatement aprés la signature de la présente, les troupes du Roy prendront possession des portes et posteront les gardes necessaires pour maintenir le bon ordre dans la ville.[3]

ART. 2.

The troops and the militia, who are in garrison in the town of Montreal, shall go out of the gate of[4] ——— with all the honors of war, six pieces of canon and one mortar, which shall be put on board the vessel on which the Marquis de Vaudreuil shall embark, with ten rounds for each piece. The same treatment shall be extended to the garrison of Three Rivers, as to the honors of war.

ART. 3.

The troops and militia, who shall be in garrison in the fort of Jacques Cartier and in the Island of St. Helen, and other forts, shall be treated in the same manner, and shall have the same honors; and these troops shall go to Montreal, or to Three Rivers, or to Quebec, to be all there embarked for the first sea port in France, by the shortest way. The troops who are in our posts situated on our frontiers, on the side of Acadia, at Detroit, Michilimakinac, and other posts, shall enjoy the same honors, and be treated in the same manner.

Toutes ces troupes ne doivent point servir pendant la présente guerre, et mettront pareillement les armes bas ; le reste est accordé.

Art. 4.

Les milices après estre sorties des villes, et des forts et postes cy dessus, retourneront chez elles, sans pouvoir estre inquiettées, sous quelque prétexte que ce soit, pour avoir porté les armes.

"Granted."

Art. 5.

Les troupes qui tiennent la campagne leveront leur camp, marcheront tambour battant, armes, bagages, et avec leur artillerie, pour se joindre à la garnison de Montreal, et auront en tout le même traitement.

"These troops, as well as the others, must lay down their arms."

Art. 6.

Les sujets de sa Majesté Britanique et de sa Majesté Très Chrétienne soldats, miliciens, ou matelots, qui auront déserté,[6] ou laissé le service de leur souverain, et porté les armes dans l'Amérique Septentrionale, seront de part et d'autre pardonés de leur crime. Ils seront respectivement rendus à leur patrie, sinon ils resteront chacun où ils sont, sans qu' ils puissent estre recherchés ni inquiettés.

"Refused."

Art. 7.

Les magazins, l'artillerie, fusils, sabres, munitions de guerre, et généralement tout ce qui apartient à S. M. T. C., tant dans les villes de Montreal et 3 Rivières, que dans les forts et postes mentionés en l'article 3, seront livrés par des inventaires exacts, aux commissaires qui seront préposés pour les recevoir au nom de S. M. B. Il sera remis au Mis de Vaudreuil des expeditions en bonne forme des d'inventaires.

"This is everything that can be asked on this article."

Art. 8.

Les officiers, soldats, miliciens, matelots, et même les sauvages détenus pour cause de leurs blessures ou maladie, tant dans les hopitaux que dans les maisons particulières, jouiront des privilèges du cartel, et traittées conséquament.

"The sick and wounded shall be treated the same as our own people."

Art. 9.

Le Général Anglois s'engagera de renvoyer chez eux les sauvages Indiens,[7] et Monaigans,[8] qui font nombre de ses armées, d'abord après la signature de la présente capitulation. Et cependant, pour prévenir tous désordres de la part de ceux qui ne seroient pas partis, il sera donné

THE CAPITULATION OF MONTREAL.

Art. 4.

The militia, after evacuating the above towns, forts, and posts, shall return to their homes without being molested on any pretence whatever, on account of their having borne arms.

Accordé.

Art. 5.

The troops who keep the field shall raise their camp, shall march, drums beating, with their arms, bagage, and artillery, to join the garrison of Montreal, and shall have in every respect the same treatment.

Ces troupes doivent, comme les autres, mettre bas les armes.

Art. 6.

The subjects of his Britannic Majesty, and of his Most Christian Majesty, soldiers, militia, or seamen, who shall have deserted[a] or left the service of their sovereign, and borne arms in North America, shall be on both sides pardoned for their crime. They shall be respectively returned to their country; if not, each shall remain where he is without being called to account or molested,

Refusé.

Art. 7.

The magazines, the artillery, firelocks, sabres, ammunition, and in general everything that belongs to his Most Christian Majesty, as well in the towns of Montreal and Three Rivers as in the forts and posts mentioned in article 3, shall be delivered up, according to exact inventories, to the commissaries who shall be appointed to receive them in the name of his Britannic Majesty. Duplicates of the said inventories in due form shall be given to the Marquis de Vaudreuil.

C'est tout ce qu'on peut demander sur cette article.

Art. 8.

The officers, soldiers, militia, seamen, and even the savages, detained on account of their wounds or sickness, as well in the hospitals as in private houses, shall enjoy the privileges of the cartel, and shall be treated accordingly,

Les malades et blessés seront traités de même que nos propres gens.

Art. 9.

The British General shall engage to send back to their own homes the savage Indians[7] and Monäigans,[8] who make part of his armies, immediately after the signing of the present capitulation; and in the meantime, in order to prevent all disorders on the part of those who may not have gone

par ce Général des sauve-gardes aux personnes qui en demanderont, tant en ville que dans les campagnes.

"The first part refused. There never have been any cruelties committed by the Indians of our army, and good order will be preserved."

Art. 10.

Le Général de Sa Majesté Britanique garentira tous désordres de la part de ses troupes ; les assujetira à payer les domages qu'elles pouroient faire, tant dans les villes que dans les campagnes.

"Answered by the preceding article."

Art. 11.

Le Général Anglois ne poura obliger le Marquis de Vaudreuil de sortir de la ville de Montreal avant le ————, et on ne poura loger personne dans son hôtel jusqu'à son départ. M. le Ch^{er} Levis comandant les troupes de terre, les officiers principaux, et majors des troupes de terre et de la colonie, les ingénieurs, officiers d'artillerie, et comissaire des guerres,[9] resteront pareillement à Montreal jusqu'au d. jour, et y conserveront leur logemens. Il en sera usé de même à l'égard de M. Bigot, Intendant, des comissaires de la marine, et officiers de plume, dont mond: s.[10] Bigot aura besoin : et on ne poura également loger personne à l'intendance avant le départ de cet Intendant.

"The Marquis de Vaudreuil, and all these gentlemen, shall be masters of their houses, and shall embark when the King's ships shall be ready to sail for Europe : and all possible conveniences [11] shall be granted them."

Art. 12.

Il sera destiné pour le passage en droiture au premier port de mer en France, du Marquis de Vaudreuil, le vaisseau le plus comode qui se trouvera ; il y sera pratiqué les logemens nécessaires pour lui, Mad^e la Marquise de Vaudreuil, M. de Rigaud, Gouverneur de Montreal, et la suitte de ce Général. Ce vaisseau sera pourvû de subsistances convenables au dépens de Sa M^{te} Britanique, et le Mis de Vaudreuil emportera avec lui ses papiers, sans qu'ils puissent estre visites, et il embarquera ses equipages, vaisselle, bagages, et ceux de sa suitte.

"Granted, except the archives which shall be necessary for the government of the country."

Art. 13.

Si avant ou après l'embarquement du Mis de Vaudreuil, la nouvelle de la paix arrivoit,[12] et que par le traitté le Canada reste à Sa M^{te} T. C., le Mis de Vaudreuil reviendroit à Québec ou à Montreal, toutes choses

away, the said General shall give safe-guards to such persons as shall desire them, as well in the town as in the country.

Le premier refusé. Il n'y a point eu des cruautés commises par les sauvages de notre armée : et le bon ordre sera maintenu.

Art. 10.

His Britannic Majesty's general shall be answerable for all disorders on the part of his troops, and shall oblige them to pay the damages they may do, as well in the towns as in the country.

Répondu par l'article précédent.

Art. 11.

The English general shall not oblige the Marquis de Vaudreuil to leave the town of Montreal before————, and no person shall be quartered in his house till he is gone. The Chevalier de Levis, commander of the land forces, the principal officers and majors of the land forces and colony troops, the engineers, officers of artillery, and commissary of war,[9] shall also remain at Montreal till the said day, and shall keep their lodgings. The same shall be observed with regard to M. Bigot, Intendant, to the commissaries of marine, and the writers whom the said M. Bigot shall require; and similarly no one shall be lodged at the Intendant's house before his departure.

Le Marquis de Vaudreuil et tous ces messieurs seront maitres de leurs maisons, et s'embarqueront dès que les vaisseaux du Roy seront prêts à faire voile pour l'Europe ; et on leur accordera toutes les commodités[11] qu' on pourra.

Art. 12.

The most convenient vessel that can be found shall be appointed to convey the Marquis de Vaudreuil by the straitest passage to the first seaport in France ; there shall be furnished the accommodations necessary for him, the Marchioness de Vaudreuil, M. de Rigaud, the Governor of Montreal, and the suite of that general. This vessel shall be properly victualled at the expense of his Britannic Majesty, and the Marquis de Vaudreuil shall take with him his papers without their being examined, and shall put on board his equipages, plate, baggage, and also those of his retinue.

Accordé ; excepté les archives qui pouront être nécessaires pour le gouvernement du pais.

Art. 13.

If before or after the embarkation of the Marquis de Vaudreuil, news of peace arrives,[12] and Canada by treaty remains to his Most Christian Majesty, the Marquis de Vaudreuil shall return to Quebec or Montreal ; everything shall return to its former state under the dominion of

rentreroient dans leur premier estat sous la domination de Sa M^{té} T. C., et la présente capitulation deviendroit nulle et sans effets quelconques.

" Whatever the King may have done on this subject shall be obeyed."

Art. 14.

Il sera destiné deux vaisseaux pour le passage en France de M. le Ch^{er} de Levis, des officiers principaux, et estat major général des troupes de terre, ingénieurs, officiers d'artillerie, et gens qui sont à leur suitte. Ces vaisseaux seront également pourvûs de subsistances ; il y sera pratiqué les logemens nécessaires. Ces officiers pouront emporter leurs papiers, qui ne seront point visités, leurs equipages et bagages. Ceux de ces officiers qui seront mariés auront la liberté d'emmener avec eux leurs femmes et enfans, et la subsistance leur sera fournie.

" Granted ; except that the Marquis de Vaudreuil and all the officers, of whatever rank they may be, shall faithfully deliver to us all the charts and plans of the country."

Art. 15.

Il en sera de même destiné un pour le passage de Mr Bigot, Intendant, et de sa suitte, dans lequel vaisseau il sera fait les aménagemens convenables pour lui et les personnes qu'il emmenera. Il y embarquera également ses papiers, qui ne seront point visités, ses equipages, vaisselle, et bagages, et ceux de sa suitte. Ce vaisseau sera pourvû de subsistances comme il est dit cy devant.

" Granted, with the same reserve as in the preceding article."

Art. 16.

Le Général Anglois fera aussi fournir pour M. de Longueüil, Gouverneur des 3 Rivières, pour les estats majors de la colonie, et les comissaires de la marine, les vaisseaux nécessaires pour se rendre en France, et le plus comodement qu'il sera possible. Ils pouront y embarquer leur familles, domestique, bagages, equipages ; et la subsistance leur sera fournie pendant la traversée sur un pied convenable, aux dépens de Sa M^{té} Britanique.

" Granted."

Art. 17.

Les officiers et soldats, tant des troupes de terre que de la colonie, ainsi que les officiers marins et matelots, qui se trouveront dans la colonie seront aussi embarqués pour France dans les vaisseaux qui leur seront destinés en nombre suffisant, et le plus comodement que faire se poura. Les officiers de troupes et marins, qui seront mariés, pouront emmener avec eux leurs familles, et tous auront la liberté d'embarquer leurs

his Most Christian Majesty, and the present capitulation shall become null and of no effect.

Ce que le Roy pouroit avoir fait à ce sujet, sera obëi.

Art. 14.

Two ships shall be appointed for the passage to France of the Chevalier de Levis, of the principal officers and staff of the land forces, engineers, officers of artillery, and the members of their suite. Those vessels shall likewise be victualled, and the necessary accommodation shall be provided in them. Those officers shall be allowed to take with them their papers, which shall not be examined, their equipages and baggage. Such of the said officers as shall be married shall have liberty to take with them their wives and children, and subsistence shall be furnished for them.

Accordé: excepté que M. le Mis de Vaudreuil, et tous les officiers de quelque rang qu'ils puissent être, nous remettront de bonne foy toutes les cartes et plans du païs.

Art. 15.

A vessel shall also be appointed for the passage of M. Bigot, the Intendant, and of his suite, in which vessel the proper accommodation shall be made for him and the persons whom he shall take with him. He shall likewise take on board with him his papers, which shall not be examined, his equipages, plate, and baggage, and those of his suite. This vessel shall be victualled, as before mentioned.

Accordé; avec la même réserve que par l'article precedent.

Art. 16.

The English general shall also cause to be provided for M. de Longueuil, Governor of Three Rivers, for the staff of the colony, and the commissaries of marine, the vessels necessary for their transportation to France in the most convenient way possible. They shall embark therein their families, servants, baggage, and equipages; and subsistence on a suitable footing shall during the voyage be furnished for them at the expense of his Britannic Majesty.

Accordé.

Art. 17.

The officers and soldiers, as well of the land forces as of the colony, and also the marine officers and seamen who shall be in the colony, shall likewise be embarked for France in vessels appointed for them in sufficient numbers, and in the most convenient way possible. The married officers of the land forces and marines shall be allowed to take with them their families, and all of them shall have liberty

domestiques et bagages. Quant aux soldats et matelots, ceux qui seront mariés pouront emmener avec eux leurs femmes et enfans, et tous embarqueront leur havresacs et bagages. Il sera embarqué dans ces vaisseaux les subsistances convenables et suffisantes aux dépens de Sa M^{te} Britanique.

"Granted."

Art. 18.

Les officiers, soldats, et tous ceux qui sont à la suitte des troupes, qui auront leurs bagages dans les campagnes, pouront les envoyer chercher avant leur départ, sans qu'il leur soit fait aucun tort, ni empeschement.

"Granted."

Art. 19.

Il sera fourni par le Général Anglois un bâtiment d'hôpital pour ceux des officiers, soldats, et matelots blessés ou malades, qui seront en estat d'estre transportés en France, et la subsistance leur sera également fournie aux dépens de sa M^{te} Britanique. Il en sera usé de même à l'égard des autres officiers, soldats, et matelots, blessés ou malades, aussitost qu'ils seront rétablis. Les uns et les autres pouront emmener leurs femmes, enfans, domestiques, et bagages; et lesd.[?] soldats et matelots ne pouront être solicités ni forcés à prendre parti dans le service de sa M^{te} Britanique.

"Granted."

Art. 20.

Il sera laissé un comissaire, et un écrivain de Roy pour avoir soin des hopitaux, et veiller à tout ce qui aura raport au service de sa M^{te} Très Chrétienne.

"Granted."

Art. 21.

Le Général Anglois fera également fournir des vaisseaux pour le passage en France des officiers du Conseil Supérieur, de Justice, Police, de l'Amirauté, et tous autres officiers ayant comissions ou brevets de sa M^{te} Très Chrétienne, pour eux, leurs familles, domestiques, et equipages, comme pour les autres officiers; et la subsistance leur sera fournie de même au dépens de sa M^{te} Britanique. Il leur sera cependant libre de rester dans la colonie, s'il le jugent apropos, pour y arranger leurs affaires, ou de se retirer en France quand bon leur semblera.

"Granted, but if they have papers relating to the government of the country, they are to be delivered up to us."

Art. 22.

S'il y a des officiers militaires dont les affaires exigent leur présence dans la colonie jusqu' à l'année prochaine, ils pouront y rester après en

to embark their servants and baggage. As to the soldiers and seamen, those who are married shall take with them their wives and children, and all of them shall embark their haversacks and baggage; there shall be put on board these vessels at the expense of his Britannic Majesty, suitable and sufficient subsistence.

Accordé.

Art. 18.

The officers, soldiers, and all the followers of the troops, who shall have their baggage in the fields, may send for it before their departure, without harm or hindrance.

Accordé.

Art. 19.

There shall be furnished by the English general an hospital ship for such of the wounded or sick officers, soldiers, and seamen as shall be in a condition to be carried to France, and subsistence shall likewise be furnished for them at the expense of his Britannic Majesty. The same treatment shall be extended to the other wounded or sick officers, soldiers, and seamen, as soon as they shall have recovered. They shall all be allowed to take with them their wives, children, servants, and baggage; and the said soldiers and sailors shall not be solicited nor forced to take part in the service of his Britannic Majesty.

Accordé.

Art. 20.

A commissary and one of the King's writers shall be left to take care of the hospitals, and to attend to whatever may relate to the service of his Most Christian Majesty.

Accordé.

Art. 21.

The English general shall also cause ships to be provided for the passage to France of the officers of the Supreme Council, of justice, of police, admiralty, and all other officers having commissions or brevets from his Most Christian Majesty for them—their families, servants, and equipages, as for the other officers; and subsistence for them likewise shall be furnished at the expense of his Britannic Majesty. They shall, however, be free to remain in the colony, if they think proper, to settle their affairs, or to withdraw to France whenever they think fit.

Accordé, mais s'ils ont des papiers qui concernent le gouvernement du pais, ils doivent nous les remettre.

Art. 22.

If there are any military officers, whose affairs require their presence in the colony till the next year, they shall have liberty to stay in it after

avoir eu la permission du Mis de Vaudreuil, et sans qu'ils puissent estre réputés prisoniers de guerre.

" All those whose private affairs shall require their stay in the country, and who shall have the Marquis de Vaudreuil's leave for so doing, shall be allowed to remain till their affairs are settled."

Art. 23.

Il sera permis au munitionaire des vivres du Roy de demeurer en Canada jusqu'à l'année prochaine, pour estre en estat de faire face aux dettes qu'il a contractées dans la colonie, relativement à ses fournitures ; si néantmoins il préfère de passer en France cette année, il sera obligé de laisser, jusqu'à l'année prochaine une personne pour faire ses affaires. Ce particulier conservera et pourra emporter tous ses papiers, sans estre visités. Ses comis auront la liberté de rester dans la colonie, ou de passer en France ; et dans ce dernier cas, le passage et la subsistance leur seront accordés sur les vaisseaux de sa M^{te} Britanique pour eux, leurs familles, et leurs bagages.

" Granted."

Art. 24.

Les vivres et autres aprovisionements qui se trouveront en nature dans les magasins du munitionaire, tant dans les villes de Montreal et des 3 Rivières, que dans les campagnes, lui seront conservés, lesd. vivres lui appartenant et non au Roy, et il lui sera loisible de les vendre aux Francois ou aux Anglois.

" Everything that is actually in the magazines, destined for the use of the troops, is to be delivered to the British commissary, for the King's forces."

Art. 25.

Le passage en France sera également accordé sur les vaisseaux de sa M^{te} Britanique, ainsi que la subsistance, à ceux des officiers de la compagnie des Indes[14] qui voudront y passer, et ils emmeneront leurs familles, domestiques, et bagages. Sera permis à l'agent principal de lad^{te}[15] compagnie, supposé qu'il voulut passer en France, de laisser telle personne qu'il jugera apropos jusques à l'année prochaine pour terminer les affaires de lad^{te} comp^{ie} et faire le recouvrement des sommes qui lui sont dues. L'agent principal conservera tous les papiers de lad^{te} compagnie, et ils ne pouront estre visités.

" Granted."

Art. 26.

Cette compagnie sera maintenue dans la propriété des ecarlatines[16] et castors, qu'elle peut avoir dans la ville de Montreal ; il n'y sera point

having obtained the permission of the Marquis de Vaudreuil for that purpose, and without being reputed prisoners of war.

Tous ceux dont les affaires particulières exigent qu' ils restent dans le païs, et qui en ont la permission de M. Vaudreüil, seront permis de rester jusque' à ce que leurs affaires soient terminées.

Art. 23.

The commissary for the King's provisions shall be permitted to stay in Canada till next year, in order to be able to answer for the debts he has contracted in the colony on account of what he has furnished; if, nevertheless, he prefers to go to France this year, he shall be obliged to leave till next year a person to transact his business. This person shall preserve, and have liberty to carry off, all his papers without being inspected. His clerks shall have leave to stay in the colony, or to go to France; and in this latter case a passage and subsistence shall be allowed them on the ships of his Britannic Majesty, for them, their families, and their baggage.

Accordé.

Art. 24.

The provisions and other stores, which shall be found in kind in the magazines of the commissary, as well in the towns of Montreal and Three Rivers as in the country, shall be preserved to him, the said provisions belonging to him and not to the King; and he shall be at liberty to sell them to the French and English.

Tout ce qui se trouve dans les magazins destinés à l'usage des troupes doit être delivré au commissaire Anglois pour les troupes du Roy.

Art. 25.

A passage to France shall likewise be granted on board of his Britannic Majesty's ships, as well as victuals, to such officers of the India Company[14] as shall be willing to go thither, and they shall take with them their families, servants, and baggage. The chief agent of the said company, in case he should choose to go to France, shall be allowed to leave such person as he shall think proper till next year, to settle the affairs of the said company, and to collect such sums as are due to them. The chief agent shall keep possession of all the papers of the said company, and they shall not be liable to inspection.

Accordé.

Art. 26.

This company shall be maintained in the ownership of the Ecarlatines[16] and the beavers they may have in the town of Montreal; they shall not

touché sous quelque prétexte que ce soit, et il sera donné à l'agent principal les facilités necessaires pour faire passer cette année en France ses castors sur les vaisseaux de Sa M^te Britanique, en payant le fret sur le pied que les Anglois le payeroient.

"Granted with regard to what may belong to the company, or to private persons; but if his Most Christian Majesty has any share in it, that must become the property of the King."

Art. 27.

Le libre exercise de la Religion Catolique, apostolique, et Romaine, subsistera en son entier; en sorte que tous les estats et les peuples des villes et des campagnes, lieux et postes éloignés pouront continuer de s'assembler dans les èglises, et de fréquenter les sacramens comme cy devant, sans estre inquieté en aucun manière, directement ou indirectement. Ces peuples seront obligées par le Gouvernement Anglois à payer aux prêtres qui en prendront soin les dixmes, et tous les droits qu'ils avoient coutume de payer sous le gouvernement de sa M^te Très Chrétienne.

"Granted as to the free exercise of their religion; the obligation of paying the tithes¹⁷ to the priests will depend on the King's pleasure."

Art. 28.

Le Chapitre, les prestres, curés, et missionaires, continueront avec entière liberté leurs exercises et fonctions curiales dans les paroisses des villes et des campagnes.

"Granted."

Art. 29.

Les Grands Vicaires només par le Chapitre pour administrer le Dioceze pendant la vacance du siège episcopal pouront demeurer dans les villes ou paroisses des campagnes, suivant qu'ils le jugeront àpropos. Ils pouront en tout temps visiter les differentes paroisses du Dioceze, avec les cérémonies ordinaires, et exercer toute la jurisdiction qu'ils exercoient sous la domination Françoise. Ils jouiront des mêmes droits en cas de mort du futur evesque, dont il sera parlé à l'article suivant.

"Granted, except what regards the following article."

Art. 30.

Si par le Traitté de Paix, le Canada restoit au pouvoir de sa M^te Britanique, sa M^te Très Chrétiene continueroit a nomer l'évesque de la Colonie, qui seroit toujours de la comunion Romaine, et sous l'autorité duquel les peuples exerceroient la religion Romaine.

"Refused."

be touched under any pretence whatever, and there shall be given to the chief agent the necessary facilities to send this year his beavers to France on board his Britannic Majesty's ships, paying the freight on the same footing as the British would pay it.

Accordé pour ce qui peut appartenir a la compagnie ou aux particuliers, mais si Sa Majesté Trés Chrétienne y a aucune part, elle doit être au profit du Roy.

Art. 27.

The free exercise of the Catholic, Apostolic, and Roman religion shall subsist entire, in such manner that all classes and peoples of the towns and rural districts, places, and distant posts may continue to assemble in the churches, and to frequent the sacraments as heretofore, without being molested in any manner, directly or indirectly. These people shall be obliged by the English Government to pay to the priests, who shall have the oversight of them, the tithes and all the dues they were accustomed to pay under the Government of his Most Christian Majesty.

Accordé pour le libre exercise de leur Religion. L'obligation de payer la dixme[17] aux prêtres dependra de la volonté du Roy.

Art. 28.

The Chapter, priests, curés and missionaries shall continue with entire freedom their parochial services and functions in the parishes of the towns and rural districts.

Accordé.

Art. 29.

The Grand Vicars named by the Chapter to administer the diocese during the vacancy of the episcopal see shall have liberty to dwell in the towns or country parishes, as they shall think proper. They shall at all times be free to visit the different parishes of the diocese with the ordinary ceremonies, and exercise all the jurisdiction they exercised under the French dominion. They shall enjoy the same rights in case of the death of the future Bishop, of which mention will be made in the following article.

Accordé, excepté ce qui regarde l'article suivant.

Art. 30.

If by the treaty of peace Canada should remain in the power of his Britannic Majesty, His Most Christian Majesty shall continue to name the Bishop of the colony, who shall always be of the Roman communion, and under whose authority the people shall exercise the Roman religion.

Refusé.

Art. 31.

Poura le Seigneur Evesque etablir dans le besoin de nouvelles paroisses, et pourvoir au rétablissement de sa Cathédrale et de son palais episcopal ; et il aura en attendant la liberté de demeurer dans les villes, ou paroisses, comme il le jugera àpropos. Il poura visiter son diocèze avec les cérémonies ordinaires, et exercer toute la jurisdiction que son predecesseur exerçoit sous la domination françoise, sauf à exiger de lui le serment de fidelité, ou promesse de ne rien faire, ni rien dire contre le service de sa M^{te} Britanique.

"This article is comprised under the foregoing."

Art. 32.

Les comunautés de filles seront conservées dans leurs constitutions et privilèges. Elles continueront d'observer leur règles. Elles seront exemptes du logement de gens de guerre, et il sera fait deffenses de les troubler dans les exercises de pieté qu'elles pratiquent, ni d'entrer chez elles. On leur donnera même des sauve-gardes, si elles en demandent.

"Granted."

Art. 33.

Le précédent article sera pareillement executé à l'égard des Jesuites et Recolets, et de la maison des prêtres de St. Sulpice à Montreal. Ces derniers et les Jesuites conserveront le droit qu'ils ont de nomer à certaines cures et missions, comme cy devant.

"Refused, till the King's pleasure be known."

Art. 34.

Toutes les comunautés, et tous les prestres conserveront leurs meubles, la proprieté, et l'usufruit des seigneuries, et autres biens que les uns et les autres possedent dans la colonie, de quelque nature qu'ils soient, et lesd. biens seront conservés dans leurs privilèges, droits, honeurs, et exemptions.

"Granted."

Art. 35.

Si les chanoines, prestres, missionaires, les prestres du seminaire des missions etrangères et de St. Sulpice, ainsi que les Jesuites et les Recolets, veulent passer en France, le passage leur sera accordé sur les vaisseaux de sa Majesté Britanique, et tous auront la liberté de vendre, en total ou partie, les biens fonds et mobiliers qu'ils possedent dans la colonie, soit aux François ou aux Anglois, sans que le Gouvernement Britanique puisse

Art. 31.

The Bishop shall in case of need establish new parishes, and provide for the re-erection of his cathedral and of his episcopal palace ; and he shall have in the meantime liberty to dwell in the towns or parishes, as he shall think fit. He shall be permitted to visit his diocese with the usual ceremonies, and to exercise all the jurisdiction which his predecessor exercised under the French dominion, save that an oath of fidelity, or a promise not to do or say anything against the service of his Britannic Majesty may be required of him.

C'est Article¹ˢ est compris sous le précédent.

Art. 32.

The communities of nuns shall be preserved in their constitutions and privileges. They shall continue to observe their rules. They shall be exempt from lodging any military, and it shall be forbidden to molest them in the religious exercises which they practise, or to enter their convents. Safe-guards shall even be given them, if they demand them.

Accordé.

Art. 33.

The preceding article shall likewise be executed with regard to the communities of Jesuits and Recollets, and to the house of the priests of St. Sulpice at Montreal. These latter and the Jesuits shall be left in possession of the right, which they have, to nominate to certain cures and missions, as heretofore.

" Refusé jusqû à ce que le plaisir du Roy soit connu."

Art. 34.

All the communities and all the priests shall keep their movables, the ownership and usufruct of the seigniories, and other property which both possess in the colony, of whatever nature it may be, and the said property shall be maintained in its privileges, rights, honors, and exemptions.

" Accordé."

Art. 35.

If the canons, priests, missionaries, the priests of the Seminary of the Foreign Missions and of St. Sulpice, as well as the Jesuits and the Recollets, wish to go to France, passage will be given them on the vessels of his Britannic Majesty, and all shall have leave to sell, in whole or in part, the fixed and movable property which they possess in the Colony, either to the French or to the English, without the British Government

y mettre le moindre empeschment ni obstacle. Ils pouront emporter avec eux, ou faire passer en France le produit, de quelque nature qu'il soit, desd. biens vendus, en payant le fret comme il est dit à l'article 26, et ceux d'entre ces prestres qui voudront passer cette année seront nourris pendant la traversée aux dépens de sa M^{te} Britanique, et pouront emporter avec eux leurs bagages.

"They shall be masters to dispose of their estates, and to send the produce thereof, as well as their persons, and all that belongs to them to France."

Art. 36.

Si par le traitté de paix le Canada reste à sa M^{te} Britanique, tous les François, Canadiens, Accadiens, comerçans, et autres personnes qui voudront se retirer en France, en auront la permission du Général Anglois qui leur procurera le passage. Et néantmoins si d'icy âcette decision il se trouvoit des comerçans, François ou Canadiens, ou autres personnes qui voulussent passer en France, le Général Anglois leur en donneroit egalement la permission. Les uns et les autres emmeneront avec eux leurs familles, domestiques, et bagages.

"Granted."

Art. 37.

Les seigneurs de terre, les officiers militaires et de justice, les Canadiens tant des villes que des campagnes, les François établis ou comerçant dans toute l'etendue de la colonie de Canada, et toutes autres personnes que ce puisse estre, conserveront l'entière paisible propriété et possession de leurs biens, seigneuriaux et roturiers, meubles et immeubles, marchandises, pelleteries, et autres effets, même de leurs batimens de mer ; il n'y sera point touché ni fait le moindre domage sous quelque prétexte que ce soit. Il leur sera libre de les conserver, louer, vendre, soit aux François, ou aux Anglois, d'en emporter le produit au lettres de change, pelleteries, espèces sonantes, ou autres retours, lorsqu'ils jugeront àpropos de passer en France, en payant le fret, comme à l'article 26. Ils jouiront aussi des pelleteries qui sont dans les postes d'en haut, & qui leur apartiennent, et qui peuvent même estre en chemin de se rendre à Montreal. Et à cet effet il leur sera permis d'envoyer dès cette année, ou la prochaine, des canots equipés pour chercher celles de ces pelleteries qui auront restées dans ces postes.

"Granted, as in the 26th article."

Art. 38.

Tous les peuples sortis de l'Accadie, qui se trouveront en Canada, y compris les frontières du Canada du costé de l'Accadie,[19] auront le

being able to impose the least hindrance or obstacle. They may take with them, or send to France, the produce, of whatsoever nature it be, of the said property sold, on paying the freight as mentioned in article 26, and those of the priests who wish to go this year shall be maintained during the voyage at the expense of his Britannic Majesty, and shall be allowed to take with them their baggage.

Ils seront les maitres de disposer de leur biens, et d'en passer le produit, ainsi que leurs personnes, et tout ce qui leur appartient, en France,

ART. 36.

If by the treaty of peace Canada remains to his Britannic Majesty, all the French, Canadians, Acadians, merchants and other persons who wish to withdraw to France, shall have permission to do so from the English general, who shall procure them a passage. And, nevertheless, if between now and that decision, any merchants, French or Canadian, or other persons, wish to go to France, the English general shall likewise grant them permission. Both shall take with them their families, servants, and baggage.

Accordé.

ART. 37.

The Seigneurs, the military officers and the officers of justice, the Canadians in both the towns and the rural districts, the French settled or trading in the whole extent of the colony of Canada, and all other persons whatsoever, shall keep the entire peaceable ownership and possession of their property, seignorial and common, movable and immovable, merchandise, furs, and other effects, even their ships; it shall not be touched, nor shall the least damage be done to it under any pretext whatever. They shall be free to keep, let, or sell it to the French or to the English, to take away the produce of it in bills of exchange, furs, specie, or other returns, when they think fit to go to France, paying the freight as in article 26. They shall likewise have the furs which are in the posts above belonging to them, and those which may be on the way to be delivered at Montreal. And for this purpose they shall be permitted to send, this year or next, canoes fitted out to bring such of those furs as shall have remained in those posts.

Accordé comme par l'article 26.

ART. 38.

All the people gone from Acadia, who shall be found in Canada, including the frontiers of Canada on the side of Acadia,[19] shall have

même traitement que les Canadiens, et jouiront des mêmes privilèges qu'eux.

"The king is to dispose of his ancient subjects; in the meantime they shall enjoy the same privilege as the Canadians."

Art. 39.

Aucuns Canadiens, Accadiens, ni François, de ceux qui sont présentement en Canada, et sur les frontières de la colonie du costé de l'Accadie, du Detroit, Michilimakinac, et autres lieux et postes des pays d'en haut, ni les soldats mariés et non mariés, restant en Canada, ne pouront estre portés ni transmigrés dans les colonies Angloises, ni en l'ancienne Angleterre, et ils ne pouront estre recherchés pour avoir pris les armes.

"Granted, except with regard to the Acadians."

Art. 40.

Les sauvages ou Indiens alliés de sa M^{te} Très Chrétienne seront maintenus dans les terres qu'ils habitent, s'ils veulent y rester; ils ne pouront estre inquietés sous quelque prétexte que se puisse estre, pour avoir pris les armes et servi sa M^{te} Très Chrétienne. Ils auront, comme les François, la liberté de religion et conserveront leurs missionnaires. Il sera permis aux vicaires généraux actuels, et à l'evêque, lorsque le siege episcopal sera rempli, de leur envoyer de nouveaux missionnaires, lorsqu'ils le jugeront nécessaire.

"Granted, except the last article, which has been already refused."

Art. 41.

Les François, Canadiens, et Accadiens, qui resteront dans la colonie, de quelque estat et condition qu'ils soient, ne seront, ni ne pouront estre forcés à prendre les armes contre sa M^{te} Très Chrétienne, ni ses alliés, directement ni indirectement, dan quelque occasion que ce soit. Le Gouvernement Britanique ne poura exiger d'eux qu'une exacte neutralité.

"They become subjects of the King."

Art. 42.

Les François et Canadiens continueront d'estre gouvernés suivant la coutume de Paris et les loix et usages etablis pour ce pays, et ils ne pouront estre assujettis à d'autres impots qu'à ceux estoient établis sous la domination Françoise.[20]

"Answered by the preceding articles, and particularly by the last."

the same treatment as the Canadians, and shall enjoy the same privileges as they.

C'est au Roy à disposer de ses anciens sujets: en attendant ils jouiront de mêmes privileges que les Canadiens.

Art. 39.

No Canadians, Acadians, or French, of those who are now in Canada and on the frontiers of the colony on the side of Acadia, Detroit, Michillimackinac, and in other places and posts of the upper country, nor soldiers married and unmarried remaining in Canada, shall be carried or transported into the English colonies, or to Old England, and they shall not be molested for having taken arms.

Accordé excepté à l égard des Acadiens.

Art. 40.

The savage or Indian allies of his Most Christian Majesty shall be maintained in the lands they occupy if they wish to remain there; they shall not be disturbed on any pretext whatever for having taken arms and served his Most Christian Majesty. They shall have, like the French, liberty of religion, and shall keep their missionaries. It shall be permitted to the actual Vicars General, and to the Bishop, when the episcopal see shall be filled, to send new missionaries to them when they think it necessary to do so.

Accordé, à la reserve du dernier article qui a deja été refusé.

Art. 41.

The French, Canadians, and Acadians, who shall remain in the colony, of whatever state and condition they may be, shall not be forced to take arms against either his Most Christian Majesty or his allies, directly or indirectly, on any occasion whatever. The British Government shall require of them only an exact neutrality.

Ils deviennent sujets du Roy.

Art. 42.

The French and Canadians shall continue to be governed according to the custom of Paris, and the laws and usages established for this country; and they shall not be subjected to any other imposts than those which were established under the French dominion.[20]

Repondu par les articles précédents, et particulièrement par le dernièr

Art. 43.

Les papiers du gouvernement resteront sans exception au pouvoir du M¹ˢ de Vaudreuil, et passeront en France avec lui. Ces papiers ne pouront estre visités sous quelque prétexte que ce soit.

" Granted, with the reserve already made."

Art. 44.

Les papiers de l'Intendance, des Bureaux du Controle de la Marine, des Trésoriers ancien et nouveau, des Magazins du Roy, du Bureau du Domaine et des forges St. Maurice, resteront au pouvoir de M. Bigot, Intendant, et ils seront embarqués pour France dans le vaisseau ou il passera. Ces papiers ne seront point visités.

" The same in this article."

Art. 45.

Les Registres et autres papiers du Conseil Supérieur[21] de Quebec, de la Prevosté et Amirauté de la même ville, ceux des jurisdictions Royales des trois Rivières et de Montreal; ceux des jurisdictions seigneuriales de la colonie; les minutes des actes des notaires des villes et des campagnes, et généralement les actes et autres papiers qui peuvent servir à justifier l'estat et la fortune des citoyens, resteront dans la colonie dans les greffes des jurisdictions dont ces papiers dépendent.

" Granted."

Art. 46.

Les habitans et négocians jouiront de tous les privilèges du commerce aux mêmes faveurs et conditions accordées au sujets de sa Majesté Britanique, tant dans les pays d'en haut que dans l'intérieur de la colonie.

" Granted."

Art. 47.

Le negres et panis[22] des deux sexes resteront en leur qualité d'esclaves, en la possession des François et Canadiens à qui ils apartiennent; il leur sera libre de les garder à leur service dans la colonie, ou de les vendre, et ils pourront aussi continuer à les faire elever dans la Religion Romaine.

" Granted, except those who shall have been made prisoners."

Art. 48.

Il sera permis au M¹ˢ de Vaudreuil, aux officiers généraux et supérieurs des troupes de terre, aux Gouverneurs et etats majors des différentes

THE CAPITULATION OF MONTREAL.

Art. 43.

The papers of the Government shall remain without exception in the power of the Marquis de Vaudreuil, and shall go to France with him. Those papers shall not be examined under any pretext whatever.

Accordé avec la reserve déjà faite.

Art. 44.

The papers of the Intendancy, of the offices of Control of Marine, of the old and new Treasuries, of the King's magazines, of the officers of the Revenue and Forges of St. Maurice, shall remain in the power of M. Bigot, the Intendant, and they shall be shipped for France in the vessel in which he goes. Those papers shall not be examined.

Il en est de même de cet article.

Art. 45.

The registers and other papers of the Supreme Council[21] of Quebec, of the Prevôté and Admiralty of the same city; those of the Royal jurisdictions of Three Rivers and Montreal; those of the Seignorial jurisdictions of the colony; the minutes of the acts of the notaries of the towns and of the rural districts, and, generally, the acts and other papers that may serve to prove the estates and the fortune of the citizens, shall remain in the colony in the rolls of the jurisdictions on which those papers depend.

Accordé.

Art. 46.

The inhabitants and merchants shall enjoy all the privileges of trade on the same favors and conditions granted to the subjects of his Britannic Majesty, as well in the upper districts, as in the interior of the colony.

Accordé.

Art. 47.

The negroes and panis[22] of both sexes shall remain in their quality of slaves, in the possession of the French and Canadians to whom they belong; they shall be free to keep them in their service in the colony, or to sell them, and they may also continue to have them brought up in the Roman religion.

Accorde, excepté ceux qui auront étés faits prisonniers.

Art. 48.

The Marquis de Vaudreuil, the general and superior officers of the land troops, the governors and the staff officers of the different places of the

places de la colonie, aux officiers militaires et de justice, et à toutes autres personnes qui sortiront de la colonie, ou qui sont déja absents, de nommer et établir des procureurs pour agir pour eux, et en leur nom, dans l'administration de leurs biens, meubles et immeubles, jusqu'à ce que la paix soit faite. Et si par le traitté des deux couronnes le Canada ne rentre point sous la domination Françoise, ces officiers, ou autres personnes, ou procureurs pour eux, auront l'agrément de vendre leurs seigneuries, maisons, et autres biens fonds, leurs meubles et effets, &ca, d'en emporter ou faire passer le produit en France, soit en lettres de change, espèces sonantes, pelleteries, ou autres retours, comme il est dit à l'article 37.

"Granted."

ART. 49.

Les habitans ou autres personnes qui auront souffert quelque domage en leurs biens meubles ou immeubles, restés à Quebec sous le foy de la capitulation de cet ville, pourront faire leurs représentations au Gouvernement Britanique, qui leur rendra la justice, qui leur sera due contre qui il apartiendra.

"Granted."

ART. 50, et DERNIER.

La présente capitulation sera inviolablement exécutée en tous les articles, de part et d'autre, et de bonne foy, non obstant toute infraction et tout autre prétexte par raport aux précédentes capitulations, et sans pouvoir servir de représailles."

P. S.

ART. 51.

Le Général Anglois s'engagera en cas qu'il reste des sauvages, après la redition de cette ville, à empêcher qu'ils n'entrent dans les villes, et qu'ils n'insultent en aucune manière les sujets de sa M^{té} Très Chrétienne.

"Care shall be taken that the Indians do not insult any of the subjects of his Most Christian Majesty."

ART. 52.

Les troupes et autres sujets de sa M^{té} Très Chrétienne, qui doivent passer en France, seront embarquées quinze jours au plus tard après la signature de la présente capitulation.

"Answered by the 11th article."

ART. 53.

Les troupes et autres sujets de sa M^{té} Très Chrétienne, qui devront passer en France, resteront logées, ou campées dans la ville de Montreal

colony, the military and civil officers, and all other persons who shall go from the colony, or who are already absent, shall have leave to name and appoint attorneys to act for them and in their name, in the administration of their effects movable and immovable, until the peace be made. And if by the treaty between the two crowns Canada does not come again under French rule, those officers or other persons, or attorneys for them, shall have leave to sell their seignories, houses, and other estates, their movables and effects, &c., to carry away or send to France the produce thereof, either in bills of exchange, specie, furs, or other returns, as mentioned in article 37.

Accordé.

Art. 49.

The inhabitants or other persons, who shall have suffered any damage in their goods, movable or immovable, left at Quebec under the faith of the capitulation of that city, may make their representations to the British Government, who shall render them due justice against those whom it may concern.

Accordé.

Art. 50, and last.

The present capitulation shall be inviolably executed in all its articles, on both sides, and in good faith, notwithstanding any infraction and any other pretext with regard to preceding capitulations, and without resorting to reprisals.[23]

Accordé.

POSTSCRIPT.

Art. 51.

The English general shall undertake, in case there remain any savages after the surrender of this town, to prevent them from entering into the towns, and from insulting in any way the subjects of his Most Christian Majesty.

On aura soin que les sauvages n'insulte[24] aucun des sujets de sa M^{té} Très Chrétienne.

Art. 52.

The troops and other subjects of his Most Christian Majesty, who are to go to France, shall be embarked at latest fifteen days after the signing of the present capitulation.

Repondu par l'article 11.

Art. 53.

The troops and other subjects of his Most Christian Majesty, who are to go to France, shall remain lodged or encamped in the town of Montreal

et autres postes qu'elles occupent présentement jusqu'au moment où elles seront embarquées pour le départ. Il sera néantmoins accord des passeports à ceux qui en auront besoin, pour les differens lieux de la colonie pour aller vaquer à leurs affaires.

"Granted."

Art. 54.

Tous les officiers et soldats des troupes au service de France, qui sont prisonniers à la Nouvelle Angleterre, et faits en Canada, seront renvoyés le plustost qu'il sera possible en France, où il sera traitté de leur rançon, ou échange, suivant le cartel; et si quelques uns de ces officiers avoient des affaires en Canada, il leur sera permis d'y venir.

"Granted."

Art. 55.

Quant aux officiers de milices, aux miliciens, et aux Accadiens qui sont prisoniers à la nouvelle Angleterre, ils seront renvoyés sur leurs terres.

Fait à Montreal le 8 Sept. 1760.

VAUDREUIL.

"Granted, except what regards the Acadians.[10]

Done in the camp before Montreal the 8th September, 1760.

(Sgd)

JEFF. AMHERST.

Endorsed :—

Copy—Articles of capitulation granted to the Marquis de Vaudreuil, 8th Sept., 1760. [25]

NOTES TO THE CAPITULATION OF MONTREAL.

[1] The left hand page contains the contract of surrender, the stipulations of the French Governor being in French, and the replies of the British Commander-in-chief in English. The right hand page contains English and French translations of these articles, respectively. The French text in both columns is printed from a certified copy of the original document in the "Colonial Office Papers" under the title of "America and the West Indies," vol. 93. The French text have been carefully collated with those printed in Vol. O of the "Statutes of Lower Canada." The text of the British concessions is taken from Knox's "Historical Journal of the Campaign in North America" (Vol. II, p. 423), and its correctness is sufficiently attested by the fact that it is almost literally identical with the text printed in the "Annual Register" for 1760 (p. 222), and with that given in the "Documents Relative to the Colonial History of the State of New York" (Vol. X, p. 1107). The latter is copied from the original in the Government Archives at Paris. Captain Knox no doubt took his copy at Montreal while the articles were under negotiation. The editor of the "Annual Register" was

THE CAPITULATION OF MONTREAL.

and other posts which they now occupy, until the time when they shall be embarked for their departure. Passports, however, shall be granted to those who shall want them, for the different places of the colony, to go and attend to their affairs.

Accordé.

ART. 54.

All the officers and soldiers of the troops in the service of France, who are prisoners in New England, and were taken in Canada, shall be sent back as soon as possible to France, where negotiations will be entered into for their ransom or exchange, according to the cartel; and if any of those officers had affairs in Canada, they shall have leave to come thither.

Accordé.

ART. 55.

As to the officers of the militia, the militia-men, and the Acadians who are prisoners in New England, they shall be sent back to their countries.

Done at Montreal, the 8th of September, 1760.

VAUDREUIL.

Accordé à la reserve de ce qui regarde les Acadiens.[1][8]

Fait au camp devant Montreal ce 8e Septembre, 1760.

JEFF. AMHERST.

Edmund Burke, who probably obtained his copy from the original in the Colonial office. In the translation of the French articles use has been made of the version given by Knox, and also of the version given in the New York "Documents," which in some respects differs from it. The translation in the "Annual Register" is substantially identical with the one given by Knox. The shortness of the time which elapsed between the first communication from De Vaudreuil to Amherst, and the submission of the former's stipulations for the latter's consideration seems to show that De Vaudreuil, as in the case of Quebec, had for some time been meditating the surrender of the place and had prepared the articles beforehand. Negotiations were opened on the morning of the 7th of September, and by noon Gen. Amherst had returned the French stipulations with his own conditions appended. The remainder of that day was consumed in correspondence, and the articles were signed on the following day.

2 The Marquis de Vaudreuil protested against the severity of these terms, but in vain. The Chevalier de Levis, who commanded the French troops, absolutely refused to submit to them, until ordered to do so by the Governor. An English version of the Chevalier's protest and the Governor's order is given in the New York "Documents" (Vol. X, p. 1106). The order is brief enough to be quoted:

"Whereas the interest of the colony does not permit us to reject the conditions "proposed by the English general, which are favorable to a country whose lot is "confided to me, I order Chevalier de Levis to conform himself to the said capitula- "tion, and to make the troops lay down their arms."
VAUDREUIL.
Montreal, 8th September, 1760.

De Levis sent to Gen. Amherst a spirited remonstrance on his own account, as a soldier to a soldier, but his messenger was silenced and told by Amherst "that he was fully resolved, for the infamous part the troops of France had "acted in exciting the savages to perpetrate the most horrid and unheard of "barbarities in the whole progress of the war, and for other open treacheries "as well as flagrant breaches of faith, to manifest to all the world, by this "capitulation, his detestation of such ungenerous practices, and disapprobation "of their conduct," (Knox's "Historical Journal," Vol. II, p. 418).

In a letter sent to Marshal de Belle Isle after he landed in France, De Levis asserted that the regular troops "merited more attention from the Marquis de Vaudreuil and more esteem from Gen. Amherst, and added that his protest against what he considered harsh terms had prevented an exchange of the civilities "usual on such meeting between generals." New York "Documents"(Vol. X, p. 1123).

3 Gen. Amherst in a letter to the Marquis de Vaudreuil (Knox's "Historical Journal," Vol. II, p. 420), stated, before the articles were signed, that he would leave the question of taking possession of the gates and of posting guards to the Governor's "own convenience," as he had proposed these precautions "only with a view of maintaining good order, and to prevent with greater certainty anything being attempted against the good faith and terms of capitulation."

4 In the New York "Documents" the blank is filled with the word "Quebec" in brackets. In Knox's English version—he does not give the French text— "Quebec" is inserted without brackets. It is similarly inserted in the text in the "Statutes of Lower Canada."

5 Knox gives this remark but it is wanting in the colonial office French version, and also in the articles printed in the "Annual Register." Its omission from the articles in the New York "Documents" shows that it is wanting also in the original in the French Archives. In the text in the "Statutes of Lower Canada" there is an obvious error in the French version, in the use of the word "precédent."

6 In his letter to Marshal de Belle Isle (see Note 2 above), De Levis attributes the large number of French deserters to the fact that the soldiers had been permitted to marry and settle on land, and that they had been led to expect their discharge at the conclusion of the war.

7 The object De Vaudreuil had in view in the insertion of this stipulation was to prevent the perpetration of outrages on the French people by the Indians who formed part of the armies commanded by General Haviland and by Gen. Amherst. The latter had been joined at Oswego by Sir William Johnson, who, according to Knox ("Historical Journal," Vol. II, p. 40), had under his command 1330 Indian warriors, mostly Iroquois. All but a few of these on the way to Montreal abandoned Amherst's army in disgust because the general would not permit scalping and other savage atrocities.

8 This name appears in Knox's "Historical Journal," in the "Annual Register," and in the New York "Documents," as "Moraigans." The Marquis de Vaudreuil in a despatch, of which a translation is given in the New York "Documents," (Vol. II, p. 579), twice spells the name "Moraingans." Who these Monaigans or

Moraigans were cannot now be indisputably ascertained. The weight of authority seems to favor the view that they were the Mohicans. Knox ("Historical Journal," Vol. II. p. 400), mentions the "Mohians" in the list of tribes which were represented in Johnson's army, and Colden in his "History of the Five Nation Indians" states that the French name "Mourigan" is the equivalent of the English name "Mahikander," which was given to a tribe on the Hudson River, below Albany. That Knox's "Mohians" and Colden's "Mahikanders" were the Indians commonly called "Mohicans" is probable, as is also the identity of Colden's "Mourigan," with Vaudreuil's "Moraigans" and "Moraigans" Colden wrote his history while he was surveyor-general of the Province of New York, and it was published just ten years before the capitulation of Montreal.

9 In the "Statutes of Lower Canada." 'Commissaires des guerre.' That there was only one "Commissary of War" appears from the versions given in Knox's "Historical Journal" and the New York "Documents." De Levis in his letter to Marshal de Belle Isle (see note 2) gives his name and title "Commissary Bernier."

10 "Mon dit Sieur."

11 General Amherst did his best to keep this pledge, but as a matter of fact the French officers and soldiers suffered a good deal of hardship on the voyage. For an account of their sufferings see De Levis' letter to De Belle Isle referred to in Note 3. The French general does not charge the English general with want of good faith, and he admits that when Amherst, on account of insufficient vessel accommodation, desired to send the battalion by way of New York, he opposed it on the ground that it would have been "annihilated on that route by voluntary desertion or insubordination."

12 The war between the British and the French in America was but an episode in the "Seven Years War," which was waged from 1757 to 1763. Hostilities came permanently to an end in America with the surrender of Canada, but they continued for two years longer in Europe. The original belligerents, Prussia and Austria, settled their differences by the treaty of Hubertsberg, which was signed on the 15th of February, 1763; and Great Britain, France, and Spa n did the same thing by the treaty of Paris, which was signed on the 10th of February, 1763.

13 "Les dits."

14 For an account of the various companies organized to carry on the fur trade, see Kingsford's "History of Canada," Vol. II , pp. 504-508. See also Vol. I., p. 331 of the same work.

15 "La dite."

16 "Scarlet cloths" in the translation in the New York "Documents."

17 Compare with this concession, Art. 6 of the terms of capitulation of Quebec, Art. 4 of the treaty of Paris, 1763; sec. 5 of the Quebec Act, 1774; sec. 35 of the Constitutional Act, 1791; and sec. 42 of the Union Act, 1840.

18 Cet article.

19 See Notes to the treaty of Utrecht, and "papers" relating to Nova Scotia.

20 Compare with this stipulation the terms of the Royal Proclamation of 1763, of section 4 of the Quebec Act of 1774, and of the Act of Parliament of Upper Canada which restored English law in that Province (Appendix D).

21 In 1663 Louis XIV. constituted as the governing body of New France " Le Conseil Souverain," with powers similar to those of the Parliament of Paris. The title of this body was in 1703 changed to " Le Conseil Supérieur." For a learned discussion of the nature of this council, see the " Introduction " by P. J. O. Chauveau, prefixed to the collection of " Jugements et Deliberations du Conseil Souve-

rain de la Nouvelle France," published in 1885 under the auspices of the Legislature of Quebec.

22 Capt. Knox in a footnote to this article in his "Historical Journal,' says: "I believe this implies convicts, or malefactors condemned to slavery."

23 Compare article 11 of the Capitulation of Quebec, and see Note 7 upon it.

24 " N' insultent."

25 The endorsation of the copy translated for the New York "Documents" is as follows: " Certified to be true, according to the original signed by the Marquis de Vaudreuil, and collated by Mr. Appy, secretary of M. Amherst."

True copy

(Signed)   VAUDREUIL.

III. EXTRACTS FROM THE TREATY OF PARIS, 1763.[1]

The Definitive Treaty of Peace and Friendship, between his Britannic Majesty, the Most Christian King, and the King of Spain; concluded at Paris, the 10th day of February, 1763. To which the King of Portugal acceded on the same day.

I. There shall be a Christian, universal, and perpetual peace, as well by sea as by land, and a sincere and constant friendship shall be re-established between their Britannic, Most Christian, Catholic, and Most Faithful Majesties.[2]   *   *   *

II. The treaties[3] of Westphalia of 1648; those of Madrid, between the Crowns of Great Britain and Spain, of 1667 and 1670; the treaties of peace of Nimeguen of 1678 and 1679; of Ryswick of 1697; those of peace and of commerce of Utrecht of 1713; that of Baden of 1714; the treaty of the triple alliance of the Hague of 1717; that of the quadruple alliance of London of 1718; the treaty of peace of Vienna of 1738; the definitive treaty of Aix-la-Chapelle of 1748; and that of Madrid, between the Crowns of Great Britain and Spain of 1750; as well as the treaties between the Crowns of Spain and Portugal, of the 13th of February, 1668, of the 6th of February, 1715, and of the 12th of February, 1761; and that of the 19th of April, 1713, between France and Portugal, with the guaranties of Great Britain: serve as a basis and foundation to the peace, and to the present treaty: and for this purpose they are all renewed and confirmed in the best form, as well as all the treaties in general, which subsisted between the high contracting parties before the war, as if they were inserted here word for word, so that they are to be exactly observed, for the future, in their whole tenor, and religiously executed on all sides, in all their points which shall not be derogated from by the present treaty, notwithstanding all that may have been stipulated to the contrary by any of the high contracting parties; and all the said parties declare, that they will not suffer any privilege, favour, or indulgence to subsist, contrary to the treaties above confirmed, except what shall have been agreed and stipulated by the present treaty.

IV. His Most Christian Majesty renounces all pretensions which he has heretofore formed, or might form, to Nova Scotia or Acadia, in all its parts,[4] and guaranties the whole of it, with all its dependencies, to the King of Great Britain: moreover, his Most Christian Majesty cedes and guaranties to his said Britannic Majesty, in full right, Canada with all its dependencies, as well as the Island of Cape Breton,[5] and all the other islands and coasts in the gulph and river St. Lawrence, and, in general, everything that depends on the said countries, lands, islands and coasts, with the sovereignty, property, possession, and all rights acquired by treaty or otherwise, which the Most Christian King and the Crown of France have had till now over the said countries, islands, places, coasts, and their inhabitants, so that the Most Christian King cedes and makes over to the said King and to the Crown of Great Britain, and that in the most ample manner and form, without restriction and without any liberty to depart from the said cession and guaranty, under any pretence, or to disturb Great Britain in the possessions above-mentioned. His Britannic Majesty on his side agrees to grant the liberty of the Catholic religion to the inhabitants of Canada: he will consequently give the most precise and most effectual orders, that his new Roman Catholic subjects may profess the worship of their religion, according to the rites of the Romish Church, as far as the laws of Great Britain permit.[a] His Britannic Majesty further agrees, that the French inhabitants, or others who had been subjects of the Most Christian King in Canada, may retire with all safety and freedom wherever they shall think proper, and may sell their estates, provided it be to subjects of his Britannic Majesty, and bring away their effects, as well as their persons, without being restrained in their emigration, under any pretence whatsoever except that of debts or of criminal prosecutions: the term limited for this emigration shall be fixed to the space of eighteen months, to be computed from the day of the exchange of the ratifications of the present treaty.

V. The subjects of France shall have the liberty of fishing and drying, on a part of the coasts of the Island of Newfoundland, such as it is specified in the XIIIth article of the Treaty of Utrecht; which article is renewed and confirmed by the present treaty, except what relates to the island of Cape Breton, as well as to the other islands and coasts in the mouth and in the gulph of St. Lawrence: and his Britannic Majesty consents to leave to the subjects of the Most Christian King the liberty of fishing in the gulph of St. Lawrence, on condition that the subjects of France do not exercise the said fishery but at the distance of three leagues from all the coasts belonging to Great Britain, as well those of the continent as those of the islands situated in the said gulph of St. Lawrence. And as to what relates to the fishery on the coasts of the island of Cape Breton out of the said gulph, the subjects of the Most Christian King shall not be permitted to exercise the said fishery but at the distance of fifteen leagues from the coasts of the island of Cape Breton; and the fishery on the coast of Nova Scotia or Acadia, and everywhere else out of the said gulph, shall remain on the foot of former treaties.[7]

VI. The King of Great Britain cedes the islands of St. Pierre and Miquelon in full right to his Most Christian Majesty, to serve as a shelter to the French fishermen: and his said Most Christian Majesty engages not to fortify the said islands; to erect no buildings upon them, but merely for the convenience of the fishery; and to keep upon them a guard of fifty men only for the police.

VII. In order to re-establish peace on solid and durable foundations, and to remove for ever all subject of dispute with regard to the limits of the British and French territories on the continent of America, it is agreed that for the future the confines between the dominions of his Britannic Majesty, and those of his Most Christian Majesty, in that part of the world, shall be fixed irrevocably by a line drawn along the middle of the river Mississippi, from its source[a] to the river Iberville, and from thence, by a line drawn along the middle of this river, and the lakes Maurepas and Pontchartrain, to the sea; and for this purpose, the Most Christian King cedes in full right, and guaranties to his Britannic Majesty, the river and port of the Mobile, and everything which he possesses, or ought to possess, on the left side of the river Mississippi, except the town of New Orleans, and the island in which it is situated, which shall remain to France; provided that the navigation of the river Mississippi shall be equally free, as well to the subjects of Great Britain as to those of France, in its whole breadth and length, from its source to the sea, and expressly that part which is between the said island of New Orleans and the right bank of that river, as well as the passage both in and out of its mouth. It is further stipulated, that the vessels belonging to the subjects of either nation shall not be stopped, visited, or subjected to the payment of any duty whatsoever. The stipulations inserted in the IVth article in favor of the inhabitants of Canada shall also take place with regard to the inhabitants of the countries ceded by this article.

VIII. The King of Great Britain shall return to France the islands of Guadeloupe, of Marie Galante, of Desirade, of Martinico, and of Belle-isle; and the fortresses of these islands shall be restored in the same condition they were in when they were conquered by the British arms; provided that his Britannic Majesty's subjects, who shall have settled in the said islands, or those who shall have any commercial affairs to settle there, or in the other places restored to France by the present treaty, shall have liberty to sell their lands and their estates, to settle their affairs, to recover their debts, and to bring away their effects, as well as their persons, on board vessels which they shall be permitted to send to the said islands and other places restored as above, and which shall serve for this use only, without being restrained on account of their religion, or under any other pretence whatsoever, except that of debts or of criminal prosecutions: * * *

IX. The Most Christian King cedes and guaranties to his Britannic Majesty, in full right, the islands of Grenada,[b] and of the Grenadines, with the same stipulations in favor of the inhabitants of this colony inserted in the IVth article for those of Canada : and the partition of the islands called Neutral is agreed and fixed, so that those of St. Vincent, Dominica, and Tobago shall remain in full right to Great Britain, and that of St. Lucia shall be delivered to France, to enjoy the same likewise in full right; and the high contracting parties guaranty the partition so stipulated.

XVII. His Britannic Majesty shall cause to be demolished all the fortifications which his subjects shall have erected in the Bay of Honduras, and other places of the territory of Spain in that part of the world, four months after the ratification of the present treaty; and his Catholic Majesty shall not permit his Britannic Majesty's subjects, or their workmen, to be disturbed or molested, under any pretence whatsoever in the said places in their occupation of cutting, loading, and carrying away logwood; and for this purpose they may build without hindrance and occupy without interruption the houses and magazines which are necessary for them, for their families, and for their effects; and his Catholic Majesty assures to them by this article, the full enjoyment of those advantages and powers on the Spanish coasts and territories, as above stipulated, immediately after the ratification of the present treaty.

XVIII. His Catholic Majesty desists, as well for himself as for his successors, from all pretension which he may have formed in favor of the Guipuscoans and other his subjects, to the right of fishing in the neighbourhood of the island of Newfoundland.

XIX. The King of Great Britain shall restore to Spain all the territory which he has conquered in the island of Cuba, with the fortress of the Havana, and this fortress, as well as all the other fortresses of the said island, shall be restored in the same condition they were in when conquered by his Britannic Majesty's arms; provided that his Britannic Majesty's subjects, who shall have settled in the said island, restored to Spain by the present treaty, or those who shall have any commercial affairs to settle there, shall have liberty to sell their lands and their estates, to settle their affairs, to recover their debts, and to bring away their effects as well as their persons on board vessels which they shall be permitted to send to the said island restored as above, and which shall serve for that use only, without being restrained on account of their religion, or under any pretence whatsoever, except that of debts or of criminal prosecutions;   *   *   *   * .

XX. In consequence of the restitution stipulated in the preceding article, his Catholic Majesty cedes and guaranties, in full right, to his Britannic Majesty, Florida with Fort St. Augustin and the Bay of Pensacola, as well as all that Spain possesses on the continent of North America to the east or to the south-east of the river Mississippi; and, in general, everything that depends on the said countries and lands, with the sovereignty, property, possession, and all rights, acquired by treaties or otherwise, which the Catholic King and the Crown of Spain have had, till now, over the said countries, lands, places, and their inhabitants; so that the Catholic King cedes and makes over the whole to the said King, and to the Crown of Great Britain, and that in the most ample manner and form. His Britannic Majesty agrees, on his side, to grant to the inhabitants of the countries above ceded the liberty of the Catholic religion; he will consequently give the most express and the most effectual orders, that his new Roman Catholic subjects may profess the worship of their religion, according to the rites of the Romish church, as far as the laws of Great Britain permit: His Britannic Majesty further agrees that the Spanish inhabitants or others, who had been subjects of the Catholic King in the said countries, may retire with all safety and freedom whenever they think proper; and may sell their estates, provided it be to His Britannic Majesty's subjects, and bring away their effects as well as their persons, without being restrained in their emigration under any pretence whatsoever except that of debts or of criminal prosecutions: * * * * * * * *

XXII. All the papers, letters, documents, and archives, which were found in the countries, territories, towns, and places that are restored, and those belonging to the countries ceded, shall be respectively and *bona fide* delivered or furnished at the same time, if possible, that possession is taken, or at latest four months after the exchange of the ratifications of the present treaty, in whatever places the said papers or documents may be found.[10]

NOTES TO THE TREATY OF PARIS, 1763.

¹ The extracts selected contain all that is essential from a Canadian point of view in the treaty. The text is reprinted from the "Collection of Treaties between Great Britain and other Powers," published in London in 1790, by George Chalmers, who states that this Treaty of Paris " is printed from the copy which was published by authority in 1763." Three "separate articles," having " the same force as if they were inserted in the treaty," are appended to it. The second of these is as follows: "It has been agreed and determined that the French language, made use of in all the copies of the present treaty, shall not become an example which may be alledged or made a precedent of, or prejudice in any manner any of the contracting Powers; and that they shall conform themselves for the future to what has been observed, and ought to be observed, with regard to and on the part of Powers who are used, and have a right, to give and to receive copies of like treaties in another language than French; the present treaty having still the same force and effect as if the aforesaid custom had been therein observed."

² The titles by courtesy of George III. of Great Britain, Louis XV. of France, Charles III. of Spain, and Joseph Emmanuel of Portugal, respectively. The first of the "separate articles," referred to in Note 1, provides that "some of the titles made use of by the contracting Powers * * * not being generally acknowledged, it has been agreed that no prejudice shall ever result therefrom to any of the said contracting parties, and that the titles taken or omitted on either side * * * shall not be cited or quoted as a precedent."

³ For extracts from these treaties, relating to Canada, see Appendix A.

⁴ For the extent of Acadia, see note 5 to the Treaty of Utrecht.

⁵ See Article XIII of the Treaty of Utrecht.

⁶ Compare the corresponding stipulation in Article XX. of this treaty, and also the one in Article XIV. of the Treaty of Utrecht.

⁷ See note 7 to the Treaty of Utrecht.

⁸ Compare the description of the boundary of Quebec given in the Quebec Act, 1774. For a list of French settlements on the Upper Mississippi, see the Ontario Sessional Papers, Vol. XI., No. 31, pp. 445-446.

⁹ This cession of Grenada is of importance in connection with Lord Mansfield's judgment in *Campbell* v. *Hall*.

¹⁰ In a declaration by the British plenipotentiary appended to the Treaty of Paris, it is undertaken that "the letters of exchange and bills, which had been delivered to the Canadians for the necessaries furnished to the French troops," shall be paid "agreeably to a liquidation made in a convenient time." See Articles 23, 24 of the Capitulation of Montreal.

IV. ROYAL PROCLAMATION¹ UNDER THE TREATY OF PARIS, 1763.

BY THE KING.

A PROCLAMATION.

GEORGE R.

WHEREAS we have taken into our Royal consideration the extensive and valuable acquisitions in America, secured to our Crown by the late definitive treaty of peace concluded at Paris the tenth day of February last; and being desirous that all our loving subjects, as well of our kingdoms as of our colonies in America, may avail themselves with all convenient speed of the great benefits and advantages which must accrue therefrom to their commerce, manufactures, and navigation; we have thought fit, with the advice of our Privy Council, to issue this our Royal Proclamation, hereby to publish and declare to all our loving subjects, that we have, with the advice of our said Privy Council, granted our letters patent under our Great Seal of Great Britain, to erect within the countries and islands ceded and confirmed to us by the said treaty, four distinct and separate governments, stiled and called by the names of QUEBEC, EAST FLORIDA, WEST FLORIDA, and GRENADA, and limited and bounded as follows, viz:

Firstly. The Government of QUEBEC, bounded² on the Labrador Coast by the River St. John, and from thence by a line drawn from the head of that river, through the Lake St. John, to the south end of the Lake Nipissim; from whence the said line, crossing the River St. Lawrence, and the Lake Champlain in forty-five degrees of north latitude, passes along the high lands which divide the rivers that empty themselves into the said River St. Lawrence, from those which fall into the sea; and also along the north coast of the Baye des Chaleurs, and the coast of the Gulph of St. Lawrence to Cape Rosieres, and from thence crossing the mouth of the River St. Lawrence by the west end of the Island of Anticosti, terminates at the aforesaid River St. John.

Secondly. The Government of EAST FLORIDA, bounded to the westward by the Gulph of Mexico and the Apalachicola River; to the northward, by a line drawn from that part of the said river where the Catahouchee and Flint Rivers meet, to the source of the St. Mary's River, and by the course of the said river to the Atlantic

H.C.C.—5

Ocean; and to the east and south by the Atlantic Ocean and the Gulph of Florida, including all the islands within six leagues of the sea coast.

Thirdly. The Government of WEST FLORIDA, bounded to the southward by the Gulph of Mexico, including all islands within six leagues of the coast from the River Apalachicola to Lake Pontchartrain; to the westward, by the said lake, the Lake Maurepas, and the River Mississippi; to the northward, by a line drawn east from that part of the River Mississippi which lies in thirty-one degrees north latitude, to the River Apalachicola, or Catahouchee; and to the eastward by the said river.

Fourthly. The Government of GRENADA,³ comprehending the island of that name, together with the Grenadines, and the islands of Dominico, St. Vincent and Tobago.

And to the end that the open and free fishing of our subjects may be extended to and carried on upon the coast of Labrador, and the adjacent islands, we have thought fit, with the advice of our said Privy Council, to put all that coast, from the River St. John's to Hudson's Streights, together with the islands of Anticosti and the Magdeleine, and all smaller islands lying upon the said coast, under the care and inspection of our Governor of Newfoundland.⁴

We have also, with the advice of our Privy Council, thought fit to annex the islands of St. John and Cape Breton, or Isle Royale, with the lesser islands adjacent thereto, to our Government of Nova Scotia.⁵

We have also, with the advice of our Privy Council aforesaid, annexed to our Province of Georgia, all the lands lying between the rivers Attamaha and St. Mary's.

And whereas it will greatly contribute to the speedy settling our said New Governments, that our loving subjects should be informed of our paternal care for the security of the liberty and properties of those who are, and shall become, inhabitants thereof; we have thought fit to publish and declare, by this our Proclamation, that we have in the letters patent under our Great Seal of Great Britain, by which the said Governments are constituted, given express power and direction to our governors of our said colonies respectively, that so soon as the state and circumstances of the said colonies will admit thereof, they shall, with the advice and consent of the members of our Council, summon and call general assemblies⁶ within the said governments respectively, in such manner and form as is used and directed in those colonies and provinces⁷ in America, which are under our immediate government; and we have also given power to the said governors, with the consent of our said councils and the representatives of the people so to be summoned as aforesaid, to make, constitute, and ordain laws, statutes, and ordinances for the public peace, welfare, and good government of our said colonies, and of the people and inhabitants thereof, as near as may be, agreeable to the laws of England, and under such regulations and restrictions as are used in other colonies, and in the meantime, and until such assemblies can be called as aforesaid, all persons inhabiting in or resorting to our said colonies may confide in our Royal protection for the enjoyment of the benefit of the laws of our realm of England:* for which purpose we have given power under our great seal to the governors of our said colonies respectively to enact and constitute, with the advice of our said councils respectively, courts of judicature and public justice within our said colonies for the hearing and determining all causes as well criminal as civil according to law and equity, and, as near as may be, agreeable to the laws of England, with liberty to all persons who may think themselves aggrieved by the sentence of such courts in all civil cases to appeal under the usual limitations and restrictions to us in our Privy Council.*

We have also thought fit, with the advice of our Privy Council as aforesaid, to give unto the governors and councils of our said three new colonies upon the continent full power and authority to settle and agree with the inhabitants of our said new colonies, or any other person who shall resort thereto, for such lands, tenements and hereditaments as are now or hereafter shall be in our power to dispose of, and them to grant to any such person or persons, upon such terms and under such moderate quit rents, services, and acknowledgments as have been appointed and settled in other colonies, and under such other conditions as shall appear to us to be necessary and expedient for the advantage of the grantees and the improvement and settlement of our said colonies.

And whereas we are desirous upon all occasions to testify our Royal sense and approbation of the conduct and bravery of the officers and soldiers of our armies, and to reward the same. We do hereby command and empower our governors of our said three new colonies, and other our governors of our several Provinces on the continent of North America, to grant without fee or reward to such reduced officers as have served in North America during the late war, and are actually residing there, and shall personally apply for the same, the following quantities of land, subject at the expiration of ten years to the same quit rents as other lands are subject to in the Province within which they are granted, as also subject to the same conditions of cultivation and improvement, viz:

To every person having the rank of a field officer.... 5,000 acres.
To every captain................................. 3,000 acres.
To every subaltern or staff officer................. 2,000 acres.
To every non-commissioned officer .... 200 acres.
To every private man .... 50 acres.

We do likewise authorize and require the Governors and Commanders-in-Chief of all our said Colonies upon the Continent of North America, to grant the like quantities of land and upon the same conditions to such reduced officers of our navy of like rank as served on board our ships of war in North America, at the times of the reduction of Louisburg and Quebec in the late war, and who shall personally apply to our respective Governors for such grants.

And whereas it is just and reasonable, and essential to our interest and the security of our colonies, that the several nations or tribes of Indians[10] with whom we are connected, and who live under our protection, should not be molested or disturbed in the possession of such parts of our dominions and territories as, not having been ceded to us, are reserved to them, or any of them, as their hunting-grounds; we do therefore, with the advice of our Privy Council, declare it to be our Royal will and pleasure that no Governor or Commander-in-Chief in any of our colonies of QUEBEC, EAST FLORIDA, or WEST FLORIDA, do presume upon any pretence whatever to grant warrants of survey, or pass any patents for lands beyond the bounds of their respective governments as described in their commissions: as also that no Governor or Commander-in-Chief of our other colonies or plantations in America do presume for the present, and until our further pleasure be known, to grant warrants of survey, or pass any patents for lands beyond the heads or sources of any of the rivers which fall into the Atlantic Ocean from the west or northwest; or upon any lands whatever which, not having been ceded to or purchased by us, as aforesaid, are reserved to the said Indians or any of them.

And we do further declare it to be our Royal will and pleasure, for the present as aforesaid, to reserve under our sovereignty, protection, and dominion, for the use of the said Indians, all the land and territories not included within the limits of our said three new governments, or within the limits of the territory granted to the Hudson's Bay Company; as also the land and territories lying to the westward of the sources of the rivers which fall into the sea from the west and northwest as aforesaid; and we do hereby strictly forbid, on pain of our displeasure, all our loving subjects from making any purchases or settlements whatever, or taking possession of any of the lands above reserved, without our special leave and licence for that purpose first obtained.

And we do further strictly enjoin and require all persons whatsoever, who have either wilfully or inadvertently seated themselves upon any lands within the countries above described, or upon any other lands which, not having been ceded to or purchased by us, are still reserved to the said Indians as aforesaid, forthwith to remove themselves from such settlements.

And whereas great frauds and abuses have been committed in the purchasing lands of the Indians, to the great prejudice of our interests and to the great dissatisfaction of the said Indians ; in order, therefore, to prevent such irregularities for the future, and to the end that the Indians may be convinced of our justice and determined resolution to remove all reasonable cause of discontent, we do, with the advice of our Privy Council, strictly enjoin and require that no private person do presume to make any purchase from the said Indians of any lands reserved to the said Indians within those parts of our colonies where we have thought proper to allow settlement; but that, if at any time any of the said Indians should be inclined to dispose of the said lands, the same shall be purchased only for us, in our name, at some public meeting or assembly of the said Indians, to be held for that purpose by the Governor or Commander-in-Chief of our colony respectively, within which they shall lie: and, in case they shall be within the limits of any proprietaries,[11] conformable to such directions and instructions as we or they shall think proper to give for that purpose : and we do, by the advice of our Privy Council, declare and enjoin that the trade of the said Indians shall be free and open to all our subjects whatever, provided that every person who may incline to trade with the said Indians, do take out a licence for carrying on such trade, from the Governor or Commander-in-Chief of any of our colonies respectively, where such person shall reside, and also give security to observe such regulations as we shall at any time think fit, by ourselves or commissaries to be appointed for this purpose, to direct and appoint for the benefit of the said trade; and we do hereby authorize, enjoin and require the Governors and Commanders-in-Chief of all our colonies respectively, as well those under our immediate government as those under the government and direction of proprietaries, to grant such licenses without fee or reward, taking special care to insert therein a condition that such licence shall be void, and the security forfeited, in case the person to whom the same is granted shall refuse or neglect to observe such regulations as we shall think proper to prescribe, as aforesaid.

And we do further expressly enjoin and require all officers whatever, as well military as those employed in the management and direction of Indian affairs within the territories reserved as aforesaid for the use of the said Indians, to seize and apprehend all persons whatever who, standing charged with treason, misprision of treason, murder, or other felonies or misdemeanors, shall fly from justice and take refuge in the said territory, and to send them under a proper guard to the colony where the crime was committed, of which they shall stand accused, in order to take their trial for the same.

Given at our Court, at St. James's, the seventh day of October, one thousand seven hundred and sixty-three, in the third year of our Reign.

GOD SAVE THE KING.

NOTES TO THE ROYAL PROCLAMATION, 1763.

1 By the judgment of Lord Chief Justice Mansfield in the case of *Campbell* v. *Hall*, which has never been reversed by or questioned in a court of law, this Proclamation is declared to have been the Imperial Constitution of Canada during the years 1763-1774. In the latter year it was superseded by the Quebec Act. The text is reprinted from the "Annual Register" for 1763, a contemporary authority, but it has been compared with other reprints.

2 Compare the boundaries of Quebec as given in the Quebec Act, 1774, as modified by the Treaty of Paris, 1783, and as authoritatively declared for the western and northern limits of the former Province of Quebec by the Imperial Act of 1889, to declare the boundaries of the Province of Ontario in the Dominion of Canada (52 and 53 Vict. Chap. 28).

3 See Lord Chief Justice Mansfield's judgment in *Campbell* v. *Hall*, for a statement of the facts connected with the establishment of British Government in Grenada.

4 Compare the Quebec Act, 1774, and the Constitutional Act, 1791. For the treaty stipulations with France respecting the fisheries see the Treaty of Utrecht, 1713, the Treaty of Paris, 1763, and the Treaty of Versailles, 1783.

5 "St. John" was the former name of Prince Edward Island. With respect to Nova Scotia and Cape Breton, compare the Treaty of Utrecht, 1713; the Treaty of Aix-la-Chapelle, 1748; and the Treaty of Paris, 1763.

6 The commission to Governor Melville of Grenada was issued on the 9th of April, 1764, and the one to Governor Murray of Quebec on the 21st of November, 1763. Each authorized the Governor to call an Assembly, but in the case of Quebec this authorization was not acted upon. With respect to Grenada see Note 3, above.

7 See Note 15 to "Representative Assemblies in the Maritime Provinces."

8 For contemporary opinion as to the extent to which English law, civil and criminal, was really introduced by this proclamation, see Maseres' "Collection of Commissions."

9 The appellate jurisdiction of the King-in-Council was declared illegal by the Petition of Right and the Act of 1640 for all causes arising in Great Britain. It was recognized after the Restoration, first for the Islands of Jersey and Guernsey, and afterwards for all the Colonies, for which the Judicial Committee of the Privy Council is still the tribunal of last resort.

10 The nature of the Indian title to lands occupied by nomad tribes has from very early times in America, been a subject of both political and legal importance. For all British Colonies all controversy on the question has been finally set at rest by the judgment of the Judicial Committee of the Privy Council in the well-known case, "*St. Catherines' Milling and Lumber Company* v. *The Queen*." The judgment in that case (Appeal Cases, Vol. XIV., pp. 46-61) was delivered by Lord Watson, according to whom the terms of this Proclamation "show that the tenure of the Indians was a personal and usufructuary right, dependent on the good will of the Sovereign," and "the Crown has all along had a present proprietary estate in the land, upon which the Indian title was a mere burden." The theory on which the British colonists in America acted is lucidly stated in a formal opinion given jointly by several colonial authorities, and printed in the "Documents relating to

the Colonial History of the State of New York," Vol. XIII., p. 486: "Tho' it hath been and still is the usual practice of all Proprietors to give their Indians some recompence for their land, and seem to purchase it of them, yet that is not done for want of sufficient title from the King or Prince who hath the right of discovery but out of prudence and Christian charity, least otherwise the Indians might have destroyed the first planters (who are usually too few to defend themselves) or refuse all commerce and conversation with the planters, and thereby all hopes of converting them to the Christian faith would be lost." The judgment of the Privy Council above cited was given on an appeal from the judgment of the Supreme Court of Canada in the same case (Supreme Coutr Reports, Vol. XIII., p. 577), dismissing an appeal from the Ontario Court of Appeal (Appeal Reports, Vol. XIII., pp. 148-173), and the judgment of the latter Court dismissed the appeal from the original judgment of Chancellor Boyd, who held that, "the claim of the Indians by virtue of their original occupation is not such as to give any title to the land itself, but only serves to commend them to the consideration and liberality of the Government upon their displacement," and that "the surrender to the Crown by the Indians of any territory adds nothing in law to the strength of the title paramount," (Ontario Reports, Vol. X., p. 234). The various judgments in the Canadian Courts contain very full discussions of the whole question in its historical aspects.

11 Settlements or plantations, of which the territory had been granted to individuals or companies by Royal charters.

COMMISSION[1] OF GOVERNOR MURRAY, 1763.

George the Third, by the Grace of God, of Great Britain, France, and Ireland, King, Defender of the Faith, and so forth, to our trusty and well-beloved JAMES MURRAY,[2] Esquire, Greeting:

We, reposing especial trust and confidence in the prudence, courage, and loyalty of you, the said James Murray, of our especial grace, certain knowledge, and mere motion, have thought fit to constitute and appoint, and by these premises do constitute and appoint you, the said James Murray, to be our Captain General and Governor in Chief in and over our province of Quebec[3] in America; bounded on the Labrador Coast by the river St. John; and from thence by a line drawn from the head of that river through the lake St. John to the south end of the lake Nipissim, from whence the said line crossing the river St. Lawrence and the lake Champlain, in forty-five degrees of northern latitude, passes along the high lands which divide the rivers that empty themselves into the said river St. Lawrence from those which fall into the sea; and also along the north coast of the Baye des Chaleurs and the coast of the gulf of St. Lawrence to Cape Rosieres; and from thence crossing the mouth of the river St. Lawrence by the west end of the island of Anticosti, terminates at the aforesaid river St. John; together with all the rights, members, and appurtenances whatsoever thereunto belonging.

And we do hereby require and command you to do and execute all things in due manner that shall belong to your said command and the trust we have reposed in you, according to the several powers and directions granted or appointed you by this present commission and the instructions and authorities herewith given unto you, or by such other powers, instructions, and authorities as shall at any time hereafter be granted or appointed under our signet and sign manual, or by our order in our privy Council, and according to such reasonable laws and statutes as shall hereafter be made and agreed upon by you with the advice and consent of the council and assembly of our said province under your government, in such manner and form as is herein after expressed.

* * * * *

And we do hereby give and grant unto you, the said James Murray, full power and authority, with the advice and consent of our said council to be appointed as aforesaid, so soon as the situation and circumstances of our said province under your government will admit thereof, and when and as often as need shall require, to summon and call general assemblies[1] of the freeholders and planters within your government, in such manner as you in your discretion shall judge most proper; or according to such further powers, instructions and authorities as shall be at any time hereafter granted or appointed you under our signet or sign manual or by our order in our privy Council.

And our will and pleasure is that the persons thereupon duly elected by the major part of the freeholders of the respective parishes or precincts, and so returned, shall, before their sitting, take the oaths mentioned in the said act, intituted "An Act for the further security of his Majesty's person and government, and the succession of the Crown in the heirs of the late Princess Sophia, being Protestants, and for extinguishing the hopes of the pretended Prince of Wales, and his open and secret abettors;" as also make and subscribe the fore-mentioned declaration; which oaths and declaration you shall commissionate fit persons under the public seal of that our province to tender and administer unto them; and, until the same shall be so taken and subscribed, no person shall be capable of sitting, though elected.

And we do hereby declare that the persons so elected and qualified shall be called "The Assembly of that our Province of Quebec"; and that you, the said James Murray, by and with the advice and consent of our said Council and Assembly, or the major part of them, shall have full power and authority to make, constitute and ordain laws, statutes, and ordinances for the public peace, welfare, and good government of our said province, and of the people and inhabitants thereof, and such others as shall resort thereunto, and for the benefit of us, our heirs, and successors; which said laws, statutes, and ordinances are not to be repugnant, but as near as may be agreeable to the laws and statutes of this our kingdom of Great Britain.

* * * * *

And we do by these presents give and grant unto you, the said James Murray, full power and authority, with the advice and consent of our said Council, to erect, constitute, and establish such and so many courts of judicature and public justice[5] within our said province under your government as you and they shall think fit and necessary, for the hearing and determining of all causes, as well criminal as civil, according to law and equity, and for awarding execution thereupon, with all reasonable and necessary powers, authorities, fees, and privileges belonging thereto.

* * * * *

And we do hereby grant unto you full power and authority to constitute and appoint judges, and, in cases requisite, commissioners of oyer and terminer, justices of the peace, and other necessaroy fficers and ministers[6] in our said province for the better administration of justice and putting the laws in execution; and |to administer, or cause to be administered, unto them such oath or oaths as are usually given for the due execution and performance of offices and places, and for clearing the truth in judicial causes.

And we do hereby give and grant unto you full power and authority when you shall see cause, or shall judge any offender or offenders in criminal matters, or for any fines or forfeitures due unto us, fit objects of our mercy, to pardon all such offenders and remit all such offences, fines and forfeitures, treason and wilful murder only excepted; in which cases you shall likewise have power upon extraordinary occasions to grant reprieves to the offenders until, and to the intent that, our royal pleasure may be known therein.

And we do by these presents give and grant unto you full power and authority to collate any person or persons to any churches, chapels, or other ecclesiastical benefices within our said province, as often as any of them shall happen to be void.

. . . .

And we do hereby require and command all officers and ministers, civil and military, and all other inhabitants of our said province, to be obedient, aiding and assisting unto you, the said James Murray, in the execution of this our commission and of the powers and authorities therein contained; and in case of your death or absence from our said province and government, to be obedient, aiding and assisting to the commander in chief for the time being; to whom we do therefore by these presents give and grant all and singular the powers and authorities herein granted, to be by him executed and enjoyed during our pleasure, or until your arrival within our said province.

And in case of your death or absence from our said province our will and pleasure is that our lieutenant governour of Montreal or Trois Rivieres, according to the priority of their commissions of lieutenant governours, do execute our said commission with all the powers and authorities therein mentioned as aforesaid. And in case of the death or absence of our lieutenant governours of Montreal and Trois Rivieres from our said province, and that there shall be no person within our said province appointed by us to be lieutenant governour or commander in chief of our said province, our will and pleasure is that the eldest councillor, who shall be at the time of your death or absence residing within our said province, shall take upon him the administration of the government, and execute our said commission and instructions, and the several powers and authorities therein contained, in the same manner to all intents and purposes as other our governour or commander in chief should or ought to do, in case of your absence, or until your return, or in all cases until our further pleasure be known.

And we do hereby declare, ordain, and appoint that you, the said James Murray, shall and may hold, execute, and enjoy the office and place of our Captain General and Governour in Chief in and over our said Province of Quebec and all the territories depending thereon, with all and singular the powers and authorities hereby granted unto you, for and during our will and pleasure. In witness whereof we have caused these our letters to be made patent.

Witness ourself at Westminster, the twenty-first day of November, in the fourth year of our reign.

By writ of Privy Seal.

(Signed)   YORKE & YORKE.[5]

NOTES TO GOVERNOR MURRAY'S COMMISSION.

[1] The text of this Commission is reprinted from "A Collection of Several Commissions and other Public Instruments," by Francis Maseres, who became Attorney-General of the Province of Quebec in 1766. The "Collection" was published in London in 1772. The omitted passages deal with the oaths to be taken by the Governor and to be administered by him to other officials, the custody of the public seal, the disallowance of statutes and ordinances, the Governor's veto, the raising of armed forces and erection of fortifications, the punishment of offences committed by marines, the appropriation of public moneys, the management of the public lands, and the establishment of markets and harbors. They are *mutatis mutandis*, practically identical with the passages that deal with the same subjects in the Commission of Governor Cornwallis.

[2] Gen. Murray took part in the seige of Quebec in 1759, and was commandant of that city after its capture. In the summer of 1760 he ascended the St. Lawrence with an army to meet Gen. Amherst at Montreal. He was one of the British Generals who administered the country by military rule until this commission was issued to him as the first civil Governor after the capitulation. The other generals were Haldimand, who commanded at Three Rivers, and Gage who commanded at Montreal. Murray retired from Canada in 1767.

[3] See the Royal Proclamation, 1763.

[4] No assembly was ever called together under this commission, as had been done from 1758 under the similar commissions to the Governors of Nova Scotia. There is reason to believe that in declining to act on the authority contained in his commission, Gov. Murray followed the advice given by Chief Justice Hey, Attorney-General Maseres, and Lieutenant-Governor Carleton.

[5] The assumption was that English law, both civil and criminal, had been introduced by the Royal Proclamation of 1763. For illustrations of the state of confusion which ensued in the administration of Justice see Smith's "History of Canada from its First Discovery to the year 1791," and especially the report, there

given in full, of Crown Law Officers Yorke and DeGrey to the Lords of Trade and Plantations on certain memorials and petitions sent from both British and French residents in Quebec. See also Attorney-General Maseres' "Draught" of a report in 1769 on the same subject in the collection mentioned in Note 1 above. This draft was not acceptable to Governor Carleton, who favored the revival of "the whole body of the French laws that were in use there before the conquest with respect to civil matters." This policy of Governor Carleton's, in spite of the opposition of Maseres and of Chief Justice Hey, was afterwards embodied in the Quebec Act.

6 The first judge appointed under this commission was Chief Justice Gregory, who was recalled on the representation of Gov. Murray (Smith's "History"). He was succeeded by Chief Justice Hey, whose commission was issued by Gov. Carleton in 1766, and is given in full by Maseres in his "Collection," as is also that issued in the same year to Maseres himself as Attorney-General.

7 In 1768 George III. issued a mandate requiring the Governor to appoint three Church of England Clergymen as Rectors of the parish churches of Quebec, Montreal, and Three Rivers respectively. Maseres gives in his "Collection" the draft of a commission that was intended to be issued to the Rev. David Francis de Montmollin as Rector of the church of Quebec, adding that instead of commissions as Rectors, licenses to preach were afterwards substituted, on account of "the peculiar and delicate situation of the Province with respect to religion."

8 See Note 18 to "Representative Assemblies in the Maritime Provinces."

V. LORD MANSFIELD'S JUDGMENT[1] IN CAMPBELL v. HALL, 1774.

The case of the Island of Grenada ; in relation to the payment of four and one-half in the hundred of goods imported therefrom ; between Alexander[2] Campbell, Esq., Plaintiff, and Wm. Hall, Esq., Defendant, in the Court of King's-Bench, before Lord Chief-Justice Mansfield : 15 George III., A. D. 1774.

November 28.[3]

The unanimous judgment of the Court was this day given by Lord Mansfield, as follows :

This is an action brought by the plaintiff, Alexander Campbell, who is a natural-born subject of Great Britain, and who, upon the third of May,[4] 1763, purchased lands in the island of Grenada ; and it is brought against the defendant, William Hall, who was collector for His Majesty at the time of levying the import of a duty of four and a half per cent. upon goods exported from the island of Grenada. The action is to recover a sum of money, which was levied by the defendant and paid by the plaintiff, as this duty of four and a half per cent. upon sugars, which were exported from the island of Grenada, from the estate and by the consignment of the plaintiff.

The action is an action for money had and received ; and it is brought upon this ground, namely, that the money was paid to the defendant without consideration, the duty for which he received it not having been imposed by lawful or sufficient authority to warrant the same.

And it is stated in the special verdict[5] that the money is not paid over, but continues in the defendant's hands, by consent of the Attorney-General, for His Majesty, in order that the question may be tried.

The special verdict states Grenada to have been conquered by the British arms from the French King in 1762 ; that the island was ceded by capitulation ; and that the capitulation upon which it surrendered was by reference to the capitulation upon which the island of Martinico had been surrendered on the 7th of February, 1762.

The special verdict then states some articles of that capitulation, particularly the fifth, which grants that Martinico should continue to be governed by its own laws till His Majesty's pleasure be known. It next states the sixth article, where, to a demand of the inhabitants of Grenada requiring that they, as also the religious orders of both sexes, should be maintained in the property of their effects, moveable and immoveable, of what nature soever, and that they should be preserved in their priviledges, rights, honours, and exemptions, the answer is that the inhabitants, being subjects of Great Britain, will enjoy their properties and the same privileges as in the other His Majesty's Leeward Islands.⁶

Then it states another article of the capitulation, namely, the 7th article, by which they demand that they shall pay no other duties than what they before paid to the French King; that the capitation tax shall be the same, and that the expenses of the courts of justice, and of the administration of government should be paid out of the King's demesne: in answer to which they are referred to the answer I have stated, as given in the foregoing article; that is, being subjects they will be entitled in like manner as the other His Majesty's subjects in the British Leeward Islands.

The next thing stated in the special verdict is the treaty of peace signed on the 10th of February, 1763; and it states that part of the treaty of peace by which the island of Grenada is ceded, and other articles not material.

The next and material instrument which they state is a proclamation under the Great Seal, bearing date the 7th of October, 1763, reciting thus:⁷

"Whereas it will greatly contribute to the settling of our said islands "of which Grenada is one, that they be informed of our love and paternal "care for the liberties and rights of those who are, or shall be inhabitants "thereof; we have thought fit to publish and declare by this our procla- "mation, that we have by our letters patent under our Great Seal of "Great Britain, whereby our said Governments are constituted, given "express power and direction to our governors of our said colonies re- "spectively, that so soon as the state and circumstances of the said "colonies will admit thereof, they shall, with the advice and consent of "our said council, call and summon general assemblies,⁸ in such manner "and form as is used in the other colonies under our immediate govern- "ment. And we have also given power to the said governors, with the "advice and consent of our said council and assembly of representatives "as aforesaid, to make, constitute, and ordain laws, statutes, and ordin- "ances for the public peace, welfare and good government of our said "colonies and the inhabitants thereof, as near as may be agreeable to the "laws of England, and under such regulations and restrictions as are "used in our other colonies."

Then follow letters patent under the Great Seal, or rather a proclamation of the 26th of March, 1764, whereby the King recites, that he had ordered a survey and division of the ceded islands, as an invitation to all purchasers to come and purchase upon certain terms and conditions specified in that proclamation.

The next instrument stated in the verdict is the letters patent bearing date the 9th of April, 1764. In these letters there is a commission appointing General Melville Governor of the island of Grenada, with power to summon an assembly as soon as the situation and circumstances of the island would admit; and to make laws in all the usual forms with reference to the manner of the other assemblies of the King's Provinces in America.

The Governor arrived in Grenada on the 14th of December, 1764; before the end of 1765, the particular day not stated, an assembly actually met: but before the arrival of the Governor at Grenada, indeed, before his departure from London, there is another instrument upon the validity of which the whole question turns, which instrument contains letters patent under the Great Seal, bearing date the 20th of July, 1764, and reciting that in Barbadoes, and in all the British Leeward islands, a duty of four and a half per cent. was paid upon goods exported; and reciting further:

" Whereas it is reasonable and expedient, and of importance to our
" other sugar islands, that the like duties should take place in our said
" island of Grenada ; we have thought fit, and our royal will and pleasure
" is, and we do hereby, by virtue of our prerogative Royal, order, direct,
" and appoint that an import or custom of four and a half per cent. in
" specie, shall, from and after the 29th day of September next ensuing
" the date of these presents be raised and paid to us, our heirs and suc-
" cessors, for and upon all dead commodities of the growth or produce of
" our said island of Grenada that shall be shipped off from the same, in
" lieu of all customs and impost[10] duties hitherto collected upon goods
" imported and exported into and out of the said island, under the
" authority of his Most Christian Majesty, and that the same shall be
" collected, &c."; then it goes on with reference to the island of Barbadoes, and the other Leeward islands.

The jury find that in fact such duty of four and a half per cent. is paid to his Majesty in all the British Leeward islands. And they find several Acts of Assembly which are relative to the several islands, and which I shall not state, as they are public, and every gentleman may have access to them.

These letters patent of the 20th of July, 1764, with what I stated in the opening, are all that is material in this special verdict.

Upon the whole of the case this general question arises, being the substance of what is submitted to the Court by the verdict: " Whether these letters patent of the 20th of July, 1764, are good and valid to abrogate the French duties, and in lieu thereof to impose this duty of four and a half per cent., which is paid by all the Leeward islands subject to his Majesty."

That the letters are void has been contended at the bar, upon two points: (1) That although they had been made before the Proclamation of the 7th of October, 1763, the King by his prerogative could not have imposed them; and (2) that, although the King had sufficient authority before the 7th of October, 1763, he had divested himself of that authority by the Proclamation of that date.

A great deal has been said, and authorities have been cited relative to propositions in which both sides exactly agree, or which are too clear to be denied. The stating of these will lead us to the solution of the first point.

I will state the propositions at large:

1 A country conquered by the British arms becomes a dominion of the King in the right of his crown, and therefore necessarily subject to the legislative power of the Parliament of Great Britain.

2. The conquered inhabitants once received into the conqueror's protection becomes subjects; and are universally to be considered in that light, not as enemies or aliens.

3. Articles of capitulation, upon which the country is surrendered, and treaties of peace by which it is ceded, are sacred and inviolate, according to their true intent and meaning.

4. The law and legislation of every dominion equally affects all persons and property within the limits thereof, and is the true rule for the decision of all questions which arise there. Whoever purchases, sues, or lives there, puts himself under the laws of the place, and in the situation of its inhabitants   An Englishman in Ireland, Minorca, the Isle of Man, or the Plantations, has no privilege distinct from the natives while he continues there.

5. The laws of a conquered country continue in force until they are altered by the conqueror. The justice and antiquity of this maxim are incontrovertible; and the absurd exception as to pagans mentioned in Calvin's case,[11] shows the universality and antiquity of the maxim. That exception could not exist before the Christian era, and in all probability arose from the mad enthusiasm of the Crusades. In the present case the capitulation expressly provides and agrees that they shall continue to be governed by their own laws, until his Majesty's pleasure be further known.

6. If the King has power (and, when I say " the King," I mean in this case " the King without the concurrence of Parliament ") to alter the old and to make new laws for a conquered country—this being a power subordinate to his own authority as a part of the supreme legislature and parliament—he can make none which are contrary to fundamental principles; he cannot exempt an inhabitant from the laws of trade, or the authority of Parliament, or give him privileges exclusive of his other subjects; and so in many other instances that might be put.

The present Proclamation is an Act of this subordinate legislative power. If it had been made before the 7th of October, 1763, it would have been made on the most reasonable and equitable grounds, putting the island of Grenada as to duties on the same footing as the other islands.

If Grenada paid more duties, the injury would have been to her; if less, it must have been detrimental to the other islands; nay, it would have been carrying the capitulation into execution, which gave the people of Grenada hopes that if any new duties were laid on, their condition would be the same as that of the other Leeward islands.

The only question which remains on this first point then is, whether the King of himself had power to make such a change between the 10th of February, 1763, the day the treaty was signed, and the 7th of October,[12] 1763.

Taking the above propositions to be granted, he has a legislative power over a conquered country, limited to him by the constitution, and subordinate to the constitution and parliament. It is left by the constitution to the King's authority to grant or refuse a capitulation. If he refuses, and puts the inhabitants to the sword, or exterminates them, all the lands belong to him; and if he plants a colony, the new settlers share the land between them, subject to the prerogative of the conqueror. If he receives the inhabitants under his protection and grants them their property, he has power to fix such terms and conditions as he thinks proper. He is entrusted with making peace at his discretion; and he may retain the conquest, or yield it up, on such condition as he pleases. These powers no man ever disputed, neither has it hitherto been controverted that the King might change part or the whole of the law or political form of government of a conquered nation.

To go into the history of conquests made by the crown of England.

The alteration of the laws of Ireland has been much discussed by lawyers and writers of great fame at different periods of time; but no man ever said the change was made by the parliament of England; no man, unless perhaps Mr. Molyneux,[13] ever said the King could not do it. The fact, in truth, after all the researches that have been made, comes out clearly to be as laid down by Lord Chief Justice Vaughan, that Ireland received the laws of England by the charters and commands of Henry II., King John, Henry III., and he adds an *et cetera* to take in Edward I., and the successors of the princes named. That the charter of 12 King John was by assent of a parliament of Ireland, he shows clearly to be a mistake. Whenever the first parliament was called in Ireland, that change in their constitution was without an act of the parliament of England, and therefore must have been derived from the King.

Mr. Barrington is well warranted in saying that the 12th of Edward I., called the "Statute of Wales," is certainly no more than a regulation made by the King as conqueror, for the government of the country, which, the preamble says, was then totally subdued; and, however for purposes of policy he might think fit to claim it as a fief appertaining to the realm of England, he could never think himself entitled to make laws without assent of parliament to bind the subjects of any part of the realm. Therefore as he did make laws for Wales without assent of parliament, the clear consequence[14] is that he governed it as a conquest: which was his title in fact, and the feudal right was but a fiction.

Berwick, after the conquest of it, was governed by charters from the crown, till the reign of James I., without interposition of parliament.

Whatever changes were made in the laws of Gascony, Guyenne, and Calais must have been under the King's authority; if by act of parliament, that act would be extant, for they were conquered in the reign of King Edward III.; and all the acts from that reign to the present time are extant; and in some acts of parliament there are commercial regulations relative to each of the conquests which I have named; none making any change in their constitution and laws, and particularly with regard to Calais, which is alluded to as if its laws were considered as given by the Crown. Yet as to Calais, there was a great change made in the constitution: for the inhabitants were summoned by writ to send burgesses to the English parliament; and, as this was not by act of parliament, it must have been by the sole act of the King.

Besides the garrison there are inhabitants, property, and trade at Gibraltar; the King, ever since that conquest, has from time to time made orders and regulations suitable to the condition of those who live, trade, or enjoy property in a garrison town.

Mr. Attorney-General[15] has alluded to a variety of instances, several within these twenty years, in which the King has exercised legislation over Minorca. In Minorca, it has appeared lately, there are and have been for years back a great many inhabitants of worth and a great trade carried on. If the King does it there as coming in the place of the King of Spain, because their old constitution continues (which by the by is another proof that the constitution of England does not necessarily follow a conquest by the King of England) the same argument applies here; for before the 7th of October, 1763, the constitution of Grenada continued, and the King stood in the place of their former sovereign.

After the conquest of New York, in which most of the old Dutch inhabitants remained, King Charles II. changed its constitution and political form of government, and granted it to the Duke of York, to hold from his crown under all the regulations contained in the letters patent.

It is not to be wondered that an adjudged case in point is not to be found; no dispute ever was started before upon the King's legislative right over a conquest; it never was denied in a court of law or equity in Westminster-hall, never was questioned in parliament. Lord Coke's report of the arguments and resolutions of the judges in Calvin's case lays it down as clear (and that strange extra judicial opinion, as to a conquest from a pagan country, will not make reason not to be reason, and law not to be law as to the rest). The book says, that "if a King"—I omit the distinction between a Christian and an infidel kingdom, which as to this purpose is wholly groundless, and most deservedly exploded— "If a King comes to a kingdom by conquest, he may, at his pleasure, alter and change the laws of that kingdom; but, until he doth make an alteration of those laws the ancient laws of that kingdom remain; but if a King hath a kingdom by title of descent, then, seeing that by the laws of that kingdom he doth inherit the kingdom, he cannot change those laws of himself without consent of parliament." It is plain that he speaks of his own country where there is a parliament. Also, "if a King hath a kingdom by conquest, as King Henry the Second had Ireland, after King John had given to them, being under his obedience and subjection, the laws of England for the government of that country, no succeeding King could alter the same without parliament." Which is very just, and it necessarily includes that King John himself could not alter the grant of the laws of England.

Besides this, the authority of two great names has been cited, who took the proposition for granted. And though opinions of counsel, whether acting officially in a public charge or in private, are not properly authority on which to found a decision, yet I cite them;—not to establish so clear a point, but to shew that when it has been matter of legal enquiry, the answer it has received, by gentlemen of eminent character and abilities in the profession, has been immediate and without hesitation, and conformable to these principles. In 1722, the assembly of Jamaica refusing the usual supplies, it was referred to Sir Philip Yorke, and Sir Clement Wearg,[16] what was to be done if they should persist in this refusal. Their answer is—"If Jamaica was still to be considered as a conquered island, the King had a right to levy taxes upon the inhabitants; but, if it was to be considered in the same light as the other colonies, no tax could be imposed upon the inhabitants, but by an assembly of the island, or by an act of parliament." The distinction in law between a conquered country and a colony they held to be clear and indisputable; whether, as to the case before them of Jamaica, that island remained a conquest or was made a colony, they had not examined. I have, upon former occasions, traced the constitution of Jamaica as far as there are books or papers in the offices; I cannot find that any Spaniard remained upon the island so late as the Restoration; if any, they were very few. A gentleman to whom I put the question on one of the arguments in this cause, said he knew of no Spanish names[17] among the white inhabitants of

Jamaica; but there were amongst the negroes. The King, I mean Charles the Second, after the Restoration invited settlers by proclamation, promising them his protection. He made grants of land. He appointed at first a governor and council only; afterwards he granted a commission to the governor to call an assembly. The constitution of every province immediately under the King has arisen in the same manner; not by the grants, but by commissions, to call assemblies. And therefore, all the Spaniards having left the island, or having been killed or driven out of it, Jamaica from the first settling was an English colony, who under the authority of the King planted a vacant island, belonging to him in right of his crown; like the cases of the islands of St. Helena and St. John, mentioned by Mr. Attorney-General.

A maxim of constitutional law, as declared by all the judges in Calvin's case, and which two such men in modern times as Sir Philip Yorke and Sir Clement Wearg took for granted, will acquire some authority, even if there were anything which otherwise [made it doubtful; but on the contrary no book, no saying of a judge, no, not even an opinion of any counsel, public or private, has been cited; no instance is to be found in any period of our history where it was ever questioned.

The counsel for the plaintiff undoubtedly labored this point from a diffidence of what might be our opinion on the second question. But upon the second point, after full consideration, we[1] are of opinion that before the letters patent of the 20th of July, 1764, the King had precluded himself from an exercise of the legislative authority which he had before by virtue of his prerogative over the island of Grenada.

The first and material instrument is the proclamation of the 7th of October, 1763. See what it is that the King there says, and with what view he says it; how and to what he engages himself and pledges his word: " Whereas it will greatly contribute to the speedy settling our said new governments, that our loving subjects should be informed of our paternal care for the security of the liberty and properties of those who are, and shall become, inhabitants thereof; we have thought fit to publish and declare by this our proclamation, that we have in the letters patent under our Great Seal of Great Britain, by which the said governments are constituted, given express power and direction to our governors of our said colonies respectively, that, so soon as the state and circumstances of the said colonies will admit thereof, they shall, with the advice and consent of the members of our council, summon and call general assemblies" (and then follow the directions for that purpose.) And to what end? "To make, constitute, and ordain laws, statutes, and ordinances for the public peace, welfare, and good government of our said colonies," of which this of Grenada is one, "and of the people and inhabitants thereof, as near as may be agreeable to the laws of

England." With what view is the promise given? To invite settlers; to invite subjects. Why? The reason is given. They may think their liberties and properties more secure when they have a legislative assembly than under a governor and council only. The governor and council depending on the King, he can recall them at pleasure, and give a new frame to the constitution; but not so of the other, which has a negative on those parts of the legislature which depend on the King. Therefore that assurance is given them for the security of their liberty and properties, and with a view to invite them to go and settle there after this proclamation that assured them of the constitution under which they were to live.

The next act is of the 26th of March, 1764, which, the constitution having been established by proclamation, invites further such as shall be disposed to come and purchase, to live under the constitution. It states certain terms and conditions on which the allotments were to be taken, established with a view to permanent colonization and the increase and cultivation of the new settlement. For further confirmation of all this, on the 9th of April, 1764, three months before the impost in question was imposed, there is an actual commission to Governor Melville, to call an assembly as soon as the state and circumstances of the island should admit.—You will observe in the proclamation there is no legislature reserved to be exercised by the King, or by the governor and council under his authority, or in any other method or manner, until the assembly should be called: the promise imports the contrary; for whatever construction is to be put upon it, (which perhaps it may be somewhat difficult to pursue through all the cases to which it may be applied) it apparently considers laws then in being in the island, and to be administered by courts of justice; not an interposition of legislative authority between the time of the promise and of calling the assembly. It does not appear from the special verdict when the first assembly was called; it must have been in about a year at farthest from the governor's arrival, for the jury find he arrived in December, 1764, and that an assembly was held about the latter end of the year 1765. So that there appears to have been nothing in the state and circumstances of the island to prevent calling an assembly.

We therefore think that, by the two proclamations and the commission to Governor Melville, the King had immediately and irrevocably granted to all who were or should become inhabitants, or who had or should have property, in the island of Grenada—in general to all whom it might concern—that the subordinate legislation over the island should be exercised by an assembly, with the consent of the governor and council, in like manner as in the other provinces under the King.

Therefore, though the right of the King to have levied taxes on a conquered country, subject to him in right of his crown, was good, and the duty reasonable, equitable, and expedient, and, according to the finding of the verdict, paid in Barbadoes and all the other Leeward islands ; yet by the inadvertency of the King's servants in the order in which the several instruments passed the office (for the patent of the 20th of July, 1764, for raising the impost stated, should have been first), the order is inverted, and the last we think contrary to and a violation of the first, and therefore void. How proper soever the thing may be respecting the object of these letters patent of the 20th of July, 1764, it can only now be done, to use the words of Sir Philip Yorke and Sir Clement Wearg, " by the assembly of the island, or by an act of the Parliament of Great Britain."

The consequence is, judgment must be given for the plaintiff.[10]

NOTES TO LORD MANSFIELD'S JUDGMENT.

[1] This judgment is to be found in Cowper's " Reports of Cases adjudged in the Court of King's Bench ; " in Lofft's "Reports," etc.; and in Vol. XX. of Howell's "Complete Collection of State Trials." Cowper gives the judgment only; Lofft gives the "special verdict" referred to in the judgment, and also a very full summary of the arguments of counsel before the King's Bench, which heard it argued three separate times with different counsel on each side on each occasion. The text given here is taken mainly from Lofft, whose report has been used in compiling the "State Trials," but there are in it many inaccuracies which a comparison with Cowper's text will expose. The judgment appears to have been an oral one, for Lofft explains in a note that he used a contemporary printed summary to correct errors and supply omissions in his own notes.

[2] Cowper's Report has " James Campbell."

[3] The Quebec Act, 1774, which in Canada superseded the Royal Proclamation of 1763, became law on the 22nd of June.

[4] In Cowper's Reports, "the third of March."

[5] In July, 1773, the case of *Campbell* v. *Hall* was first tried at the Guildhall, before Lord Chief Justice Mansfield and a jury. The latter returned a "special verdict," embodying in it simply the ascertained facts of the case, and expressly leaving the legal or constitutional question at issue to be decided by the Court.

[6] Compare with this stipulation and reply those found in the Articles of Capitulation of Quebec, 1759, and of Montreal, 1760, and the corresponding provisions of the Treaties of Utrecht, 1713, and of Paris, 1763.

[7] This paragraph from the Royal Proclamation is not quoted literally. See the correct text on pp. 68-69.

[8] See Note 15 to " Representative Assemblies in the Maritime Provinces."

[9] The form of this Commission was similar to that of Governor Cornwallis' of Nova Scotia (pp. 9-16).

[10] Cowper's " Reports " has " import."

[11] Lord Chief Justice Coke gives an abstract of the Calvin case in the seventh book of his " Reports." A lucid and interesting account of it is given by Masores in the "Canadian Freeholder," Vol. II., pp. 312-322. For the benefit of those who have not access to these works it may be stated that Calvin was an infant born in

Scotland three years after James VI. of that country became James I. of England, and the question at issue in the case was whether, having been born after the union of the Crowns, he was an alien in England, as he undoubtedly would have been if he had been born before it. Lord Chancellor Ellesmere and twelve out of fourteen Judges decided that Calvin was not an alien, and Lord Coke in his judgment, in the course of a discussion of the nature of alienage, uttered the dictum quoted by Lord Mansfield respecting the legislative authority of the King over conquered countries. Maseres ingeniously contends that Lord Coke's dictum makes against, rather than for Lord Mansfield's opinion on this point.

12 The day the Royal Proclamation was issued.

13 In his "Case of Ireland Against England."

14 That is, "inference."

15 Thurlow.

16 Attorney-General and Solicitor-General, respectively, under George I.

17 The word "slave" occurs instead of "names" in the report in the "State Trials."

18 The report in the "State Trials" has "we are all of opinion;" Maseres, in the the "Canadian Freeholder," (Vol. II., pp. 343-346), raises, but does not settle, the question whether Lord Mansfield's colleagues of the King's Bench concurred in the former part of his judgment, namely, that the King had a prerogative right to legislate for a conquered country until he lost that right either by surrendering it to the conquered people or by the legislative intervention of the British Parliament. The compiler of the "State Trials" (Vol. XX., p. 1389), gives the following statement, as an addendum to the text of the Report in the Grenada case: "Mr. Baron Maseres has told me he was informed by Mr. Justice Miller himself, that he did not concur in the doctrine which Lord Mansfield in the case of *Campbell* v. *Hull*, laid down respecting the right of the Crown to legislate antecedently to a renunciation of such right for a conquered colony." It is somewhat peculiar that Lord Mansfield here for the first time in his judgment associates his colleagues with himself in the finding of the Court.

19 For a full, learned, and interesting discussion of this judgment in all its aspects—historical, political, and legal—see Maseres' second dialogue in Vol. II. of the "Canadian Freeholder." See also "State Trials" (Vol. XX. p. 331), for the opinion of Sergeant Marshall on the view of the constitution given by Lord Mansfield. The second part of the judgment has always been regarded as an important charter of colonial liberties, all the more so because Lord Mansfield in Parliament, as well as on the Bench, was a thorough-going asserter of royal prerogative and of imperial sovereignty over the colonies. See his speech, made in the House of Lords on the 3rd of February, 1866, on the adoption of the motion declaring the right of Great Britain to tax her American colonies.

THE QUEBEC ACT, 1774, AND SUPPLEMENTARY ACTS.

An Act, for making more effectual provision for the Government of the Province of Quebec in North America.

Preamble.

WHEREAS his Majesty, by his Royal Proclamation, bearing date the seventh day of October, in the third year of his reign, thought fit to declare the provisions which had been made in respect to certain countries, territories, and islands in America, ceded to his Majesty by the definitive treaty of peace, concluded at Paris on the tenth day of February, one thousand seven hundred and sixty three; and whereas by the arrangements made by the said Royal Proclamation, a very large extent of country, within which there were several colonies and settlements of the subjects of France,[2] who claimed to remain therein under the faith of the said treaty, was left without any provision being made for the administration of civil government therein; and certain parts of the territory of Canada, where sedentary fisheries had been established and carried on by the subjects of France, inhabitants of the said Province of Canada, under grants and concessions from the Government thereof, were annexed to the Government of Newfoundland, and thereby subjected to regulations inconsistent with the nature of such fisheries. May it therefore please your Most Excellent Majesty that it may be enacted, and be it enacted by the King's Most Excellent Majesty, by and with the advice and consent of the Lords Spiritual and Temporal, and Commons, in this present Parliament assembled, and by the authority of the same:

The territories, islands, and countries in North America, belonging to Great Britain,

That all the territories, islands, and countries in North America, belonging to the Crown of Great Britain, bounded on the south by a line from the Bay of Chaleurs, along the high lands which divide the rivers that empty themselves into the River St. Lawrence from those which fall into the sea, to a point in forty-five degrees of Northern latitude on the Eastern bank of the River Connecticutt, keeping the same latitude directly west through the Lake Champlain until, in the same latitude, it meets the

River St. Lawrence; from thence up the Eastern bank of the said River to the Lake Ontario; thence through the Lake Ontario, and the River commonly called Niagara; and thence along by the Eastern and South-Eastern bank of Lake Erie, following the said bank until the same shall be intersected by the Northern boundary granted by the charter of the Province of Pennsylvania, in case the same shall be so intersected; and from thence along the said Northern and Western boundaries of the said Province until the said Western boundary strike the Ohio: But in case the said bank of the said Lake shall not be found to be so intersected, then following the said bank until it shall arrive at that point of the said bank which shall be nearest to the northwest angle of the said Province of Pennsylvania, and thence by a right line to the said northwest angle of the said Province, and thence along the Western boundary of the said Province, until it strike the River Ohio; and along the Bank of the said River westward to the banks of the Mississippi, and Northward^a to the Southern boundary of the territory granted to the Merchants Adventurers of England trading to Hudson's Bay; and also all such territories, islands, and countries, which have since the tenth of February, one thousand seven hundred and sixty-three been made part of the Government of Newfoundland—be, and they are hereby, during his Majesty's pleasure, annexed to and made part and parcel of the Province of Quebec, as created and established by the said Royal Proclamation of the seventh of October, one thousand seven hundred and sixty-three. *Annexed to the Province of Quebec.*

II. Provided always, that nothing herein contained, relative to the boundary of the Province of Quebec shall in any wise affect the boundaries of any other colony. *Not to affect the boundaries of any other Colony;*

III. Provided always, and be it enacted, that nothing in this Act shall extend, or be construed to extend, to make void or to vary or alter any right, title, or possession derived under any grant, conveyance, or otherwise howsoever, of or to any lands within the said Province or the Provinces thereto adjoining; but that the same shall remain, and be in force, and have effect as if this Act had never been made. *nor to make void other rights formerly granted.*

IV. And whereas the provisions made by the said Proclamation in respect to the civil government of the said Province of Quebec, and the powers and authorities given to the Governor and other civil officers of the said Province by the grants and commissions issued in consequence *Former provisions for the Province to be null and void after May 1st, 1775.*

thereof, have been found upon experience to be inapplicable to the state and circumstances of the said Province, the inhabitants whereof amounted at the conquest to above sixty-five thousand persons professing the religion of the Church of Rome, and enjoying an established form of constitution and system of laws by which their persons and property had been protected, governed, and ordered for a long series of years from the first establishment of the said Province of Canada;⁴ be it therefore enacted by the Authority aforesaid, that the said Proclamation, so far as the same relates to the said Province of Quebec, and the Commission under the authority whereof the Government of the said Province is at present administered, and all and every the Ordinance and Ordinances made by the Governor and Council of Quebec for the time being relative to the civil government and administration of justice in the said Province, and all Commissions to judges and other officers thereof, be, and the same are hereby revoked, annulled, and made void⁵ from and after the first day of May, one thousand seven hundred and seventy-five.

Inhabitants of Quebec may profess the Romish religion, subject to the King's supremacy, as by Act I. Eliz.; and the Clergy enjoy their accustomed dues.

V. And for the more perfect security and ease of the minds of the inhabitants of the said Province it is hereby declared, that his Majesty's subjects professing the religion of the Church of Rome, of and in the said Province of Quebec, may have, hold and enjoy the free exercise of the religion of the Church of Rome, subject to the King's supremacy, declared and established by an Act⁶ made in the first year of the Reign of Queen Elizabeth over all the Dominions and Countries which then did, or thereafter should, belong to the Imperial Crown of this Realm; and that the clergy⁷ of the said Church may hold, receive, and enjoy their accustomed dues and rights with respect to such persons only as shall profess the said religion.

Provision may be made by his Majesty for the support of the Protestant Clergy.

VI. Provided, nevertheless, that it shall be lawful for his Majesty, his heirs or successors, to make such provision out of the rest of the said accustomed dues and rights, for the encouragement of the Protestant Religion, and for the maintenance and support of a Protestant clergy⁸ within the said Province, as he or they shall from time to time think necessary or expedient.

No person professing the Romish religion obliged

VII. Provided always, and be it enacted, that no person professing the religion of the Church of Rome and residing in the said Province shall be obliged to take the Oath⁹ required by the said statute passed in the first year of the reign of Queen Elizabeth, or any other oaths substituted by any other Act in the place thereof; but that every such person, who by the said statute is required to take the oath therein mentioned, shall be obliged, and is hereby required, to take and subscribe the following oath before the Governor, or such other Person, in such Court of Record as his Majesty shall appoint, who are hereby authorized to administer the same; *vidilicet*, {*to take the Oath of I. Elizabeth; but to take before the Governor, etc., the following Oath:*}

> "I A. B. do sincerely promise and swear that I will be faithful, "and bear true allegiance to his Majesty King George, and him will "defend to the utmost of my power, against all traitorous con-"spiracies and attempts whatsoever, which shall be made against "his person, crown, and dignity; and I will do my utmost endea-"vour to disclose and make known to his Majesty, his heirs and "successors, all treasons and traitorous conspiracies and attempts, "which I shall know to be against him or any of them; and all this "I do swear without any equivocation, mental evasion, or secret "reservation, and renouncing all pardons and dispensations from "any Power or Person whomsoever to the contrary.
> "So help me GOD." {*The Oath.*}

And every such person, who shall neglect or refuse to take the said oath before mentioned, shall incur and be liable to the same penalties, forfeitures, disabilities, and incapacities as he would have incurred and been liable to for neglecting or refusing to take the oath required by the said statute passed in the first year of the reign of Queen Elizabeth. {*Persons refusing the Oath to be subject to the penalties by Act I. Eliz.*}

VIII. And be it further enacted by the Authority aforesaid, that all his Majesty's Canadian subjects within the Province of Quebec, the religious orders and communities only excepted,[10] may also hold and enjoy their property and possessions, together with all customs and usages relative thereto, and all others their civil rights, in as large, ample, and beneficial manner as if the said Proclamation, Commissions, Ordinances, and other Acts and Instruments had not been made, and as may consist with their allegiance to his Majesty, and subjection to the Crown and Parliament of Great Britain; and that in all matters of controversy relative to property and civil rights, resort shall be had to the laws of Canada[11] as the rule for the decision of the same; and all causes that shall hereafter be instituted in any of the courts of justice, to be appointed within and for the said Province by his Majesty, his heirs and successors, shall with respect to such property and rights be determined agreeably to the said laws and customs of Canada, until they shall be varied or altered by any Ordinance that shall from time to time be passed in the said Province by the {*His Majesty's Canadian subjects (religious orders excepted) may hold all their possessions, etc., and in matters of controversy resort may be had to the Laws of Canada for decision.*}

Governor, Lieutenant-Governor, or Commander-in-Chief for the time being, by and with the advice and consent of the Legislative Council of the same, to be appointed in manner hereinafter mentioned.

<small>Not to extend to lands granted by His Majesty in common soccage.</small>

IX. Provided always, that nothing in this Act contained shall extend, or be construed to extend, to any lands that have been granted by his Majesty, or shall hereafter be granted by his Majesty, his heirs and successors, to be holden in free and common soccage.[1][2]

<small>Owners of goods may alienate the same by will, etc., if executed according to the Laws of Canada.</small>

X. Provided also, that it shall and may be lawful to and for every person that is owner of any lands, goods or credits in the said Province, and that has a right to alienate the said lands, goods or credits in his or her lifetime, by deed of sale, gift, or otherwise, to devise or bequeath the same at his or her death, by his or her last will and testament; any law, usage, or custom heretofore or now prevailing in the Province, to the contrary hereof in anywise notwithstanding; such will being executed either according to the Laws of Canada, or according to the forms prescribed by the Laws of England.

<small>Criminal Law of England to be continued in the Province.</small>

XI. And whereas the certainty and lenity of the Criminal Law of England, and the benefits and advantages resulting from the use of it, have been sensibly felt by the inhabitants from an experience of more than nine years, during which it has been uniformly administered; be it therefore further enacted by the Authority aforesaid, that the same shall continue to be administered, and shall be observed as law in the Province of Quebec, as well in the description and quality of the offence as in the method of prosecution and trial, and the punishments and forfeitures thereby inflicted, to the exclusion of every other rule of criminal law or mode of proceeding thereon, which did or might prevail in the said Province before the year of our Lord one thousand seven hundred and sixty-four; everything in this Act to the contrary thereof in any respect notwithstanding; subject nevertheless to such alterations and amendments[13] as the Governor, Lieutenant-Governor, or Commander-in-Chief for the time being, by and with the advice and consent of the Legislative Council of the said Province, hereafter to be appointed, shall from time to time cause to be made therein, in manner hereinafter directed.

<small>His Majesty may appoint a Council for</small>

XII. And whereas it may be necessary to ordain many regulations for the future welfare and good government of the Province of Quebec, the occasions of which cannot now be foreseen, nor without much delay and inconvenience be provided for, without intrusting that authority for a certain time and under proper restrictions to persons resident there: and whereas it is at present inexpedient to call an Assembly,[14] be it therefore enacted by the Authority aforesaid, that it shall and may be lawful for his Majesty, his heirs and successors, by warrant under his or their signet or sign manual, and with the advice of the Privy Council, to constitute and appoint a Council for the affairs of the Province of Quebec, to consist of such persons resident there, not exceeding twenty-three nor less than seventeen, as his Majesty, his heirs and successors shall be pleased to appoint; and, upon the death, removal, or absence of any of the members of the said Council, in like manner to constitute and appoint such and so many other person or persons as shall be necessary to supply the vacancy or vacancies; which Council so appointed and nominated, or the major part thereof, shall have power and authority to make Ordinances for the peace, welfare, and good government of the said Province, with the consent of his Majesty's Governor, or, in his absence, of the Lieutenant-Governor or Commander-in-Chief for the time being. *[the affairs of the Province; Which Council may make Ordinances, with consent of the Governor.]*

XIII. Provided always that nothing in this Act contained shall extend to authorize or impower the said Legislative Council to lay any taxes or duties within the said Province, such rates and taxes only excepted as the inhabitants of any town or district within the said Province may be authorized by the said Council to assess, levy, and apply, within the said town or district, for the purpose of making roads, erecting and repairing public buildings, or for any other purpose respecting the local convenience and œconomy of such town or district.[15] *[The Council are not impowered to lay taxes, public roads or buildings excepted.]*

XIV. Provided also, and be it enacted by the Authority aforesaid, that every Ordinance so to be made shall within six months be transmitted by the Governor, or in his absence by the Lieutenant-Governor, or Commander-in-Chief for the time being, and laid before his Majesty for his Royal Approbation; and if his Majesty shall think fit to disallow thereof, the same shall cease and be void from the time that his Majesty's order-in-council thereupon shall be promulgated at Quebec. *[Ordinances made to be laid before His Majesty for his approbation.]*

Ordinances touching religion not to be in force without His Majesty's approbation.

XV. Provided also that no Ordinance touching religion, or by which any punishment may be inflicted greater than fine or imprisonment for three months, shall be of any force or effect, until the same shall have received his Majesty's approbation.

When Ordinances are to be passed by a majority.

XVI. Provided also that no Ordinance shall be passed at any meeting of the Council where less than a majority of the whole Council is present, or at any time except between the first day of January and the first day of May, unless upon some urgent occasion, in which case every member thereof resident at Quebec, or within fifty miles thereof, shall be personally summoned by the Governor, or in his absence by the Lieutenant-Governor, or Commander-in-Chief for the time being, to attend the same.

Nothing to hinder his Majesty to constitute Courts of Criminal, Civil, and Ecclesiastical Jurisdiction.

XVII. And be it further enacted by the Authority aforesaid, that nothing herein contained shall extend, or be construed to extend, to prevent or hinder his Majesty, his heirs and successors, by his or their letters patent under the Great Seal of Great Britain, from erecting, constituting and appointing such Courts of Criminal, Civil, and Ecclesiastical jurisdiction within and for the said Province of Quebec, and appointing from time to time the judges and officers thereof, as his Majesty, his heirs and successors, shall think necessary and proper for the circumstances of the said Province.

All Acts formerly made are hereby inforced within the Province.

XVIII. Provided always, and it is hereby enacted, that nothing in this Act contained shall extend, or be construed to extend, to repeal or make void within the said Province of Quebec any Act or Acts of the Parliament of Great Britain heretofore made for prohibiting, restraining, or regulating the trade or commerce of his Majesty's Colonies and Plantations in America; but that all and every the said Acts, and also all Acts of Parliament heretofore made concerning or respecting the said Colonies and Plantations, shall be, and are hereby declared to be in force within the said Province of Quebec, and every part thereof.[10]

The Quebec Revenue Act, 1774.

An Act[17] to establish a fund towards further defraying the charges of the Administration of Justice, and support of the Civil Government within the Province of Quebec in America.

Whereas certain duties[18] were imposed by the authority of his Most Christian Majesty upon wine, rum, brandy, *eau de vie de liqueur*, imported into the Province of Canada, now called the Province of Quebec, and also a duty of three pounds *per centum ad valorem* upon all dry goods imported into and exported from the said Province, which duties subsisted at the time of the surrender of the said Province to your Majesty's forces in the late war: And whereas it is expedient that the said duties should cease and be discontinued, and that in lieu and instead thereof other duties should be raised by the authority of Parliament for making a more adequate provision for defraying the charge of the administration of justice and the support of civil Government in the said Province: We, your Majesty's most dutiful and loyal subjects, the Commons of Great Britain in Parliament assembled, do most humbly beseech your Majesty that it may be enacted, and be it enacted by the King's most Excellent Majesty, by and with the advice and consent of the Lords Spiritual and Temporal and Commons, in this present Parliament assembled, and by the authority of the same: That from and after the fifth day of April, one thousand, seven hundred, and seventy-five, all the duties which were imposed upon rum, brandy, *eau de vie de liqueur*, within the said Province, and also of three pounds *per centum ad valorem* on dried goods imported into or exported from the said Province under the authority of his most Christian Majesty, shall be and are hereby discontinued; and that in lieu and instead thereof there shall from and after the said fifth day of April, one thousand seven hundred and seventy-five be raised, levied, collected, and paid unto his Majesty, his heirs and successors, for

Preamble.
Certain duties imposed by his most Christian Majesty upon rum, brandy, etc., imported into Quebec.

After April 5, 1775, to be discontinued within the Province,

and instead of which the following duties to be paid to His Majesty.

and upon the respective goods hereinafter mentioned, which shall be imported or brought into any part of the said Province, over and above all other duties now payable in the said Province, by any Act or Acts of Parliament, the several rates and duties following: that is to say,

The rates.

For every gallon of brandy, or other spirits, of the manufacture of Great Britain, three-pence.

For every gallon of rum, or other spirits, which shall be imported or brought from any of his Majesty's sugar colonies in the West Indies, six-pence.

For every gallon of rum, or other spirits which shall be imported or brought from any other of his Majesty's colonies or dominions in America, nine-pence.[19]

For every gallon of foreign brandy, or other spirits of foreign manufacture imported or brought from Great Britain, one shilling.

For every gallon of rum or spirits of the produce or manufacture of any of the Colonies or Plantations in America, not in the possession or under the dominion of his Majesty imported from any other place except Great Britain, one shilling.

For every gallon of molasses and syrups which shall be imported or brought into the said Province in ships or vessels belonging to his Majesty's subjects in Great Britain or Ireland, or to his Majesty's subjects in the said Province, three-pence.

For every gallon of molasses and syrups, which shall be imported or brought into the said Province in any other ships or vessels in which the same may be legally imported, six-pence; and after those rates for any greater or less quantity of such goods respectively.

Rates deemed sterling money of Great Britain;

II. And it is hereby further enacted by the authority aforesaid, that the said rates and duties charged by this Act shall be deemed, and are hereby declared, to be sterling money of Great Britain, and shall be collected, recovered, and paid, to the amount of the value of[20] which such nominal sums bear in Great Britain; and that such monies may be received and taken according to the proportion and value of five shillings and sixpence the ounce in silver; and that the said duties hereinbefore granted

How they are to be levied, etc.

shall be raised, levied, collected, paid, and recovered, in the same manner and form, and by such rules, ways, and means, and under such penalties and forfeitures, except in such cases where any alteration is made by this Act, as any other duties payable to his Majesty upon goods imported into any British Colony or Plantation in America are or shall be raised, levied, collected, paid, and recovered, by any Act or Acts of Parliament, as fully and effectually, to all intents and purposes, as if the several clauses, powers, directions, penalties, and forfeitures relating thereto, were particularly repeated and again enacted in the body of this present Act: and that all the monies that shall arise by the said duties (except the necessary charges of raising, collecting, levying, recovering, answering, paying, and accounting for the same), shall be paid by the Collector of his Majesty's Customs, into the hands of his Majesty's Receiver-General in the said Province for the time being, and shall be applied in the first place in making a more certain and adequate provision towards defraying the expences of the administration of justice and of the support of Civil Government in the said Province; and that the Lord High Treasurer, or Commissioners of his Majesty's Treasury, or any three or more of them for the time being, shall be, and is, or are hereby impowered, from time to time, by any warrant or warrants under his or their hand or hands, to cause such money to be applied out of the said produce of the said duties, towards defraying the said expences; and that the residue of the said duties shall remain and be reserved in the hands of the said Receiver-General, for the future disposition of Parliament.[21] *to whom they are to be paid, and how to be applied.*

III. And it is hereby further enacted by the authority aforesaid that if any goods chargeable with any of the said duties herein-before mentioned shall be brought into the said Province by land carriage, the same shall pass and be carried through the port of St. John's, near the River Sorrel; or if such goods shall be brought into the said Province by any inland navigation other than upon the River St. Lawrence, the same shall pass and be carried upon the said River Sorrel by the said port, and shall be there entered with, and the said respective rates and duties paid for the same, to such officer or officers of his Majesty's Customs as shall be there appointed for that purpose; and if any such goods coming by land carriage or inland navigation, as aforesaid, shall pass by or beyond the said place before named, without entry or payment of the said rates and duties, or shall be brought into any part of the said Province by or through any other place whatsoever, the said goods shall be forfeited; and every person who shall be assisting, or otherwise concerned in the bringing or removing such goods, or to whose hands the same shall come, knowing that they were brought or removed contrary to this Act, shall forfeit *Regulations with respect to goods brought into the Province chargeable with the duties before mentioned.*

II.C.C.—7

treble the value of such goods, to be estimated and computed according to the best price that each respective commodity bears in the Town of Quebec, at the time such offence shall be committed; and all the horses, cattle, boats, vessels, and other carriages whatsoever, made use of in the removal, carriage, or conveyance of such goods, shall also be forfeited and lost, and shall and may be seized by any officer of his Majesty's Customs, and prosecuted as hereinafter mentioned.

<small>Penalties and forfeitures when to be prosecuted for, etc.</small>

IV. And it is hereby further enacted by the authority aforesaid, that the said penalties and forfeitures by this Act inflicted, shall be sued for and prosecuted in any Court of Admiralty, or Vice-Admiralty,[22] having jurisdiction within the said Province, and the same shall and may be recovered and divided in the same manner and form, and by the same rules and regulations in all respects as other penalties and forfeitures for offences against the laws relating to the customs and trade of his Majesty's Colonies in America shall or may, by any Act or Acts of Parliament be sued for, prosecuted, recovered, and divided.

<small>Any person keeping a house of public entertainment to pay £1 16s for a license.</small>

V. And be it further enacted by the authority aforesaid, that there shall from and after the fifth day of April, one thousand seven hundred and seventy-five, be raised, levied, collected and paid unto his Majesty's Receiver-General of the said Province for the use of his Majesty, his heirs and successors, a duty of one pound sixteen shillings, sterling money of Great Britain, for every licence that shall be granted by the Governor, Lieutenant-Governor, or Commander in Chief of the said Province to any person or persons for keeping a house or any other place of publick entertainment, or for the retailing wine, brandy, rum, or any other spirituous liquors within the said Province; and any person keeping any such house or place of entertainment, or retailing any such liquors without such licence shall forfeit and pay the sum of ten pounds for every such offence, upon conviction thereof; one moiety to such person as shall inform or prosecute for the same, and the other moiety shall be paid into the hands of the Receiver-General of the Province for the use of his Majesty.

<small>Penalty of £10 for every offence.</small>

<small>Not to make void French revenues, etc., reserved at the conquest.</small>

VI. Provided always that nothing herein contained shall extend or be construed to extend to discontinue, determine, or make void any part of the territorial[23] or casual revenues, fines, rents, or profits whatsoever, which were reserved to, and belonged to his Most Christian Majesty, before and at the time of the conquest and surrender thereof to his Majesty, the King of Great Britain; but that the same and every one of them, shall remain and be continued to be levied, collected, and paid in the same manner as if this Act had never been made; anything therein contained to the contrary notwithstanding.

VII. And be it further enacted by the authority aforesaid, that if any action or suit shall be commenced against any person or persons for anything done in pursuance of this Act, and if it shall appear to the Court or judge where or before whom the same shall be tried, that such action or suit is brought for anything that was done in pursuance of, and by the authority of this Act, the defendant or defendants shall be indemnified and acquitted for the same; and if such defendant or defendants shall be so acquitted; or if the plaintiff shall discontinue such action or suit, such Court or judge shall award to the defendant or defendants treble costs.

In suits brought pursuant to this Act, defendants to have treble costs.

The Quebec Revenue Act, 1775.

An Act[24] for amending and explaining an Act,[25] passed in the fourteenth year of his Majesty's reign, intituled "An Act to establish a Fund towards further defraying the charges of the Administration of Justice and support of the Civil Government within the Province of Quebec, in America."

Preamble.
Clause in Act 14 Geo. III., recited.

Whereas by an Act passed in the fourteenth year of his Majesty's reign (intituled, "An Act to establish a fund towards further defraying the charges of the administration of justice and support of the Civil Government within the Province of Quebec in America"), it is amongst other things enacted, that if any goods, chargeable with any of the duties in the said Act mentioned, shall be brought into the said Province by land carriage, the same shall pass and be carried through the Port of Saint John's, near the River Sorrel; or if such goods shall be brought into the said Province by any inland navigation other than that upon the River Saint Lawrence, the same shall pass and be carried upon the said River Sorrel by the said port, and shall be there entered with, and the said respective rates and duties paid for the same to, such officer or officers of his Majesty's customs as shall there be appointed for that purpose; and if any such goods, coming by land carriage or inland navigation, as aforesaid, shall pass by or beyond the said place before named, without entry or payment of the said rates and duties, or shall be brought into any part of the said Province by or through any other place whatsoever, the said goods shall be forfeited; and every person who shall be assisting, or otherwise concerned in the bringing or removing such goods, or to whose hands the same shall come, knowing that they were brought or removed contrary to this Act, shall forfeit treble the value of such goods; to be estimated and computed according to the best price that each respective commodity bears in the town of Quebec at the time such offence shall be committed; and all the horses, cattle, boats, vessels, and other carriages whatsoever, made use of in the removal, carriage, or conveyance of such goods, shall be forfeited and lost, and shall and may be seized by any officer of his Majesty's Customs, and prosecuted as thereinafter mentioned: And whereas there is reason to apprehend that the regulations and restrictions contained in the said hereinbefore recited clause, so far as they relate to the bringing of rum, brandy, or other spirits into the Province of Quebec by land carriage, may, without further explanation, operate to the prejudice and disadvantage of the commerce carried on with the Indians[26] in the upper or interior parts of the said Province: We, your Majesty's most dutiful and loyal subjects, the Commons of Great Britain in Parliament assembled, do most humbly beseech your Majesty that it may be enacted; and be it enacted by the King's Most Excellent Majesty, by and with the advice and consent of the Lords Spiritual and Temporal, and Commons, in this present Parliament assembled, and by the authority of the same, That it shall and may be lawful to and for all his Majesty's subjects freely to bring, carry or convey, by land carriage or inland navigation, into any ports of the Province of Quebec,[27] not heretofore comprehended within the limits thereof by his Majesty's Royal Proclamation of the seventh of October, one thousand seven hundred and sixty-three, any quantity of rum, brandy, or other spirits, anything contained in the before-recited Act of Parliament to the contrary thereof in any wise notwithstanding.

His Majesty's subjects may bring, by land or inland navigation, into any ports of Quebec not heretofore comprehended in the Royal Proclamation of Oct. 7, 1763, any quantity of rum, brandy, etc.

The Colonial Tax Repeal Act, 1778.

An Act[2] for removing all doubts and apprehensions concerning taxation by the Parliament of Great Britain in any of the Colonies, Provinces, and Plantations in North America and the West Indies: and for repealing so much of an Act, made in the seventh year of the reign of his present Majesty, as imposes a duty on tea imported from Great Britain into any Colony or Plantation in America, or relates thereto.

Preamble.

Whereas taxation by the Parliament of Great Britain, for the purpose of raising a revenue in his Majesty's Colonies, Provinces, and Plantations in North America,[29] has been found by experience to occasion great uneasiness and disorders among his Majesty's faithful subjects, who may nevertheless be disposed to acknowledge the justice of contributing to the common defence of the Empire, provided such contribution should be raised under the authority of the General Court,[30] or General Assembly, of each respective Colony, Province, or Plantation: And whereas, in order as well to remove the said uneasiness, and to quiet the minds of his Majesty's subjects who may be disposed to return to their allegiance, as to restore the peace and welfare of all his Majesty's Dominions, it is expedient to declare that the King and Parliament of Great Britain will[31] not impose any duty, tax, or assessment, for the purpose of raising a revenue in any of the Colonies, Provinces, or Plantations: May it please your Majesty that it may be declared and enacted,

No tax to be hereafter imposed by the King and Parliament of Great Britain on any of the Colonies in North America or the West Indies; except, etc.

and it is hereby declared and enacted by the King's Most Excellent Majesty, by and with the advice and consent of the Lords Spiritual and Temporal, and Commons, in this present Parliament assembled, and by the authority of the same, that from and after the passing of this Act the King and Parliament of Great Britain will not impose any duty, tax, or assessment whatever, payable in any of his Majesty's Colonies, Provinces, and Plantations in North America or the West Indies; except only such duties as it may be expedient to impose for the regulation of commerce; the net produce of such duties to be always paid and applied to and for the use of the Colony, Province, or Plantation, in which the same shall be respectively levied, in such manner as other duties collected by the authority of the respective General Courts, or General Assemblies, of such Colonies, Provinces, or Plantations, are ordinarily paid and applied.

II. And be it further enacted by the authority aforesaid, that from and after the passing of this Act, so much of an Act³² made in the seventh year of his present Majesty's reign, intituled "An Act for granting certain duties in the British Colonies and Plantations in America; for allowing a drawback of the duties of Customs upon the exportation from this kingdom of coffee and cocoanuts of the produce of the said Colonies or Plantations ; for discontinuing the drawbacks payable on China earthenware exported to America; and for more effectually preventing the clandestine running of goods in said Colonies or Plantations," as imposes a duty on tea imported from Great Britain into any Colony or Plantation in America, or has relation to the said duty, be, and the same is hereby repealed. *So much of an Act, 7 Geo. III., as imposes a duty on tea imported from Great Britain into America repealed.*

Canadian Revenue Control Act, 1831.

An Act[33] to amend an Act of the fourteenth year of His Majesty King George the Third, for establishing a fund towards defraying the charges of the administration of justice and support of the civil government within the Province of Quebec in America.

22ND SEPTEMBER, 1831.

14 G. 3, cap. 88. Whereas by an Act passed in the fourteenth year of the reign of his late Majesty, King George the Third, intituled "An Act to establish a Fund towards further defraying the charges of the administration of justice and support of the Civil Government within the Province of Quebec in America," it was amongst other things enacted that from and after the fifth day of April, one thousand, seven hundred and seventy-five, there should be raised, levied, collected and paid unto his said late Majesty, his heirs and successors, for and upon the respective goods thereinafter mentioned, which should be imported and brought into any port of the said Province, over and above all other duties then payable in the said Province by any Act or Acts of Parliament, the several rates and duties therein mentioned; (that is to say,) for every gallon of brandy or other spirits of the manufacture of Great Britain, three-pence; for every gallon of rum or other spirits, which should be imported or brought from any of his Majesty's sugar colonies in the West Indies, six-pence; for every gallon of rum or other spirits which should be imported or brought from any other of his Majesty's colonies or dominions in America, nine-pence; for every gallon of foreign brandy, or other spirits of foreign manufacture, imported or brought from Great Britain, one shilling; for every gallon of rum or of the produce or manufactures of any of the Colonies or Plantations in America not in the possession or under the Dominion of his Majesty imported from any other place except Great Britain, one shilling; for every gallon of molasses and syrups which should be imported or brought in the said Province in ships or vessels belonging to his Majesty's subjects in Great Britain or Ireland, or to his Majesty's subjects in the said

Province, three-pence; for every gallon of molasses and syrups which should be imported or brought into the said Province in any other ships or vessels in which the same might be legally imported, six-pence; and after those rates for any greater or less quantity of such goods respectively; and it was thereby further enacted that all the monies that should arise by the said duties (except the necessary charges of raising, collecting, levying, recovering, answering, paying, and accounting for the same, should be paid by the Collector of his Majesty's customs into the hands of his Majesty's Receiver-General in the said Province for the time being, and should be applied in the first place in making a more certain and adequate provision towards defraying the expenses of the administration of justice and of the support of the Civil Government in the said Province; and that the Lord High Treasurer, or the Commissioners of his Majesty's Treasury, or any three or more of them for the time being should be and they were thereby empowered from time to time by any warrant or warrants under his or their hand or hands, to cause such money to be applied out of the said produce of the said duties towards defraying said expenses: and it was thereby enacted that the residue of the said duties should remain and be reserved in the hands of the said Receiver-General for the future dispositions of Parliament: And whereas the said Province of Quebec hath since the enactment of the said Act been divided into the two Provinces of Upper Canada and Lower Canada: And whereas it is expedient to make further provision for the appropriation of the duties raised, levied and collected under the said Act; be it therefore enacted by the King's Most Excellent Majesty, by and with the advice and consent of the Lords Spiritual and Temporal and Commons, in this present Parliament assembled, and by the authority of the same, that it shall and may be lawful for the Legislative Councils and Assemblies of the said Provinces of Upper Canada and Lower Canada[a4] respectively, by any Acts to be by them from time to time passed and assented to by his Majesty, his heirs, and successors, or on his or their behalf, to appropriate[a5] in such manner, and to such purposes as to them respectively shall seem meet, all the monies that shall hereafter arise by, or be produced from the said duties, except so much of such monies as shall be necessarily defrayed for the charges of raising, collecting, levying, recovering, answering, paying, and accounting for the same.

Legislative Councils of Upper and Lower Canada may appropriate certain revenues thereof as shall seem meet to them.

NOTES TO THE QUEBEC ACT, 1774, AND SUPPLEMENTARY ACTS.

¹ This Act is 14 Geo. III., Cap. 83. The text is reprinted from the Imperial "Statutes at Large," London, 1776. The best account of the proceedings connected with its progress through the British Parliament is given in Sir Henry Cavendish's "Debates on the Canada Bill in 1774," London, 1839. For many interesting documents relating to the state of affairs in Quebec see Maseres' "Account of the Proceedings of the British and other Protestant Inhabitants of the Province of Quebeck in North America, in order to obtain an House of Assembly in that Province," and also his "Additional Papers Concerning the Province of Quebeck." In his "Canadian Freeholder" he discusses fully the policy which prompted the passing of the Act. The author had been Attorney General of Quebec from 1766 to 1772. See also Garneau's "History of Canada" Book XI, Cap. I.

² Some of these "settlements" are referred to in Art. 39 of the Montreal Capitulation. For a very full list of these "colonies and settlements," see the Ontario Sessional Papers of 1879, No. 31, p. 445. They were distributed along the great lakes, over the region between Lake Erie and the Ohio River as far west as the Mississippi, over the territory between Lake Michigan and the Mississippi, and over the district tributary to the Red River and Lake Winnipeg. How much of all this vast area was included in the Montreal Capitulation cannot now be ascertained, for the Marquis de Vaudreuil, in a letter written in 1761, denied having ever given the British authorities any definite boundary of the surrendered territory. On this point see the collection of documents entitled "Ontario Boundaries before the Privy Council, 1884," and the "Annual Register" for 1761. The French settlers on the Illinois were especially urgent in their requests for some regular form of government.

³ This word played a very important part in the controversies which took place between 1867 and 1889, about the western limit of the Province of Ontario. If taken to mean "due north" that limit would have been placed as far east as Thunder Bay. Taking it to mean "in a northerly direction"—*i.e.*, along the Mississippi towards its source—the Judicial Committee of the Privy Council in 1884 placed the limit at the "Northwest Angle" on the Lake of the Woods, and this finding was in 1889 confirmed by Act of the Imperial Parliament.

⁴ In a memorial sent to the Earl of Dartmouth in 1774 by a number of the French inhabitants of Quebec the petitioners make this statement: "In the year 1764, your Majesty deigned to bring to a close the military Government in this Province for the purpose of introducing the civil government, and from the time of this change we realise 1 the inconvenience which resulted from the British laws, which, until that time, were totally unknown to us." In the same memorial the population is estimated to be upwards of 100,000, and the British Government is petitioned to annex to Quebec "all the upper districts known under the names of Missilimackinac, Detroit, and other adjacent places as far as the River Mississippi," with a view to the regulation of trade and the collection of debts.

⁵ For copies of some of the commissions to judges and other officers see Maseres' "Collection of Commissions." As to the right of Parliament to make void the Royal Proclamation see Lord Mansfield's judgment in *Campbell* v. *Hall*.

6 This Act is 1 Elizabeth, cap. 1, and is entitled "An Act to restore to the Crown the Ancient Jurisdiction over the Estate Ecclesiastical and Spiritual, and abolishing all foreign powers repugnant to the same." The citation here is from section 16, which enacts: "that no foreign prince, person, prelate, state or potentate, spiritual or temporal, shall at any time, after the last day of this session of Parliament, use, enjoy, or exercise any manner of power, jurisdiction, superiority, authority, preheminence or privilege, spiritual or ecclesiastical, within this realm, or within any other your Majesty's dominions or countries that now be, or hereafter shall be, but from thenceforth the same shall be clearly abolished out of this realm, and all other your Highness' dominions for ever; any statute, ordinance, custom, constitutions, or any other matter or cause whatsoever, to the contrary notwithstanding."

7 Compare Article 27 of the Capitulation of Montreal.

8 Compare the provisions respecting the support of a Protestant Clergy in the Constitutional Act, 1791. Tithes were abolished in Upper Canada by Act of the Parliament of that Province (2 Geo. IV., cap. 32).

9 Section 19 of the Act of Supremacy (1 Eliz., cap. 1) prescribes the oath here referred to, which all "ecclesiastical persons and officers" were bound to take. The text is here given for convenience of comparison with the one substituted for it:—"I, A. B., do utterly testify and declare in my conscience, that the Queen's Highness is the only Supreme Governor of this realm, and of all other her Highness' "dominions and countries, as well in all spiritual or ecclesiastical things or causes, "as temporal; and that no foreign prince, person, prelate, state or potentate, hath "or ought to have any jurisdiction, power, superiority, preheminence, or authority, "ecclesiastical or spiritual within this realm; and therefore I do utterly renounce "and forsake all foreign jurisdictions, powers, superiorities and authorities, and "do promise that from henceforth I shall bear faith and true allegiance to the "Queen's Highness, her Heirs and lawful successors, and to my power shall assist "and defend all jurisdictions, preheminences, privileges and authorities granted or "belonging to the Queen's Highness, her Heirs and Successors, or united and "annexed to the Imperial Crown of this realm. So help me God, and by the "contents of this Book." This oath of Supremacy was abolished by the "Promissory Oaths Act, 1868" (31 & 32 Vict. Cap. 72).

10 Compare Art. 33 of the Montreal Capitulation, and Art. 4 of the Treaty of Paris, 1763

11 The "benefit of the laws" of England was by the Royal Proclamation of 1763 conferred on the inhabitants of Quebec. As to the extent to which English law was by this means introduced, see Note 5 to Governor Murray's Commission. English law was reintroduced into Upper Canada in 1792 by the first Parliament of that Province (32 Geo. III., cap. 1).

12 The land of Canada was granted during the French period on feudal tenures, for a description of which see Parkman's "Old Régime in Canada," and Kingsford's "History of Canada," Book III., Chapter 4. For some time after the conquest the British Government contemplated making further grants on this tenure, and actually instructed Governor Carleton in 1775, and again in 1786 to do so; but ultimately this policy was abandoned, and efforts were made to bring about the abolition of feudal tenures. This was accomplished by Act of the Canadian Parliament in 1854 (18 Vict., cap. 3). Tenure in free and common soccage was not effectually introduced till 1789, in spite of the efforts of U. E. Loyalist immigrants. See Bouchette's "British Dominions in North America," Vol. I., Chapter 14.

13 For such "alterations and amendments" see the ordinances in vol. O. of the "Statutes of Lower Canada."

14 For an explanation of the alleged inexpediency of calling an Assembly see Cavendish's "Debates," and Maseres' "Account" and "Papers" mentioned in Note 1.

15 For the means of raising a Provincial revenue see 14 Geo. III., cap 88. Four years after the passing of that Act there was passed another (18 George III., cap. 12), which declared that the King and Parliament of Great Britain would no longer tax the colonies, but this declaration did not take effect in Quebec. For ordinances passed by the Council dealing with municipal matters see vol. O. of the "Statutes of Lower Canada." No municipal machinery was ever organized for the Province under this section. In Appendix C to Lord Durham's Report will be found an account of the general character of the municipal legislation of the Council of 1774-1791 and of the Assembly of 1791-1837

16 The Imperial Parliament had always assumed the right to regulate the trade and commerce of all the colonies, as well as to tax them. The very statute (18 George III., cap. 12), which in 1778 announced the abandonment of the latter claim, reasserted the former.

17 The text is reprinted from the Imperial "Statutes at Large," London, 1776. The statute is 14 George III., cap. 88.

18 The date of the imposition of these duties could not be definitely ascertained after the cession of Canada to Great Britain, as appears from an account given by Maseres, in his "Collection of Several Commissions," of two unsuccessful attempts made by the British Government to enforce by law the payment of new duties imposed by Governor Murray. The French duties were said to have been paid for at least fifty years before the conquest.

19 This discrimination against trade with the other British Provinces could not fail to aggravate the ill-feeling already aroused by the Quebec Act.

20 So in the text of the "Statutes at Large."

21 See Act 1 & 2 William IV., cap. 23.

22 The Commission to General Murray to act as Vice-Admiral was issued on the 19th of March, 1764. It is given in full in Maseres' "Collection of Several Commissions."

23 Referring chiefly to the payments by seigneurs to the Crown under the feudal tenures, but including also escheats.

24 This statute is 15 George III., cap. 40. The text is reprinted from the Imperial "Statutes at Large," London, 1775.

25 The Act amended and explained is 14 George III., cap. 88. The text of it immediately precedes this Act.

26 Alcoholic liquors from a very early period in the history of both the French and the English colonies, played an important part in the fur trade with the Indians. In Canada there were constant disputes about the matter between the Bishop and the Governor. See Kingsford's "History of Canada," Book II., chap. 11; Book III, chaps. 5 and 8; Book X, chap. 2; and other passages.

27 This opened up to the liquor traffic the routes from New York and Albany to the Canadian Northwest and to the upper Mississippi.

28 This Act is 18 George III., cap. 12 The text is taken from the Imperial "Statutes at Large," London, 1780. It was the outcome of a vain attempt to win back the revolting colonies to their allegiance to Great Britain, and, though apparently broad enough in its title to include Quebec, it was obviously not intended to repeal the Quebec Revenue Act of 1774 (14 George III., cap. 88. above).

29 The right of the Imperial Parliament to tax the colonies was first practically asserted by the passage of the Stamp Act in 1765 (5 George III., cap. 12) This is

was repealed the following year (6 George III., cap. 11), and at the same time an Act (6 George III., cap. 12), was passed declaring that the legislative authority of Great Britain extended to all the colonies, in all cases whatsoever. It was in the debate on this declaratory Act that Lord Mansfield made his celebrated speech to prove the "right" of Great Britain to tax her colonies, and that William Pitt (afterwards Lord Chatham) made his equally celebrated speech to prove the "expediency" of refraining from the exercise of that right. In 1767 an Act (7 Geo. III., cap. 46) was passed imposing certain customs duties on goods imported into the colonies, and in 1770 this was repealed, by 10 Geo. III., cap. 17, as to several of the duties; the duty on tea was maintained till the Act of 1778 was passed.

30 The name given to the Provincial Legislatures of Massachusetts and Connecticut.

31 Compare with this preamble the language of the declaratory Act referred to in Note 29 above, which affirms that the King, Lords, and Commons in Parliament assembled, "had, hath, and of right ought to have, full power and authority to make laws and statutes of sufficient force and validity to bind the colonies and people of America, subjects of the Crown of Great Britain, in all cases whatsoever." In 1775 Burke introduced a bill embodying the main features of this Act, but it was then defeated in the House of Commons by a majority of 210 to 105.

32 7 George III., cap. 46.

33 This Act is 1 & 2 William IV., cap. 23. The text is reprinted from the Imperial "Statutes at Large," London, 1832. It was passed in compliance with a demand from Upper and Lower Canada for the privilege of controlling the expenditure of their own revenues. Compare with the provisions of this Act, sections 46 and 47 of the Constitutional Act, 1791.

34 See the Constitutional Act 1791.

35 On the use made by the Legislatures of this power see Lord Durham's Report, and Christie's "History of Lower Canada."

THE CONSTITUTIONAL ACT, 1791, AND SUPPLEMENTARY ACTS.

An Act[1] to repeal certain parts of an Act, passed in the fourteenth year of His Majesty's reign, intituled " An Act for making more effectual provision for the Government of the Province of Quebec, in North America," and to make further provision for the Government of the said Province.

Preamble.
14 Geo. III., cap. 83 recited.

WHEREAS an Act was passed in the fourteenth year of the reign of his present Majesty, intituled " An Act for making more effectual provision for the Government of the Province of Quebec in North America " : And whereas it is expedient and necessary that further provision should now be made for the good Government and prosperity thereof : May it therefore please your most Excellent Majesty that it may be enacted ; and be it enacted by the King's Most Excellent Majesty, by and with the advice and consent of the Lords Spiritual and Temporal, and Commons in this present Parliament assembled, and by the authority of the same, that

So much of recited Act as relates to the appointment of a Council for Quebec, or its powers, repealed.

so much of the said Act as in any manner relates to the appointment of a Council for the affairs of the said Province of Quebec, or to the power given by the said Act to the said Council, or to the major part of them, to make ordinances for the peace, welfare, and good Government of the said Province, with the consent of His Majesty's Governor, Lieutenant-Governor, or Commander in Chief for the time being, shall be, and the same is hereby repealed.

II. And whereas his Majesty has been pleased to signify, by his message to both Houses of Parliament, his Royal intention to divide his Province of Quebec into two separate Provinces, to be called the Province of Upper Canada and the Province of Lower Canada :[2] Be it enacted by the

Within each of the intended Provinces a Legislative Council and Assembly to

authority aforesaid, that there shall be within each of the said Provinces respectively a Legislative Council and an Assembly,[3] to be severally composed and constituted in the manner hereinafter described ; and that in each of the said

Provinces respectively, His Majesty, His Heirs, and Successors, shall have power during the continuance of this Act, by and with the advice and consent of the Legislative Council and Assembly of such Provinces respectively, to make laws for the peace, welfare and good Government thereof, such laws not being repugnant to this Act; and that all such laws, being passed by the Legislative Council and Assembly of either of the said Provinces respectively, and assented to by His Majesty, His Heirs or Successors, or assented to in His Majesty's name by such person as His Majesty, His Heirs or Successors, shall from time to time appoint to be the Governor or Lieutenant-Governor of such Province, or by such person as His Majesty, His Heirs or Successors, shall from time to time appoint to administer the Government within the same, shall be, and the same are hereby declared to be, by virtue of and under this Act, valid and binding, to all intents and purposes whatever, within the Province in which the same shall have been so passed.

be constituted, by whose advice his Majesty may make laws for the Government of the Province.

III. And be it further enacted by the authority aforesaid, that for the purpose of constituting such Legislative Council as aforesaid, in each of the said Provinces respectively, it shall and may be lawful for his Majesty, his heirs, or successors, by an instrument under his or their sign manual, to authorize and direct the Governor or Lieutenant-Governor, or person administering the Government, in each of the said Provinces respectively, within the time herein after mentioned, in His Majesty's name, and by an instrument under the Great Seal of such Province, to summon to the said Legislative Council, to be established in each of the said Provinces respectively, a sufficient number of discreet and proper persons, being not fewer than seven, to the Legislative Council for the Province of Upper Canada, and no fewer than fifteen to the Legislative Council for the Province of Lower Canada; and that it shall also be lawful for his Majesty, his heirs or successors, from time to time, by an instrument under his or their sign manual, to authorize and direct the Governor or Lieutenant-Governor, or person administering the Government in each of the said Provinces respectively, to summon to the Legislative Council of such Province in like manner such other persons as his Majesty, his heirs or successors, shall think fit; and that every person who shall be so summoned to the Legislative Council of either of the said Provinces respec-

His Majesty may authorize the Governor or Lieutenant-Governor of each Province to summon members to the Legislative Council.

tively, shall thereby become a member of such Legislative Council, to which he shall have been so summoned.

No person under 21 years of age, etc., to be summoned.

IV. Provided always, and be it enacted by the authority aforesaid, that no person shall be summoned to the Legislative Council, in either of the said Provinces, who shall not be of the full age of twenty-one years, and a natural born subject of his Majesty, or a subject of his Majesty naturalized by Act of the British Parliament,[4] or a subject of his Majesty having become such by the conquest and cession of the Province of Canada.

Members to hold their seats for life.

V. And be it further enacted by the authority aforesaid, that every member of each of the said Legislative Councils shall hold his seat therein for the term of his life, but subject nevertheless to the provisions hereinafter contained for vacating the same, in the cases hereinafter specified.

His Majesty may annex to hereditary titles of honor the right of being summoned to the Legislative Council.

VI. And be it further enacted by the authority aforesaid, that whenever his Majesty, his heirs or successors, shall think proper to confer upon any subject of the Crown of Great Britain, by letters patent under the Great Seal of either of the said Provinces, any hereditary title of honor, rank, or dignity of such Province, descendible according to any course of descent limited in such letters patent, it shall and may be lawful for his Majesty, his heirs or successors, to annex thereto by the said letters patent, if his Majesty, his heirs or successors shall so think fit, an hereditary right of being summoned to the Legislative Council of such Province, descendible according to the course of descent so limited with respect to such title, rank, or dignity; and that every person on whom such right shall be so conferred, or to whom such right shall severally so descend, shall thereupon be entitled to demand from the Governor, Lieutenant Governor, or person administering the Government of such Province, his writ of summons to such Legislative Council at any time after he shall have attained the age of twenty-one years, subject nevertheless to the provision hereinafter contained.[5]

Such descendible right forfeited, and

VII. Provided always, and be it further enacted by the authority aforesaid, that when and so often as any person to whom such hereditary right shall have descended shall, without the permission of his Majesty, his heirs or successors, signified to [the Legislative Council of the Province by the Governor, Lieutenant-Governor, or person administering the Government there, have been absent from the said Province for the space of four years continually, at any time between the date of his succeeding to such right and the time of his applying for such writ of summons, if he shall have been of the age of twenty-one years or upwards at the time of his so succeeding, or at any time between the date of his attaining the said age and the time of his so applying, if he shall not have been of the said age at the time of his so succeeding; and also when and so often as any such person shall, at any time before his applying for such writ of summons have taken any oath of allegiance or obedience to any foreign prince or power, in any such case such person shall not be entitled to receive any writ of summons to the Legislative Council by virtue of such hereditary right, unless his Majesty, his heirs or successors, shall at any time think fit, by instrument under his or their sign manual, to direct that such person should be summoned to the said Council; and the Governor, Lieutenant-Governor, or person administering the Government in the said Provinces respectively, is hereby authorized and required, previous to granting such writ of summons to any person applying for the same, to interrogate such person upon oath, touching the said several particulars before such Executive Council as shall have been appointed by his Majesty, his heirs or successors, within such Province for the affairs thereof.

VIII. Provided also, and be it further enacted by the authority aforesaid, that if any member of the Legislative Councils of either of the said Provinces respectively, shall leave such Province, and shall reside out of the same for the space of four years continually, without the permission of his Majesty, his heirs or successors, signified to such Legislative Council by the Governor, or Lieutenant-Governor, or person administering his Majesty's Government there, or for the space of two years continually without the like permission, or the permission of the Governor, Lieutenant-Governor, or person administering the Government of such Province, signified to such Legislative Council in the manner aforesaid; or if any such member shall take any oath of allegiance or obedience to any foreign prince or power, his seat in such Council shall thereby become vacant.

Seats in Council vacated in certain cases.

IX. Provided also, and be it further enacted by the authority aforesaid, that in every case where a writ of sum-

Hereditary rights and seats so for-

THE CONSTITUTIONAL ACT

feited, or vacated, to remain suspended during the lives of the parties, but on their deaths to go to the persons next entitled thereto.

mons to such Legislative Council shall have been lawfully withheld from any person to whom such hereditary right, as aforesaid, shall have descended, by reason of such absence from the Province as aforesaid, or of his having taken an oath of allegiance or obedience to any foreign prince or power, and also in every case where the seat in such Council of any member thereof, having such hereditary right as aforesaid, shall have been vacated by reason of any of the causes hereinbefore specified, such hereditary right shall remain suspended during the life of such person unless his Majesty, his heirs or successors, shall afterwards think fit to direct that he be summoned to such Council; but that on the death of such person such right, subject to the provisions herein contained, shall descend to the person who shall next be entitled thereto, according to the course of descent limited in the letters patent by which the same shall have been originally conferred.

Seats in Council forfeited, and hereditary rights extinguished, for treason.

X. Provided also, and be it further enacted by the authority aforesaid, that if any member of either of the said Legislative Councils shall be attainted for treason in any Court of law within any of his Majesty's dominions, his seat in such Council shall thereby become vacant, and any such hereditary right as aforesaid then vested in such person, or to be derived to any other person through him, shall be utterly forfeited and extinguished.

Questions respecting the right to be summoned to Council, etc., to be determined as herein mentioned.

XI. Provided also, and be it enacted by the authority aforesaid, that whenever any question shall arise respecting the right of any person to be summoned to either of the said Legislative Councils respectively, or respecting the vacancy of the seat in such Legislative Council of any person having been summoned thereto, every such question shall by the Governor or Lieutenant-Governor of the Province, or by the person administering the Government there, be referred to such Legislative Council to be by the said Council heard and determined; and that it shall and may be lawful, either for the person desiring such writ of summons, or respecting whose seat such question shall have arisen, or for his Majesty's Attorney-General of such Province in his Majesty's name, to appeal from the determination of the said Council in such case to his Majesty in his Parliament of Great Britain: and that the judgment thereon of his Majesty in his said Parliament shall be final and conclusive to all intents and purposes whatever.

XII. And be it further enacted by the authority aforesaid, that the Governor or Lieutenant-Governor of the said Provinces respectively, or the person administering His Majesty's Government therein respectively, shall have power and authority from time to time, by an instrument under the great Seal of such Province, to constitute, appoint and remove the Speakers of the Legislative Councils of such Provinces respectively. *The Governor of the Province may appoint and remove the Speaker.*

XIII. And be it further enacted by the authority aforesaid, that for the purpose of constituting such Assembly as aforesaid in each of the said Provinces respectively, it shall and may be lawful for his Majesty, his heirs or successors, by an instrument under his or their sign manual, to authorize and direct the Governor or Lieutenant-Governor, or person administering the Government in each of the said Provinces respectively, within the time hereinafter mentioned, and thereafter from time to time as occasion shall require, in his Majesty's name and by an instrument under the Great Seal of such Province, to summon and call together an Assembly in and for such Province. *His Majesty may authorize the Governor to call together the Assembly.*

XIV. And be it further enacted by the authority aforesaid, that for the purpose of electing the member of such Assemblies respectively it shall and may be lawful for his Majesty, his heirs or successors, by an instrument under his or their sign manual, to authorize the Governor or Lieutenant-Governor of each of the said Provinces respectively, or the person administering the Government therein, within the time hereinafter mentioned, to issue a proclamation[6] dividing such Province into districts, or counties, or circles, and towns or townships, and appointing the limits thereof, and declaring and appointing the number of representatives to be chosen by each of such districts, or counties, or circles, and towns or townships respectively; and that it shall also be lawful for his Majesty, his heirs or successors, to authorize such Governor or Lieutenant-Governor, or person administering the Government, from time to time to nominate and appoint proper persons to execute the office of returning-officer in each of the said districts, or counties, or circles, and towns or townships respectively; and that such division of the said Provinces into districts, or counties, or circles, and towns or townships, and such declaration and appointment of the number of representatives to be chosen by each of the said districts, or counties, or circles, *and, for the purpose of electing the members, to issue a proclamation dividing the Province into Districts, etc.*

and towns or townships, respectively, and also such nomination and appointment of returning-officers in the same, shall be valid and effectual to all the purposes of this Act, unless it shall at any time be otherwise provided by any Act of the Legislative Council and Assembly of the Province, assented to by his Majesty, his heirs, or successors.

Power of the Governor to appoint returning officers to continue two years from the commencement of this Act.

XV. Provided nevertheless, and be it further enacted by the authority aforesaid, that the provision hereinbefore contained for empowering the Governor, Lieutenant-Governor, or person administering the Government of the said Provinces respectively, under such authority as aforesaid from his Majesty, his heirs or successors, from time to time to nominate and appoint proper persons to execute the office of returning-officer in the said districts, counties, circles, and towns or townships, shall remain and continue in force in each of the said Provinces respectively for the term of two years from and after the commencement of this Act within such Province, and no longer; but subject nevertheless to be sooner repealed or varied by any Act of the Legislative Council and Assembly of the Province, assented to by his Majesty, his heirs or successors.

No person obliged to serve as returning officer more than once unless otherwise provided by an Act of the Province.

XVI. Provided always, and be it further enacted by the authority aforesaid, that no person shall be obliged to execute the said office of returning-officer for any longer time than one year, or oftener than once, unless it shall at any time be otherwise provided by any Act of the Legislative Council and Assembly of the Province, assented to by his Majesty, his heirs or successors.

Number of members in each Province.

XVII. Provided also, and be it enacted by the authority aforesaid, that the whole number of members to be chosen in the Province of Upper Canada shall not be less than sixteen, and the whole number of members to be chosen in Lower Canada shall not be less than fifty.

Regulations for issuing writs for the election of members to serve in the Assemblies.

XVIII. And be it further enacted by the authority aforesaid, that writs[7] for the election of members to serve in the said Assemblies respectively shall be issued by the Governor, Lieutenant-Governor, or person administering his Majesty's Government within the said Provinces respectively, within fourteen days after the sealing of such instrument as aforesaid for summoning and calling together such Assembly, and that such writs shall be directed to the respective returning-officers of the said districts, or counties, or circles, and towns or townships, and that such writs shall be made returnable within fifty days at farthest from the day on which they shall bear date, unless it shall at any time be otherwise provided by any Act of the Legislative Council and Assembly of the Province, assented to by his Majesty, his heirs or successors; and that writs shall in like manner and form be issued for the election of members, in the case of any vacancy which shall happen by the death of the person chosen, or by his being summoned to the Legislative Council of either Province, and that such writs shall be made returnable within fifty days at farthest from the day on which they shall bear date, unless it shall at any time be otherwise provided by any Act of the Legislative Council and Assembly of the Province, assented to by his Majesty, his heirs or successors; and that in the case of any such vacancy which shall happen by the death of the person chosen, or by reason of his being so summoned as aforesaid, the writ for the election of a new member shall be issued within six days after the same shall be made known to the proper officer for issuing such writs of election.

XIX. And be it further enacted by the authority aforesaid, that all and every the returning-officers so appointed as aforesaid, to whom any such writs as aforesaid shall be directed, shall, and they are hereby authorized and required duly to execute such writs. *Returning officers to execute writs.*

XX. And be it further enacted by the authority aforesaid, that the members for the several districts, or counties, or circles of the said Provinces respectively shall be chosen by the majority of votes of such persons as shall severally be possessed, for their own use and benefit, of lands or tenements within such district, or county, or circle, as the case shall be, such lands being by them held in freehold, or in fief, or in roture, or by certificate derived under the authority of the Governor and Council of the Province of Quebec, and being of the yearly value of forty shillings sterling or upwards, over and above all rents and charges payable out of or in respect of the same; and that the members for the several towns or townships within the said Provinces respectively shall be chosen by the majority of votes of such persons as either shall be severally possessed for their own use and benefit of a dwelling house and lot of ground in such town or township, such dwelling house and lot of ground being by them held in like manner as aforesaid, and being *By whom the members are to be chosen.*

of the yearly value of five pounds sterling or upwards, or as having been resident within the said town or township for the space of twelve calendar months next before the date of the writ of summons for the election, shall *bona fide* have paid one year's rent for the dwelling house in which they shall have so resided, at the rate of ten pounds sterling per annum or upwards.

Certain persons not eligible to the Assemblies.

XXI. Provided always, and be it further enacted by the authority aforesaid, that no person shall be capable of being elected a member to serve in either of the said Assemblies, or of sitting and voting therein, who shall be a member of either of the said Legislative Councils to be established as aforesaid in the said two Provinces, or who shall be a minister of the Church of England, or a minister, priest, ecclesiastic, or teacher, either according to the rites of the Church of Rome, or under any other form or profession of religious faith or worship.

No person under 21 years of age, etc., capable of voting or of being elected;

XXII. Provided also, and be it further enacted by the authority aforesaid, that no person shall be capable of voting at any election of a member to serve in such Assembly, in either of the said Provinces, or of being elected at any such election who shall not be of the full age of twenty-one years, and a natural born subject of his Majesty, or a subject of his Majesty naturalized* by Act of the British Parliament, or a subject of his Majesty having become such by the conquest and cession of the Province of Canada.

nor any person attainted for treason or felony.

XXIII. And be it also enacted by the authority aforesaid, that no person shall be capable of voting at any election of a member to serve in such Assembly in either of the said Provinces, or of being elected at any such election, who shall have been attainted for treason or felony in any Court of law within any of his Majesty's dominions, or who shall be within any description of persons disqualified by any Act of the Legislative Council and Assembly of the Province, assented to by his Majesty, his heirs or successors.

Voters, if required, to take the following Oath,

XXIV. Provided also, and be it further enacted by the authority aforesaid, that every voter before he is admitted to give his vote at any such election shall, if required by any of the candidates, or by the returning-officer, take the following oath, which shall be administered in the English or French language, as the case may require:

I, A. B., do declare and testify, in the presence of Almighty God, that I am, to the best of my knowledge and belief, of the full age of twenty-one years, and that I have not voted before at this election. Oath,

And that every such person shall also, if so required as aforesaid, make oath previous to his being admitted to vote that he is, to the best of his knowledge and belief, duly possessed of such lands and tenements, or of such a dwelling house and lot of ground, or that he has *bona fide* been so resident and paid such rent for his dwelling house as entitles him, according to the provisions of this Act, to give his vote at such election for the county, or district, or circle, or for the town or township, for which he shall offer the same. and to make oath to the particulars herein specified.

XXV. And be it further enacted by the authority aforesaid, that it shall and may be lawful for his Majesty, his heirs or successors, to authorize the Governor or Lieutenant-Governor, or person administering the Government within each of the said Provinces respectively, to fix the time and place of holding such elections, giving not less than eight days' notice of such time, subject nevertheless to such provisions as may hereafter be made in these respects, by any Act of the Legislative Council and Assembly of the Province, assented to by his Majesty, his heirs, or successors. His Majesty may authorize the Governor to fix the term and place for holding elections,

XXVI. And be it further enacted by the authority aforesaid, that it shall and may be lawful for his Majesty, his heirs or successors, to authorize the Governor or Lieutenant-Governor of each of the said Provinces respectively, or the person administering the Government therein, to fix the places and times⁹ of holding the first and every other session of the Legislative Council and Assembly of such Province, giving due and sufficient notice thereof, and to prorogue the same from time to time, and to dissolve the same by proclamation or otherwise, whenever he shall judge it necessary or expedient. and of holding the Sessions of the Council and Assembly, etc.

XXVII. Provided always, and be it further enacted by the authority aforesaid, that the said Legislative Council and Assembly in each of the said Provinces shall be called together once at the least in every twelve calendar months, and that every Assembly shall continue for four years from the day of the return of the writs for choosing the same, and no longer,¹⁰ subject nevertheless to be sooner prorogued or dissolved by the Governor or Lieutenant-Governor of the Province, or person administering his Majesty's Government therein. Council and Assembly to be called together once in twelve months, etc.,

and all questions therein to be decided by the majority of votes.	XXVIII. And be it further enacted by the authority aforesaid, that all questions which shall arise in the said Legislative Councils or Assemblies respectively shall be decided by the majority of voices of such members as shall be present; and that in all cases where the voices shall be equal the Speaker of such Council or Assembly, as the case may be, shall have a casting voice.
No member to sit or vote till he has taken the following	XXIX. Provided always, and be it enacted by the authority aforesaid, that no member either of the Legislative Council or Assembly, in either of the said Provinces, shall be permitted to sit or vote therein until he shall have taken and subscribed the following oath, either before the Governor or Lieutenant-Governor of such Province, or person administering the Government therein, or before some person or persons authorized by the said Governor or Lieutenant-Governor, or other person as aforesaid, to administer such oath, and that the same shall be administered in the English or French language, as the case may require:
Oath.	I, A. B., do sincerely promise and swear that I will be faithful and bear true allegiance to his Majesty, King George, as lawful Sovereign of the Kingdom of Great Britain, and of these Provinces dependent on and belonging to the said Kingdom; and that I will defend him to the utmost of my power against all traitorous conspiracies and attempts whatever which shall be made against his person, crown, and dignity; and that I will do my utmost endeavour to disclose and make known to his Majesty, his heirs or successors, all treasons and traitorous conspiracies and attempts which I shall know to be against him, or any of them; and all this I do swear without any equivocation, mental evasion, or secret reservation, and renouncing all pardons and dispensations from any person or power whatever to the contrary—So help me God.
Governor may give or withhold his Majesty's assent to bills passed by the Legislative Council and Assembly, or reserve them for his Majesty's pleasure.	XXX. And be it further enacted by the authority aforesaid, that whenever any bill, which has been passed by the Legislative Council and by the House of Assembly in either of the said Provinces respectively, shall be presented for his Majesty's assent to the Governor or Lieutenant-Governor of such Province, or person administering his Majesty's Government therein, such Governor or Lieutenant-Governor, or person administering the Government shall, and he is hereby authorized and required to declare, according to his discretion, but subject nevertheless to the provisions contained in this Act, and to such instructions as may from time to time be given in that behalf by his Majesty, his heirs or successors, that he assents to such bill in his Majesty's name, or that he withholds his Majesty's

assent from such bill, or that he reserves such bill for the signification of his Majesty's pleasure thereon.

XXXI. Provided always, and be it further enacted by the authority aforesaid, that whenever any bill which shall have been so presented for his Majesty's assent to such Governor, Lieutenant-Governor, or person administering the Government, shall by such Governor, Lieutenant-Governor, or person administering the Government, have been assented to in his Majesty's name, such Governor, Lieutenant-Governor, or person as aforesaid shall, and he is hereby required, by the first convenient opportunity to transmit to one of his Majesty's principal Secretaries of State, an authentic copy of such bill so assented to; and that it shall and may be lawful, at any time within two years after such bill shall have been so received by such Secretary of State for his Majesty, his heirs or successors, by his or their Order-in-Council to declare his or their disallowance of such bill, and that such disallowance, together with a certificate under the hand and seal of such Secretary of State testifying the day on which such bill was received as aforesaid, being signified by such Governor, Lieutenant-Governor, or person administering the Government, to the Legislative Council and Assembly of such Province, or by proclamation, shall make void and annul the same, from and after the date of such signification.

Governor to transmit to the Secretary of State copies of such bills as have been assented to, which his Majesty in Council may declare his disallowance of within two years from the receipt.

XXXII. And be it further enacted by the authority aforesaid, that no such bill which shall be so reserved for the signification of his Majesty's pleasure thereon, shall have any force or authority within either of the said Provinces respectively until the Governor, or Lieutenant-Governor, or person administering the Government shall signify, either by speech or message, to the Legislative Council and Assembly of such Province, or by proclamation, that such bill has been laid before his Majesty in Council, and that his Majesty has been pleased to assent to the same; and that an entry shall be made in the journals of the said Legislative Council of every such speech, message, or proclamation; and a duplicate thereof duly attested shall be delivered to the proper officer to be kept amongst the public records of the Province; and that no such bill, which shall be so reserved as aforesaid shall have any force or authority within either of the said Provinces respectively unless his Majesty's assent thereto shall have been so signified as

Bills reserved for his Majesty's pleasure not to have any force till his Majesty's assent be communicated to the Council and Assembly.

aforesaid, within the space of two years from the day on which such bill shall have been presented for his Majesty's assent, to the Governor, Lieutenant-Governor, or person administering the Government of such Province.

Laws in force at the commencement of this Act to continue so, except repealed or varied by it, etc.

XXXIII. And be it further enacted by the authority aforesaid, that all laws, statutes, and ordinances which shall be in force on the day to be fixed in the manner herein after directed for the commencement of this Act, within the said Provinces, or either of them, or in any part thereof respectively, shall remain and continue to be of the same force, authority, and effect in each of the said Provinces respectively as if this Act had not been made, and as if the said Province of Quebec had not been divided; except in so far as the same are expressly repealed or varied by this Act, or in so far as the same shall or may hereafter by virtue of and under the authority of this Act be repealed or varied by his Majesty, his heirs, or successors by and with the consent of the Legislative Councils and Assemblies of the said Provinces respectively, or in so far as the same may be repealed or varied by such temporary laws or ordinances as may be made in the manner hereinafter specified.

Establishment of court of civil jurisdiction in each Province.

XXXIV. And whereas by an ordinance passed in the Province of Quebec the Governor and Council of the said Province were constituted a Court of civil jurisdiction for hearing and determining appeals in certain cases therein specified, be it further enacted by the authority aforesaid, that the Governor, or Lieutenant-Governor, or person administering the Government of each of the said Provinces respectively, together with such Executive Council as shall be appointed by his Majesty for the affairs of such Province, shall be a Court of civil jurisdiction, within each of the said Provinces respectively, for hearing and determining appeals within the same, in the like cases, and in the like manner and form, and subject to such appeal therefrom as such appeals might, before the passing of this Act, have been heard and determined by the Governor and Council of the Province of Quebec; but subject nevertheless to such further or other provisions[11] as may be made in this behalf by any Act of the Legislative Council and Assembly of either of the said Provinces respectively, assented to by his Majesty, his heirs, or successors.

14 George III, cap. 83, and

XXXV. And whereas by the above mentioned Act passed in the fourteenth year of the reign of his present Majesty it was declared that the clergy of the Church of Rome in the Province of Quebec might hold, receive, and enjoy their accustomed dues and rights, with respect to such persons only as should profess the said religion; provided nevertheless that it should be lawful for his Majesty, his heirs or successors, to make such provision out of the rest of the said accustomed dues and rights for the encouragement of the Protestant religion and for the maintenance and support of a Protestant clergy within the said Province as he or they should from time to time think necessary and expedient: And whereas by his Majesty's Royal instruction, given under his Majesty's Royal sign manual on the third of January in the year of our Lord one thousand seven hundred and seventy-five to Guy Carleton, Esquire, now Lord Dorchester, at that time his Majesty's Captain-General and Governor in Chief in and over his Majesty's Province of Quebec, his Majesty was pleased amongst other things to direct that no incumbent professing the religion of the Church of Rome, appointed to any parish in the said Province, should be entitled to receive any tythes for lands or possessions occupied by a Protestant, but that such tythes should be received by such persons as the said Guy Carleton, Esquire, his Majesty's Captain-General and Governor in Chief in and over his Majesty's said Province of Quebec, should appoint, and should be reserved in the hands of his Majesty's Receiver-General of the said Province for the support of a Protestant clergy in his Majesty's said Province to be actually resident within the same, and not otherwise, according to such directions as the said Guy Carleton, Esquire, his Majesty's Captain-General and Governor in Chief in and over his Majesty's said Province, should receive from his Majesty in that behalf; and that in like manner all growing rents and profits of a vacant benefice should during such vacancy be reserved for and applied to the like uses; and whereas his Majesty's pleasure has likewise been signified to the same effect in his Majesty's Royal instructions given in like manner to Sir Frederick Haldimand, Knight of the most honorable Order of the Bath, late his Majesty's Captain-General and Governor in Chief in and over his Majesty's said Province of Quebec; and also in his Majesty's Royal instructions given in like manner to the said Right Honorable Guy Lord Dorchester, now his Majesty's Captain-General and Governor in Chief in and over his Majesty's said Province of Quebec; be it enacted by the authority aforesaid that the said declaration

instructions of January 3rd, 1775, to Guy Carleton, Esq. etc., and

Sir Frederick Haldimand,

and to Lord Dorchester recited,

and the declaration and provisions therein

respecting the clergy of the Church of Rome to continue in force.

and provision contained in the said above mentioned Act, and also the said provision so made by his Majesty in consequence thereof by his instructions above recited, shall remain and continue to be of full force and effect in each of the said two Provinces of Upper Canada and Lower Canada respectively, except in so far as the said declaration or provisions respectively, or any part thereof, shall be expressly varied or repealed by any Act[12] or Acts which may be passed by the Legislative Council and Assembly of the said Provinces respectively, and assented to by his Majesty, his heirs or successors, under the restriction hereinafter provided.

His Majesty's message to Parliament recited.

His Majesty may authorize the Governor to make allotments of land for the support of a Protestant clergy in each Province;

XXXVI. And whereas his Majesty has been graciously pleased, by message to both Houses of Parliament, to express his Royal desire to be enabled to make a permanent appropriation of land in the said Provinces for the support and maintenance of a Protestant clergy within the same, in proportion to such lands as have been already granted within the same by his Majesty: And whereas his Majesty has been graciously pleased by his said message further to signify his Royal desire that such provision may be made with respect to all future grants of land within the said Provinces respectively as may best conduce to the due and sufficient support and maintenance of the Protestant clergy within the said Provinces, in proportion to such increase as may happen in the population and cultivation thereof; therefore, for the purpose of more effectually fulfilling his Majesty's gracious intentions as aforesaid, and of providing for the due execution of the same in all time to come, be it enacted by the authority aforesaid that it shall and may be lawful for his Majesty, his heirs or successors, to authorize the Governor, or Lieutenant-Governor of each of the said Provinces respectively, or the person administering the Government therein, to make from and out of the lands of the Crown within such Provinces such allotment and appropriation of lands for the support and maintenance of a Protestant clergy within the same as may bear a due proportion to the amount of such lands within the same as have at any time been granted by or under the authority of his Majesty: And that, whenever any grant of lands within either of the said Provinces shall hereafter be made by or under the authority of his Majesty, his heirs or successors, there shall at the same time be made, in respect of the same, a proportionable allotment and appropriation of lands for the

above mentioned purpose, within the township or parish to
which such lands so to be granted shall appertain or be
annexed, or as nearly adjacent thereto as circumstances will
admit; and that no such grant shall be valid or effectual
unless the same shall contain a specification of the lands so
allotted and appropriated, in respect of the lands to be
thereby granted; and that such lands so allotted and appropriated shall be, as nearly as the circumstances and nature
of the case will admit, of the like quality as the lands in
respect of which the same are so allotted and appropriated,
and shall be, as nearly as the same can be estimated at the
time of making such grant, equal in value to the seventh
part of the lands so granted.

XXXVII. And be it further enacted by the authority aforesaid that all and every the rents, profits, or emoluments, which may at any time arise from such lands so allotted and appropriated as aforesaid, shall be applicable solely to the maintenance and support of a Protestant clergy within the Province in which the same shall be situated, and to no other purpose whatever.[13] *and the rents arising from such allotment to be applicable to that purpose solely.*

XXXVIII. And be it further enacted by the authority aforesaid that it shall and may be lawful for his Majesty, his heirs and successors, to authorize the Governor or Lieutenant-Governor of each of the said Provinces respectively, or the person administering the Government therein, from time to time, with the advice of such Executive Council as shall have been appointed by his Majesty, his heirs or successors, within such Province for the affairs thereof, to constitute and erect within every township or parish which is now or hereafter may be formed, constituted, or erected within such Province, one or more parsonage or rectory, or parsonages or rectories, according to the establishment of the Church of England; and from time to time by instrument under the great Seal of such Province to endow every such parsonage or rectory with so much or such a part of the lands so allotted and appropriated as aforesaid, in respect of any lands with such township or parish which shall have been granted subsequent to the commencement of this Act or of such lands as may have been allotted and appropriated for the same purpose, by or in virtue of any instruction which may be given by his Majesty in respect of any lands granted by his Majesty before the commencement of this Act, as such Governor, Lieutenant-Governor, or *His Majesty may authorize the Governor, with the advice of the Executive Council, to erect parsonages and endow them,* person administering the Government shall, with the advice of the said Executive Council, judge to be expedient under the then existing circumstances of such township or parish.

and the Governor to present incumbents to them, who are to enjoy the same as incumbents in England.

XXXIX. And be it further enacted by the authority aforesaid, that it shall and may be lawful for his Majesty, his heirs or successors, to authorize the Governor, Lieutenant-Governor, or person administering the Government of each of the said Provinces respectively, to present to every such parsonage or rectory an incumbent or minister of the Church of England, who shall have been duly ordained according to the rites of the said Church, and to supply from time to time such vacancies as may happen therein; and that every person so presented to any such parsonage or rectory shall hold and enjoy the same, and all rights, profits, and emoluments thereunto belonging or granted, as fully and amply, and in the same manner, and on the same terms and conditions, and liable to the performance of the same duties, as the incumbent of a parsonage or rectory in England.

Presentations to parsonages and the enjoyment of them to be subject to the jurisdiction granted to the Bishop of Nova Scotia, etc.

XL. Provided always, and be it further enacted by the authority aforesaid, that every such presentation of an incumbent or minister to any such parsonage or rectory, and also the enjoyment of any such parsonage or rectory, and of the rights, profits, and emoluments thereof, by any such incumbent or minister, shall be subject and liable to all rights of institution, and all other spiritual and ecclesiastical jurisdiction and authority, which have been lawfully granted by his Majesty's Royal letters patent to the Bishop of Nova Scotia, or which may hereafter by his Majesty's Royal authority be lawfully granted or appointed to be administered and executed within the said Provinces, or either of them respectively, by the said Bishop of Nova Scotia, or by any other person or persons, according to the laws and canons of the Church of England which are lawfully made and received in England.[14]

Provisions respecting the allotment of lands for the support of a Protestant clergy, etc., may be varied or repealed by the Legislative Council and Assembly.

XLI. Provided always, and be it further enacted by the authority aforesaid, that the several provisions hereinbefore contained, respecting the allotment and appropriation of lands for the support of a Protestant clergy within the said Provinces, and also respecting the constituting, erecting, and endowing parsonages or rectories within the said Provinces, and also respecting the presentation of incumbents or ministers to the same, and also respecting the manner in which such incumbents or ministers shall hold and enjoy the same shall be subject to be varied or repealed be any express provisions for that purpose contained in any Act or Acts which may be passed by the Legislative Council and Assembly of the said Provinces respectively, and assented to by his Majesty, his heirs or successors, under the restriction herein after provided.¹⁵

XLII. Provided nevertheless, and be it further enacted by the authority aforesaid, that whenever any Act or Acts shall be passed by the Legislative Council and Assembly of either of the said Provinces, containing any provisions to vary or repeal the above recited declaration and provision contained in the said Act passed in the fourteenth year of the reign of his present Majesty; or to vary or repeal the above recited provision contained in his Majesty's Royal instructions given on the third day of January in the year of our Lord one thousand seven hundred and seventy-five to the said Guy Carleton, Esquire, now Lord Dorchester; or to vary or repeal the provisions herein before contained for continuing the force and effect of the said declaration and provisions; or to vary or repeal any of the several provisions herein before contained respecting the allotment and appropriation of lands for the support of a Protestant clergy within the said Provinces ; or respecting the constituting, erecting, or endowing parsonages or rectories within the said Provinces; or respecting the presentations of incumbents or ministers to the same ; or respecting the manner in which such incumbents or ministers shall hold and enjoy the same : And also that whenever any Act or Acts shall be so passed, containing any provisions which shall in any manner relate to or affect the enjoyment or exercise of any religious form or mode of worship; or shall impose or create any penalties, burthens, disabilities, or disqualifications in respect of the same; or shall in any manner relate to or affect the payment, recovery, or enjoyment of any of the accustomed dues or rights herein before mentioned ; or shall in any manner relate to the granting, imposing, or recovering any other dues or stipends, or emoluments whatever, to be paid to or for the use of any minister, priest, ecclesiastic, or teacher according to any religious form or mode of worship, in respect of of his said office or function; or shall in any manner relate to or affect the establishment or discipline of the Church of England amongst the ministers and members

Acts of the Legislative Council and Assembly containing provisions to the effect herein mentioned to be laid before Parliament previous to receiving his Majesty's assent, etc.

thereof within the said Provinces; or shall in any manner relate to or affect the King's prerogative touching the granting of waste lands of the Crown within the said Provinces; every such Act or Acts shall, previous to any declaration or signification of the King's assent thereto, be laid before both Houses of Parliament in Great Britain; and that it shall not be lawful for his Majesty, his heirs or successors, to signify his or their assent to any such Act or Acts, until thirty days after the same shall have been laid before the said houses, or to assent to any such Act or Acts in case either House of Parliament shall within the said thirty days address his Majesty, his heirs or successors, to withhold his or their assent from such Act or Acts; and that no such Act shall be valid or effectual to any of the said purposes within either of the said Provinces unless the Legislative Council and Assembly of such Province shall, in the session in which the same shall have been passed by them, have presented to the Governor, Lieutenant-Governor, or person administering the Government of such Province, an address or addresses specifying that such Act contains provisions for some of the said purposes herein before specially described, and desiring that, in order to give effect to the same, such Act should be transmitted to England without delay for the purpose of being laid before Parliament previous to the signification of his Majesty's assent thereto.

<small>Lands in Upper Canada to be granted in free and common soccage, and also in Lower Canada, if desired.</small> XLIII. And be it further enacted by the authority aforesaid, that all lands which shall be hereafter granted within the said Province of Upper Canada shall be granted in free and common soccage, in like manner as lands are now holden in free and common soccage in that part of Great Britain called England; and that in every case where lands shall be hereafter granted within the said Province of Lower Canada, and where the grantee thereof shall desire the same to be granted in free and common soccage, the same shall be so granted; but subject nevertheless to such alterations with respect to the nature and consequences of such tenure of free and common soccage, as may be established by any law or laws which may be made by his Majesty, his heirs or successors, by and with the advice and consent of the Legislative Council and Assembly of the Province.[16]

<small>Persons holding lands in Upper Canada may have fresh grants.</small> XLIV. And be it further enacted by the authority aforesaid, that if any person or persons holding lands in the said Province of Upper Canada[17] by virtue of any certificate of

occupation derived under the authority of the Governor and Council of the Province of Quebec, and having power and authority to alienate the same, shall at any time from and after the commencement of this Act surrender the same into the hands of his Majesty, his heirs or successors, by petition to the Governor, or Lieutenant-Governor, or person administering the Government of the said Province, setting forth that he, she, or they, is or are desirous of holding the same in free and common soccage, such Governor, or Lieutenant-Governor, or person administering the Government shall thereupon cause a fresh grant to be made to such person of such lands to be holden in free and common soccage.

XLV. Provided nevertheless, and be it further enacted by the authority aforesaid, that such surrender and grant shall not avoid or bar any right or title to any such lands so surrendered, or any interest in the same, to which any person or persons other than the person or persons surrendering the same shall have been entitled either in possession, remainder, or reversion, or otherwise, at the time of such surrender; but that every such surrender and grant shall be made subject to such right, title, and interest, and that every such right, title, or interest shall be as valid and effectual as if such surrender and grant had never been made. *Such fresh grants not to bar any right or title to the lands.*

XLVI. And whereas by an Act[s] passed in the eighteenth year of the reign of his present Majesty, intituled "An Act for removing all doubts and apprehensions concerning taxation by the Parliament of Great Britain in any of the Colonies, Provinces, and Plantations in North America and the West Indies; and for repealing so much of an Act made in the seventh year of his present Majesty as imposes a duty on tea imported from Great Britain into any Colony or Plantation in America, or relates thereto," it has been declared that the King and Parliament of Great Britain will not impose any duty, tax, or assessment whatever, payable in any of his Majesty's Colonies, Provinces, and Plantations in North America, or the West Indies, except only such duties as it may be expedient to impose for the regulation of commerce, the net produce of such duties to be always paid and applied to and for the use of the Colony, Province, or Plantation, in which the same shall be respectively levied, in such manner as other duties collected by the authority of the respective General Courts or General Assemblies of such Colonies, Provinces, or Plantations are ordinarily paid and *16 Geo. III., cap. 22, recited.*

applied": And whereas it is necessary for the general benefit of the British Empire, that such power of regulation of commerce should continue to be exercised by his Majesty, his heirs or successors, and the Parliament of Great Britain, subject nevertheless to the conditions herein before recited with respect to the application of any duties which may be imposed for that purpose: Be it therefore enacted by the authority aforesaid, that nothing in this Act contained shall extend, or be construed to extend, to prevent or affect the execution of any law which hath been or shall at any time be made by his Majesty, his heirs or successors, and the Parliament of Great Britain, for establishing regulations or prohibitions, or for imposing, levying, or collecting duties for the regulation of navigation, or for the regulation of the commerce to be carried on between the said two Provinces,[19] or between either of the said Provinces and any other part of his Majesty's dominions, or between either of the said Provinces and any foreign country or state, or for appointing and directing the payment of drawbacks of such duties so imposed, or to give to his Majesty, his heirs or successors, any power or authority, by and with the advice and consent of such Legislative Councils and Assemblies respectively, to vary or repeal any such law or laws, or any part thereof, or in any manner to prevent or obstruct the execution thereof.

This Act not to prevent the operation of any Act of Parliament establishing prohibitions or imposing duties for the regulation of navigation and commerce, etc.

XLVII. Provided always, and be it enacted by the authority aforesaid, that the net produce of all duties which shall be so imposed shall at all times hereafter be applied to and for the use of each of the said Provinces respectively, and in such manner only as shall be directed by any law or laws which shall be made by his Majesty, his heirs or successors, by and with the advice and consent of the Legislative Council and Assembly of such Province.

Such duties to be applied to the use of the respective Provinces.

XLVIII. And whereas, by reason of the distance of the said Provinces from this country, and of the change to be made by this Act in the Government thereof, it may be necessary that there should be some interval of time between the notification of this Act to the said Provinces respectively, and the day of its commencement within the said Provinces respectively; be it therefore enacted by the authority aforesaid, that it shall and may be lawful for his Majesty, with the advice of the Privy Council, to fix and declare, or to authorize the Governor or Lieutenant-Governor of the Pro-

His Majesty in Council to fix and declare the commencement of the Act, etc.

vince of Quebec, or the person administering the Government there to fix and declare the day of the commencement of this Act within the said Provinces respectively, provided that such day shall not be later than the thirty-first day of December, in the year of our Lord one thousand seven hundred and ninety-one.²⁰

XLIX. And be it further enacted by the authority aforesaid, that the time to be fixed by his Majesty, his heirs or successors, or under his or their authority by the Governor, Lieutenant-Governor, or person administering the Government in each of the said Provinces respectively, for issuing the writs of summons and election, and calling together the Legislative Councils and Assemblies of each of the said Provinces respectively, shall not be later than the thirty-first day of December, in the year of our Lord one thousand seven hundred and ninety-two.²¹ *Time for issuing the writs of summons and election, etc., not to be later than 31st December, 1792.*

L. Provided always, and be it further enacted by the authority aforesaid, that during such interval as may happen between the commencement of this Act within the said Provinces respectively, and the first meeting of the Legislative Council and Assembly of each of the said Provinces respectively, it shall and may be lawful for the Governor or Lieutenant-Governor of such Province, or for the person administering the Government therein, with the consent of the major part of such Executive Council as shall be appointed by his Majesty for the affairs of such Province, to make temporary laws and ordinances for the good government, peace, and welfare of such Province, in the same manner and under the same restrictions as such laws or ordinances might have been made by the Council for the affairs of the Province of Quebec constituted by virtue of the above mentioned Act of the fourteenth year of the reign of his present Majesty; and that such temporary laws shall be valid and binding within such Province until the expiration of six months after the Legislative Council and Assembly of such Province shall have been first assembled by virtue of and under the authority of this Act; subject nevertheless to be sooner repealed or varied by any law or laws which may be made by his Majesty, his heirs or successors, by and with the advice and consent of the said Legislative Council and Assembly. *Between the commencement of this Act and the first meeting of the Legislative Council and Assembly, temporary laws may be made.*

The Constitutional Act Amendment Act, 1830.

An Act[22] to amend so much of an Act of the thirty-first year of his late Majesty, for making more effectual provision for the Government of the Province of Quebec.

[16TH JULY, 1830.]

31 Geo. III., cap. 31.

Whereas by an Act passed in the thirty-first year of the reign of his late Majesty, King George the Third, intituled, "An Act to repeal certain parts of an Act passed in the fourteenth year of his Majesty's reign, intituled, 'An Act for making more effectual provision for the Government of Quebec in North America,' and to make further provision for the Government of the said Province," it is amongst other things enacted[23] that no person shall be summoned to the Legislative Council in either of the Provinces of Upper Canada and Lower Canada who shall not be of the full age of twenty-one years, and a natural-born subject of his Majesty, or a subject of his Majesty naturalized by Act of the British Parliament, or a subject of his Majesty having become such by the conquest and cession of the Province of Canada; and it is thereby further provided that no person shall be capable of voting at any election of a member to serve in the Legislative Assembly in either of the said Provinces of Upper Canada or Lower Canada, or of being elected at any such election, who shall not be of the full age of twenty-one years, and a natural-born subject of his Majesty, or a subject of his Majesty's naturalized by an Act of the British Parliament, or a subject of his Majesty, having become such by the conquest and cession of the Province of Canada: And whereas it is expedient[24] that persons naturalized by any Act of the Legislative Council and Assembly of the Province of Lower Canada assembled by his Majesty, his heirs, or successors should be enabled to be summoned to the Legislative Council of the said Province of Lower Canada, and of voting at the elections to serve in the Legislative Assembly of the said Province, or of being elected at any such election; Be it therefore enacted by the King's Most Excellent Majesty, by and with the advice and consent of the Lords Spiritual and Temporal, and Commons, in this present Parliament assembled, and by the authority of the same, that all persons naturalized by any Act of the Legislative Council and Assembly of the Province of Lower Canada, assented to by his Majesty, his heirs or successors, shall henceforth be and be deemed competent in the law to be summoned to the Legislative Council of the said Province of Lower Canada, and to vote at the elections of members to serve in the Legislative Assembly of the said Province, and to be elected at any such election.

Persons naturalized may sit in Assembly of Lower Canada, and in Legislative Council.

II. Provided nevertheless, and be it further enacted, that whenever any bill which has been passed by the Legislative Council and by the House of Assembly in the said Province of Lower Canada, for the naturalization of any persons or person, shall be presented for his Majesty's assent to the Governor or Lieutenant-Governor of the said Province, or to the person administering his Majesty's Government therein, such Governor or Lieutenant-Governor, or person administering the Government, shall and he is hereby required to reserve every such bill for the signification of his Majesty's pleasure thereon; and no such bill shall have any force or authority within the said Province of Lower Canada until the Governor or Lieutenant-Governor, or person administering the Government, shall signify, either by speech or message to the Legislative Council and Assembly of the said Province, or by proclamation, that such bill has been laid before his Majesty in Council, and that his Majesty has been pleased to assent to the same; and no such bill shall have any force or authority within the said Province unless his Majesty's assent thereto shall have been so signified as aforesaid within the space of two years from the day on which such bill shall have been presented for his Majesty's assent to the Governor, Lieutenant-Governor, or person administering the Government.

Act of naturalization not to have force or authority unless his Majesty's assent be signified to the same.

The Constitutional Act Suspension Act, 1838.

An Act[25] to make temporary provision for the Government of Lower Canada.

10TH FEBRUARY, 1838.

31 Geo. III., cap. 31.

Whereas in the present state of the Province of Lower Canada the House of Assembly of the said Province, constituted under the Act passed in the thirty-first year of his Majesty, King George the Third, intituled "An Act to repeal certain parts of an Act passed in the fourteenth year of his Majesty's reign, intituled 'An Act for making more effectual provision for the Government of the Province of Quebec in North America,' and to make further provision for the Government of the said Province" cannot be called together without serious detriment to the interests of the said Province,[26] by reason whereof the Government of the said Province cannot be duly administered according to the provisions of the said Act: And whereas it is expedient to make temporary provision for the Government of Lower Canada, in order that Parliament may be enabled, after mature deliberation, to make permanent arrangements[27] for the Constitution and Government of the said Province, upon such a basis as may best secure the rights and liberties and promote the interests of all classes of her Majesty's subjects in the said Province: Be it therefore enacted by the Queen's Most Excellent Majesty, by and with the consent of the Lords Spiritual and Temporal, and Commons, in this present Parliament assembled, and by the authority of the same, that from the proclamation of this Act in the said Province as hereinafter provided, until the first day of November in the year one thousand eight hundred and forty, so much of the said Act of the thirty-first year of King George the Third, and of any other Act or Acts of Parliament, as constitutes or provides for the constitution or calling of a Legislative Council or Legislative Assembly for the Province of Lower Canada, as confers any powers or functions upon the said Legislative Council and Legislative

The powers of the present Legislature of Lower Canada suspended.

Assembly, or either of those bodies, shall cease and be of no force.

II. And be it enacted that it shall be lawful for her Majesty, by any commission or commissions to be from time to time issued under the Great Seal of the United Kingdom, or by any instructions under her Majesty's signet or sign manual, and with the advice of her Privy Council, to constitute a special Council[28] for the affairs of Lower Canada, and for that purpose to appoint or authorize the Governor of the Province of Lower Canada to appoint such and so many Special Councillors as to her Majesty shall seem meet, and to make such provision as to her Majesty shall seem meet for the removal, suspension, or resignation of all or any such Councillors: Provided always that no member of the said special Council shall be permitted to sit or vote therein until he shall have taken and subscribed before the Governor of the Province of Lower Canada, or before some person authorized by the said Governor to administer such Oath, the same Oath which is now required to be taken by the members of the Legislative Council and Assembly before sitting or voting therein respectively. *Her Majesty may appoint a Special Council for the affairs of Lower Canada. Members of the Council to take an Oath.*

III. And be it enacted that from and after such proclamation as aforesaid, and until the first day of November in the year one thousand eight hundred and forty, it shall be lawful for the Governor of the Province of Lower Canada, with the advice and consent of the majority of the said Councillors present at a meeting or meetings to be for that purpose from time to time convened by the Governor of the said Province, to make such laws or ordinances for the peace, welfare, and good Government of the said Province of Lower Canada as the Legislature of Lower Canada, as now constituted, is empowered to make; and that all laws or ordinances so made, subject to the provisions hereinafter contained for disallowance thereof by her Majesty, shall have the like force and effect as laws passed before the passing of this Act by the Legislative Council and Assembly of the said Province of Lower Canada, and assented to by her Majesty, or in her Majesty's name by the Governor of the said Province: Provided always that no such law or ordinance shall be made unless the same shall have been first proposed by the said Governor for adoption by the Council, nor unless the said Governor and five at least of the said Councillors shall be actually present when such law or ordinance *The Governor and Council may make Laws or Ordinances for the Government of Lower Canada. Such laws to be proposed by the Governor.*

138 THE CONSTITUTIONAL ACT

Limiting their duration.

Proviso as to imposing taxes.

Laws or Ordinances not to affect the existing laws respecting Rights of Election, etc.

shall be made: Provided also, that no law or ordinance so made shall continue in force beyond the first day of November in the year one thousand eight hundred and forty-two, unless continued by competent authority: Provided also, that it shall not be lawful by any such law or ordinance to impose any tax, duty, rate, or impost, save only in so far as any tax, duty, rate, or impost which at the passing of this Act is payable within the said Province may be thereby continued: Provided also, that it shall not be lawful, by any such law or ordinance, to alter in any respect the law now existing in the said Province respecting the constitution or composition of the Legislative Assembly thereof, or respecting the right of any person to vote at the election of any member of the said Assembly, or respecting the qualifications of such voters, or respecting the division of the said Province into counties, cities, and towns for the purpose of such elections; nor shall it be lawful by any such law or ordinance to repeal, suspend, or alter any provision of any Act of the Parliament of Great Britain or of the Parliament of the United Kingdom, or of any Act of the Legislature of Lower Canada as now constituted, repealing or altering any such Act of Parliament.

No law, etc., to appropriate the monies in hand for repayment of the sum of £142,160 unless on certificate of Commissioners of Treasury; nor to an amount exceeding the appropriation of 1832.

IV. Provided always, and be it enacted, that it shall not be lawful by any such law or ordinance to appropriate any monies which now are or which shall hereafter be in the hands of the Receiver-General of the said Province of Lower Canada towards the repayment of any sum or sums of money which shall have been issued out of the sum of one hundred and forty-two thousand one hundred and sixty pounds, fourteen shillings, and sixpence, granted to her Majesty by an Act passed in the last session of Parliament for advances on account of charges for the administration of justice and of the Civil Government of the Province of Lower Canada, unless upon a certificate from three or more of the Commissioners of her Majesty's Treasury, setting forth the several sums which shall have been so advanced for any of the purposes aforesaid: Provided also, that, exclusive of any such repayment as aforesaid, no appropriation to be made by any such law or ordinance of the monies aforesaid in respect of the public service for any one year shall exceed the total amount of the sums appropriated by law within the said Province for the public service thereof for the year one thousand eight hundred and thirty-two.

V. And be it enacted that the Governor of the said Province is hereby required, by the first convenient opportunity, to transmit to one of her Majesty's Principal Secretaries of State an authentic copy of every law or ordinance made under the authority of this Act; and that it shall be lawful, at any time within two years after such law or ordinance shall have been so received by such Secretary of State, for her Majesty, her heirs or successors, by her or their Order in Council, to declare her or their disallowance of such law or ordinance; and that such disallowance, together with a certificate under the hand and Seal of such Secretary of State, testifying the day on which such law or ordinance was received as aforesaid, being signified by such Governor by proclamation within the said Province, shall make void and annul the same from and after the date of such signification. *Laws or Ordinances may be disallowed by her Majesty in Council.*

VI. And be it enacted that nothing herein contained shall be taken to affect or invalidate any law, statute or ordinance now in force within the said Province of Lower Canada, or in any part thereof, except in so far as the same is repugnant to this Act. *This Act not to affect laws, etc., now in force, etc.*

VII. And be it enacted that this Act shall be proclaimed by the Governor of the said Province of Lower Canada within the said Province, and shall commence and take effect within the said Province from the proclamation thereof. *Proclamation of this Act.*

VIII. And be it enacted, that for the purposes of this Act any person authorized to execute the commission of Governor of the Province of Lower Canada shall be taken to be the Governor thereof. *The term "Governor" defined.*

IX. And be it enacted that this Act may be altered or repealed by any Act to be passed in the present session of Parliament. *Act may be altered, etc.*

The Indemnity Act, 1838.

An Act[20] for indemnifying those who have issued or acted under certain parts of a certain Ordinance made under colour of an Act passed in the present session of Parliament, intituled "An Act to make temporary Provision for the Government of Lower Canada."

16TH AUGUST, 1838.

1 Vict., cap. 9

Whereas an Act was made this present session of Parliament, intituled "An Act to make temporary provision for the Government of Lower Canada": And whereas a certain Law or Ordinance hath been made and published by the Governor of the said Province, by and with the advice and consent of the Special Council, bearing date the twenty-eighth day of June last, intituled "An Ordinance[30] to provide for the security of the Province of Lower Canada," which Ordinance cannot be justified by law, but was so much intended for the Security of the said Province that it is expedient that all persons advising or acting under or in obedience to so much of the same as relates to the sending of certain persons to Bermuda, who are stated in the same to have made certain confessions, and to the subjecting such persons to restraint, should be indemnified by Parliament in the manner and to the extent herein-after provided for: Be it enacted by the Queen's Most Excellent Majesty, by and with the advice and consent of the Lords Spiritual and Temporal and Commons, in this present Parliament assembled, and by the authority of the same, that all personal actions and suits, indictments, informations, and all prosecutions and proceedings whatsoever, which have been or shall be prosecuted or commenced in any Court or before any tribunal in any part of her Majesty's Dominions, against any person or persons for or by reason of any act, matter, or thing advised, commanded, appointed, or done in relation to the premises before the pro-

Indemnity for persons advising or acting under an Ordinance of the Governor and Council of Lower Canada, of the 28th of June last

clamation of this Act in the said Province of Lower Canada and in the Islands of Bermuda respectively, or elsewhere, in manner hereinafter provided, be, are, and shall be discharged and made void by virtue of this Act; and that if any action or suit shall be prosecuted or commenced against any person or persons for any such act, matter or thing so advised, commanded, appointed, or done, he, she, or they may plead the general issue, and give this Act and the special matter in evidence; and if the plaintiff or plaintiffs in any action or suit so to be prosecuted or commenced, except in that part of Great Britain called Scotland, after the first day of October next, shall become nonsuit, or forbear further prosecution, or suffer discontinuance, or if a verdict pass against such plaintiff or plaintiffs, the defendant or defendants shall recover his, her, or their double costs, for which he, she, or they shall have the like remedy as in cases where costs by law are given to defendants; and if any such action or suit as aforesaid shall be commenced or prosecuted after the first day of October next in that part of Great Britain called Scotland, the Court before whom such action or suit shall be commenced or prosecuted shall allow to the defender the benefit of the discharge and indemnity hereby provided, and shall further allow to him his double costs of suit in all such cases as aforesaid.

II. And be it enacted that this Act shall be proclaimed in the said Province of Lower Canada and in the said Islands of Bermuda by the Governor, or by the person authorized to execute the Commission of Governor of the said Province and of the said Islands respectively, forthwith after he shall have received a copy of the same from one of her Majesty's Principal Secretaries of State.[3,1]

This Act to be proclaimed in Lower Canada and Bermuda respectively.

The Suspension Act Amendment Act, 1839.

An Act[32] to amend an Act of the last session of Parliament for making temporary Provision for the Government of Lower Canada.

(17TH AUGUST, 1839.)

31 Geo. III., cap. 31.

Whereas an Act was passed in the thirty-first year of the reign of his Majesty, King George the Third, intituled " An Act to repeal certain parts of an Act passed in the fourteenth year of his Majesty's reign, intituled 'An Act for making more effectual provision for the Government of the Province of Quebec in North America,' and to make further provision for the Government of the said Province," whereby among other things it was enacted that there should be within each of the Provinces of Upper Canada and Lower Canada respectively a Legislative Council and an Assembly, to be constituted in manner therein described, and with such powers and authorities as therein mentioned : And whereas an Act was passed in the last session of Parliament, intituled "An Act to make temporary Provision for the Government of Lower Canada," whereby it was enacted that from the proclamation of the Act until the first day of November one thousand eight hundred and forty so much of the said Act of the thirty-first year of the reign of his Majesty, King George the Third, and of any other Act or Acts of Parliament, as provides for the Constitution or calling of a Legislative Council or Assembly for the Province of Lower Canada, or confers any powers or functions upon them or either of them, should cease ; and by the said Act now in recital provision is made in the meantime for the appointment by his Majesty of a Special Council for the affairs of Lower Canada, and for the making of laws or ordinances for the Government of the said Province by the Governor thereof, with the advice and consent of the majority of the Councillors present at any meeting of the Council : And whereas it is expedient that some of the provisions contained in the said lastly-recited Act should be altered : Be it therefore enacted by the

Queen's most Excellent Majesty, by and with the advice and consent of the Lords Spiritual and Temporal, and Commons, in this present Parliament assembled, and by the authority of the same, that the number of Councillors forming the Special Council in manner provided by the said Act passed in the last session of Parliament shall not be less than twenty, and that no business shall be transacted at any meeting of the said Special Council at which there are not present at least eleven Councillors." *The Special Council to consist of not less than twenty members, and no business to be transacted unless eleven be present.*

II. And be it enacted that from and immediately after the passing of this Act so much of the said recited Act passed in the last Session of Parliament as provides that no law or ordinance made by the Governor of the said Province of Lower Canada, with such advice and consent as therein mentioned, shall continue in force beyond the first day of November, one thousand eight hundred and forty-two, unless continued by competent authority, shall be and the same is hereby repealed: Provided always that every law or ordinance which by the terms and provisions thereof shall be made to continue in force after the said first day of November, one thousand eight hundred and forty-two, shall be laid before both Houses of Parliament within thirty days after a copy thereof shall be received by one of her Majesty's Principal Secretaries of State, under the provisions of the said Act of the last Session of Parliament, if Parliament shall be then sitting, or otherwise within thirty days after the then next meeting of Parliament; and no such law or ordinance shall be confirmed or declared to be left to its operation by her Majesty until such law or ordinance shall first have been laid for thirty days before both Houses of Parliament, or in case either House of Parliament shall, within the said thirty days, address her Majesty to disallow any such law or ordinance. *Repeal of provision of 1 & 2 Vict., cap. 9, preventing the making of permanent laws; but all permanent laws to be laid for thirty days before Parliament previous to being confirmed.*

III. And be it enacted that from and immediately after the passing of this Act so much of the said recited Act passed in the last Session of Parliament as provides that it shall not be lawful, by any such law or ordinance as therein mentioned to impose any tax, duty, rate, or impost, save only in so far as any tax, duty, rate, or impost, which at the passing of that Act was payable within the said Province of Lower Canada, might be continued, shall be and the same is hereby repealed: Provided always that it shall not be lawful for the said Governor, with such advice and consent *Repeal of the provision of 1 & 2 Vict., cap. 9, prohibiting taxation; but no new tax to be levied except for public works and objects of municipal government; and such taxes not to be appropriated by Government.*

as aforesaid, to make any law or ordinance imposing, or authorizing the imposition of any new tax, duty, rate, or impost, except for carrying into effect local improvements within the said Province of Lower Canada, or any district or other local division thereof, or for the establishment or maintenance of police, or other objects of municipal government, within any city or town or district or other local division of the said Province: Provided also that in every law or ordinance imposing or authorizing the imposition of any such new tax, duty, rate or impost, provision shall be made for the levying, receipt, and appropriation thereof by such person or persons as shall be thereby appointed or designated for that purpose, but that no such new tax, rate, duty, or impost shall be levied by or made payable to the Receiver-General or any other public officer employed in the receipt of her Majesty's ordinary revenue in the said Province; nor shall any such law or ordinance as aforesaid provide for the appropriation of any such new tax, duty, rate, or impost by the said Governor, either with or without the advice of the Executive Council of the said Province, or by the Commissioners of her Majesty's treasury, or by any other officer of the Crown employed in the receipt of her Majesty's ordinary revenue.

Repeal of the provision of 1 & 2 Vict., cap. 9, prohibiting the alteration of Acts of Parliament; but no law to be made affecting the Temporal or Spiritual rights of Ecclesiastics, or the law of tenure.

IV. And be it enacted that from and after the passing of this Act so much of the said recited Act passed in the last session of Parliament as provides that it shall not be lawful for any such law or ordinance as therein mentioned to repeal, suspend, or alter any provision of any Act of the Parliament of Great Britain, or of the Parliament of the United Kingdom, or of any Act of the Legislature of Lower Canada, as then constituted, repealing or altering any such Act of Parliament, shall be and the same is hereby repealed: Provided always, that it shall not be lawful for the said Governor, with such advice and consent as aforesaid, to make any law or ordinance altering or affecting the Temporal or Spiritual rights of the Clergy of the United Church of England and Ireland, or of the Ministers of any other religious communion, or altering or affecting the tenure of land within the said Province of Lower Canada, or any part thereof, save so far as the tenure of land may be altered or affected by any law or ordinance which may be made by the said Governor, with such advice and consent as aforesaid, to provide for the extinction of any Seignorial rights and dues now vested in or claimed by the Ecclesiastics of the Seminary of Saint Sulpice at Montreal within the said Province, or to provide for the extinction of any Seignorial rights and dues vested in or claimed by any other person or persons or body or bodies corporate or politic, within the Island of Montreal, or the island called Isle Jesus, within the said Province.

V. And be it enacted that every law or ordinance to be made by the said Governor, with such advice and consent as aforesaid, shall, before the passing or enactment thereof, be published at length in the public Gazette of the said Province of Lower Canada. *Laws, etc., to be published in Gazette.*

VI. And be it enacted that for the purposes of this Act the person authorized to execute the Commission of Governor of the Province of Lower Canada shall be taken to be the Governor thereof.[34] *Definition of Governor.*

VII. And be it enacted that this Act may be amended or repealed by any Act to be passed during the present session of Parliament.[35] *Act may be amended, etc.*

NOTES TO THE CONSTITUTIONAL ACT AND SUPPLEMENTARY ACTS.

1 This statute is 31 George III., cap. 31. The text is reprinted from the Imperial "Statutes at Large," London, 1794. For a full report of the debates on the measure while it was in progress through the British Parliament see Clarendon's "Parliamentary Chronicle," Vol. III. One of the chief causes of the passage of this Act was the influx of British immigrants, known as "United Empire Loyalists," who settled at various points along the north shore of Lake Ontario, and in the Niagara peninsula.

2 This intention was not carried out till after the Act was passed. On the 24th of August, 1791, two "Orders" were passed by the King in Council, one making the division of Quebec into Upper and Lower Canada by a boundary defined in the "Order;" the other citing this "Order" and enjoining the issue of a warrant authorizing the Governor of Quebec to fix a day for the Act to go into operation. Both Orders in Council are given at length in the collection of papers entitled "Ontario Boundaries before Privy Council, 1881." Lieutenant-Governor Clarke, in the absence of Lord Dorchester, proclaimed the 26th of December, 1791, as the day when the division of the Province should take effect. The text of his proclamation is given in Vol. O. of the "Statutes of Lower Canada."

3 See Note 1 to "Representative Assemblies in the Maritime Provinces."

4 See 11 George IV. & 1 William IV., cap. 53, appended to this Act.

5 For arguments for and against this design to create a political aristocracy see the debates in Clarendon's "Parliamentary Chronicle," Vol. III. The proposal emanated from Pitt and was endorsed by Burke, but was opposed by Fox, who declared his preference for an elective Council.

6 The proclamation dividing Lower Canada into electoral districts was issued at Quebec by Lieutenant-Governor Clarke on the 7th of May, 1792; the text will be found in Vol. O. of the "Statutes of Lower Canada." The proclamation dividing Upper Canada was issued at Kingston by Lieutenant-Governor Simcoe on the 16th of July, 1792, and the text of it is given in full in Thomson and McFarlane's collection of "Statutes of Upper Canada, 1791-1831," (Kingston, 1831).

7 Lieutenant-Governor Clarke's proclamation announcing the issue of writs for the election of the first Lower Canadian Assembly was dated the 14th of May, 1792, and the writs were made returnable on the 10th of July following. The text of the proclamation is given in Vol. O. of the "Statutes of Lower Canada."

8 See Note 4 above.

The first Parliament of Lower Canada met at Quebec on the 17th of December, 1792. For an account of its organization and work see Christie's "History of the Late Province of Lower Canada," Vol. I., cap. IV. The first Parliament of Upper Canada met at Niagara, then Newark, on the 17th of September, 1792. An account of its work will be found in Read's "Life of Governor Simcoe."

10 Compare sections 50, 85, 86, and 88, of the British North America Act, 1867; sections 3 and 4 of chapter 11 of the Revised Statutes of Ontario, 1887; and article 110 of the Revised Statutes of Quebec, 1888.

11 The ordinance above referred to is 32 George III., cap. 1. It was passed as a temporary measure, and its operation was prolonged in Lower Canada by Act of the first Parliament, 33 George III., cap. 3. This was in turn repealed by 34 George III., cap. 6. In Upper Canada a Court of Appeal was established by 34 George III., cap. 2.

12 Tithes payable to the clergy of "the Protestant Church" were abolished by Act of the Upper Canadian Legislature (2 George IV., cap. 32).

13 The Imperial Statutes dealing further with the Clergy Reserves are the following: 6 George IV., cap. 59; 7 & 8 George IV., cap. 62; 3 & 4 Vict., cap. 78; and 16 & 17 Vict., cap. 21.

14 Under the authority of these clauses Sir John Colborne, when Lieutenant-Governor of Upper Canada, in 1836 issued letters patent creating fifty-seven rectories. The text of the instrument which created and endowed the "Parsonage or Rectory of St. James," in the township of York, is given in full in the bill filed in Chancery in the "Rectories Case," August 25th, 1852, by Attorney-General Richards. The prayer of the bill was that the letters patent should be declared void and that the lands constituting the endowment should be given up. The decision of the Court was that the Lieutenant-Governor had authority under these sections to create and endow rectories, and this decision has never since been reversed. See the volume known as "The Rectories Case, Upper Canada," containing the bill in Chancery and many other documents; Vols. V. and VI. of Grant's Chancery Reports, Upper Canada; "Religious Endowments in Canada," by Sir Francis Hincks (London, 1869); and "Reminiscences of His Public Life," by the same author.

15 The "clergy reserves" were secularized in 1854 by Act of the Canadian Parliament, 18 Vict., cap. 2. Later enactments dealt with the uses to which the funds obtained by the sale of the lands should be put.

16 The boundary line between Upper and Lower Canada from the St. Lawrence to the Ottawa river (see Appendix) was located with a view to excluding from Upper Canada as many as possible of the existing Seignories. This design of converting feudal tenures into free and common soccage holdings, was the motive of several subsequent enactments of the Imperial Parliament. See 3 George IV., cap. 119; 6 George IV., cap 59; and 1 William IV., cap 20. The Canadian Statutes dealing with the same subject are 8 Vict., cap. 42; 12 Vict., cap. 49; and 18 Vict., cap. 3. The last of these is "The Seignorial Act" of 1854, which abolished "all feudal rights and duties in Lower Canada." See note 12 to the "Quebec Act, 1774."

17 The instructions to Governor Carleton in 1775, and to the same officer as Lord Dorchester in 1786, authorized him to grant lands anywhere in the then Province of Quebec on feudal tenures.

18 See "Colonial Taxation Act" above.

19 Disputes soon arose between Upper and Lower Canada over the division of the revenue from customs duties on goods imported by way of the St. Lawrence. An agreement was arrived at in 1817, that one-fifth of all the duties collected in Lower Canada should be paid to Upper Canada, and this was ratified in the following year by Act of Parliament of Lower Canada (58 George III., cap. 4), and by Act of Parliament of Upper Canada (58 George III., cap. 13). The Lower Canadian Statute expired on the first of July, 1819, and the Assembly refused to renew it. This refusal ultimately led to the passage of the Imperial Statute known as 'The Canada Trade Act" (3 George IV., cap 119), which made permanent the agreement that one-fifth of the duties should go to Upper Canada. See Christie's "History of Lower Canada," Vol II., cap. 23.

20 See Note 2 above.

21 See Notes 7 and 9 above.

22 This Act is 11 George IV. & 1 William IV., cap. 53. The text is reprinted from the Imperial "Statutes at Large," London, 1832.

23 See "The Constitutional Act, 1791," section 4.

24 The English "Hansard" does not give any of the discussions on this measure in its progress through Parliament, and the Canadian histories are silent as to the reasons for its enactment.

H.C.C.

25 This Statute is 1 & 2 Vict., cap. 9. The text is reprinted from the Imperial "Statutes at Large," London, 1838.

26 For an account of the state of the Province which led to the passing of this Act see Christie's "History of Lower Canada," Vol. IV.; Garneau's "Histoire du Canada," Vol. III.; and Lord Durham's Report. On the 6th of March, 1836, the British House of Commons adopted a series of resolutions which declared it inexpedient to comply with the demand of the Legislative Assembly for an elective Legislative Council. When the Assembly met the following year it accepted these resolutions as "a formal and total refusal of the reforms and improvements" demanded by that House. The Legislature met on the 18th of August, 1837, and on the 26th of the same month it was prorogued by Lord Gosford never to be summoned again. The immediate result was a resort to arms on the part of the leaders of the Assembly, and a more remote one was the passage of this Act by the British Parliament in February, 1838, and its proclamation in Lower Canada on the 29th of March following.

27 The permanent arrangements here contemplated were not made till the Union Act was passed in 1840. The intention was to make such arrangements during the same session. See section IX. of this Act.

28 The first Council, which was called by Sir John Colborne as administrator, pending Lord Durham's arrival, was composed of eleven French and eleven English members; their names are given in Christie's "History of Lower Canada," Vol. V., p. 53.

29 This Act is 1 & 2 Vict., cap. 112. It is reprinted from the Imperial "Statutes at Large," London, 1838.

30 When Lord Durham arrived in Lower Canada, as Governor, he found many of the insurgents still in prison, and in order to get rid as easily as possible of the difficulty created by their detention he secured the previous consent of the leaders of the movement to their own banishment, and had this ordinance passed by his "Special Council" on the 28th of June, 1838. The text of the document will be found in the collection entitled "Ordinances Made and Passed by the Governor-General and Special Council for the Affairs of the Province of Lower Canada," Vol. II. It is given in Christie's "History of Lower Canada," Vol. V., pp. 166-171. It enacted that Wolfred Nelson and seven others then in prison should be banished to the Bermudas and be detained there, and that Louis Joseph Papineau, George Etienne Cartier, and fourteen others, then fugitives from justice, should not be permitted to return except by special permission from the Governor. The clause providing for the detention of the insurgents in the Bermudas was made the ground for declaring the ordinance *ultra vires* of the Governor and the Special Council, a view put forward by Lord Brougham and endorsed by Attorney-General (afterwards Lord Chancellor) Campbell.

31 The passage of this Act chagrined Lord Durham to such an extent that he soon afterwards retired to England.

32 This statute is 2 & 3 Vict., cap. 53. It is reprinted from the Imperial "Statutes at Large," London, 1841.

33 See Note 28 above. Lord Durham's Council, which passed the Ordinance under which Nelson and others were banished, was composed of Vice-Admiral Paget, who was then on a visit from Halifax to Quebec; Major-General MacDonnell, Lieut.-Col. Grey, Col. Cowper, and Hon. Charles Buller. Not one of these members was a Canadian.

34 Sir John Colborne succeeded Lord Durham in the administration of the Government of Lower Canada.

35 No amending Act was passed during that session; the next statute dealing with the constitution was the Union Act of 1840.

THE UNION ACT, 1840, AND SUPPLEMENTARY ACTS.

An Act[1] to re-unite the Provinces of Upper and Lower Canada, and for the government of Canada.

[23RD JULY, 1840.

Whereas it is necessary that provision be made for the good government of the Provinces of Upper and Lower Canada, in such manner as may secure the rights and liberties and promote the interests of all classes of her Majesty's subjects within the same: And whereas to this end it is expedient[2] that the said Provinces be reunited to form one Province for the purposes of executive government and legislation: Be it therefore enacted by the Queen's Most Excellent Majesty, by and with the advice and consent of the Lords Spiritual and Temporal, and Commons, in the present Parliament assembled, and by the authority of the same, that it shall be lawful for her Majesty, with the advice of her Privy Council, to declare, or to authorize the Governor-General of the said two Provinces of Upper and Lower Canada to declare by proclamation[3] that the said Provinces upon, from, and after a certain day in such proclamation to be appointed, which day shall be within fifteen calendar months next after the passing of this Act, shall form and be one Province under the name of the Province of Canada, and thenceforth the said Provinces shall constitute and be one Province under the name aforesaid upon, from, and after the day so appointed, as aforesaid. *Declaration of Union.*

II. And be it enacted that so much of an Act[4] passed in the session of Parliament held in the thirty-first year of the reign of George the Third, intituled, " An Act to repeal certain parts of an Act passed in the fourteenth year of His Majesty's Reign, intituled ' An Act for making more effectual Provision for the Government of the Province of Quebec in North America,' and to make further Provision for the Government of the said Province," as provides for constituting and composing a Legislative Council and Assembly within each of the said Provinces respectively, and for the *Repeal of Acts, 31 G. 3, c. 31.*

making of laws; and also the whole of an Act[5] passed in the session of Parliament held in the first and second years of the reign of her present Majesty, intituled "An Act to make Temporary Provision for the Government of Lower Canada;" and also the whole of an Act[6] passed in the session of Parliament held in the second and third years of the reign of her present Majesty, intituled "An Act to Amend an Act of the last Session of Parliament for making Temporary Provision for the Government of Lower Canada;" and also the whole of an Act[7] passed in the session of Parliament held in the first and second years of the reign of his late Majesty, King William the Fourth, intituled "An Act to amend an Act of the fourteenth year of His Majesty, King George the Third, for establishing a fund towards defraying the Charges of the Administration of Justice and the Support of Civil Government in the Province of Quebec in America;" shall continue and remain in force until the day on which it shall be declared by proclamation, as aforesaid, that the said two Provinces shall constitute and be one Province as aforesaid, and shall be repealed on, from, and after such day: Provided always that the repeal of the said several Acts of Parliament shall not be held to revive or give any force or effect to any enactment which has by the said Acts, or any of them, been repealed or determined.

Composition and Powers of Legislature.

III. And be it enacted that from and after the reunion of the said two Provinces there shall be within the Province of Canada one Legislative Council and one Assembly to be severally constituted and composed in the manner hereinafter prescribed, which shall be called "The Legislative Council and Assembly of Canada;" and that within the Province of Canada her Majesty shall have power, by and with the advice and consent of the said Legislative Council and Assembly, to make laws for the peace, welfare, and good government of the Province of Canada, such laws not being repugnant to this Act, or to such parts of the said Act[8] passed in the thirty-first year of the reign of his said late Majesty as are not hereby repealed, or to any Act of Parliament made or to be made and not hereby repealed, which does or shall by express enactment or by necessary intendment extend to the Provinces of Upper and Lower Canada, or to either of them, or to the Province of Canada; and that all such laws being passed by the said Legislative Council and Assembly and assented to by her Majesty, or assented to in her Majesty's name by the Governor of the Province of Canada, shall be valid and binding to all intents and purposes within the Province of Canada.

IV. And be it enacted that for the purpose of composing the Legislative Council of the Province of Canada it shall be lawful for her Majesty, before the time to be appointed for the first meeting of the said Legislative Council and Assembly, by an instrument under the sign manual, to authorize the Governor in her Majesty's name, by an instrument under the Great Seal of the said Province, to summon to the said Legislative Council of the said Province such persons, being not fewer than twenty, as her Majesty shall think fit; and that it shall also be lawful for her Majesty from time to time to authorize the Governor in like manner to summon to the said Legislative Council such other person or persons as her Majesty shall think fit, and that every person who shall be so summoned shall thereby become a member of the Legislative Council of the Province of Canada: Provided always, that no person shall be summoned to the said Legislative Council of the Province of Canada who shall not be of the full age of twenty-one years, and a natural-born subject of her Majesty, or a subject of her Majesty naturalized by Act of the Parliament of Great Britain, or by Act of the Parliament of the United Kingdom of Great Britain and Ireland, or by an Act of the Legislature of either of the Provinces of Upper or Lower Canada, or by an Act of the Legislature of the Province of Canada. *Appointment of Legislative Councillors.* *Qualification of Legislative Councillors.*

V. And be it enacted that every member of the Legislative Council of the Province of Canada shall hold his seat therein for the term of his life," but subject nevertheless to the provisions hereinafter contained for vacating the same. *Tenure of office of Councillor.*

VI. And be it enacted that it shall be lawful for any member of the Legislative Council of the Province of Canada to resign his seat in the said Legislative Council, and upon such resignation the seat of such Legislative Councillor shall become vacant. *Resignation of Legislative Councillor.*

VII. And be it enacted that if any Legislative Councillor of the Province of Canada shall for two successive sessions of the Legislature of the said Province fail to give his attendance in the said Legislative Council, without the permission *Vacating seat by absence.*

of her Majesty or of the Governor of the said Province signified by the said Governor to the Legislative Council, or shall take any oath or make any declaration or acknowledgment of allegiance, obedience, or adherence to any foreign prince or power, or shall do, concur in, or adopt any Act whereby he may become entitled to the rights, privileges, or immunities of a subject or citizen of any foreign state or power, or shall become bankrupt, or take the benefit of any law relating to insolvent debtors, or become a public defaulter, or be attainted of treason, or be convicted of felony or of any infamous crime, his seat in such Council shall thereby become vacant.

Trial of questions.
VIII. And be it enacted that any question which shall arise respecting any vacancy in the Legislative Council of the Province of Canada, on occasion of any of the matters aforesaid, shall be referred by the Governor of the Province of Canada to the said Legislative Council, to be by the said Legislative Council heard and determined: Provided always that it shall be lawful, either for the person respecting whose seat such question shall have arisen, or for her Majesty's Attorney-General for the said Province on her Majesty's behalf, to appeal from the determination of the said Council in such case to her Majesty, and that the judgment of her Majesty, given with the advice of her Privy Council thereon, shall be final and conclusive to all intents and purposes.

Appointment of Speaker.
IX. And be it enacted that the Governor of the Province of Canada shall have power and authority from time to time, by an instrument under the Great Seal of the said Province, to appoint one member of the said Legislative Council to be Speaker of the said Legislative Council, and to remove him and appoint another in his stead.

Quorum.

Division.

Casting vote.
X. And be it enacted that the presence of at least ten members of the said Legislative Council, including the Speaker, shall be necessary to constitute a meeting for the exercise of its powers; and that all questions which shall arise in the said Legislative Council shall be decided by a majority of voices of the members present other than the Speaker, and when the voices shall be equal the Speaker shall have the casting vote.

XI. And be it enacted that for the purpose of constituting the Legislative Assembly of the Province of Canada it shall be lawful for the Governor of the said Province, within the time hereinafter mentioned and thereafter from time to time as occasion shall require, in her Majesty's name and by an instrument or instruments under the Great Seal of the said Province, to summon and call together a Legislative Assembly in and for the said Province. *Convoking the Assembly.*

XII. And be it enacted that in the Legislative Assembly of the Province of Canada, to be constituted as aforesaid, the parts of the said Province which now constitute the Provinces of Upper and Lower Canada respectively, shall, subject to the provisions hereinafter contained, be represented by an equal number of representatives to be elected for the places and in the manner hereinafter mentioned. *Representatives for each Province.*

XIII. And be it enacted that the County of Halton in the Province of Upper Canada shall be divided into two ridings, to be called respectively the East Riding and the West Riding; and that the East Riding of the said County shall consist of the following townships, namely: Trafalgar, Nelson, Esquesing, Nassagaweya, East Flamborough, West Flamborough, Ering, Beverley; and that the West Riding of the said County shall consist of the following towships, namely: Garafraxa, Nichol, Woolwich, Guelph, Waterloo, Wilmot, Dumfries, Puslinch, Eramosa; and that the East Riding and West Riding of the said County shall each be represented by one member in the Legislative Assembly of the Province of Canada. *County of Halton.*

XIV. And be it enacted that the County of Northumberland in the Province of Upper Canada shall be divided into two ridings, to be called respectively the North Riding and the South Riding; and that the North Riding of the last-mentioned County shall consist of the following townships, namely: Monaghan, Otonabee, Asphodel, Smith, Douro, Dummer, Belmont, Methuen, Burleigh, Harvey, Emily, Gore, Ennismore; and that the South Riding of the last-mentioned County shall consist of the following townships, namely: Hamilton, Haldimand, Cramak, Murray, Seymour, Percy; and the North Riding and South Riding of the last-mentioned County shall each be represented by one member in the Legislative Assembly of the Province of Canada. *County of Northumberland.*

THE UNION ACT

County of Lincoln.

XV. And be it enacted that the County of Lincoln in the Province of Upper Canada shall be divided into two ridings, to be called respectively the North Riding and the South Riding; and that the North Riding shall be formed by uniting the First Riding and Second Riding of the said County, and the South Riding by uniting the Third Riding and Fourth Riding of the said County; and that the North and South Ridings of the last-mentioned County shall each be represented by one member in the Legislative Assembly of the Province of Canada.

Other county constituency of Upper Canada.

XVI. And be it enacted that every county and riding, other than those herein-before specified, which at the time of the passing of this Act was by law entitled to be represented in the Assembly of the Province of Upper Canada, shall be represented by one member in the Legislative Assembly of the Province of Canada.

Town constituency of Upper Canada.

XVII. And be it enacted that the City of Toronto shall be represented by two members, and the towns of Kingston, Brockville, Hamilton, Cornwall, Niagara, London, and Bytown shall each be represented by one member in the Legislative Assembly of the Province of Canada.

County constituency of Lower Canada, 1 & 2 Vict. c. 9.

XVIII. And be it enacted that every county which before and at the time of the passing of the said Act of Parliament, intituled "An Act to make temporary provision for the Government of Lower Canada" was entitled to be represented in the Assembly of the Province of Lower Canada, except the Counties of Montmorency, Orleans, L'Assomption, La Chesnaye, L'Acadie, Laprairie, Dorchester, and Beauce hereinafter mentioned, shall be represented by one member in the Legislative Assembly of the Province of Canada.

Further provision as to constituency of Lower Canada.

XIX. And be it enacted that the said counties of Montmorency and Orleans shall be united into and form one county to be called the County of Montmorency; and that the said Counties of L'Assomption and La Chesnaye shall be united into and form one county to be called the County of Leinster; and that the said Counties of L'Acadie and Laprairie shall be united into and form one county to be called the County of Huntingdon; and that the Counties of Dorchester and Beauce shall be united into and form one county to be called the County of Dorchester; and that each of the said Counties of Montmorency, Leinster, Huntingdon, and Dorchester shall be represented by one member in the Legislative Assembly of the said Province of Canada.

XX. And be it enacted that the Cities of Quebec and Montreal shall each be represented by two members, and the Towns of Three Rivers and Sherbrooke shall each be represented by one member in the Legislative Assembly of the Province of Canada. Town constituency of Lower Canada.

XXI. And be it enacted that for the purpose of electing their several representatives to the said Legislative Assembly, the cities and towns hereinbefore mentioned shall be deemed to be bounded and limited in such manner as the Governor of the Province of Canada, by letters patent under the Great Seal of the Province to be issued within thirty days after the union of the said Provinces of Upper Canada and Lower Canada shall set forth and describe; and such parts of any such city or town (if any), which shall not be included within the boundary of such city or town respectively by such letters patent for the purposes of this Act, shall be taken to be a part of the adjoining county or riding for the purpose of being represented in the said Legislative Assembly. Boundaries of cities and towns to be settled by the Governor.

XXII. And be it enacted that for the purpose of electing the members of the Legislative Assembly of the Province of Canada it shall be lawful for the Governor of the said Province from time to time to nominate proper persons to execute the office of Returning Officer in each of the said counties, ridings, cities, and towns, which shall be represented in the Legislative Assembly of the Province of Canada, subject nevertheless to the provisions hereinafter contained. Returning Officers.

XXIII. And be it enacted that no person shall be obliged to execute the said office of Returning Officer for any longer term than one year, or oftener than once, unless it shall be at any time otherwise provided by some Act or Acts of the Legislature of the Province of Canada. Term of office of Returning Officer.

XXIV. And be it enacted that writs for the election of members to serve in the Legislative Assembly of the Province of Canada shall be issued by the Governor of the said Writs of election.

Province within fourteen days after the sealing of such instrument, as aforesaid, for summoning and calling together such Legislative Assembly; and that such writs shall be directed to the returning officers of the said counties, ridings, cities, and towns respectively; and that such writs shall be made returnable within fifty days at farthest from the day on which they shall bear date, unless it shall at any time be otherwise provided by any Act of the Legislature of the said Province; and that writs shall in like manner and form be issued for the election of members in the case of any vacancy which shall happen by the death or resignation of the person chosen, or by his being summoned to the Legislative Council of the said Province, or from any other legal cause; and that such writs shall be made returnable within fifty days at farthest from the day on which they shall bear date, unless it shall be at any time otherwise provided by any Act of the Legislature of the said Province; and that in any case of any such vacancy which shall happen by the death of the person chosen, or by reason of his being so summoned as aforesaid, the writ for the election of a new member shall be issued within six days after notice thereof shall have been delivered to or left at the office of the proper officer for issuing such writs of election.

Time and place of holding elections.
XXV. And be it enacted that it shall be lawful for the Governor of the Province of Canada for the time being to fix the time and place of holding elections of members to serve in the Legislative Assembly of the said Province, until otherwise provided for as hereinafter mentioned, giving not less than eight days' notice of such time and place.

Power to alter system of representation.
XXVI. And be it enacted that it shall be lawful for the Legislature of the Province of Canada, by any Act or Acts[11] to be hereafter passed, to alter the divisions and extent of the several counties, ridings, cities, and towns which shall be represented in the Legislative Assembly of the Province of Canada, and to establish new and other divisions of the same, and to alter the apportionment of representatives to be chosen by the said counties, ridings, cities, and towns respectively, and make a new and different apportionment of the number of representatives to be chosen in and for those parts of the Province of Canada which now constitute the said Provinces of Upper and Lower Canada respectively, and in and for the several districts, counties, ridings, and towns in

the same, and to alter and regulate the appointment of
returning officers in and for the same, and make provision
in such manner as they may deem expedient for the issuing
and return of writs for the election of members to serve in
the said Legislative Assembly, and the time and place of
holding such elections: Provided always that it shall not be Proviso.
lawful to present to the Governor of the Province of Canada
for her Majesty's assent any bill of the Legislative Council
and Assembly of the said Province by which the number of
representatives in the Legislative Assembly may be altered,
unless the second and third reading of such bill in the Legislative Council and the Legislative Assembly shall have been
passed with the concurrence of two-thirds of the members
for the time being of the said Legislative Council, and of two-
thirds of the members for the time being of the said Legislative Assembly respectively, and the assent of her Majesty
shall not be given to any such bill unless addresses shall have
been presented by the Legislative Council and the Legislative Assembly respectively to the Governor, stating that
such bill has been so passed.

XXVII. And be it enacted that until provisions shall The present
otherwise be made by an Act or Acts of the Legislature of election laws
the Province of Canada all the laws which at the time of the vinces to apply
passing of this Act are in force in the Province of Upper until altered.
Canada, and all the laws which at the time of the passing of
the said Act[12] of Parliament, intituled "An Act to make 1 & 2 Vict. c. 9.
temporary provision for the Government of Lower Canada"
were in force in the Province of Lower Canada, relating to
the qualification and disqualification of any person to be
elected, or to sit or vote as a member of the Assembly in the
said Provinces respectively, (except those which require a
qualification of property in candidates for election, for which
provision is hereinafter made), and relating to the qualification and disqualification of voters at the election of members
to serve in the Assemblies of the said Provinces respectively,
and to the oaths to be taken by any such voters, and to the
powers and duties of returning officers, and the proceedings
at such elections, and the period during which such elections
may be lawfully continued, and relating to the trial of controverted elections and the proceedings incident thereto, and
to the vacating of seats of members, and the issuing and
execution of new writs in case of any seat being vacated
otherwise than by a dissolution of the Assembly, shall

respectively be applied to elections of members to serve in the Legislative Assembly of the Province of Canada for places situated in those parts of the Province of Canada for which such laws were passed.

Qualification of Members.

XXVIII. And be it enacted that no person shall be capable of being elected a member of the Legislative Assembly of the Province of Canada who shall not be legally or equitably seised as of freehold, for his own use and benefit, of lands or tenements held in free and common soccage, or seised or possessed, for his own use and benefit, of lands or tenements held in fief or in roture, within the said Province of Canada, of the value of five hundred pounds of sterling money of Great Britain, over and above all rents, charges, mortgages, and incumbrances charged upon and due and payable out of or affecting the same; and that every candidate at such election, before he shall be capable of being elected, shall, if required by any other candidate, or by any elector, or by the returning officer, make the following declaration:

Declaration of candidates for election.

"I, A. B., do declare and testify that I am duly seised at law or in "equity as of freehold, for my own use and benefit, of lands or "tenements held in free and common soccage 'or duly seised or "possessed for my own use and benefit, of lands or tenements held "in fief or in roture (as the case may be),] in the Province of Canada, "of the value of five hundred pounds of sterling money of Great "Britain, over and above all rents, mortgages, charges, and incum- "brances charged upon, or due and payable out of, or affecting the "same; and that I have not collusively or colourably obtained a "title to or become possessed of the said lands and tenements, or "any part thereof, for the purpose of qualifying or enabling me to "be returned a member of the Legislative Assembly of the Province "of Canada."

Persons making false declaration liable to the penalties of perjury.

XXIX. And be it enacted that if any person shall knowingly and wilfully make a false declaration respecting his qualification as a candidate at any election as aforesaid, such person shall be deemed to be guilty of a misdemeanor, and being thereof lawfully convicted shall suffer the like pains and penalties as by law are incurred by persons guilty of wilful and corrupt perjury in the place in which such false declaration shall have been made.

Place and times of holding Parliament.

XXX. And be it enacted that it shall be lawful for the Governor of the Province of Canada for the time being to fix such place or places[15] within any part of the Province of Canada, and such times for holding the first and every other session of the Legislative Council and Assembly of the said Province as he may think fit, such times and places to be afterwards changed or varied as the Governor may judge advisable and most consistent with general convenience and the public welfare, giving sufficient notice thereof; and also to prorogue the said Legislative Council and Assembly from time to time, and dissolve the same, by proclamation or otherwise, whenever he shall deem it expedient.

XXXI. And be it enacted that there shall be a session of the Legislative Council and Assembly of the Province of Canada once at least in every year, so that a period of twelve calendar months shall not intervene between the last sitting of the Legislative Council and Assembly in one session and the first sitting of the Legislative Council and Assembly in the next session; and that every Legislative Assembly of the said Province hereafter to be summoned and chosen shall continue for four years from the day of the return of the writs for choosing the same, and no longer, subject nevertheless to be sooner prorogued or dissolved by the Governor of the said Province. *Duration of Parliament.*

XXXII. And be it enacted that the Legislative Council and Assembly of the Province of Canada shall be called together for the first time at some period[14] not later than six calendar months after the time at which the Provinces of Upper and Lower Canada shall become reunited as aforesaid. *First calling together of the Legislature.*

XXXIII. And be it enacted that the members of the Legislative Assembly of the Province of Canada shall, upon the first assembling after every general election, proceed forthwith to elect one of their number to be Speaker; and in case of his death, resignation, or removal by a vote of the said Legislative Assembly, the said members shall forthwith proceed to elect another of such members to be such Speaker; and the Speaker so elected shall preside at all meetings of the said Legislative Assembly. *Election of the Speaker.*

XXXIV. And be it enacted that the presence of at least twenty members of the Legislative Assembly of the Province of Canada, including the Speaker, shall be necessary to constitute a meeting of the said Legislative Assembly for the exercise of its powers; and that all questions which *Quorum.* *Division.*

shall arise in the said Assembly shall be decided by the majority of voices of such members as shall be present, other than the Speaker, and when the voices shall be equal the Speaker shall have the casting voice.

XXXV. And be it enacted that no member, either of the Legislative Council or of the Legislative Assembly of the Province of Canada, shall be permitted to sit or vote therein until he shall have taken and subscribed the following oath before the Governor of the said Province, or before some person or persons authorized by such Governor to administer such oath:

"I, A. B., do sincerely promise and swear that I will be faithful "and bear true allegiance to her Majesty, Queen Victoria, as lawful "Sovereign of the United Kingdom of Great Britain and Ireland, "and of this Province of Canada, dependent on and belonging to "the said United Kingdom; and that I will defend her to the utmost "of my power against all traitorous conspiracies and attempts "whatever, which shall be made against her person, crown, and "dignity; and that I will do my utmost endeavour to disclose and "make known to her Majesty, her heirs and successors, all treasons "and traitorous conspiracies and attempts which I shall know to "be against her or any of them; and all this I do swear without any "equivocation, mental evasion, or secret reservation, and renounc- "ing all pardons and dispensations from any person or persons "whatever to the contrary,

SO HELP ME GOD."

XXXVI. And be it enacted that every person authorized by law to make an affirmation instead of taking an oath may make such affirmation in every case in which an oath is hereinbefore required to be taken.

XXXVII. And be it enacted that whenever any bill which has been passed by the Legislative Council and Assembly of the Province of Canada shall be presented for her Majesty's assent to the Governor of the said Province, such Governor shall declare according to his discretion, but subject nevertheless to the provisions contained in this Act, and to such instructions as may from time to time be given in that behalf by her Majesty, her heirs or successors, that he assents to such bill in her Majesty's name, or that he withholds her Majesty's assent, or that he reserves such bill for the signification of her Majesty's pleasure thereon.

XXXVIII. And be it enacted that whenever any bill, which shall have been presented for her Majesty's assent to the Governor of the said Province of Canada, shall by such Governor have been assented to in her Majesty's name, such Governor shall by the first convenient opportunity transmit to one of her Majesty's principal Secretaries of State an authentic copy of such bill so assented to; and that it shall be lawful at any time within two years after such bill shall have been so received by such Secretary of State, for her Majesty by Order in Council to declare her disallowance of such bill; and that such disallowance, together with a certificate under the hand and seal of such Secretary of State certifying the day on which such bill was received as aforesaid, being signified by such Governor to the Legislative Council and Assembly of Canada by speech or message to the Legislative Council and Assembly of the said Province, or by proclamation, shall make void and annul the same from and after the day of such signification.

XXXIX. And be it enacted that no bill which shall be reserved for the signification of her Majesty's pleasure thereon shall have any force or authority within the Province of Canada until the Governor of the said Province shall signify, either by speech or message to the Legislative Council and Assembly of the said Province, or by proclamation, that such bill has been laid before her Majesty in Council and that her Majesty has been pleased to assent to the same; and that an entry shall be made in the journals of the said Legislative Council of every such speech, message, or proclamation, and a duplicate thereof duly attested shall be delivered to the proper officer to be kept amongst the records of the said Province; and that no bill which shall be so reserved as aforesaid shall have any force or authority in the said Province unless her Majesty's assent thereto shall have been so signified as aforesaid within the space of two years from the day on which such bill shall have been presented for her Majesty's assent to the Governor as aforesaid. *Assent to bills reserved.*

XL. Provided always, and be it enacted that nothing herein contained shall be construed to limit or restrain the exercise of her Majesty's prerogative in authorizing, and that, notwithstanding this Act and any other Act or Acts passed in the Parliament of Great Britain, or in the Parliament of the United Kingdom of Great Britain and Ireland, or of the Legislature of the Province of Quebec, or of the *Authority of the Governor.*

Provinces of Upper or Lower Canada respectively, it shall be lawful for her Majesty to authorize the Lieutenant-Governor of the Province of Canada to exercise and execute, within such parts of the said Province as her Majesty shall think fit, notwithstanding the presence of the Governor within the Province, such of the powers, functions, and authority, as well judicial as other, which before and at the time of passing of this Act were and are vested in the Governor, Lieutenant-Governor, or person administering the Government of the Provinces of Upper and Lower Canada respectively, or of either of them, and which from and after the said reunion of the said two Provinces shall become vested in the Governor of the Province of Canada; and to authorize the Governor of the Province of Canada to assign, depute, substitute, and appoint any person or persons, jointly or severally, to be his deputy or deputies within any part or parts of the Province of Canada, and in that capacity to exercise, perform and execute during the pleasure of the said Governor such of the powers, functions, and authorities, as well judicial as other, as before and at the time of the passing of this Act were and are vested in the Governor, Lieutenant-Governor, or person administering the Government of the Provinces of Upper and Lower Canada respectively, and which from and after the union of the said Provinces shall become vested in the Governor of the Province of Canada, as the Governor of the Province of Canada shall deem to be necessary or expedient: Provided always, that by the appointment of a deputy or deputies as aforesaid the power and authority of the Governor of the Province of Canada shall not be abridged, altered, or in any way affected otherwise than as her Majesty shall think proper to direct.

Language of Legislative records.

XLI. And be it enacted that from and after the said reunion of the said two Provinces, all writs, proclamations, instruments for summoning and calling together the Legislative Council and Legislative Assembly of the Province of Canada and for proroguing and dissolving the same, and all writs of summons and election, and all writs and public instruments whatsoever relating to the said Legislative Council and Legislative Assembly or either of them, and all returns to such writs and instruments, and all journals, entries, and written or printed proceedings of what nature soever of the said Legislative Council and Legislative Assembly and each of them respectively, and all written or printed proceedings and reports of committees of the said Legislative Council and Legislative Assembly respectively, shall be in the English language only :[15] Provided always, that this enactment shall not be construed to prevent translated copies of any such documents being made, but no such copy shall be kept among the records of the Legislative Council or Legislative Assembly, or be deemed in any case to have the force of an original record.

XLII. And be it enacted that whenever any bill or bills shall be passed by the Legislative Council and Assembly of the Province of Canada containing any provisions to vary or repeal any of the provisions now in force contained in an Act of the Parliament of Great Britain passed in the fourteenth year of the reign of his late Majesty King George the Third, intituled "An Act for making more effectual provision for the Government of the Province of Quebec in North America," or in the aforesaid Act of Parliament passed in the thirty-first year of the same reign, respecting the accustomed dues and rights of the clergy of the Church of Rome; or to vary or repeal any of the several provisions contained in the said last mentioned Act respecting the allotment and appropriation of lands for the support of the Protestant clergy within the Province of Canada,[16] or respecting the constituting, erecting, or endowing of parsonages or rectories within the Province of Canada, or respecting the presentation of incumbents or ministers of the same, or respecting the tenure on which such incumbents or ministers shall hold or enjoy the same[17]; and also that whenever any bill or bills shall be passed containing any provisions which shall in any manner relate to or affect the enjoyment or exercise of any form or mode of religious worship, or shall impose or create any penalties, burdens, disabilities, or disqualifications in respect of the same, or shall in any manner relate to or affect the payment, recovery, or enjoyment of any of the accustomed dues or rights hereinbefore mentioned, or shall in any manner relate to the granting, imposing, or recovering of any other dues, or stipends, or emoluments to be paid to or for the use of any minister, priest, ecclesiastic, or teacher according to any form or mode of religious worship, in respect of his said office or function; or shall in any manner relate to or affect her Majesty's prerogative touching the granting of waste lands of the Crown within the said

Ecclesiastical and Crown rights.

14 G. 3, c. 83.

Province; every such bill or bills shall, previously to any declaration or signification of her Majesty's assent thereto, be laid before both Houses of Parliament of the United Kingdom of Great Britain and Ireland; and that it shall not be lawful for her Majesty to signify her assent to any such bill or bills until thirty days after the same shall have been laid before the said Houses, or to assent to any such bill or bills in case either House of Parliament shall within the said thirty days address her Majesty to withhold her assent from any such bill or bills; and that no such bill shall be valid or effectual to any of the said purposes within the said Province of Canada unless the Legislative Council and Assembly of such Province shall, in the session in which the same shall have been passed by them, have presented to the Governor of the said Province an address or addresses specifying that such bill or bills contains provisions for some of the purposes hereinbefore specially described, and desiring that, in order to give effect to the same such bill or bills may be transmitted to England without delay, for the purpose of its being laid before Parliament previously to the signification of her Majesty's assent thereto.

Colonial Taxation.

18 G. 3, c. 12.

XLIII. And whereas by an Act[18] passed in the eighteenth year of the reign of his late Majesty King George the Third, intituled "An Act for removing all Doubts and Apprehensions concerning Taxation by the Parliament of Great Britain in any of the Colonies, Provinces, and Plantations in North America and the West Indies; and for repealing so much of an Act made in the seventh year of the reign of his present Majesty as imposes a duty on Tea imported from Great Britain into any Colony or Plantation in America, or relating thereto," it was declared that " the " King and Parliament of Great Britain would not impose " any duty, tax, or assessment whatever, payable in any of " his Majesty's Colonies, Provinces, and Plantations in " North America or the West Indies, except only such duties " as it might be expedient to impose for the regulation of " commerce, the net produce of such duties to be always " paid and applied to and for the use of the Colony, Province, " or Plantation in which the same shall be respectively " levied, in such manner as other duties collected by the " authority of the respective General Courts[19] or General " Assemblies of such Colonies, Provinces, or Plantations " were ordinarily paid and applied ": And whereas it is necessary for the general benefit of the Empire that such power of regulation of commerce should continue to be exercised by her Majesty and the Parliament of the United Kingdom of Great Britain and Ireland, subject nevertheless to the conditions hereinbefore recited with respect to the application of any duties which may be imposed for that purpose ; be it therefore enacted that nothing in this Act contained shall prevent or affect the execution of any law which hath been or shall be made in the Parliament of the said United Kingdom for establishing regulations and prohibitions, or for the imposing, levying, or collecting duties for the regulation of navigation, or for the regulation of the commerce between the Province of Canada and any other part of her Majesty's Dominions, or between the said Province of Canada or any other part thereof and any foreign country or state, or for appointing and directing the payment of drawbacks of such duties so imposed, or to give to her Majesty any power or authority, by and with the advice and consent of such Legislative Council and Assembly of the said Province of Canada, to vary or repeal any such law or laws, or any part thereof, or in any manner to prevent or obstruct the execution thereof : Provided always, that the net produce of all duties which shall be so imposed shall at all times hereafter be applied to and for the use of the said Province of Canada, and (except as hereinafter provided) in such manner only as shall be directed by any law or laws which may be made by her Majesty, by and with the advice and consent of the Legislative Council and Assembly of such Province.

XLIV. And whereas by the laws now in force in the said Province of Upper Canada the Governor, Lieutenant-Governor, or person administering the Government of the said Province, or the Chief Justice of the said Province, together with any two or more of the members of the Executive Council of the said Province, constitute and are a Court of Appeal for hearing and determining all appeals from such judgments or sentences as may be lawfully brought before them : And whereas by an Act of the Legislature of the said Province of Upper Canada, passed in the thirty-third year of the reign of his late Majesty King George the Third, intituled "An Act to establish a Court of Probate in the said Province, and also a Surrogate Court in every District thereof," there was and is established a Court of Probate in the said Province, in which Act it was enacted that the Gov- *(Courts of Appeal, Probate, Queen's Bench and Chancery in Upper Canada ; and Court, of Appeal in Lower Canada.*

(Laws of Upper Canada, 33 G. 3, Sess. 2, c. 8.)

ornor, Lieutenant-Governor, or person administering the Government of the said last-mentioned Province should preside, and that he should have the powers and authorities in the said Act specified: And whereas by an Act of the Legislature of the said Province of Upper Canada, passed in the second year of the reign of his late Majesty King William the Fourth, intituled " An Act respecting the Time and Place of Sitting of the Court of King's Bench," it was amongst other things enacted that his Majesty's Court of King's Bench in that Province should be holden in a place certain; that is, in the city, town, or place which should be for the time being the seat of the Civil Government of the said Province, or within one mile therefrom : And whereas by an Act of the Legislature of the said Province of Upper Canada passed in the seventh year of the reign of his late Majesty King William the Fourth, intituled " An Act to establish a Court of Chancery in this Province," it was enacted that there should be constituted and established a Court of Chancery to be called and known by the name and style of " The Court of Chancery for the Province of Upper Canada," of which Court the Governor, Lieutenant-Governor, or person administering the Government of the said Province should be Chancellor; and which Court, it was also enacted, should be holden at the seat of Government in the said Province, or in such other place as should be appointed by proclamation of the Governor, Lieutenant-Governor, or person administering the Government of the said Province: And whereas by an Act of the Legislature of the Province of Lower Canada, passed in the thirty-fourth year of the reign of his late Majesty George the Third, intituled " An Act for the Division of the Province of Lower Canada, for amending the Judicature thereof, and for repealing certain Laws therein mentioned," it was enacted that the Governor, Lieutenant-Governor, or person administering the Government, the members of the Executive Council of the said Province, the Chief Justice thereof and the Chief Justice to be appointed for the Court of King's Bench at Montreal, or any five of them, the Judges of the Court of the District wherein the judgment appealed from was given excepted, should constitute a Superior Court of Civil Jurisdiction or Provincial Court of Appeals, and should take cognizance of, hear, try, and determine all causes, matters, and things appealed from all civil jurisdictions and Courts wherein an appeal is by law allowed; be it enacted that until otherwise

(Laws of Upper Canada, 2 W. 4, c. 8.)

(Laws of Upper Canada, 7 W. 4, c. 2.)

(Laws of Lower Canada, 34 G. 3.)

provided by an Act of the Legislature of the Province of Canada, all judicial and ministerial authority which before and at the time of passing this Act was vested in or might be exercised by the Governor, Lieutenant-Governor, or person administering the Government of the said Province of Upper Canada, or the members or any number of the members of the Executive Council of the same Province, or was vested in or might be exercised by the Governor, Lieutenant-Governor, or the person administering the Government of the Province of Lower Canada, and the members of the Executive Council of that Province, shall be vested in and may be exercised by the Governor, Lieutenant-Governor, or person administering the Government of the Province of Canada, and in the members or the like number of the members of the Executive Council of the Province of Canada respectively; and that until otherwise provided by Act or Acts of the Legislature of the Province of Canada the said Court of King's Bench, now called the Court of Queen's Bench of Upper Canada, shall from and after the Union of the Provinces of Upper and Lower Canada be holden at the City of Toronto, or within one mile from the municipal boundary of the said City of Toronto: Provided always, that until otherwise provided by Act or Acts of the Legislature of the Province of Canada, it shall be lawful for the Governor of the Province of Canada, by and with the advice and consent of the Executive Council of the same Province, by his proclamation to fix and appoint such other place as he may think fit, within that part of the last-mentioned Province which now constitutes the Province of Upper Canada, for the holding of the said Court of Queen's Bench.

XLV. And be it enacted that all powers, authorities, and functions which by the said Act passed in the thirty-first year of the reign of his late Majesty, King George the Third, or by any other Act of Parliament, or by any Act of the Legislature of the Provinces of Upper and Lower Canada respectively, are vested in or are authorized or required to be exercised by the respective Governors or Lieutenant-Governors of the said Provinces, with the advice or with the advice and consent of the Executive Council of such Provinces respectively, or in conjunction with such Executive Council or with any number of the members thereof, or by the said Governors or Lieutenant-Governors individually and alone, shall, in so far as the same are not repugnant to *[Powers to be exercised by Governor, with the Executive Council, or alone.]*

or inconsistent with the provisions of this Act, be vested in and may be exercised by the Governor of the Province of Canada, with the advice or with the advice and consent of, or in conjunction as the case may require with such Executive Council, or any members thereof, as may be appointed by her Majesty for the affairs of the Province of Canada, or by the said Governor of the Province of Canada individually and alone in cases when the advice, consent, or concurrence of the Executive Council is not required.

Existing laws saved.

XLVI. And be it enacted that all laws, statutes, and ordinances which at the time of the union of the Provinces of Upper and Lower Canada shall be in force within the said Provinces or either of them, or any part of the said Provinces respectively, shall remain and continue to be of the same force, authority, and effect in those parts of the Province of Canada which now constitute the said Provinces respectively as if this Act had not been made, and as if the said two Provinces had not been united as aforesaid, except in so far as the same are repealed or varied by this Act, or in so far as the same shall or may hereafter by virtue and under the authority of this Act be repealed or varied by any Act or Acts of the Legislature of the Province of Canada.

Courts of Justice, Commissions, Officers, etc.

XLVII. And be it enacted that all the courts of civil and criminal jurisdiction within the Provinces of Upper and Lower Canada at the time of the union of the said Provinces, and all legal commissions, powers, and authorities, and all officers, judicial, administrative, or ministerial, within the said Provinces respectively, except in so far as the same may be abolished, altered, or varied by or may be inconsistent with the provisions of this Act, or shall be abolished, altered, or varied by any Act or Acts of the Legislature of the Province of Canada, shall continue to subsist within those parts of the Province of Canada which now constitute the said two Provinces respectively, in the same form and with the same effect as if this Act had not been made, and as if the said two Provinces had not been reunited as aforesaid.

Provision respecting temporary Acts.

XLVIII. And whereas the Legislatures of the said Provinces of Upper and Lower Canada have from time to time passed enactments, which enactments were to continue in force for a certain number of years after the passing thereof, " and from thence to the end of the then next ensuing session of the Legislature of the Province in which the same were passed"; be it therefore enacted that whenever the words, "and from thence to the end of the then next ensuing session of the Legislature," or words to the same effect, have been used in any temporary Act of either of the said two Provinces which shall not have expired before the reunion of the said two Provinces, the said words shall be construed to extend and apply to the next session of the Legislature of the Province of Canada.

XLIX. And whereas by a certain Act passed in the third year of the reign of his late Majesty, King George the Fourth, intituled, "An Act to regulate the Trade of the Provinces of Upper and Lower Canada, and for other purposes relating to the said Provinces," certain provisions were made for appointing arbitrators with power to hear and determine certain claims of the Province of Upper Canada upon the Province of Lower Canada, and to hear any claim which might be advanced on the part of the Province of Upper Canada to a proportion of certain duties therein mentioned, and for prescribing the course of proceeding to be pursued by such arbitrators[20]; be it enacted that the said recited provisions of the said last-mentioned Act, and all matters in the same Act contained, which are consequent to or dependent upon the said provisions or any of them, shall be repealed. *Repeal of part of 3 G. 4, c. 119.*

L. And be it enacted that upon the union of the Provinces of Upper and Lower Canada, all duties and revenues over which the respective Legislatures of the said Provinces before and at the time of the passing of this Act had and have power of appropriation,[21] shall form one consolidated revenue fund to be appropriated for the public service of the Province of Canada in the manner and subject to the charges hereinafter mentioned. *Revenues of the two Provinces to form a Consolidated Revenue Fund.*

LI. And be it enacted that the said consolidated revenue fund of the Province of Canada shall be permanently charged with all the costs, charges, and expences incident to the collection, management, and receipt thereof, such costs, charges, and expences, being subject nevertheless to be reviewed and audited in such manner as shall be directed by any Act of the Legislature of the Province of Canada. *Consolidated Revenue Fund to be charged with expense of collection, etc.*

LII. And be it enacted that out of the consolidated revenue fund of the Province of Canada there shall be pay- *£45,000 to be granted permanently for* the Services in Schedule A, and £30,000 for the life of her Majesty and five years following, for those in Schedule B.

able in every year to her Majesty, her heirs and successors, the sum of forty-five thousand pounds²² for defraying the expence of the several services and purposes named in the Schedule marked A. to this Act annexed; and during the life of her Majesty, and for five years after the demise of her Majesty, there shall be payable to her Majesty, her heirs and successors, out of the said consolidated revenue fund, a further sum of thirty thousand pounds, for defraying the expence of the several services and purposes named in the Schedule marked B to this Act annexed; the said sums of forty-five thousand pounds and thirty thousand pounds to be issued by the Receiver-General in discharge of such warrant or warrants as shall be from time to to time directed to him under the hand and seal of the Governor; and the said Receiver-General shall account to her Majesty for the same, through the Lord High Treasurer or Lords Commissioners of her Majesty's Treasury, in such form and manner as her Majesty shall be graciously pleased to direct.

How the appropriation of sums granted may be varied.

LIII. And be it enacted that, until altered by any Act of the Legislature of the Province of Canada, the salaries of the Governor and of the Judges shall be those respectively set against their several offices in the said Schedule A.; but that it shall be lawful for the Governor to abolish any of the offices named in the said Schedule B., or to vary the sums appropriated to any of the services or purposes named in the said Schedule B.; and that the amount of saving which may accrue from any such alteration in either of the said schedules shall be appropriated to such purposes connected with the administration of the Government of the said Province as to her Majesty shall seem fit; and that accounts in detail of the expenditure of the several sums of forty-five thousand and thirty thousand pounds hereinbefore granted, and of every part thereof, shall be laid before the Legislative Council and Legislative Assembly of the said Province within thirty days next after the beginning of the session after such expenditure shall have been made: Provided always that not more than two thousand pounds shall be payable at the same time for pensions to the judges out of the said sum of forty-five thousand pounds, and that not more than five thousand pounds shall be payable at the same time for pensions out of the said sum of thirty thousand pounds; and that a list of all such pensions and of the persons to whom the same shall have been granted, shall be laid in every year before the said Legislative Council and Legislative Assembly.

LIV. And be it enacted that during the time for which the said several sums of forty-five thousand pounds and thirty thousand pounds are severally payable the same shall be accepted and taken by her Majesty by way of Civil List, instead of all territorial and other revenues now at the disposal of the Crown, arising in either of the said Provinces of Upper Canada or Lower Canada, or in the Province of Canada, and that three-fifths of the net produce of the said territorial and other revenues now at the disposal of the Crown within the Province of Canada shall be paid over to the account of the said consolidated revenue fund; and also during the life of her Majesty and for five years after the demise of her Majesty the remaining two-fifths of the net produce of the said territorial and other revenues and at the disposal of the Crown within the Province of Canada shall be also paid over in like manner to the account of the said consolidated revenue fund. *Surrender of Hereditary Revenues of the Crown.*

LV. And be it enacted that the consolidation of the duties and revenues of the said Province shall not be taken to affect the payment out of the said consolidated revenue fund of any sum or sums heretofore charged upon the rates and duties already raised, levied, and collected to and for the use of either of the said Provinces of Upper Canada or Lower Canada, or of the Province of Canada, for such time as shall have been appointed by the several Acts of the Legislature of the Province by which such charges were severally authorized. *Charges already created in either Province.*

LVI. And be it enacted that the expences of the collection, management, and receipt of the said consolidated revenue fund shall form the first charge thereon; and that the annual interest of the Public Debt of the Provinces of Upper and Lower Canada, or of either of them, at the time of the reunion of the said Provinces shall form the second charge thereon; and that the payments to be made to the clergy of the United Church of England and Ireland, and to clergy of the Church of Scotland, and to ministers of other Christian denominations, pursuant to any law or usage whereby such payments before or at the passing of this Act were or are legally or usually paid out of the *The order of charges on the Consolidated Fund to be:— 1st. Expense of collection; 2nd. Interest of the debt; 3rd. Payments to the Clergy;*

public or Crown revenue of either of the Provinces of Upper and Lower Canada, shall form the third charge upon the said consolidated revenue fund; and that the said sum of forty-five thousand pounds shall form the fourth charge thereon; and that the said sum of thirty thousand pounds, so long as the same shall continue to be payable, shall form the fifth charge thereon; and that the other charges upon the rates and duties levied within the said Province of Canada hereinbefore reserved shall form the sixth charge thereon, so long as such charges shall continue to be payable.

<small>4th and 5th. Civil List.</small>

<small>6th. Other charges already made on the Public Revenue.</small>

<small>Subject to the above charges, the Consolidated Revenue Fund to be appropriated by the Provincial Legislature, by bills, etc.</small>

LVII. And be it enacted that, subject to the several payments hereby charged on the said Consolidated Revenue Fund, the same shall be appropriated by the Legislature of the Province of Canada for the public service in such manner as they shall think proper: Provided always that all bills for appropriating any part of the surplus of the said consolidated revenue fund, or for imposing any new tax or import, shall originate in the Legislative Assembly of the said Province of Canada: Provided also that it shall not be lawful for the said Legislative Assembly to originate or pass any vote, resolution, or bill for the appropriation of any part of the surplus of the said consolidated revenue fund, or of any other tax or impost, to any purpose which shall not have been first recommended by a message of the Governor to the said Legislative Assembly during the session in which such vote, resolution, or bill shall be passed.

<small>Townships to be constituted.</small>

LVIII. And be it enacted that it shall be lawful for the Governor, by an instrument or instruments to be issued by him for that purpose under the Great Seal of the Province, to constitute townships[23] in those parts of the Province of Canada in which townships are not already constituted, and to fix metes and bounds thereof, and to provide for the election and appointment of township officers therein, who shall have and exercise the like powers as are exercised by the like officers in the townships already constituted in that part of the Province of Canada now called Upper Canada; and every such instrument shall be published by proclamation, and shall have the force of law from a day to be named in each case in such proclamation.

<small>Powers of Governor how to be exercised.</small>

LIX. And be it enacted that all powers and authorities expressed in this Act to be given to the Governor of the

Province of Canada shall be exercised by such Governor in conformity with and subject to such orders, instructions, and directions as her Majesty shall from time to time see fit to make or issue

LX. And whereas his late Majesty King George the Third, by his Royal Proclamation[24] bearing date the seventh day of October in the third year of his reign, was pleased to declare that he had put the coast of Labrador from the River St. John to Hudson's Straits, with the islands of Anticosti and Madelaine and all other smaller islands lying on the said coast, under the care and inspection of the Governor of Newfoundland ; And whereas by an Act passed in the fourteenth year of the reign of his said late Majesty, intituled " An Act for making more effectual provision for the Government of the Province of Quebec in North America," all such territories, islands, and countries, which had since the tenth day of February in the year one thousand seven hundred and sixty-three been made part of the Government of Newfoundland, were during his Majesty's pleasure annexed to and made part and parcel of the Province of Quebec as created and established by the said proclamation[25] ; be it hereby declared and enacted that nothing in this or any other Act contained shall be construed to restrain her Majesty, if she shall be so pleased, from annexing the Magdalen Islands in the Gulf of St. Lawrence to her Majesty's Island of Prince Edward. *Magdalen Islands may be annexed to the Island of Prince Edward.*

LXI. And be it enacted that in this Act, unless otherwise expressed therein, the words " Act of the Legislature of the Province of Canada " are to be understood to mean " Act of her Majesty, her Heirs or Successors, enacted by her Majesty, or by the Governor on behalf of her Majesty, with the advice and consent of the Legislative Council and Assembly of the Province of Canada "; and the words " Governor of the Province of Canada " are to be understood as comprehending the Governor, Lieutenant-Governor, or person authorized to execute the Office or the functions of Governor of the said Province. *Interpretation clause.*

LXII. And be it enacted that this Act may be amended or repealed by any Act to be passed in the present session of Parliament[26]. *Act may be amended, etc.*

SCHEDULES.

SCHEDULE A.

Governor	£7000
Lieutenant-Governor	1000

Upper Canada.

1 Chief Justice	1500
4 Puisne Judges, at £900 each	3600
1 Vice-Chancellor	1125

Lower Canada.

1 Chief Justice, Quebec	1500
3 Puisne Judges, Quebec, at £900 each	2700
1 Chief Justice, Montreal	1100
3 Puisne Judges, Montreal, at £900 each	2700
1 Resident Judge at Three Rivers	900
1 Judge of the Inferior District of St. Francis	500
1 Judge of the Inferior District of Gaspé	500
Pensions to the Judges, salaries of the Attornies and Solicitors General, and contingent and miscellaneous expences of Administration of Justice throughout the Province of Canada	20875
	£45000

SCHEDULE B.

Civil Secretaries and their Offices	£8000
Provincial Secretaries and their Offices	3000
Receiver-General and his Office	3000
Inspector-General and his Office	2000
Executive Council	3000
Board of Works	2000
Emigrant Agent	700
Pensions	5000
Contingent Expences of Public Offices	3300
	£30000

The Union Act Amendment Act, 1848.

An Act[27] to repeal so much of an Act of the Third and Fourth Years of Her present Majesty, to re-unite the Provinces of Upper and Lower Canada, as relates to the use of the English Language in Instruments relating to the Legislative Council and Legislative Assembly of the Province of Canada.

[14TH AUGUST, 1848.

Whereas by an Act past in the session of Parliament held 3 & 4 Vict. c. 35. in the third and fourth years of Her Present Majesty, intituled "An Act to re-unite the Provinces of Upper and Lower Canada, and for the Government of Canada," it is amongst other things enacted that from and after the said reunion of the said two Provinces, all writs, proclamations, instruments for summoning and calling together the Legislative Council and Legislative Assembly of the Province of Canada, and for proroguing and dissolving the same, and all writs of summons and elections, and all writs and public instruments whatsoever relating to the said Legislative Council and Legislative Assembly, or either of them, and all returns to such writs and instruments, and all journals, entries, and written or printed proceedings, of what nature soever, of the said Legislative Council and Legislative Assembly, and of each of them respectively, and all written or printed proceedings and reports of Committees of the said Legislative Council and Legislative Assembly respectively, shall be in the English language only: Provided always that the said enactment shall not be construed to prevent translated copies of any such documents being made, but no such copy should be kept among the records of the Legislative Council or Legislative Assembly, or be deemed in any case to have the force of an original record: And whereas it is expedient to alter the law in this respect, in order that the Legislature of the Province of Canada, or the said Legislative Council and Legislative Assembly respectively, may have power to make such regulations herein as to them may seem advisable: Be it therefore enacted by the Queen's most excellent Majesty, by and with the So much of recited Act as enacts that all writs, etc., shall be in English repealed.

advice and consent of the Lords Spiritual and Temporal, and Commons, in this present Parliament assembled, and by the authority of the same, that from and after the passing of this Act so much of the said recited Act as is hereinbefore recited shall be repealed.[2][3]

Act may be amended, etc.

II. And be it enacted that this Act, or any part thereof, may be repealed, altered, or varied at any time during the present session of Parliament.

The Union Act Amendment Act, 1854.

An Act[29] to empower the Legislature of Canada to alter the Constitution of the Legislative Council for that Province, and for other purposes.

[11TH AUGUST, 1854.

Whereas an Act[30] of the session of Parliament holden in the third and fourth years of her Majesty, chapter thirty-five, " to reunite the Provinces of Upper and Lower Canada, and for the Government of Canada," provides amongst other things for the establishment of a Legislative Council in the Province of Canada, consisting of members summoned thereto by the Governor, under the authority of her Majesty as therein specified : And whereas it is expedient[31] that the Legislature of the said Province should be empowered to alter the constitution of the said Legislative Council : And whereas the said Act requires amendment in other respects: Be it enacted by the Queen's most excellent Majesty, by and with the consent of the Lords Spiritual and Temporal, and Commons, in this present Parliament assembled, and by the authority of the same, as follows :

I. It shall be lawful for the Legislature of Canada, by any Act or Acts to be hereinafter for that purpose passed, to alter the manner of composing the Legislative Council of the said Province, and to make it consist of such number of members appointed or to be appointed or elected by such persons and in such manner as to the said Legislature may seem fit, and to fix the qualifications of the persons capable of being so appointed or elected, and by such Act or Acts to make provision, if they shall think fit, for the separate dissolution, by the Governor of the said Legislative Council and Legislative Assembly respectively, and for the purposes aforesaid to vary and repeal in such manner as to them may seem fit all or any of the sections of the said recited Act, and of any other Act of Parliament now in force, which relate to the constitution of the Legislative Council of Canada: Provided always that any bill or bills which shall be passed by the present Legislative Council and Assembly of Canada for all or any of the purposes

[marginal note: Power to the Legislature of Canada to alter the Constitution of the Legislative Council.]

aforesaid shall be reserved by the said Governor,[32] unless he think fit to withhold her Majesty's assent thereto, for the signification of her Majesty's pleasure, and shall be subject to the enactments of the said recited Act of the third and fourth years of her Majesty, chapter thirty-five, section thirty-nine, which relate to bills so reserved for the signification of her Majesty's pleasure.

Provisions of former Acts of Parliament to apply to the new Legislative Council.

II. As soon as the constitution of the Legislative Council of the Province of Canada shall have been altered under such Act or Acts so assented to by her Majesty as aforesaid, all provisions of the said recited Act of Parliament of the third and fourth years of her Majesty, chapter thirty-five, and of any other Act of Parliament now in force relating to the Legislative Council of Canada, shall be held to apply to the Legislative Council of Canada so altered, except so far as such provisions may have been varied or repealed by such Act or Acts of the Legislature of Canada so assented to as aforesaid.

Legislature of Canada may vary Acts constituting the new Legislative Council;

III. It shall be lawful for the Legislature of Canada from time to time to vary and repeal all or any of the provisions of the Act or Acts altering the constitution of the said Legislative Council: Provided always, that any bill for any such purpose, which shall vary the qualification of councillors, or the duration of office of such councillors, or the power of the Governor to dissolve the Council or Assembly, shall be reserved by the Governor for the signification of her Majesty's pleasure in manner aforesaid.

and may vary, etc., the property qualification of members of Assembly.

IV. It shall be lawful for the Legislature of Canada, by any Act or Acts reserved for the signification of her Majesty's pleasure, and whereto her Majesty shall have assented as hereinbefore provided, to vary or repeal any of the provisions of the recited Act of Parliament of the third and fourth years of her Majesty, which relate to the property qualification of members of the Legislative Assembly.[33]

Proviso in section 26 of 3 & 4 Vict. c. 35 repealed.

V. So much of the twenty-sixth section of the said recited Act of Parliament as provides that it shall not be lawful to present to the Governor of the Province of Canada, for her Majesty's assent, any bill of the Legislative Council and Assembly of the said Province by which the number of representatives in the Legislative Assembly may be altered unless the second and third readings of such bill in the Legislative Council and Legislative Assembly shall have been passed with the concurrence of two-thirds of the members for the time being of the said Legislative Council, and of two-thirds of the members for the time being of the said Legislative Assembly respectively, and that the assent of her Majesty shall not be given to any such bill unless addresses shall have been presented by the Legislative Council and the Legislative Assembly respectively to the Governor stating that such bill has been so passed, is hereby repealed.

VI. The forty-second section of the said recited Act of Parliament, providing that in certain cases Bills of the Legislative Council and Assembly of Canada shall be laid before both Houses of Parliament of the United Kingdom, is hereby repealed; and notwithstanding anything in the said Act of Parliament, or in any other Act of Parliament contained, it shall be lawful for the Governor to declare that he assents in her Majesty's name to any bill of the Legislature of Canada, or for her Majesty to assent to any such bill if reserved for the signification of her pleasure thereon, although such bill shall not have been laid before the said Houses of Parliament; and no Act heretofore passed, or to be passed by the Legislature of Canada shall be held invalid or ineffectual by reason of the same not having been laid before the said Houses, or by reason of the Legislative Council and Assembly not having presented to the Governor such address as by the said Act of Parliament is required. *Section 42 of 3 & 4 Vict. c. 35 repealed.*

VII. That in this Act the word "Governor" is to be understood as comprehending the Governor and in his absence the Lieutenant-Governor, or person authorized to execute the office or the functions of the Governor of Canada. *Interpretation of terms.*

The Union Act Amendment Act, 1859.

An Act⁴ to empower the Legislature of Canada to make laws regulating the appointment of a Speaker of the Legislative Council.

[8TH AUGUST, 1856.]

WHEREAS by an Act passed in the Session of Parliament, holden in the third and fourth years of Her Majesty, chapter thirty-five, " to re-unite the Provinces of Upper and Lower Canada, and for the Government of Canada," it is amongst other things provided that the Governor of the Province of Canada shall have power and authority, from time to time, by an instrument under the Great Seal of the said Province, to appoint one member of the said Legislative Council to be Speaker of the said Legislative Council, and to remove him and appoint another in his stead : And, whereas by an Act passed in the Session of Parliament holden in the seventeenth and eighteenth years of Her Majesty, chapter one hundred and eighteen, " to empower the Legislature of Canada to alter the constitution of the Legislative Council for that Province, and for other purposes," power was given to the Legislature of Canada to alter the manner of composing the Legislative Council for that Province, and to make it consist of such number of persons appointed, or to be appointed, or elected by such persons and in such manner as to the said Legislature may seem fit, in the manner and subject to the conditions by that Act provided, and for the purpose aforesaid to vary and repeal, in such manner as to them may seem fit, all or any of the provisions of the first-recited Act, and of any other Act of Parliament now in force which relate to the constitution of the Legislative Council of Canada; and it was thereby further enacted, that the Speaker of the Legislative Council should, as theretofore, be appointed by the Governor : And, whereas the said Legislature, in pursuance of the powers conferred on them by the said last-recited Act, have, by an Act of the Province of Canada passed in the Session of the said Legislature holden in the nineteenth and twentieth years of Her Majesty,³⁵ " to change the constitution of the Legislative Council by rendering the same elective," provided for the election of members of the said Council, and for the gradual substitution of elective for appointed members thereof: And, whereas doubts have been entertained whether it is lawful for the Legislature of Canada, under the powers given to them by the said last-recited Act of Parliament, to provide for the appointment or election of a Speaker of the Legislative Council, and it is expedient that such doubts should be removed, be it enacted by the Queen's Most Excellent Majesty, by and with the advice and consent of the Lords Spiritual and Temporal, and Commons, in this present Parliament assembled, and by the authority of the same, as follows:

I. It shall be lawful for the Legislature of Canada, by any Act[36] or Acts passed in the manner and subject to the conditions specified in the said last-recited Act of Parliament, to alter the constitution of the Legislative Council of the said Province by providing for the appointment or election of a Speaker of the said Council; and for this purpose to vary and repeal, in such manner as to them may seem fit, so much of the hereinbefore recited sections of the said Acts of Parliament, and of the provisions of the said recited or any other Acts of Parliament as relates to the appointment of such Speaker.

NOTES TO THE UNION ACT AND SUPPLEMENTARY ACTS.

1 This Act is 3 & 4 Vict. cap. 35. It is reprinted from the Imperial "Statutes at Large," London, 1841. Full reports of the discussions on the various stages of the measure in its progress through both Houses of Parliament are given in "Hansard's Parliamentary Debates," Third Series, vols. 52, 53, 54, and 55, (1840). The occasion of this legislation was the series of political disorders which culminated in the Rebellion of 1837-38. See Note 26 on the "Constitutional Act and Supplementary Acts" (p. 148). The Act was based on the recommendations contained in Lord Durham's Report, and is said to have been drafted by Chief Justice Stuart of Lower Canada under the direction of Governor Thomson, afterwards Lord Sydenham. It was strongly opposed in both the House of Commons and the House of Lords, but as Sir Robert Peel supported Lord John Russell in carrying it through the former, the opposition there was rather on specific clauses than on the principle of the bill. Protests against the third reading in the House of Lords were entered on the journals by the Duke of Wellington and Lord Ellenborough, the most prominent grounds in each case being the extent of the united provinces and the want of harmony between their populations.

2 See Lord Durham's Report, and Lord John Russell's speech on his motion for leave to introduce the measure in the House of Commons (Hansard, Third Series, vol. 52, pp. 1323-1354).

3 This proclamation was issued by Lord Sydenham on the 5th of February, 1841, and it declared that the union of the Provinces should take effect on the 10th of the same month. The text of the proclamation is given in the Journals of the Legislative Assembly for the first session of the first Provincial Parliament of Canada (1841).

4 The Constitutional Act, sections ii—xxxii. (pp. 112-123).

5 See pp. 136-139.

6 See pp. 142-145.

7 See pp. 106-107.

8 The Constitutional Act, 1791.

9 Very little objection was made to life-membership in the course of the debates on the bill in Parliament. Mr. Joseph Hume suggested that a portion of the Council should be chosen by the people, but the suggestion was not supported and was not pressed. See the "Union Act Amendment Act" of 1854 (pp. 177-179 below), which empowered the Canadian Parliament to alter the Constitution of the Legislative Council. See also the Act passed by the Canadian Parliament in 1856 (19 & 20 Vict., cap. 140), making the Legislative Council elective.

10 See pp. 136-139.

11 The effect of the operation of sections xiii-xx of the Union Act was to give Upper and Lower Canada each 42 members in the Legislative Assembly. By an Act (16 Vict., cap. 152), passed in 1853, under the authority conferred by section xxvi. of the Union Act, this number was increased to 65, and the membership of the Assembly then remained unchanged till 1867, when the British North America Act became law. The Statute of 1853 was entitled "An Act to enlarge the Representation of the People of this Province in Parliament," but it also effected an extensive redistribution of seats in the Assembly. It is worthy of note that in the same session a statute was passed extending the electoral franchise and providing a new system of registration of votes.

12 See pp. 136-139.

13 The first Parliament of Canada under the Union Act met at Kingston in 1841, but the place of meeting was changed to Montreal, where the second Parliament held its first session in 1844, in accordance with the expressed will of its predecessor. After the burning of the Parliament buildings in 1849 the Legislature resolved to meet alternately in Toronto and Quebec, and actually did so until the seat of Government became permanently fixed at Ottawa, as the result of the decision of Her Majesty, Queen Victoria, to whom the question had been referred by Parliament for arbitration. This decision was given in 1858, and in 1866 the Provincial Parliament met for the first and last time in Ottawa. For the reasons which led to the abandonment of Montreal see Walrond's "Letters and Journals of Lord Elgin," pp. 80-94. The fiction of allowing the Governor to choose the place of meeting of Parliament was kept up to the last under the Union Act (see proclamation naming Ottawa, Journals of Legislative Assembly for 1866, p. v.), but it was abolished by the Confederation Act, section 16, which fixed the seat of Government of Canada at Ottawa, subject to the Queen's pleasure.

14 The first Parliament met on the 14th of June, four months and four days after the union took effect. See Note 3.

15 This section appeared in the draft bill without the proviso, and when Mr. Charles Buller, who had, as Lord Durham's secretary, aided him in the preparation of his report, objected to the clause as "below the dignity of legislation on a great constitutional question," Lord John Russell explained that the intention was simply to require "the legal record of everything" to be in the English language. At the suggestion of Sir C. Grey the proviso, which now appears as part of the section, was added for the purpose of making it clear that there was no intention to prevent the use of translations of documents. It should be noted that neither the draft nor the section as finally passed assumed to forbid the use of the French language in debates, and as a matter of fact that language was so used from the beginning, the first Speaker, Mr. Cuvillier, being one of the French members of the first Parliament. On the 19th of June in the first session a series of "Rules" were adopted by the Legislative Assembly for the regulation of its own procedure. Rule 29 is as follows: "That copies of the Journals, translated into the French language, be laid on the table daily, for the use of the members; and also copies of Speeches from the Throne, Addresses, Messages, and Entries of other transactions and deliberations of the House, when asked for by any two members.' Rule 38 thus enacts: "When a motion is seconded, it shall be read in English and in French by the Speaker, if he is master of the two languages; if not, the Speaker shall read in either of the two languages most familiar to him; and the reading in the other language shall be at the table by the Clerk or his Deputy, before debate." In the same session an Act (4 & 5 Vic., cap. 11) was passed to provide for the translation of the Union Act and of the Provincial statutes into the French language, and their circulation among the French people. In the session of 1844-45 the Legislative Assembly resolved (Journals p. 61) that all bills and documents submitted to the House be printed in English and French, in equal proportions; but during the same session (Journals p. 265), the Speaker refused a motion written in French, on the ground that to receive it would be a violation of section xli. of the Union Act, and on an appeal to the House his decision was sustained. With reference to the repeal of section xli., see pp. 175-176 below.

16 During the session in which the Union Act was passed the Imperial Parliament passed an Act (3 & 4 Vict., cap. 78) dealing with the clergy reserves. Another Imperial Act, and the last (16 & 17 Vict., cap. 21), was passed in 1853, "to authorize the Legislature of the Province of Canada to make provision concerning the clergy reserves in that Province, and the proceeds thereof." Under the authority

conferred by the latter statute and by the Union Act, the clergy reserves were secularized in 1854 by Act of the Canadian Parliament (18 Vict., cap. 2).

17 The right of the Governor to endow rectories under the authority of the Constitutional Act, 1791, was taken away by Act of the Canadian Parliament (14 & 15 Vict., cap. 175) passed in 1851 and entitled "An Act respecting Rectories." This Act expressly left the legality of existing endowments to be settled by the courts of law, and a test case was submitted to the Court of Chancery in 1852. See note 14 to the "Constitutional Act and Supplementary Acts" (p. 147).

18 See pp. 104-105.

19 The name given to the Legislatures of Massachusetts and Connecticut.

20 See note 19 to the "Constitutional Act and Supplementary Acts" (p. 117).

21 Under the authority of 1 & 2 William IV., cap. 23. See pp. 106-107 above.

22 A motion was made in the House of Commons by Mr. Hume to cut down this amount to £25,000, and Viscount Howick suggested that the salary of the Governor should not be a charge on the revenues of the colony. Neither of these proposals was entertained by the House.

23 For the condition of Upper and Lower Canada, in the matter of municipal institutions at this date, see Lord Durham's report. The first municipal system, as that term is now used in this country, was created for Upper Canada in 1841 by Act of the first Parliament (4 & 5 Vict., cap. 10). Lord Sydenham took a warm interest in the measure, and was largely instrumental in securing its enactment. He had previously induced the Special Council of Lower Canada to establish a similar system in that Province, deeming it unlikely that the Legislature of the United Province would do so. See "Life of Lord Sydenham," by Poulett Scrope, pp. 176, 200-205, 216, 252-254. See also Sir Francis Hincks' "Reminiscences," pp. 63-68.

24 See p. 63 above.

25 See p. 91 above.

26 The only other Act of the same session dealing with Canadian affairs is the Clergy Reserve Act (3 & 4 Vict., cap. 78).

27 This Act is 11 & 12 Vict., cap. 56. For a brief account of the state of affairs which led to its passage see note 15 above. In the session of 1844-5 (see Journals, pp. 91, 223, 289, 300) an address was adopted, praying for the repeal by the Imperial Parliament of "so much of the Union Act as enacts that all public records and documents shall be in English only." In a despatch dated Feb. 3rd, 1846 (Legislative Assembly Journals p. 13), Mr. W. E. Gladstone acknowledges the receipt of the address, states that it had been "laid before the Queen," and informs Gen. Cathcart that "from regard to the wishes thus expressed by Her loyal subjects, Her Majesty is inclined to entertain the prayer of that address, and authorizes you to make a communication accordingly to the Legislative Bodies at the opening of the session." This intimation subdued the agitation, pending the passage of the Act of 1848. Hansard's "Parliamentary Debates" does not give any discussion of the bill in either House except two short speeches on the third reading in the House of Lords (Third Series, vol. 100, pp. 509-510), one by Lord Stanley deprecating the tendency the measure would probably have in raising up "a permanent barrier between two portions of the country, whose amalgamation was essential to the welfare of both"; the other by Earl Grey, containing a plea for "the principle of allowing all their local concerns to be regulated according to the wishes and feelings of the people of Canada." He added that the measure had been recommended by "three successive Governors-General."

AND SUPPLEMENTARY ACTS. 185

28 The removal of the restriction imposed by the Union Act was announced to the Canadian Parliament on the 18th of January, 1849, in a speech from the Throne, delivered by Lord Elgin, who warmly sympathized with the policy of allowing the French language to be reinstated. See Walrond's "Letters and Journals of Lord Elgin," pp. 54-57.

29 This Act is 17 & 18 Vict., cap. 118. The text is reprinted from the Imperial "Statutes at Large," London, 1855. It was passed in compliance with an address to the Queen from the Legislative Assembly of Canada, adopted, after a protracted debate and many divisions, on the second of June, 1853. See Journals of the Legislative Assembly of the session of 1852-53, pp. 197, and 922-946. For interesting debates on the Act at various stages of its progress, especially in the House of Lords, see "Hansard's Parliamentary Debates," Third Series, vol. 134, pp. 159, 501, 822, and vol. 135, p. 1319.

30 The Union Act, 1840 (sections iv-x).

31 See the address adopted by the Legislative Assembly of Canada (Journals of 1852-53, pp. 944-946); also the debates in the Imperial Parliament referred to in note 29 above.

32 See Canadian Statutes, 19 & 20 Vict., cap. 140, entitled "An Act to change the constitution of the Legislative Council by rendering the same elective." In compliance with the proviso appended to this section the Act was on the 16th of May, 1856, "reserved for the signification of Her Majesty's pleasure," but on the 24th of June of the same year it was assented to by the Queen in Council, and on the 14th of July following it was proclaimed by the Governor-General, Sir Edmund Walker Head.

33 See sections xxviii.-xxix. of the Union Act (p. 153). A property qualification continued to be required of members of the Legislative Assembly until the latter was brought to an end by the passage of the British North America Act, 1867 (see "Consolidated Statutes of Canada, 1859," cap. 6, ss. 36-37).

34 This Act is 22 & 23 Vict. cap. 10. The text is reprinted from the Imperial "Statutes at Large," London, 1860.

35 Cap. 140.

36 The Legislature of Canada did in 1860 pass an Act providing for the election of the Speaker by the Legislative Council, and the first member so elected was Sir Allan McNab (March 20, 1862.)

THE CONFEDERATION ACT, 1867, AND SUPPLEMENTARY ACTS.

An Act¹ for the Union of Canada, Nova Scotia, and New Brunswick, and the Government thereof; and for purposes connected therewith.

[29TH MARCH, 1867.

WHEREAS the Provinces of Canada, Nova Scotia, and New Brunswick² have expressed their desire to be federally united into one Dominion under the Crown of the United Kingdom of Great Britain and Ireland, with a constitution similar in principle to that of the United Kingdom :³

And whereas such a Union would conduce to the welfare of the Provinces and promote the interests of the British Empire :

And whereas on the establishment of the Union by authority of Parliament it is expedient, not only that the Constitution of the Legislative Authority in the Dominion be provided for, but also that the nature of the Executive Government therein be declared :

And whereas it is expedient that provision⁴ be made for the eventual admission into the Union of other parts of British North America :

Be it therefore enacted and declared by the Queen's most Excellent Majesty, by and with the advice and consent of the Lords Spiritual and Temporal, and Commons, in this present Parliament assembled, and by the authority of the same, as follows:

I.—PRELIMINARY.

Short title.

1. This Act may be cited as *The British North America Act, 1867.*

Application of provisions referring to the Queen.

2. The provisions of this Act referring to Her Majesty the Queen extend also to the heirs and successors of Her Majesty, Kings and Queens of the United Kingdom of Great Britain and Ireland.

II.—Union.

3. It shall be lawful for the Queen, by and with the advice of Her Majesty's Most Honourable Privy Council, to declare by Proclamation that, on and after a day therein appointed, not being more than six months after the passing of this Act, the Provinces of Canada, Nova Scotia, and New Brunswick shall form and be one Dominion under the name of Canada; and on and after that day those three Provinces shall form and be one Dominion under that name accordingly.⁵ *[Declaration of Union.]*

4. The subsequent provisions of this Act shall, unless it is otherwise expressed or implied, commence and have effect on and after the Union, that is to say, on and after the day appointed for the Union taking effect in the Queen's Proclamation; and in the same provisions, unless it is otherwise expressed or implied, the name Canada shall be taken to mean Canada as constituted under this Act. *[Construction of subsequent provisions of Act.]*

5. Canada shall be divided into four Provinces, named Ontario, Quebec, Nova Scotia, and New Brunswick. *[Four Provinces.]*

6. The parts of the Province of Canada (as it exists at the passing of this Act) which formerly constituted respectively the Provinces of Upper Canada and Lower Canada shall be deemed to be severed, and shall form two separate Provinces. The part which formerly⁶ constituted the Province of Upper Canada shall constitute the Province of Ontario; and the part which formerly constituted the Province of Lower Canada shall constitute the Province of Quebec. *[Provinces of Ontario and Quebec.]*

7. The Provinces of Nova Scotia and New Brunswick shall have the same limits as at the passing of this Act.⁷ *[Provinces of Nova Scotia and New Brunswick.]*

8. In the general census of the population of Canada, which is hereby required to be taken in the year one thousand eight hundred and seventy-one, and in every tenth year thereafter, the respective populations of the four Provinces shall be distinguished.⁸ *[Decennial Census.]*

III.—Executive Power.

9. The Executive Government and authority of and over Canada is hereby declared to continue and be vested in the Queen. *[Declaration of executive power in the Queen.]*

THE CONFEDERATION ACT

Application of provisions referring to Governor General.

10. The provisions of this Act referring to the Governor General extend and apply to the Governor General for the time being of Canada, or other the Chief Executive Officer or Administrator, for the time being carrying on the Government of Canada on behalf and in the name of the Queen, by whatever title he is designated.

Constitution of Privy Council for Canada.

11. There shall be a Council to aid and advise in the Government of Canada, to be styled the Queen's Privy Council for Canada; and the persons who are to be members of that Council shall be from time to time chosen and summoned by the Governor General and sworn in as Privy Councillors, and members thereof may be from time to time removed by the Governor General.

All powers under Acts to be exercised by Governor General with advice of Privy Council, or alone.

12. All powers, authorities, and functions which under any Act of the Parliament of Great Britain, or of the Parliament of the United Kingdom of Great Britain and Ireland, or of the Legislature of Upper Canada, Lower Canada, Canada, Nova Scotia, or New Brunswick, are at the Union vested in or exerciseable by the respective Governors or Lieutenant Governors of those Provinces, with the advice, or with the advice and consent, of the respective Executive Councils thereof, or in conjunction with those Councils, or with any number of members thereof, or by those Governors or Lieutenant Governors individually, shall, as far as the same continue in existence and capable of being exercised after the Union in relation to the Government of Canada, be vested in and exerciseable by the Governor General, with the advice or with the advice and consent of or in conjunction with the Queen's Privy Council for Canada, or any members thereof, or by the Governor General individually, as the case requires, subject nevertheless (except with respect to such as exist under Acts of the Parliament of Great Britain or of the Parliament of the United Kingdom of Great Britain and Ireland) to be abolished or altered by the Parliament of Canada.[9]

Application of provisions referring to Governor General in Council.

13. The provisions of this Act referring to the Governor General in Council shall be construed as referring to the Governor General acting by and with the advice of the Queen's Privy Council for Canada.

Power to Her Majesty to authorize Governor General to appoint Deputies.

14. It shall be lawful for the Queen, if Her Majesty thinks fit, to authorize the Governor General from time to time to appoint any person or any persons, jointly or severally, to be his Deputy or Deputies within any part or parts of Canada, and in that capacity to exercise during the pleasure of the Governor General such of the powers, authorities, and functions of the Governor General as the Governor General deems it necessary or expedient to assign to him or them, subject to any limitations or directions expressed or given by the Queen; but the appointment of such a Deputy or Deputies shall not affect the exercise by the Governor General himself of any power, authority or function.

15. The Command-in-Chief of the Land and Naval Militia, and of all Naval and Military Forces, of and in Canada, is hereby declared to continue and be vested in the Queen. Command of armed forces to continue to be vested in the Queen.

16. Until the Queen otherwise directs, the seat of Government of Canada shall be Ottawa.¹⁰ Seat of Government of Canada.

IV.—LEGISLATIVE POWER.

17. There shall be one Parliament for Canada, consisting of the Queen, an Upper House styled the Senate, and the House of Commons. Constitution of Parliament of Canada.

18. The privileges, immunities, and powers to be held, enjoyed, and exercised by the Senate and by the House of Commons, and by the members thereof respectively, shall be such as are from time to time defined by Act of the Parliament of Canada, but so that the same shall never exceed those at the passing of this Act held, enjoyed, and exercised by the Commons House of Parliament of the United Kingdom of Great Britain and Ireland and by the members thereof.¹¹ Privileges, &c. of Houses.

19. The [Parliament of Canada shall be called together not later than six months¹² after the Union. First Session of the Parliament of Canada.

20. There [shall be a Session of the Parliament of Canada once at least in every year, so that twelve months shall not intervene between the last sitting of the Parliament in one Session and its first sitting in the next Session.¹³ Yearly Session of the Parliament of Canada.

The Senate.

21. The Senate shall, subject to the provisions of this Act, consist of seventy-two¹⁴ members, who shall be styled Senators. Number of Senators.

Representation of Provinces in Senate.

22. In relation to the constitution of the Senate, Canada shall be deemed to consist of three divisions—
1. Ontario;
2. Quebec;
3. The Maritime Provinces, Nova Scotia and New Brunswick; which three divisions shall (subject to the provisions of this Act) be equally represented in the Senate as follows: Ontario by twenty-four Senators; Quebec by twenty-four Senators; and the Maritime Provinces by twenty-four Senators, twelve thereof representing Nova Scotia, and twelve thereof representing New Brunswick.[15]

In the case of Quebec each of the twenty-four Senators representing that Province shall be appointed for one of the twenty-four Electoral Divisions of Lower Canada specified in Schedule A. to chapter one of the Consolidated Statutes of Canada.

Qualifications of Senator.

23. The qualification of a Senator shall be as follows:—
(1) He shall be of the full age of thirty years:
(2) He shall be either a natural born subject of the Queen, or a subject of the Queen naturalized by an Act of the Parliament of Great Britain, or of the Parliament of the United Kingdom of Great Britain and Ireland, or of the Legislature of one of the Provinces of Upper Canada, Lower Canada, Canada, Nova Scotia, or New Brunswick, before the Union, or of the Parliament of Canada after the Union:
(3) He shall be legally or equitably seised as of freehold for his own use and benefit of lands or tenements held in free and common socage, or seised or possessed for his own use and benefit of lands or tenements held in franc-alleu or in roture, within the Province for which he is appointed, of the value of four thousand dollars, over and above all rents, dues, debts, charges, mortgages, and incumbrances due or payable out of or charged on or affecting the same:
(4) His real and personal property shall be together worth $4,000 over and above his debts and liabilities:
(5) He shall be resident in the Province for which he is appointed:

(6) In the case of Quebec he shall have his real property qualification in the Electoral Division for which he is appointed, or shall be resident in that Division.

24. The Governor General shall from time to time, in the Queen's name, by instrument under the Great Seal of Canada, summon qualified persons to the Senate ; and, subject to the provisions of this Act, every person so summoned shall become and be a member of the Senate and a Senator. *Summons of Senator.*

25. Such persons shall be first summoned to the Senate as the Queen by warrant under Her Majesty's Royal Sign Manual thinks fit to approve, and their names shall be inserted in the Queen's Proclamation of Union.[16] *Summons of first body of Senators.*

26. If at any time on the recommendation of the Governor General the Queen thinks fit to direct that three or six members be added to the Senate, the Governor General may by summons to three or six qualified persons (as the case may be), representing equally the three divisions of Canada, add to the Senate accordingly.[17] *Addition of Senators in certain cases.*

27. In case of such addition being at any time made the Governor General shall not summon any person to the Senate, except on a further like direction by the Queen on the like recommendation, until each of the three divisions of Canada is represented by twenty-four Senators and no more. *Reduction of Senate to normal number.*

28. The number of Senators shall not at any time exceed seventy-eight.[18] *Maximum number of Senators.*

29. A Senator shall, subject to the provisions of this Act, hold his place in the Senate for life. *Tenure of place in Senate.*

30. A Senator may by writing under his hand addressed to the Governor General resign his place in the Senate, and thereupon the same shall be vacant. *Resignation of place in Senate.*

31. The place of a Senator shall become vacant in any of the following cases : *Disqualification of Senators.*
(1) If for two consecutive Sessions of the Parliament he fails to give his attendance in the Senate :
(2) If he takes an oath or makes a declaration or acknowledgment of allegiance, obedience, or adherence to a foreign power, or does an act whereby he becomes a subject or citizen, or entitled to the rights or privileges of a subject or citizen of a foreign power.

(3) If he is adjudged bankrupt or insolvent, or applies for the benefit of any law relating to insolvent debtors, or becomes a public defaulter :

(4) If he is attainted of treason or convicted of felony or of any infamous crime :

(5) If he ceases to be qualified in respect of property or of residence; provided, that a Senator shall not be deemed to have ceased to be qualified in respect of residence by reason only of his residing at the seat of the Government of Canada while holding an office under that Government requiring his presence there.

Summons on vacancy in Senate.

32. When a vacancy happens in the Senate by resignation, death, or otherwise, the Governor General shall by summons to a fit and qualified person fill the vacancy.

Questions as to qualifications and vacancies in Senate.

33. If any question arises respecting the qualification of a Senator or a vacancy in the Senate the same shall be heard and determined by the Senate.

Appointment of Speaker of Senate.

34. The Governor General may from time to time, by instrument under the Great Seal of Canada, appoint a Senator to be Speaker of the Senate, and may remove him and appoint another in his stead.

Quorum of Senate.

35. Until the Parliament of Canada otherwise provides, the presence of at least fifteen Senators, including the Speaker, shall be necessary to constitute a meeting of the Senate for the exercise of its powers.

Voting in Senate.

36. Questions arising in the Senate shall be decided by a majority of voices, and the Speaker shall in all cases have a vote, and when the voices are equal the decision shall be deemed to be in the negative.

The House of Commons.

Constitution of House of Commons in Canada.

37. The House of Commons shall, subject to the provisions of this Act, consist of one hundred and eighty-one members, of whom eighty-two shall be elected for Ontario, sixty-five for Quebec, nineteen for Nova Scotia, and fifteen for New Brunswick.

Summoning of House of Commons.

38. The Governor General shall from time to time, in the Queen's name, by instrument under the Great Seal of Canada, summon and call together the House of Commons.

39. A Senator shall not be capable of being elected or of sitting or voting as a member of the House of Commons. Senators not to sit in House of Commons.

40. Until the Parliament of Canada otherwise provides, Ontario, Quebec, Nova Scotia, and New Brunswick shall, for the purposes of the election of members to serve in the House of Commons, be divided into Electoral Districts as follows:— Electoral districts of the four Provinces.

(1) Ontario shall be divided into the Counties, Ridings of Counties, Cities, parts of Cities, and Towns enumerated in the first Schedule to this Act, each whereof shall be an Electoral District, each such District as numbered in that Schedule being entitled to return one member.

(2) Quebec shall be divided into sixty-five Electoral Districts, composed of the sixty-five Electoral Divisions into which Lower Canada is at the passing of this Act divided under chapter two of the Consolidated Statutes of Canada, chapter seventy-five of the Consolidated Statutes for Lower Canada, and the Act of the Province of Canada of the twenty-third year of the Queen, chapter one, or any other Act amending the same in force at the Union, so that each such Electoral Division shall be for the purposes of this Act an Electoral District entitled to return one member.

(3) Each of the eighteen Counties of Nova Scotia shall be an Electoral District. The County of Halifax shall be entitled to return two members, and each of the other Counties one member.

(4) Each of the fourteen Counties into which New Brunswick is divided, including the City and County of St. John, shall be an Electoral District; the City of St. John shall also be a separate Electoral District. Each of those fifteen Electoral Districts shall be entitled to return one member.

41. Until the Parliament of Canada[19] otherwise provides, all laws in force in the several Provinces at the Union relative to the following matters or any of them, namely,— the qualifications and disqualifications of persons to be elected or to sit or vote as members of the House of Continuance of existing election laws until Parliament of Canada otherwise provides.

Assembly or Legislative Assembly in the several Provinces, the voters at elections of such members, the oaths to be taken by voters, the returning officers, their powers and duties, the proceedings at elections, the periods during which elections may be continued, the trial of controverted elections, and proceedings incident thereto, the vacating of seats of members, and the execution of new writs in case of seats vacated otherwise than by dissolution,—shall respectively apply to elections of members to serve in the House of Commons for the same several Provinces.

Provided that, until the Parliament of Canada otherwise provides, at any election for a Member of the House of Commons for the District of Algoma, in addition to persons qualified by the law of the Province of Canada to vote, every male British subject aged twenty-one years or upwards, being a householder, shall have a vote.

Writs for first election.

42. For the first election of members to serve in the House of Commons the Governor General shall cause writs to be issued by such person, in such form, and addressed to such returning officers as he thinks fit.

The person issuing writs under this section shall have the like powers as are possessed at the Union by the officers charged with the issuing of writs for the election of members to serve in the respective House of Assembly or Legislative Assembly of the Province of Canada, Nova Scotia, or New Brunswick; and the Returning Officers to whom writs are directed under this section shall have the like powers as are possessed at the Union by the officers charged with the returning of writs for the election of members to serve in the same respective House of Assembly or Legislative Assembly.

As to casual vacancies.

43. In case a vacancy in the representation in the House of Commons of any Electoral District happens before the meeting of the Parliament, or after the meeting of the Parliament before provision is made by the Parliament in this behalf, the provisions of the last foregoing section of this Act shall extend and apply to the issuing and returning of a writ in respect of such vacant District.

As to election of Speaker of House of Commons.

44. The House of Commons on its first assembling after a general election shall proceed with all practicable speed to elect one of its members to be Speaker.

45. In case of a vacancy happening in the office of Speaker by death, resignation or otherwise, the House of Commons shall with all practicable speed proceed to elect another of its members to be Speaker. *As to filling up vacancy in office of Speaker.*

46. The Speaker shall preside at all meetings of the House of Commons. *Speaker to preside.*

47. Until the Parliament of Canada otherwise provides, in case of the absence for any reason of the Speaker from the chair of the House of Commons for a period of forty-eight consecutive hours, the House may elect another of its members to act as Speaker,[20] and the member so elected shall during the continuance of such absence of the Speaker have and execute all the powers, privileges, and duties of Speaker. *Provision in case of absence of Speaker.*

48. The presence of at least twenty members of the House of Commons shall be necessary to constitute a meeting of the House for the exercise of its powers, and for that purpose the Speaker shall be reckoned as a member. *Quorum of House of Commons.*

49. Questions arising in the House of Commons shall be decided by a majority of voices other than that of the Speaker, and when the voices are equal, but not otherwise, the Speaker shall have a vote. *Voting in House of Commons.*

50. Every House of Commons shall continue for five years from the day of the return of the writs for choosing the House (subject to be sooner dissolved by the Governor General), and no longer. *Duration of House of Commons.*

51. On the completion of the census in the year one thousand eight hundred and seventy-one, and of each subsequent decennial census, the representation of the four Provinces shall be re-adjusted[21] by such authority, in such manner and from such time as the Parliament of Canada from time to time provides, subject and according to the following rules:— *Decennial Re-adjustment of Representation.*

(1) Quebec shall have the fixed number of sixty-five members:

(2) There shall be assigned to each of the other Provinces such a number of members as will bear the same proportion to the number of its population (ascertained at such census) as the number sixty-five bears to the number of the population of Quebec (so ascertained):

H.C.C. 13

(3) In the computation of the number of members for a Province a fractional part not exceeding one-half of the whole number requisite for entitling the Province to a member shall be disregarded; but a fractional part exceeding one-half of that number shall be equivalent to the whole number:

(4) On any such re-adjustment the number of members for a Province shall not be reduced unless the proportion which the number of the population of the Province bore to the number of the aggregate population of Canada at the then last preceding re-adjustment of the number of members for the Province is ascertained at the then latest census to be diminished by one-twentieth part or upwards:

(4) Such re-adjustment shall not take effect until the termination of the then existing Parliament.

Increase of number of House of Commons.

52. The number of members of the House of Commons may be from time to time increased by the Parliament of Canada, provided the proportionate representation of the Provinces prescribed by this Act is not thereby disturbed.

Money Votes; Royal Assent.

Appropriation and tax bills.

53. Bills for appropriating any part of the public revenue, or for imposing any tax or impost, shall originate in the House of Commons.[22]

Recommendation of money votes.

54. It shall not be lawful for the House of Commons to adopt or pass any vote, resolution, address, or bill for the appropriation of any part of the public revenue, or of any tax or impost, to any purpose that has not been first recommended to that House by message of the Governor General in the Session in which such vote, resolution, address, or bill is proposed.[23]

Royal assent to bills, &c.

55. Where a bill passed by the Houses of the Parliament is presented to the Governor General for the Queen's assent, he shall declare according to his discretion, but subject to the provisions of this Act and to Her Majesty's instructions, either that he assents thereto in the Queen's name, or that he withholds the Queen's assent, or that he reserves the bill for the signification of the Queen's pleasure.

Disallowance by Order in Council of Act

56. Where the Governor General assents to a bill in the Queen's name, he shall by the first convenient opportunity send an authentic copy of the Act to one of Her Majesty's Principal Secretaries of State, and if the Queen in Council within two years after receipt thereof by the Secretary of State thinks fit to disallow the Act, such disallowance (with a certificate of the Secretary of State of the day on which the Act was received by him) being signified by the Governor General, by speech or message to each of the Houses of the Parliament, or by proclamation, shall annul the Act from and after the day of such signification.[24] assented to by Governor General.

57. A bill reserved for the signification of the Queen's pleasure shall not have any force unless and until within two years from the day on which it was presented to the Governor General for the Queen's assent, the Governor General signifies, by speech or message to each of the Houses of the Parliament or by proclamation, that it has received the assent of the Queen in Council.[25] Signification of Queen's pleasure on bill reserved.

An entry of every such speech, message, or proclamation shall be made in the Journal of each House, and a duplicate thereof duly attested shall be delivered to the proper officer to be kept among the Records of Canada.

V.—PROVINCIAL CONSTITUTIONS.

Executive Power.

58. For each Province there shall be an officer, styled the Lieutenant Governor, appointed by the Governor General in Council by instrument under the Great Seal of Canada. Appointment of Lieutenant Governors of Provinces.

59. A Lieutenant Governor shall hold office during the pleasure of the Governor General; but any Lieutenant Governor appointed after the commencement of the first Session of the Parliament of Canada shall not be removeable within five years from his appointment, except for cause assigned,[26] which shall be communicated to him in writing within one month after the order for his removal is made, and shall be communicated by message to the Senate and to the House of Commons within one week thereafter if the Parliament is then sitting, and if not then within one week after the commencement of the next Session of the Parliament. Tenure of office of Lieutenant Governor.

60. The salaries of the Lieutenant Governors shall be fixed and provided by the Parliament of Canada. Salaries of Lieutenant Governors.

Oaths, &c., of Lieutenant Governor.	**61.** Every Lieutenant Governor shall, before assuming the duties of his office, make and subscribe before the Governor General, or some person authorized by him, oaths of allegiance and office similar to those taken by the Governor General.
Application of provisions referring to Lieutenant Governor.	**62.** The provisions of this Act referring to the Lieutenant Governor extend and apply to the Lieutenant Governor for the time being of each Province or other the chief executive officer or administrator for the time being carrying on the government of the Province, by whatever title he is designated.
Appointment of executive officers for Ontario and Quebec.	**63.** The Executive Council of Ontario and of Quebec shall be composed of such persons as the Lieutenant Governor from time to time thinks fit, and in the first instance of the following officers, namely:—The Attorney-General, the Secretary and Registrar of the Province, the Treasurer of the Province, the Commissioner of Crown Lands, and the Commissioner of Agriculture and Public Works, with in Quebec the Speaker of the Legislative Council and the Solicitor General.[27]
Executive Government of Nova Scotia and New Brunswick.	**64.** The Constitution of the Executive Authority in each of the Provinces of Nova Scotia and New Brunswick shall, subject to the provisions of this Act, continue as it exists at the Union until altered under the authority of this Act.
Powers to be exercised by Lieutenant Governor of Ontario or Quebec with advice alone.	**65.** All powers, authorities, and functions which under any Act of the Parliament of Great Britain, or of the Parliament of the United Kingdom of Great Britain and Ireland, or of the Legislature of Upper Canada, Lower Canada, or Canada, were or are before or at the Union vested in or exerciseable by the respective Governors or Lieutenant Governors of those Provinces, with the advice, or with the advice and consent, of the respective Executive Councils thereof, or in conjunction with those Councils, or with any number of members thereof, or by those Governors or Lieutenant Governors individually, shall, as far as the same are capable of being exercised after the Union in relation to the Government of Ontario and Quebec, respectively, be vested in, and shall or may be exercised by the Lieutenant Governor of Ontario and Quebec respectively, with the advice or with the advice and consent of or in conjunction with the respective Executive Councils,

or any members thereof, or by the Lieutenant Governor individually, as the case requires, subject nevertheless (except with respect to such as exist under Acts of the Parliament of Great Britain, or of the Parliament of the United Kingdom of Great Britain and Ireland), to be abolished or altered by the respective Legislatures of Ontario and Quebec.²⁸

66. The provisions of this Act referring to the Lieutenant Governor in Council shall be construed as referring to the Lieutenant Governor of the Province acting by and with the advice of the Executive Council thereof. Application of provisions referring to Lieutenant Governor in Council.

67. The Governor General in Council may from time to time appoint an administrator to execute the office and functions of Lieutenant Governor during his absence, illness, or other inability. Administration in absence, &c., of Lieutenant Governor.

68. Unless and until the Executive Government of any Province otherwise directs with respect to that Province, the seats of Government of the Provinces shall be as follows, namely,—of Ontario, the City of Toronto; of Quebec, the City of Quebec; of Nova Scotia, the City of Halifax; and of New Brunswick, the City of Fredericton.²⁹ Seats of Provincial Governments.

Legislative Power.

1. — ONTARIO.

69. There shall be a Legislature for Ontario consisting of the Lieutenant Governor and of one House,³⁰ styled the Legislative Assembly of Ontario. Legislature for Ontario.

70. The Legislative Assembly of Ontario shall be composed of eighty-two members, to be elected to represent the eighty-two Electoral Districts set forth in the first Schedule to this Act.³¹ Electoral districts.

2.—QUEBEC.

71. There shall be a Legislature for Quebec consisting of the Lieutenant Governor and of two Houses, styled the Legislative Council of Quebec and the Legislative Assembly of Quebec. Legislature for Quebec.

72. The Legislative Council of Quebec shall be composed of twenty-four members, to be appointed by the Lieutenant Governor in the Queen's name, by instrument Constitution of Legislative Council.

under the Great Seal of Quebec, one being appointed to represent each of the twenty-four Electoral Divisions of Lower Canada in this Act referred to, and each holding office for the term of his life, unless the Legislature of Quebec otherwise provides under the provisions of this Act.[32]

Qualification of Legislative Councillors.

73. The qualifications of the Legislative Councillors of Quebec shall be the same as those of the Senators for Quebec.[33]

Resignation, disqualification, &c.

74. The place of a Legislative Councillor of Quebec shall become vacant in the cases, *mutatis mutandis*, in which the place of Senator becomes vacant.[34]

Vacancies.

75. When a vacancy happens in the Legislative Council of Quebec, by resignation, death, or otherwise, the Lieutenant Governor, in the Queen's name, by instrument under the Great Seal of Quebec, shall appoint a fit and qualified person to fill the vacancy.

Questions as to vacancies, &c.

76. If any question arises respecting the qualification of a Legislative Councillor of Quebec, or a vacancy in the Legislative Council of Quebec, the same shall be heard and determined by the Legislative Council.

Speaker of Legislative Council.

77. The Lieutenant Governor may from time to time, by instrument under the Great Seal of Quebec, appoint a member of the Legislative Council of Quebec to be Speaker thereof, and may remove him and appoint another in his stead.

Quorum of Legislative Council.

78. Until the Legislature of Quebec otherwise provides, the presence of at least ten members of the Legislative Council, including the Speaker, shall be necessary to constitute a meeting for the exercise of its powers.

Voting in Legislative Council.

79. Questions arising in the Legislative Council of Quebec shall be decided by a majority of voices, and the Speaker shall in all cases have a vote, and when the voices are equal the decision shall be deemed to be in the negative.

Constitution of Legislative Assembly of Quebec.

80. The Legislative Assembly of Quebec shall be composed of sixty-five members, to be elected to represent the sixty-five Electoral Divisions or Districts of Lower Canada in this Act referred to, subject to alteration[35] thereof by the Legislature of Quebec: Provided that it shall not be lawful to present to the Lieutenant Governor of Quebec for assent any bill for altering the limits of any of the Electoral Divisions or Districts mentioned in the second Schedule to this Act, unless the second and third readings of such bill have been passed in the Legislative Assembly with the concurrence of the majority of the members representing all those Electoral Divisions or Districts, and the assent shall not be given to such bills unless an address has been presented by the Legislative Assembly to the Lieutenant Governor stating that it has been so passed.

3.--ONTARIO AND QUEBEC.

§1. The Legislatures of Ontario and Quebec respectively shall be called together not later than six months after the Union.³⁶ *First session of Legislatures.*

§2. The Lieutenant Governor of Ontario and of Quebec shall from time to time, in the Queen's name, by instrument under the Great Seal of the Province, summon and call together the Legislative Assembly of the Province. *Summoning of Legislative Assemblies.*

§3. Until the Legislature of Ontario or of Quebec otherwise provides, a person accepting or holding in Ontario or in Quebec any office, commission, or employment, permanent or temporary, at the nomination of the Lieutenant Governor, to which an annual salary, or any fee, allowance, emolument, or profit of any kind or amount whatever from the Province is attached, shall not be eligible as a member of the Legislative Assembly of the respective Province, nor shall he sit or vote as such; but nothing in this section shall make ineligible any person being a member of the Executive Council of the respective Province, or holding any of the following offices, that is to say, the offices of Attorney-General, Secretary and Registrar of the Province, Treasurer of the Province, Commissioner of Crown Lands, and Commissioner of Agriculture and Public Works, and, in Quebec, Solicitor-General³⁷, or shall disqualify him to sit or vote in the House for which he is elected, provided he is elected while holding such office. *Restriction on election of holders of offices.*

§4. Until the Legislatures of Ontario and Quebec respectively otherwise provide, all laws which at the Union are in force in those Provinces respectively, relative to the following matters, or any of them, namely,—the qualifications and disqualifications of persons to be elected or to sit or vote as members of the Assembly of Canada, the qualifications or disqualifications of voters, the oaths to be *Continuance of existing election laws.*

taken by voters, the Returning Officers, their powers and duties, the proceedings at elections, the periods during which such elections may be continued, and the trial of controverted elections*ⁿ* and the proceedings incident thereto, the vacating of the seats of members and the issuing and execution of new writs in case of seats vacated otherwise than by dissolution, shall respectively apply to elections of members to serve in the respective Legislative Assemblies of Ontario and Quebec.

Provided that until the Legislature of Ontario otherwise provides, at any election for a member of the Legislative Assembly of Ontario for the District of Algoma, in addition to persons qualified by the law of the Province of Canada to vote, every male British subject, aged twenty-one years or upwards, being a householder, shall have a vote.

<small>Duration of Legislative Assemblies.</small>

85. Every Legislative Assembly of Ontario and every Legislative Assembly of Quebec shall continue for four years from the day of the return of the writs for choosing the same (subject nevertheless to either the Legislative Assembly of Ontario or the Legislative Assembly of Quebec being sooner dissolved by the Lieutenant Governor of the Province), and no longer.

<small>Yearly session of Legislature.</small>

86. There shall be a session of the Legislature of Ontario and of that of Quebec once at least in every year, so that twelve months shall not intervene between the last sitting of the Legislature in each Province in one session and its first sitting in the next session.

<small>Speaker, quorum, &c.</small>

87. The following provisions of this Act respecting the House of Commons of Canada, shall extend and apply to the Legislative Assemblies of Ontario and Quebec, that is to say,—the provisions relating to the election of a Speaker originally and on vacancies, the duties of the Speaker, the absence of the Speaker, the quorum, and the mode of voting, as if those provisions were here re-enacted and made applicable in terms to each such Legislative Assembly.

4.—Nova Scotia and New Brunswick.

<small>Constitutions of Legislatures of Nova Scotia and New Brunswick.</small>

88. The constitution of the Legislature of each of the Provinces of Nova Scotia and New Brunswick shall, subject to the provisions of this Act, continue as it exists at the Union until altered under the authority of this Act; and the House of Assembly of New Brunswick existing at the passing of this Act shall, unless sooner dissolved, continue for the period for which it was elected.

5.—Ontario, Quebec, and Nova Scotia.

89. Each of the Lieutenant Governors of Ontario, Quebec, and Nova Scotia shall cause writs to be issued for the first election of members of the Legislative Assembly thereof in such form and by such person as he thinks fit, and at such time and addressed to such Returning Officer as the Governor General directs, and so that the first election of member of Assembly for any Electoral District or any subdivision thereof shall be held at the same time and at the same places as the election for a member to serve in the House of Commons of Canada for that Electoral District.

First election.

6.—The Four Provinces.

90. The following provisions of this Act respecting the Parliament of Canada, namely,—the provisions relating to appropriation and tax bills, the recommendation of money votes, the assent to bills, the disallowance of Acts, and the signification of pleasure on bills reserved,—shall extend and apply to the Legislatures of the several Provinces as if those provisions were here re-enacted and made applicable in terms to the respective Provinces and the Legislatures thereof, with the substitution of the Lieutenant Governor of the Province for the Governor General, of the Governor General for the Queen and for a Secretary of State, of one year for two years, and of the Province for Canada.

Application to Legislatures of provisions respecting money votes, &c.

VI.—DISTRIBUTION OF LEGISLATIVE POWERS.

Powers of the Parliament.

91. It shall be lawful for the Queen, by and with the advice and consent of the Senate and House of Commons, to make laws for the peace, order, and good government of Canada, in relation to all matters not coming within the classes of subjects by this Act assigned exclusively to the Legislatures of the Provinces; and for greater certainty, but not so as to restrict the generality of the foregoing terms of this section, it is hereby declared that (notwithstanding anything in this Act) the exclusive legislative

Legislative authority of Parliament of Canada.

authority of the Parliament of Canada extends to all matters coming within the classes of subjects next hereinafter enumerated ; that is to say,—

1. The Public Debt and Property.
2. The regulation of Trade and Commerce.39
3. The raising of money by any mode or system of Taxation.
4. The borrowing of money on the public credit.
5. Postal service.
6. The Census and Statistics.
7. Militia, Military and Naval Service, and Defence.
8. The fixing of and providing for the salaries and allowances of civil and other officers of the Government of Canada.40
9. Beacons, Buoys, Lighthouses, and Sable Island.
10. Navigation and Shipping.
11. Quarantine and the establishment and maintenance of Marine Hospitals.
12. Sea coast and inland Fisheries.41
13. Ferries between a Province and any British or Foreign country, or between two Provinces.
14. Currency and Coinage.
15. Banking, incorporation of banks, and the issue of paper money.
16. Savings Banks.
17. Weights and Measures.
18. Bills of Exchange and Promissory Notes.
19. Interest.
20. Legal tender.
21. Bankruptcy and Insolvency.
22. Patents of invention and discovery.
23. Copyrights.42
24. Indians, and lands reserved for the Indians.43
25. Naturalization and Aliens.
26. Marriage and Divorce.
27. The Criminal Law, except the Constitution of Courts of Criminal Jurisdiction, but including the Procedure in Criminal Matters.
28. The Establishment, Maintenance, and Management of Penitentiaries.
29. Such classes of subjects as are expressly excepted in the enumeration of the classes of subjects by this Act assigned exclusively to the Legislatures of the Provinces.

And any matter coming within any of the classes of subjects enumerated in this section shall not be deemed to come within the class of matters of a local or private nature comprised in the enumeration of the classes of subjects by this Act assigned exclusively to the Legislatures of the Provinces.

Exclusive Powers of Provincial Legislatures.

92. In each Province the Legislature may exclusively make laws in relation to matters coming within the classes of subjects next hereinafter enumerated; that is to say,— *Subjects of exclusive Provincial legislation.*

1. The amendment from time to time, notwithstanding anything in this Act, of the Constitution of the Province, except as regards the office of Lieutenant Governor.[44]
2. Direct Taxation within the Province in order to the raising of a Revenue for Provincial purposes.[45]
3. The borrowing of money on the sole credit of the Province.
4. The establishment and tenure of Provincial offices and the appointment and payment of Provincial officers.
5. The management and sale of the Public Lands belonging to the Province and of the timber and wood thereon.
6. The establishment, maintenance, and management of public and reformatory prisons in and for the Province.
7. The establishment, maintenance, and management of hospitals, asylums, charities, and eleemosynary institutions in and for the Province, other than marine hospitals.
8. Municipal institutions in the Province.[46]
9. Shop, saloon, tavern, auctioneer, and other licenses in order to the raising of a revenue for Provincial, local, or municipal purposes.[46]
10. Local works and undertakings other than such as are of the following classes,—
    a. Lines of steam or other ships, railways, canals, telegraphs, and other works and undertakings connecting the Province with any other or others of the Provinces, or extending beyond the limits of the Province:
    b. Lines of steamships between the Province and any British or foreign country.
    c. Such works as, although wholly situate within the Province, are before or after their execution declared by the Parliament of Canada to be for the general advantage of Canada or for the advantage of two or more of the Provinces.[47]
11. The incorporation of companies with Provincial objects.
12. The solemnization of marriage in the Province.
13. Property and civil rights in the Province.[48]
14. The administration of justice in the Province, including the constitution, maintenance, and organization of Provincial Courts, both of civil and of criminal jurisdiction, and including procedure in Civil matters in those Courts.[49]
15. The imposition of punishment by fine, penalty, or imprisonment for enforcing any law of the Province made in relation to any matter coming within any of the classes of subjects enumerated in this section.[50]
16. Generally all matters of a merely local or private nature in the Province.

Education.

Legislation respecting education.

93. In and for each Province the Legislature may exclusively make laws in relation to education, subject and according to the following provisions:

(1) Nothing in any such law shall prejudicially affect any right or privilege with respect to denominational schools which any class of persons have by law in the Province at the Union.

(2) All the powers, privileges, and duties at the Union by law conferred and imposed in Upper Canada on the separate schools and school trustees of the Queen's Roman Catholic subjects shall be and the same are hereby extended to the dissentient schools of the Queen's Protestant and Roman Catholic subjects in Quebec :

(3) Where in any Province a system of separate or dissentient schools exists by law at the Union or is thereafter established by the Legislature of the Province, an appeal shall lie to the Governor General in Council from any Act or decision of any Provincial authority affecting any right or privilege of the Protestant or Roman Catholic minority of the Queen's subjects in relation to education :[51]

(4) In case any such Provincial law as from time to time seems to the Governor General in Council requisite for the due execution of the provisions of this section is not made, or in case any decision of the Governor General in Council on any appeal under this section is not duly executed by the proper Provincial authority in that behalf, then and in every such case, and as far only as the circumstances of each case require, the Parliament of Canada may make remedial laws for the due execution of the provisions of this section and of any decision of the Governor General in Council under this section.[52]

Uniformity of Laws in Ontario, Nova Scotia, and New Brunswick.

Legislation for uniformity of laws in the three Provinces.

94. Notwithstanding anything in this Act, the Parliament of Canada may make provision for the uniformity of all or any of the laws relative to property and civil rights in Ontario, Nova Scotia, and New Brunswick, and of the procedure of all or any of the Courts in those three Provinces; and from and after the passing of any Act in that behalf the power of the Parliament of Canada to make laws in relation to any matter comprised in any such Act shall, notwithstanding anything in this Act, be unrestricted; but any Act of the Parliament of Canada making provision for such uniformity shall not have effect in any Province unless and until it is adopted and enacted as law by the Legislature thereof.[53]

Agriculture and Immigration.

95. In each Province the Legislature may make laws in relation to Agriculture in the Province, and to Immigration into the Province; and it is hereby declared that the Parliament of Canada may from time to time make laws in relation to Agriculture in all or any of the Provinces, and to Immigration into all or any of the Provinces; and any law of the Legislature of a Province relative to Agriculture or to Immigration shall have effect in and for the Province as long and as far only as it is not repugnant to any Act of the Parliament of Canada. Concurrent powers of Legislation respecting Agriculture, &c.

VII.—JUDICATURE.

96. The Governor General shall appoint the Judges of the Superior, District, and County Courts[54] in each Province, except those of the Courts of Probate in Nova Scotia and New Brunswick. Appointment of Judges.

97. Until the laws relative to property and civil rights in Ontario, Nova Scotia, and New Brunswick, and the procedure of the Courts in those Provinces, are made uniform, the Judges of the Courts of those Provinces appointed by the Governor General shall be selected from the respective Bars of those Provinces. Selection of Judges in Ontario, &c.

98. The Judges of the Courts of Quebec shall be selected from the Bar of that Province. Selection of Judges in Quebec.

99. The Judges of the Superior Courts shall hold office during good behaviour, but shall be removeable by the Governor General on address of the Senate and House of Commons.[55] Tenure of office of Judges of Superior Courts.

Salaries, &c., of Judges.

100. The salaries, allowances, and pensions of the Judges of the Superior, District, and County Courts (except the Courts of Probate in Nova Scotia and New Brunswick), and of the Admiralty Courts in cases where the Judges thereof are for the time being paid by salary, shall be fixed and provided by the Parliament of Canada.

General Court of Appeal, &c.

101. The Parliament of Canada may, notwithstanding anything in this Act, from time to time, provide for the constitution, maintenance, and organization of a general Court of Appeal for Canada, and for the establishment of any additional Courts for the better administration of the Laws of Canada.[56]

VIII.—REVENUES; DEBTS; ASSETS; TAXATION.

Creation of Consolidated Revenue Fund.

102. All duties and revenues[57] over which the respective Legislatures of Canada, Nova Scotia, and New Brunswick before and at the Union had and have power of appropriation, except such portions thereof as are by this Act reserved to the respective Legislatures of the Provinces, or are raised by them in accordance with the special powers conferred on them by this Act, shall form one Consolidated Revenue Fund, to be appropriated for the public service of Canada in the manner and subject to the charges in this Act provided.

Expenses of collection, &c.

103. The Consolidated Revenue Fund of Canada shall be permanently charged with the costs, charges, and expenses incident to the collection, management, and receipt thereof, and the same shall form the first charge thereon, subject to be reviewed and audited in such manner as shall be ordered by the Governor General in Council until the Parliament otherwise provides.

Interest of Provincial public debts.

104. The annual interest of the public debts of the several Provinces of Canada, Nova Scotia, and New Brunswick at the Union shall form the second charge on the Consolidated Revenue Fund of Canada.

Salary of Governor General.

105. Unless altered by the Parliament of Canada, the salary of the Governor General shall be ten thousand pounds sterling money[58] of the United Kingdom of Great Britain and Ireland, payable out of the Consolidated Revenue Fund of Canada, and the same shall form the third charge thereon.

106. Subject to the several payments by this Act charged on the Consolidated Revenue Fund of Canada, the same shall be appropriated by the Parliament of Canada for the public service. Appropriation from time to time.

107. All stocks, cash, banker's balances, and securities for money belonging to each Province at the time of the Union, except as in this Act mentioned, shall be the property of Canada, and shall be taken in reduction of the amount of the respective debts of the Provinces at the Union. Transfer, &c., of stocks.

108. The public works and property of each Province, enumerated in the third schedule to this Act, shall be the property of Canada. Transfer of property in schedule.

109. All lands,[50] mines, minerals, and royalties[60] belonging to the several Provinces of Canada, Nova Scotia and New Brunswick at the Union, and all sums then due or payable for such lands, mines, minerals, or royalties, shall belong to the several Provinces of Ontario, Quebec, Nova Scotia and New Brunswick in which the same are situate or arise, subject to any trusts existing in respect thereof, and to any interest other than that of the Province in the same. Property in lands, mines, &c.

110. All assets connected with such portions of the public debt of each Province as are assumed by that Province shall belong to that Province. Assets connected with Provincial debts.

111. Canada shall be liable for the debts and liabilities of each Province existing at the Union. Canada to be liable to Provincial debts.

112. Ontario and Quebec conjointly shall be liable to Canada for the amount (if any) by which the debt of the Province of Canada exceeds at the Union sixty-two million five hundred thousand dollars, and shall be charged with interest at the rate of five per centum per annum thereon. Debts of Ontario and Quebec.

113. The assets enumerated in the fourth Schedule to this Act belonging at the Union to the Province of Canada shall be the property of Ontario and Quebec conjointly. Assets of Ontario and Quebec.

114. Nova Scotia shall be liable to Canada for the amount (if any) by which its public debt exceeds at the Union eight million dollars, and shall be charged with interest at the rate of five per centum per annum thereon. Debt of Nova Scotia.

Debt of New Brunswick.

115. New Brunswick shall be liable to Canada for the amount (if any) by which its public debt exceeds at the Union seven million dollars, and shall be charged with interest at the rate of five per centum per annum thereon.

Payment of interest to Nova Scotia and New Brunswick.

116. In case the public debt of Nova Scotia and New Brunswick do not at the Union amount to eight million dollars and seven million dollars respectively, they shall respectively receive by half-yearly payments in advance from the Government of Canada interest at five per centum per annum on the difference between the actual amounts of their respective debts and such stipulated amounts.[61]

Provincial public property.

117. The several Provinces shall retain all their respective public property not otherwise disposed of in this Act, subject to the right of Canada to assume any lands or public property required for fortifications or for the defence of the country.

Grants to Provinces.

118. The following sums shall be paid yearly by Canada to the several Provinces for the support of their Governments and Legislatures :—

	Dollars.
Ontario	Eighty thousand.
Quebec	Seventy thousand.
Nova Scotia	Sixty thousand.
New Brunswick	Fifty thousand.

Two hundred and sixty thousand ;

and an annual grant in aid of each Province shall be made, equal to eighty cents per head of the population as ascertained by the census of one thousand eight hundred and sixty-one, and in the case of Nova Scotia and New Brunswick, by each subsequent decennial census until the population of each of those two Provinces amounts to four hundred thousand souls, at which rate such grant shall thereafter remain. Such grants shall be in full settlement of all future demands[61] on Canada, and shall be paid half-yearly in advance to each Province ; but the Government of Canada shall deduct from such grants, as against any Province, all sums chargeable as interest on the Public Debt of that Province in excess of the several amounts stipulated in this Act.

119. New Brunswick shall receive by half-yearly payments in advance from Canada, for the period of ten years from the Union an additional allowance of sixty-three thousand dollars per annum; but as long as the Public Debt of that Province remains under seven million dollars a deduction equal to the interest at five per centum per annum on such deficiency shall be made from that allowance of sixty-three thousand dollars. *Further grant to New Brunswick.*

120. All payments to be made under this Act, or in discharge of liabilities created under any Act of the Provinces of Canada, Nova Scotia and New Brunswick respectively, and assumed by Canada, shall, until the Parliament of Canada otherwise directs, be made in such form and manner as may from time to time be ordered by the Governor General in Council. *Form of payments.*

121. All articles of the growth, produce, or manufacture of any one of the Provinces shall, from and after the Union, be admitted free into each of the other Provinces. *Canadian manufactures, &c.*

122. The Customs and Excise Laws of each Province shall, subject to the provisions of this Act, continue in force until altered by the Parliament of Canada. *Continuance of customs and excise laws.*

123. Where Customs duties are, at the Union, leviable on any goods, wares, or merchandises in any two Provinces, those goods, wares and merchandises may, from and after the Union, be imported from one of those Provinces into the other of them on proof of payment of the Customs duty leviable thereon in the Province of exportation, and on payment of such further amount (if any) of Customs duty as is leviable thereon in the Province of importation. *Exportation and importation as between two Provinces,*

124. Nothing in this Act shall affect the right of New Brunswick to levy the lumber dues[63] provided in chapter fifteen, of title three, of the Revised Statutes of New Brunswick, or in any Act amending that Act before or after the Union, and not increasing the amount of such dues; but the lumber of any of the Provinces other than New Brunswick shall not be subjected to such dues. *Lumber dues in New Brunswick.*

125. No lands or property belonging to Canada or any Province shall be liable to taxation. *Exemption of public lands, &c.*

H.C.C. 14

Provincial Consolidated Revenue Fund.

126. Such portions of the duties and revenues over which the respective Legislatures of Canada, Nova Scotia, and New Brunswick had before the Union power of appropriation as are by this Act reserved to the respective Governments or Legislatures of the Provinces, and all duties and revenues raised by them in accordance with the special powers conferred upon them by this Act, shall in each Province form one Consolidated Revenue Fund to be appropriated for the public service of the Province.

IX.—MISCELLANEOUS PROVISIONS.

General.

As to Legislative Councillors of Provinces becoming Senators.

127. If any person being at the passing of this Act a Member of the Legislative Council of Canada, Nova Scotia, or New Brunswick, to whom a place in the Senate is offered, does not within thirty days thereafter, by writing under his hand, addressed to the Governor General of the Province of Canada, or to the Lieutenant Governor of Nova Scotia or New Brunswick (as the case may be), accept the same, he shall be deemed to have declined the same; and any person who, being at the passing of this Act a member of the Legislative Council of Nova Scotia or New Brunswick, accepts a place in the Senate, shall thereby vacate his seat in such Legislative Council.⁶³

Oath of allegiance, &c.

128. Every member of the Senate or House of Commons of Canada shall before taking his seat therein, take and subscribe before the Governor General or some person authorised by him, and every member of a Legislative Council or Legislative Assembly of any Province shall before taking his seat therein, take and subscribe before the Lieutenant Governor of the Province or some person authorized by him, the oath of allegiance contained in the fifth Schedule to this Act; and every member of the Senate of Canada and every member of the Legislative Council of Quebec shall also, before taking his seat therein, take and subscribe before the Governor General or some person authorized by him, the declaration of qualification contained in the same Schedule.

Continuance of existing laws, courts, officers, &c.

129. Except as otherwise provided by this Act, all laws in force in Canada, Nova Scotia or New Brunswick at the Union, and all courts of civil and criminal jurisdiction, and all legal commissions, powers and authorities, and all officers, judicial, administrative and ministerial, existing therein at the Union, shall continue in Ontario, Quebec, Nova Scotia, and New Brunswick respectively, as if the Union had not been made, subject nevertheless (except with respect to such as are enacted by or exist under Acts of the Parliament of Great Britain, or of the Parliament of the United Kingdom of Great Britain and Ireland), to be repealed, abolished or altered by the Parliament of Canada, or by the Legislature of the respective Province, according to the authority of the Parliament or of that Legislature under this Act.

130. Until the Parliament of Canada otherwise provides, all officers of the several Provinces having duties to discharge in relation to matters other than those coming within the classes of subjects by this Act assigned exclusively to the Legislatures of the Provinces shall be officers of Canada, and shall continue to discharge the duties of their respective offices under the same liabilities, responsibilities, and penalties as if the Union had not been made. *Transfer of officers to Canada.*

131. Until the Parliament of Canada otherwise provides, the Governor General in Council may from time to time appoint such officers as the Governor General in Council deems necessary or proper for the effectual execution of this Act. *Appointment of new officers.*

132. The Parliament and Government of Canada shall have all powers necessary or proper for performing the obligations of Canada or of any Province thereof, as part of the British Empire, towards foreign countries, arising under treaties between the Empire and such foreign countries.[64] *Treaty obligations.*

133. Either the English or the French language may be used by any person in the debates of the Houses of the Parliament of Canada and of the Houses of the Legislature of Quebec; and both those languages shall be used in the respective records and journals of those houses; and either of those languages may be used by any person or in any pleading or process in or issuing from any Court of Canada established under this Act, and in or from all or any of the Courts of Quebec. *Use of English and French languages.*

The Acts of the Parliament of Canada and of the Legislature of Quebec shall be printed and published in both those languages.⁶⁵

Ontario and Quebec.

Appointment of executive officers for Ontario and Quebec.

134. Until the Legislature of Ontario or of Quebec otherwise provides, the Lieutenant Governors of Ontario and Quebec may each appoint under the Great Seal of the Province the following officers,⁶⁶ to hold office during pleasure, that is to say,—the Attorney General, the Secretary and Registrar of the Province, the Treasurer of the Province, the Commissioner of Crown Lands, and the Commissioner of Agriculture and Public Works, and, in the case of Quebec, the Solicitor General; and may, by order of the Lieutenant Governor in Council, from time to time prescribe the duties of those officers and of the several departments over which they shall preside or to which they shall belong, and of the officers and clerks thereof; and may also appoint other and additional officers to hold office during pleasure, and may from time to time prescribe the duties of those officers, and of the several departments over which they shall preside or to which they shall belong, and of the officers and clerks thereof.

Powers, duties, &c., of executive officers.

135. Until the Legislature of Ontario or Quebec otherwise provides, all rights, powers, duties, functions, responsibilities or authorities at the passing of this Act vested in or imposed on the Attorney General, Solicitor General, Secretary and Registrar of the Province of Canada, Minister of Finance, Commissioner of Crown Lands, Commissioner of Public Works, and Minister of Agriculture and Receiver General, by any law, statute or ordinance of Upper Canada, Lower Canada, or Canada, and not repugnant to this Act, shall be vested in or imposed on any officer to be appointed by the Lieutenant Governor for the discharge of the same or any of them; and the Commissioner of Agriculture and Public Works shall perform the duties and functions of the office of Minister of Agriculture at the passing of this Act imposed by the law of the Province of Canada, as well as those of the Commissioner of Public Works.

Great Seals.

136. Until altered by the Lieutenant Governor in Council, the Great Seals of Ontario and Quebec respectively shall be the same, or of the same design, as those used in the Provinces of Upper Canada and Lower Canada respectively before their Union as the Province of Canada.

137. The words "and from thence to the end of the then next ensuing Session of the Legislature," or words to the same effect, used in any temporary Act of the Province of Canada not expired before the Union, shall be construed to extend and apply to the next Session of Parliament of Canada, if the subject matter of the Act is within the powers of the same, as defined by this Act, or to the next Sessions of the Legislatures of Ontario and Quebec respectively, if the subject matter of the Act is within the powers of the same as defined by this Act. Construction of temporary Acts.

138. From and after the Union, the use of the words "Upper Canada" instead of "Ontario," or "Lower Canada" instead of "Quebec," in any deed, writ, process, pleading, document, matter or thing, shall not invalidate the same. As to errors in names.

139. Any Proclamation under the Great Seal of the Province of Canada issued before the Union to take effect at a time which is subsequent to the Union, whether relating to that Province, or to Upper Canada, or to Lower Canada, and the several matters and things therein proclaimed shall be and continue of like force and effect as if the Union had not been made. As to issue of Proclamations before Union, to commence after Union.

140. Any Proclamation which is authorized by any Act of the Legislature of the Province of Canada to be issued under the Great Seal of the Province of Canada, whether relating to that Province, or to Upper Canada, or to Lower Canada, and which is not issued before the Union, may be issued by the Lieutenant Governor of Ontario or of Quebec, as its subject matter requires, under the Great Seal thereof; and from and after the issue of such Proclamation the same and the several matters and things therein proclaimed shall be and continue of the like force and effect in Ontario or Quebec as if the Union had not been made. As to issue of Proclamation after Union.

141. The Penitentiary of the Province of Canada shall, until the Parliament of Canada otherwise provides, be and continue the Penitentiary of Ontario and of Quebec. Penitentiary.

Arbitration respecting debts, &c.

142. The division and adjustment of the debts, credits, liabilities, properties, and assets of Upper Canada and Lower Canada shall be referred to the arbitrament of three arbitrators, one chosen by the Government of Ontario, one by the Government of Quebec, and one by the Government of Canada; and the selection of the arbitrators shall not be made until the Parliament of Canada and the Legislatures of Ontario and Quebec have met; and the arbitrator chosen by the Government of Canada shall not be a resident either in Ontario or in Quebec.[67]

Division of records.

143. The Governor General in Council may from time to time order that such and so many of the records, books, and documents of the Province of Canada as he thinks fit shall be appropriated and delivered either to Ontario or to Quebec, and the same shall henceforth be the property of that Province; and any copy thereof or extract therefrom, duly certified by the officer having charge of the original thereof shall be admitted as evidence.

Constitution of townships in Quebec.

144. The Lieutenant Governor of Quebec may from time to time, by Proclamation under the Great Seal of the Province, to take effect from a day to be appointed therein, constitute townships in those parts of the Province of Quebec in which townships are not then already constituted, and fix the metes and bounds thereof.

X.—INTERCOLONIAL RAILWAY.

Duty of Government and Parliament of Canada to make railway herein described.

145. Inasmuch as the Provinces of Canada, Nova Scotia, and New Brunswick have joined in a declaration that the construction of the Intercolonial Railway is essential to the consolidation of the Union of British North America, and to the assent thereto of Nova Scotia and New Brunswick, and have consequently agreed that provision should be made for its immediate construction by the Government of Canada: Therefore, in order to give effect to that agreement, it shall be the duty of the Government and Parliament of Canada to provide for the commencement within six months after the Union, of a railway connecting the River St. Lawrence with the City of Halifax in Nova Scotia, and for the construction thereof without intermission, and the completion thereof with all practicable speed.

XI.—Admission of Other Colonies.

146. It shall be lawful for the Queen, by and with the advice of Her Majesty's Most Honourable Privy Council, on Addresses from the Houses of Parliament of Canada, and from the Houses of the respective Legislatures of the Colonies or Provinces of Newfoundland, Prince Edward Island, and British Columbia, to admit those Colonies or Provinces,[68] or any of them, into the Union, and on Address from the Houses of the Parliament of Canada to admit Rupert's Land and the North-western Territory,[69] or either of them, into the Union, on such terms and conditions in each case as are in the Addresses expressed and as the Queen thinks fit to approve, subject to the provisions of this Act; and the provisions of any Order in Council in that behalf shall have effect as if they had been enacted by the Parliament of the United Kingdom of Great Britain and Ireland.

Power to admit Newfoundland, &c., into the Union.

147. In case of the admission of Newfoundland and Prince Edward Island, or either of them, each shall be entitled to a representation in the Senate of Canada of four members, and (notwithstanding anything in this Act) in case of the admission of Newfoundland the normal number of Senators shall be seventy-six and their maximum number shall be eighty-two; but Prince Edward Island when admitted shall be deemed to be comprised in the third of the three divisions into which Canada is, in relation to the constitution of the Senate, divided by this Act, and accordingly, after the admission of Prince Edward Island, whether Newfoundland is admitted or not, the representation of Nova Scotia and New Brunswick in the Senate shall, as vacancies occur, be reduced from twelve to ten members respectively, and the representation of each of those Provinces shall not be increased at any time beyond ten, except under the provisions of this Act for the appointment of three or six additional Senators under the direction of the Queen.[70]

As to representation of Newfoundland and Prince Edward Island in Senate.

SCHEDULES.

The FIRST SCHEDULE.

Electoral Districts of Ontario.

A

EXISTING ELECTORAL DIVISIONS.

COUNTIES.

1. Prescott.
2. Glengary.
3. Stormont.
4. Dundas.
5. Russell.
6. Carleton.
7. Prince Edward.
8. Halton.
9. Essex.

RIDINGS OF COUNTIES.

10. North Riding of Lanark.
11. South Riding of Lanark.
12. North Riding of Leeds and North Riding of Grenville.
13. South Riding of Leeds.
14. South Riding of Grenville.
15. East Riding of Northumberland.
16. West Riding of Northumberland (excepting therefrom the Township of South Monaghan).
17. East Riding of Durham.
18. West Riding of Durham.
19. North Riding of Ontario.
20. South Riding of Ontario.
21. East Riding of York.
22. West Riding of York.
23. North Riding of York.
24. North Riding of Wentworth.
25. South Riding of Wentworth.
26. East Riding of Elgin.
27. West Riding of Elgin.

28. North Riding of Waterloo.
29. South Riding of Waterloo.
30. North Riding of Brant.
31. South Riding of Brant.
32. North Riding of Oxford.
33. South Riding of Oxford.
34. East Riding of Middlesex.

Cities, Parts of Cities, and Towns.

35. West Toronto.
36. East Toronto.
37. Hamilton.
38. Ottawa.
39. Kingston.
40. London.
41. Town of Brockville, with the Township of Elizabethtown thereto attached.
42. Town of Niagara, with the Township of Niagara thereto attached.
43. Town of Cornwall, with the Township of Cornwall thereto attached.

B

New Electoral Divisions.

44. The Provisional Judicial District of ALGOMA.

The County of BRUCE, divided into two Ridings, to be called respectively the North and South Ridings:—

45. The North Riding of Bruce to consist of the Townships of Bury, Lindsay, Eastnor, Albemarle, Amable, Arran, Bruce, Elderslie, and Saugeen, and the Village of Southampton.
46. The South Riding of Bruce to consist of the Townships of Kincardine (including the Village of Kincardine), Greenock, Brant, Huron, Kinloss, Culross, and Carrick.

The County of HURON, divided into two Ridings, to be called respectively the North and South Ridings :—

47. The North Riding to consist of the Townships of Ashfield, Wawanosh, Turnberry, Howick, Morris, Grey, Colborne, Hullett, including the Village of Clinton and McKillop.
48. The South Riding to consist of the Town of Goderich and the Township of Goderich, Tuckersmith, Stanley, Hay, Usborne, and Stephen.

The County of MIDDLESEX, divided into three Ridings, to be called respectively the North, West, and East Ridings:

49. The North Riding to consist of the Townships of McGillivray and Biddulph (taken from the County of Huron), and Williams East, Williams West, Adelaide, and Lobo.

50. The West Riding to consist of the Townships of Deleware, Carradoc, Metcalfe, Mosa, and Ekfrid, and the Village of Strathroy.

[The East Riding to consist of the Townships now embraced therein, and be bounded as it is at present.]

51. The County of LAMBTON to consist of the Townships of Bosanquet, Warwick, Plympton, Sarnia, Moore, Enniskillen, and Brooke, and the Town of Sarnia.

52. The County of KENT to consist of the Townships of Chatham, Dover, East Tilbury, Romney, Raleigh, and Harwich, and the Town of Chatham.

53. The County of BOTHWELL to consist of the Townships of Sombra, Dawn, and Euphemia (taken from the County of Lambton), and the Townships of Zone, Camden with the Gore thereof, Orford and Howard (taken from the County of Kent).

The County of GREY divided into two Ridings to be called respectively the South and North Ridings:—

54. The South Riding to consist of the Townships of Bentinck, Glenelg, Artemesia, Osprey, Normanby, Egremont, Proton, and Melancthon.

55. The North Riding to consist of the Townships of Collingwood, Euphrasia, Holland, Saint Vincent, Sydenham, Sullivan, Derby, and Keppel, Sarawak and Brooke, and the Town of Owen Sound.

The County of PERTH divided into two Ridings, to be called respectively the South and North Ridings:

56. The North Riding to consist of the Townships of Wallace, Elma, Logan, Ellice, Mornington, and North Easthope, and the Town of Stratford.

57. The South Riding to consist of the Townships of Blanchard, Downie, South Easthope, Fullarton, Hibbert, and the Villages of Mitchell and St. Mary's.

The County of WELLINGTON, divided into three Ridings, to be called respectively North, South and Centre Ridings:—

58. The North Riding to consist of the Townships of Amaranth, Arthur, Luther, Minto, Maryborough, Peel, and the Village of Mount Forest.

59. The Centre Riding to consist of the Townships of Garafraxa, Erin, Eramosa, Nichol and Pilkington, and the Villages of Fergus and Elora.

60. The South Riding to consist of the Town of Guelph, and the Townships of Guelph and Puslinch.

The County of NORFOLK, divided into two Ridings, to be called respectively the South and North Ridings :—

61. The South Riding to consist of the Townships of Charlotteville-Houghton, Walsingham, and Woodhouse, and with the Gore thereof.

62. The North Riding to consist of the Townships of Middleton, Townsend, and Windham, and the Town of Simcoe.

63. The County of HALDIMAND to consist of the Townships of Oneida, Seneca, Cayuga North, Cayuga South, Rainham, Walpole, and Dunn.

64. The County of MONCK to consist of the Townships of Camborough and Moulton and Sherbrooke, and the Village of Dunnville (taken from the County of Haldimand), the Townships of Caistor and Gainsborough (taken from the County of Lincoln), and the Townships of Pelham and Wainfleet (taken from the County of Welland).

65. The County of LINCOLN to consist of the Townships of Clinton, Grantham, Grimsby, and Louth, and the Town of St. Catharines.

66. The County of WELLAND to consist of the Townships of Bertie, Crowland, Humberstone, Stamford, Thorold, and Willoughby, and the Villages of Chippewa, Clifton, Fort Erie, Thorold, and Welland.

67. The County of PEEL to consist of the Townships of Chinguacousy, Toronto, and the Gore of Toronto, and the Villages of Brampton and Streetsville.

68. The County of CARDWELL to consist of the Townships of Albion and Caledon (taken from the County of Peel), and the Townships of Adjala and Mono (taken from the County of Simcoe).

The County of SIMCOE, divided into two Ridings, to be called respectively the South and the North Ridings :—

69. The South Riding to consist of the Townships of West Gwillimbury, Tecumseth, Innisfil, Essa, Tossorontio, Mulmur, and the Village of Bradford.

70. The North Riding to consist of the Townships of Nottawasaga, Sunnidale, Vespra, Flos, Oro, Medonte, Orillia, and Matchedash, Tiny and Tay, Balaklava and Robinson, and the Towns of Barrie and Collingwood.

The County of VICTORIA, divided into two Ridings, to be called respectively the South and North Ridings :—

71. The South Riding to consist of the Townships of Ops, Mariposa, Emily, Verulam, and the Town of Lindsay.

72. The North Riding to consist of the Townships of Anson, Bexley, Carden, Dalton, Digby, Eldon, Fenelon, Hindon, Laxton, Lutterworth, Macaulay and Draper, Somerville and Morrison, Muskoka, Monck and Watt (taken from the County of Simcoe), and any other surveyed Townships lying to the north of the said North Riding.

The County of PETERBOROUGH, divided into two Ridings, to be called respectively the West and East Ridings :

73. The West Riding to consist of the Townships of South Monaghan (taken from the County of Northumberland), North Monaghan, Smith, and Ennismore, and the Town of Peterborough.

74. The East Riding to consist of the Townships of Asphodel, Belmont and Methuen, Douro, Dummer, Galway, Harvey, Minden, Stanhope and Dysart, Otonabee and Snowden, and the Village of Ashburnham, and any other surveyed Townships lying to the north of the said East Riding.

The County of HASTINGS, divided into three Ridings, to be called respectively the West, East, and North Ridings :

75. The West Riding to consist of the Town of Belleville, the Township of Sydney, and the Village of Trenton.

76. The East Riding to consist of the Townships of Thurlow, Tyendinaga, and Hungerford.

77. The North Riding to consist of the Townships of Rawdon, Huntingdon, Madoc, Elzevir, Tudor, Marmora, and Lake, and the Village of Stirling, and any other surveyed Townships lying to the north of the said North Riding.

78. The County of LENNOX to consist of the Townships of Richmond, Adolphustown, North Fredericksburgh, South Fredericksburgh, Ernest Town, and Amherst Island, and the Village of Napanee.

79. The County of ADDINGTON to consist of the Townships of Camden, Portland, Sheffield, Hinchinbrooke, Kaladar, Kennebec, Olden, Oso, Anglesea, Barrie, Clarendon, Palmerston, Effingham, Abinger, Miller, Canonto, Denbigh, Loughborough, and Bedford.

80. The County of FRONTENAC to consist of the Townships of Kingston, Wolfe Island, Pittsburgh and Howe Island, and Storrington.

The County of RENFREW, divided into two Ridings, to be called respectively the South and North Ridings :—

81. The South Riding to consist of the Townships of McNab, Bagot, Blithfield, Brougham, Herton, Admaston, Grattan, Matawatchan, Griffith, Lyndoch, Raglan, Radcliffe, Brudenell, Sebastopol, and the Villages of Arnprior and Renfrew.

82. The North Riding to consist of the Townships of Ross, Bromley, Westmeath, Stafford, Pembroke, Wilberforce, Alice, Petewawa, Buchanan, South Algona, North Algona, Fraser, McKay, Wylie, Rolph, Head, Maria, Clara, Hagarty, Sherwood, Burns, and Richards, and any surveyed Townships lying north-westerly of the said North Riding.

Every Town and incorporated Village existing at the Union, not specially mentioned in this Schedule, is to be taken as part of the County or Riding within which it is locally situate.

The SECOND SCHEDULE.

Electoral Districts of Quebec specially fixed.

COUNTIES OF—

Pontiac.
Ottawa.
Argenteuil.
Huntingdon.

Missisquoi.
Brome.
Shefford.
Stanstead.
Town of Sherbrooke.

Compton.
Wolfe and Richmond.
Megantic.

The THIRD SCHEDULE.

Provincial Public Works and Property to be the Property of Canada.

1. Canals, with Land and Water Power connected therewith.
2. Public Harbours.
3. Lighthouses and Piers, and Sable Island.
4. Steamboats, Dredges, and public Vessels.
5. Rivers and Lake Improvements.
6. Railways and Railway Stocks, Mortgages, and other Debts due by Railway Companies.
7. Military Roads.
8. Custom Houses, Post Offices, and all other Public Buildings, except such as the Government of Canada appropriate for the use of the Provincial Legislatures and Governments.
9. Property transferred by the Imperial Government and known as Ordnance Property.
10. Armouries, Drill Sheds, Military Clothing, and Munitions of War, and Lands set apart for general public purposes.

The FOURTH SCHEDULE.

Assets to be the Property of Ontario and Quebec conjointly.

Upper Canada Building Fund.
Lunatic Asylums.
Normal School.

Court Houses, ⎫
   in   ⎬ Lower Canada.
Aylmer,
Montreal,
Kamouraska. ⎭
Law Society, Upper Canada.
Montreal Turnpike Trust.
University Permanent Fund.
Royal Institution.
Consolidated Municipal Loan Fund, Upper Canada.
Consolidated Municipal Loan Fund, Lower Canada.
Agricultural Society, Upper Canada.
Lower Canada Legislative Grant.
Quebec Fire Loan.
Tamisconata Advance Account.
Quebec Turnpike Trust.
Education— East.
Building and Jury Fund, Lower Canada.
Municipalities Fund.
Lower Canada Superior Education Income Fund.

The FIFTH SCHEDULE.

OATH OF ALLEGIANCE.

I, *A.B.* do swear, That I will be faithful and bear true Allegiance to Her Majesty Queen Victoria.

Note.—The name of the King or Queen of the United Kingdom of Great Britain and Ireland for the time being is to be substituted from time to time, with proper terms of reference thereto.

DECLARATION OF QUALIFICATION.

I, *A.B.* do declare and testify, That I am by law duly qualified to be appointed a member of the Senate of Canada [*or as the case may be*], and that I am legally or equitably seised as of freehold for my own use and benefit of lands or tenements held in free and common socage [*or seised or possessed for my own use and benefit of lands or tenements held in franc-alleu or in roture (as the case may be),*] in the Province of Nova Scotia [*or as the case may be*] of the value of four thousand dollars over and above all rents, dues, debts, mortgages, charges, and incumbrances due or payable out of or charged on or affecting the same, and that I have not collusively or colourably obtained a title to or become possessed of the said lands and tenements or any part thereof for the purpose of enabling me to become a member of the Senate of Canada [*or as the case may be*], and that my real and personal property are together worth four thousand dollars over and above my debts and liabilities.

Confederation Act Amendment Act, 1871.

An Act[72] *respecting the Establishment of Provinces in the Dominion of Canada.*

[29TH JUNE, 1871.

WHEREAS[73] doubts have been entertained respecting the powers of the Parliament of Canada to establish Provinces in territories admitted, or which may hereafter be admitted, into the Dominion of Canada, and to provide for the representation of such Provinces in the said Parliament, and it is expedient to remove such doubts, and to vest such powers in the said Parliament:

Be it enacted by the Queen's Most Excellent Majesty, by and with the advice and consent of the Lords, Spiritual and Temporal, and Commons in this present Parliament assembled, and by the authority of the same, as follows:—

1. This Act may be cited for all purposes as *The British North America Act, 1871.* — Short title.

2. The Parliament of Canada may from time to time establish new Provinces in any territories forming for the time being part of the Dominion of Canada, but not included in any Province thereof, and may, at the time of such establishment, make provision for the constitution and administration of any such Province, and for the passing of laws for the peace, order and good government of such Province, and for its representation in the said Parliament. — Parliament of Canada may establish new Provinces and provide for the constitution, etc., thereof.

3. The Parliament of Canada may from time to time, with the consent of the Legislature of any Province[74] of the said Dominion, increase, diminish, or otherwise alter the limits of such Province, upon such terms and conditions as may be agreed to by the said Legislature, and may, with — Alteration of limits of Provinces.

the like consent, make provision respecting the effect and operation of any such increase or diminution or alteration of territory in relation to any Province affected thereby.

<small>Parliament of Canada may legislate for any territory not included in a Province.</small>

4. The Parliament of Canada may from time to time make provision for the administration, peace, order, and good government of any territory[75] not for the time being included in any Province.

<small>Confirmation of Acts of Parliament of Canada.</small>

5. The following Acts passed by the said Parliament of Canada, and intituled respectively:

<small>32-33 V. c. 3.</small>

" An Act for the temporary government of Rupert's Land and the North-Western Territory when united with Canada;" and

<small>33 V. c. 3.</small>

" An Act to amend and continue the Act thirty-two and thirty-three Victoria, chapter three, and to establish and provide for the government of the Province of Manitoba,"

shall be and be deemed to have been valid and effectual for all purposes whatsoever from the date at which they respectively received the assent, in the Queen's name, of the Governor General of the said Dominion of Canada.

<small>Limitation of powers of Parliament of Canada to legislate for an established Province.</small>

6. Except as provided by the third section of this Act, it shall not be competent for the Parliament of Canada to alter the provisions of the last mentioned Act of the said Parliament in so far as it relates to the Province of Manitoba, or of any other Act hereafter establishing new Provinces in the said Dominion, subject always to the right of the Legislature of the Province of Manitoba to alter from time to time the provisions of any law respecting the qualification of electors and members of the Legislative Assembly, and to make laws respecting elections in the said Province.

Confederation Act Amendment Act, 1875.

An Act[76] to remove certain doubts with respect to the powers of the Parliament of Canada, under Section 18 of the British North America Act, 1867.

[19TH JULY, 1875.]

WHEREAS by section 18 of *The British North America Act, 1867*, it is provided as follows : - "The privileges, immunities, and powers to be held, enjoyed, and exercised by the Senate and by the House of Commons, and by the members thereof respectively, shall be such as are from time to time defined by Act of the Parliament of Canada, but so that the same shall never exceed those at the passing of this Act held, enjoyed, and exercised by the Commons House of Parliament of the United Kingdom of Great Britain and Ireland, and by the members thereof."

And whereas doubts[77] have arisen with regard to the power of defining by an Act of the Parliament of Canada, in pursuance of the said section, the said privileges, powers or immunities; and it is expedient to remove such doubts :

Be it therefore enacted by the Queen's Most Excellent Majesty, by and with the advice and consent of the Lords Spiritual and Temporal, and Commons, in this present Parliament assembled, and by the authority of the same, as follows :—

1. Section 18 of *The British North America Act, 1867*, is hereby repealed, without prejudice to anything done under that section, and the following section shall be substituted for the section so repealed :— *Substitution of new section for section 18 of 30 and 31 V. c. 3.*

The privileges, immunities, and powers to be held, enjoyed and exercised by the Senate and by the House of Commons, and by the members thereof respectively, shall be such as are from time to time defined by Act of the

Parliament of Canada, but so that any Act of the Parliament of Canada defining such privileges, immunities and powers shall not confer any privileges, immunities, or powers exceeding those at the passing of such Act held, enjoyed, and exercised by the Commons House of Parliament of the United Kingdom of Great Britain and Ireland, and by the members thereof.

Confirmation of Act of Parliament of Canada.

2. The Act[78] of the Parliament of Canada passed in the thirty-first year of the reign of her present Majesty, chapter twenty-four, intituled *An Act to provide for oaths to witnesses being administered in certain cases for the purposes of either House of Parliament*, shall be deemed to be valid, and to have been valid as from the date at which the royal assent was given thereto by the Governor General of the Dominion of Canada.

Short title.

3. This Act may be cited as *The Parliament of Canada Act, 1875.*

Confederation Act Amendment Act, 1886.

An Act[79] *respecting the Representation in the Parliament of Canada of Territories which for the time being form part of the Dominion of Canada, but are not included in any Province.*

[25TH JUNE, 1886.

WHEREAS it is expedient to empower the Parliament of Canada to provide for the representation in the Senate and House of Commons of Canada, or either of them, of any territory which for the time being forms part of the Dominion of Canada, but is not included in any Province :

Be it therefore enacted by the Queen's Most Excellent Majesty, by and with the advice and consent of the Lords Spiritual and Temporal, and Commons, in the present Parliament assembled, and by the authority of the same, as follows :—

1. The Parliament of Canada may from time to time make provision for the representation in the Senate and House of Commons of Canada, or in either of them, of any territories which for the time being form part of the Dominion of Canada, but are not included in any Province thereof.

Provision by Parliament of Canada for representation of territories.

2. Any Act passed by the Parliament of Canada before the passing of this Act for the purpose mentioned in this Act shall, if not disallowed by the Queen, be, and shall be deemed to have been, valid and effectual from the date at which it received the assent, in Her Majesty's name, of the Governor-General of Canada.

Effect of Acts of Parliament of Canada.

It is hereby declared that any Act passed by the Parliament of Canada, whether before[80] or after the passing of this Act, for the purpose mentioned in this Act, or in *The British North America Act, 1871*, has effect, notwithstanding anything in *The British North America Act, 1867*, and the number[81] of Senators or the number of Members of the House of

34 and 35 V. c. 28.

30 and 31 V. c. 3.

Commons specified in the last-mentioned Act is increased by the number of Senators or of Members, as the case may be, provided by any such Act of the Parliament of Canada for the representation of any provinces or territories of Canada.

<small>Short title and construction.</small> **3.** This Act may be cited as *The British North America Act, 1886.*

<small>30 and 31 V. c. 3; 31 and 35 V. c. 28.</small> This Act, and *The British North America Act, 1867,* and *The British North America Act, 1871,* shall be construed together, and may be cited together as *The British North America Acts, 1867 to 1886.*

NOTES TO THE CONFEDERATION ACT.

1 This Act is reprinted from the collection of "Public General Statutes" issued with the "Law Reports," Vol. II, London, 1867. The text has been carefully compared with that found in the collection of "Public General Acts" issued by the Queen's Printers, London, 1867, and also with that found in the "Statutes at Large," London, 1868. The only difference amongst these various editions is in the marginal notes, and as the first two agree, they have been here followed. The Act is 30 Vict. cap. 3 in the "Law Reports," and also in the "Public General Statutes"; it is 30 & 31 Vict. cap 3 in the "Statutes at Large". In the official reprints of the Act, prefixed or appended to the Revised Statutes of Ontario, Quebec. Nova Scotia, New Brunswick, and Manitoba, the notation of the "Statutes at Large" has been followed. For a full report of the debates on the measure in its progress through the Imperial Parliament see "Hansard's Parliamentary Debates," third series, vol. 185, pp. 557, 804, 1011, 1164, and 1310. The ordinary Canadian histories give a sufficiently detailed narrative of the events which led to the confederation of the leading Provinces of British North America. For a full and valuable account of the Quebec conference of 1864, see "Confederation of Canada," (Vol. I.; Toronto, 1872) by Hon. John Hamilton Gray, one of the delegates representing New Brunswick. The debates in the Canadian Parliament, in the session of 1865, on the motion to adopt the "Quebec Resolutions," were printed in a single volume under the title of "Parliamentary Debates on the subject of the Confederation of the British North American Provinces." (Quebec, 1865). This collection of speeches by the foremost statesmen of Canada, is indispensable to the student of this part of Canadian constitutional history. For the text of the Quebec Resolutions see Appendix F.

2 In Canada and Nova Scotia the question was never submitted to popular vote In New Brunswick a general election was held to decide the matter.

3 Prof. Dicey in his "Introduction to the Law of the Constitution" (Chapter III, p. 135 of the third edition) says: "The preamble to the British North America Act, 1867, asserts with official mendacity that the Provinces of the present Dominion have expressed their desire to be united into one Dominion 'with a constitution similar in principle to that of the United Kingdom.' If preambles were intended to express the truth, for the word 'Kingdom' ought to have been substituted 'States,' since it is clear that the constitution of the Dominion is modelled on that of the Union." For a useful comparison between the constitution of Canada and that of the United States see Dr. Bourinot's "Canada and the United States" (Transactions of the "Royal Society of Canada" for 1890), and his paper under the same title in the *Scottish Review* for July, 1890. See also "Parliamentary Government in Canada, by the Hon. C. C. Colby, M P., and the *Law Quarterly Review*, Vol. III, No. 10, p. 201.

4 See sections 146 and 147 of this Act.

5 By Royal Proclamation, issued from Windsor Castle on the twenty-second of May, 1867, the first of July following was declared to be the day on which the Confederation Act should go into operation. Lord Monck, the last Governor-General of the Province of Canada under the Union Act of 1840, was appointed the first Governor-General of the Dominion of Canada under the Confederation Act of 1867, and on the first of July of that year he announced his appointment to the people of Canada by proclamation. The texts of these two documents are prefixed to the Journals of the first session (1867-68) of the House of Commons of Canada.

6 See Constitutional Act, 1791, Section II. (p. 112 above). For the legal definition of the present boundary between Ontario and Quebec, see the Imperial Act, 52 & 53 Vict. cap 28, entitled the "Canada (Ontario Boundary) Act, 1889" (Appendix B.)

7 For the boundaries of Nova Scotia and New Brunswick see Appendix B.

8 The population of each Province in the Dominion in 1871 and 1881 was as follows:—

	1871.	1881.
Ontario	1,620,851	1,923,228
Quebec	1,191,516	1,359,027
Nova Scotia	387,800	440,572
New Brunswick	285,594	321,233
Manitoba		65,954
British Columbia		49,459
Prince Edward I'd.		108,891
Territories		56,446
Total	3,485,761	4,324,810

9 For a full account of the relation sustained by the Governor-General to the Imperial Government on the one hand and to his own Privy Council on the other, see Todd's "Parliamentary Government in the British Colonies," pp. 76-123. On the exercise of the prerogative of mercy, see *ibid*, pp. 251-274.

10 See Note 13 to the Union Act, 1840, above.

11 Section 18 of "The British North America Act, 1867," was repealed by "The Parliament of Canada Act, 1875," and a new section substituted (see p. 237).

12 The first Parliament of the Dominion of Canada met on the 7th of November, 1867.

13 For the duration of Parliament see section 50.

14 This number has been increased to 80 by subsequent legislation, three of the additional members representing Manitoba (Statutes of Canada, 33 Vict. cap. 3, sec. 3; Rev. Stat. of Canada, 1886, cap. 12); three representing British Columbia (Stat. of Can., 1872, p. lxxxviii); and two representing the Northwest Territories (Stat. of Can., 50 & 51 Vict. cap. 3. For confirmatory Imperial legislation see p. 226 and p. 229 below. See section 147 as to the representation of Prince Edward Island in the Senate.

15 Compare section 147.

16 See Journals of House of Commons for 1867-68, pp. v-vii.

17 See Todd's "Parliamentary Government in the British Colonies," pp. 164-165, for a brief account of an application made in 1873 by the Canadian to the Imperial Government for the addition of six members to the Senate. See also Senate Debates for 1877, pp. 84-94; Commons Debates, same year, p. 371; and Senate Journals, same year, pp. 130-131.

18 See Note 14 above.

19 For the state of the law in regard to these matters in the Province of Canada prior to Confederation see "Consolidated Statutes of Canada," 1859, pp. 1-154, and Canadian Statutes 23 Vict. cap. 17; 27 Vict. c. 8; 27 & 28 Vict. cap. 51; and 29 Vict. cap. 1. The trial of controverted elections to the House of Commons was transferred to the Courts of law by Dominion Statute 36 Vict. cap. 23. This was replaced by 37 Vict. cap. 10, the validity of which was in 1879 declared by the Supreme

Court of the Dominion (3 Can Sup. Court Reports; Cartwright's Cases, Vol. I, p. 167), and afterwards affirmed by the Privy Council (5 Appeal Cases, 159). The trial of controverted elections to the Legislative Assembly of Ontario was transferred to the Provincial Superior Courts by Ontario Statute, 34 Vict. cap. 3.

20 The office of Deputy Speaker was created in 1885 by Dom. Stat. 48 & 49 Vict. cap. 1.

21 After the census of 1871 the representation was re-adjusted by Dom. Stat. 35 Vict. cap. 13. After the census of 1881 it was re-adjusted by Dom. Stat. 45 Vict. cap. 3.

22 See May's "Parliamentary Practice," chapter on "Supply and Ways and Means"; and Bourinot's "Parliamentary Procedure and Practice," chapter on "Committees of Supply and Ways and Means."

23 Prior to the passage of the Union Act, 1840, (sec. 57) there was no such restriction. See Scrope's "Life of Lord Sydenham," p 203, and Lord Durham's Report (p. 31 of the British Parliamentary Edition).

24 See Todd's "Parliamentary Government in the British Colonies," pp. 139-151.

25 See Note 24.

26 The only Lieutenant-Governor removed under the authority of this section was the Hon. Luc Letellier, whose dismissal from the Lieutenant-Governorship of Quebec took place in 1879. For a succint and lucid account of this important case see Todd's "Parliamentary Government in the British Colonies," pp. 405-428. See also Journals of the House of Commons of Canada, 1879, p. 85; Dom. Sess. Papers, vol. xii, No. 19; Dom. Sess. Papers, vol. xii, Nos. 18, and 18A; and Debates of the House of Commons of Canada, 1879, pp 251-409.

27 Since 1867 there have been added to the Executive Council of Ontario, a Minister of Education (39 Vic. cap. 16), and a Minister of Agriculture (51 Vict. cap. 8).

28 As to the office of Lieutenant-Governor in Ontario and Quebec see Ont. Stat. 51 Vict. cap. 5; Quebec Stat., 52 Vict. cap. 13; and the judgment of Chancellor Boyd, delivered in 1890, at Osgoode Hall, in the case of "Attorney-General of Canada v. Attorney-General of Ontario.

29 The seat of Government of Manitoba is Winnipeg; of British Columbia, Victoria; of Prince Edward Island, Charlottetown; and of the Northwest Territory, Regina.

30 Of the four Provinces which entered into Confederation in 1867, Ontario alone had only one legislative chamber. Quebec was provided with two under section 71 of this Act, and Nova Scotia and New Brunswick retained each the two it had. Of the other Provinces which now form part of the Dominion Prince Edward Island retains the two chambers which it had before its admission; Manitoba was provided with a second chamber by the Dominion Statute (33 Vic. cap. 3), which created the Province; but it was abolished by Act of the Manitoba Legislature (39 Vict. cap. 28). British Columbia occupied at the time of its admission into the Dominion a peculiar position. From 1849 to 1859 Vancouver Island was placed under the control of the Hudson Bay Company, the Governor of the colony being appointed by the British Government. The first Governor, Mr. Blanshard, appointed a legislative council of three members, and in 1856 his successor, Governor Douglass, by direction of the Secretary for the colonies, Mr. Labouchere, gave the people an opportunity of electing their first Parliament, which was made up of seven members. These two chambers continued till the union of Vancouver

Island with British Columbia in 1866, the Legislative Council having been in 1863 made partly elective. The original Province of British Columbia, which was under the same Governor with Vancouver Island from 1858 to 1864, was in the latter year granted a separate establishment, consisting of a Governor and an appointed Legislative Council. The expense of this arrangement brought about a union in 1866 under a government similar in form to that of British Columbia, namely, a Governor and an appointed Council, and this was replaced in 1871 by a constitution similar to that of Ontario, with a view to the admission of the Province into the Dominion. The statute or ordinance making this change is No. 147 in the "Laws of British Columbia (Revised), 1871." See also Macfie's "Vancouver Island and British Columbia," chap. xlii, (London, 1865). The present constitution of British Columbia is contained in chap. 22 of the "Consolidated Acts, 1888."

a The representation in the Ontario Legislative Assembly was re-adjusted in 1874 by the statute 38 Vict. cap. 2, which increased the membership to 88. It was again re-adjusted in 1885 by the statute 48 Vict. cap. 2, which increased the membership to 90. By 52 Vict., cap. 2, the number was increased to 91.

b No change has been made by the Quebec Legislature in this part of the Provincial constitution.

c See. 23 above.

d See. 31 above.

e In 1890 the Quebec Legislature passed an Act (53 Vict., cap. 3), increasing the membership of the Legislative Assembly to 72.

36 The Legislature of each of these Provinces met for the first time on the 27th of December, 1867.

37 For the law securing the independence of the members of the Legislative Assembly of Ontario, see Revised Statutes of Ontario, 1887, cap. 11., ss. 6-14. For the corresponding law for the Province of Quebec, see Revised Statutes of Quebec, 1888, articles 136-144.

38 The following statutes embody the law of Ontario in relation to the matters specified in this section: As to the qualification of members of the Legislative Assembly, R. S. O., 1887, cap. 9, s. 3; as to disqualification of members, *ibid* cap. 2, ss. 6-11; as to qualification of voters at legislative elections, 51 Vict., cap. 4 (the Manhood Suffrage Act); as to all proceedings at elections, R. S. O., 1887, cap. 9; as to the trial of controverted elections, R. S. O., 1887, cap. 10; as to vacancies, R. S. O., 1887, cap. 11. The following statutes embody the law of Quebec on the same points: As to eligibility and disqualification of members of the Legislative Assembly, R. S. Q., 1888, articles 95-99; as to the qualification of voters, 52 Vict., cap. 1; as to proceedings at elections, R. S. Q., 1888, cap. 2; as to controverted elections, R. S. Q., 1888, cap. 3; and as to vacancies, R. S. Q., 1888, articles 100-108. The Ontario Legislature by the Statute 42 Vict. cap. 4, subsequently amended by 48 Vict. cap. 2, fixed more definitely the limits of the four-year term. By the Statute 44-45 Vict. cap. 7, the Quebec Legislature extended the term to five years for that Province

39 For the interpretation of the phrase "trade and commerce," by the Courts, see Cartwright's "Cases on the British North America Act, 1867." Two of the most important decisions are those given by the Privy Council in the Citizens and the Queen Insurance Companies v. Parsons (Vol. I., p. 265), and Hodge v. the Queen (Vol. III., p. 144). Amongst other cases illustrating this point are Beard v. Steele (Vol. I., p. 680), Harris v. City of Hamilton (I., 756), Noel v. Co. of Richmond (II., 246), Angus v. City of Montreal (II., 335), Mallette v. City of Montreal (II., 340), and Coté v. Watson (II., 343).

AND SUPPLEMENTARY ACTS. 235

40 See the case of Leprohon v. City of Ottawa (Cartwright I, 592).

41 As to the nature of the control here vested in the Dominion Government over inland fisheries, see the case of Queen v. Robertson (Cartwright II., 65).

42 See the decision given by the Ontario Court of Appeal in Smiles v. Belford (Cartwright, I., 576).

43 The term "reserved" was judicially interpreted by the Privy Council in the case of the St. Catharines Milling and Lumber Co. v. the Queen (Appeal Reports XIV., 46). See also Church v. Fenton (Cartwright I., 831), and the same case in the Ontario Appeal Reports (IV., 159).

44 On the judicial interpretation of the phrase "direct taxation," see Angers v. Queen Insurance Co. (Cartwright, I., 117), and Attorney-General of Quebec v. Reed (Cartwright III., 190.

45 A number of judicial decisions have been given to determine the signification of the term "municipal institutions," including many of the so-called "liquor" cases. See amongst others Leprohon v. City of Ottawa (Cartwright, I., 592), Slavin v. Orillia (Cartwright, I., 688), Harris v. City of Hamilton (Cartwright, I., 756) Three Rivers v. Sulte (Cartwright, II, 230), *Ex parte* Pillow (Cartwright, III., 357), Windsor v. Commercial Bank (Cartwright, III, 377), and Hodge v. the Queen (Cartwright, III., 144).

46 The decided cases under this sub-section are numerous. See amongst others, the following in Cartwright's collection : Severn v. the Queen (I., 111), Regina v. Boardman (I., 676), Russell v. the Queen (II., 12), Noel v. Co. of Richmond (II., 246), Three Rivers v. Sulte (II., 280), *Ex parte* Leveillé (II., 319), Blonin v. Quebec (II., 368), Hart v. Mississquoi (II., 382), Cooey v. Brome (II., 385), De St. Aubyn v. Lafrance (II., 392), Keefe v. McLennan (II., 400), Regina v. Kings Co. Justices (II., 499), Regina v. Frawley (II., 580), Regina v. Prittie (II , 606), Regina v. Lake (II., 616), Hodge v. the Queen (III., 144), Poulin v. Quebec (III., 230), and Griffith v. Rioux (III., 348).

47 For interpretative decisions see the following cases: Bourgoin v. The Montreal, Ottawa and Occidental R.R. (Cartwright, I., 233), Credit Valley R.R. v. G. W. R.R. (I., 822), Macdougall v. Union Navigation Co. (I., 228), Regina v. Mohr (II., 257), Monkhouse v. Grand Trunk R.R. (III., 289). See also Dom. Statute 46. Vict., cap. 24, s. 6, and Revised Statutes of Canada, 1886, cap. 109, s. 121.

48 Many decisions have been given by the Courts involving a definition of this phrase, amongst others the following, all of which will be found in Cartwright's collection: Cushing v. Dupuy (I., 252), Citizens and Queen Insurance Companies v. Parsons (I., 265), Dobie v. Temporalities Board (I., 351), *Re* Goodhue (I., 560), Crombie v. Jackson (I., 685), Jones v. Canada Central R.R. Co. (I., 777), Smith v. Merchants Bank (I., 828), The Queen v. Robertson (II., 65), McClanaghan v. St. Anne's Mutual Building Society (II., 237), Cleveland v. Melbourne and Brompton Gore (II., 241), Bennett v. The Pharmaceutical Association of Quebec (II., 250), Loranger v. Colonial Building and Investment Association (III., 118), *Re* Windsor and Annapolis R.R. (III., 387).

49 The following, in Cartwright's collection, are some of the many cases decided under this sub-section: Regina v. Coote (I., 57), Valin v. Langlois (I., 158), Lenoir v. Ritchie (I., 488), The Picton (I., 557), Regina v. Roddy (I., 709), Regina v. Amer (I., 722), Regina v. Lawrence (I., 742), *Re* Squier (I., 789), The Queen v. Reno and Anderson (I., 810), Attorney-General v. Niagara Falls Bridge Co. (I., 813), Pope v. Griffith (II., 291), Page v. Griffith (II., 308), Coté v. Chauveau (II., 311), Regina v. Horner (II., 317), *Ex parte* Papin (II., 320), Page v. Griffith (II., 324), Regina v. Bennett (II., 634), Wilson v. McGuire (II., 665), Gibson v. Macdonald (III., 319).

50 Several judgments in decided cases contain *dicta* illustrative of this subsection. In the recent and important case of the Attorney-General of Canada v. the Attorney-General of Ontario it was decided by Chancellor Boyd that an Act of the Ontario Legislature (51 Vict. cap. 5), authorizing the Lieutenant-Governor to commute and remit sentences for offences against the laws of the Province or offences over which the legislative authority of the Province extends, was within the constitutional competence of the Legislature. See note 24 above.

51 Such an appeal was made by Roman Catholic inhabitants of New Brunswick against the School Act passed by the Legislature of that Province in 1871. The Governor-General-in-Council decided that there was no ground for interference, and the statute went into operation. See Todd's "Parliamentary Government in the British Colonies," pp. 346-350; and Dom. Sess. papers, 1877, No. 89. A similar appeal was made by Roman Catholic inhabitants of Prince Edward Island against the School Act passed by the Legislature of that Province in 1877, with a similar result. In 1890 the Legislature of Manitoba passed two Acts (chapters 37 and 38 of 53 Victoria), the former abolishing the dual Board of Education and the dual Superintendency of Public Instruction, the latter creating a single public school system instead of the dual system which had up to that time existed by law.

52 The Parliament of Canada was appealed to in the New Brunswick case (see note 51), but no remedial legislation was granted. See Todd's "Parliamentary Government in the British Colonies" pp. 346-350, and Dom. Sess. Papers, 1874, No. 25.

53 Nothing has been done to bring about the uniformity here provided for.

54 No provision having been made in the British North America Act for the removal of County Court Judges, the Dominion Parliament in 1882 passed an Act (45 Vict., cap. 12) dealing with the matter.

55 For proceedings taken in the House of Commons under this section, but not carried so far as to secure the removal of the judge who was assailed, see the case of Judge Lafontaine of Quebec (Commons Journals of 1867-68, pp. 297, 314 and 398; and of 1869, pp. 135 and 217); the case of Judge Loranger of Quebec (Commons Journals of 1877, pp. 20, 25, 36, 258, and Appendix No. 3); and the case of Chief Justice Wood of Manitoba, (Common Journals of 1882, pp. 176, 192, 355; Sessional Papers of 1882, No. 106; and "Debates of the House of Commons," pp. 1231-1237).

56 Prior to 1875 the only Court of Appeal against the judgments of Provincial Courts was the Judicial Committee of the Imperial Privy Council. In that year the Dominion Parliament passed an Act (38 Vict. cap. 11) "to establish a Supreme Court, and a Court of Exchequer, for the Dominion of Canada," and in the following year an Act (39 Vict. cap. 26) was passed "to make further provision in regard to the Supreme Court and the Exchequer Court of Canada." In the case of Valin v. Langlois (Supreme Court Reports, Vol. III., and Cartwright's cases Vol. I., p. 158), Supreme Court, and afterwards the Privy Council, decided that the trial of Dominion controverted elections properly devolved on the Provincial Courts. For a movement to repeal the Supreme Court Act, see Commons Journals of 1882, p. 297.

7 This was one of the great obstacles to bringing about the union of 1867. See the Resolutions of the Quebec Conference of 1864, (Appendix F), and Gray's "Confederation" of Canada, Vol. I. pp. 61-62.

8 In the first session of the Dominion Parliament a bill was passed "to fix the salary of the Governor-General," and by it the £10,000 was reduced to £6,500. It

was reserved "for the signification of Her Majesty's pleasure," and the message withholding her assent is printed as No. 73 of the Sessional Papers of 1869.

59 Including lands acquired by treaty from Indian tribes subsequent to Confederation. See the case of the St. Catharines Milling and Lumber Co. v. the Queen, (English Appeal Reports, vol. xiv., p. 46.)

60 The term "royalties" has been authoritatively defined by the Privy Council in the Mercer Case (Cartwright, vol. 3, pp. 6-15) so as to include escheats.

61 This financial settlement has been several times disturbed. "Better terms" were conceded to Nova Scotia in 1869 (Dom. Statutes, 32 & 33 Vict. cap. 3). In 1873 an Act was passed (36 Vict. cap. 30), to readjust the amounts of the Provincial debts for which the Dominion became liable, and an Act was passed the following year (37 Vict. cap. 3), confirming the "better terms" settlement made with Nova Scotia in 1869. An Act was passed in 1884 (47 Vict. cap. 53) " to re-adjust the yearly subsidies allowed by Canada to the several Provinces." In 1885 an Act (48 & 49 Vict. cap. 4) was passed authorizing the Governor-in-Council to make advances to Provinces on certain conditions. The laws relating to subsidies were consolidated in the Revised Statutes of Canada, 1886, cap. 46. The Province of Manitoba was created in 1870, with certain financial arrangements (33 Vict. cap. 3, sec. 25). These arrangements were re-adjusted by 45 Vict. cap. 5, and again by 48 & 49 Vict. cap. 50; and the latter statute was "explained" by 49 Vict. cap. 8. For the financial terms on which Prince Edward Island was admitted into Canada see the Address to the Queen adopted by the Dominion Parliament in 1873 (Com. Journals, vol. vi. p. 403). In 1887 an Act (50 & 51 Vict. cap. 8) was passed to increase the subsidy to that Province. The financial arrangements made with British Columbia on her entrance into the Dominion are contained in the address to the Queen in the Commons Journals for 1871, p. 194.

62 The adoption of the Treaty of Washington in 1871 rendered it necessary to abolish these "lumber dues," and an Act was passed by the Parliament of Canada (36 Vict. cap. 41), providing compensation to New Brunswick.

63 Ontario had no Legislative Council under the Confederation Act, and members of the Quebec Legislative Council have since served as members of Senate without vacating their seats in the Council. The same exemption from disability was allowed to the members of the Manitoba Legislative Council. In relation to dual membership of the House of Commons and of a Provincial Legislature see Dom. Statutes 35 Vict. cap. 15, and 36 Vict. cap. 2.

64 These powers were exercised in the case of the Washington Treaty of 1871 (Dom. Stat. 35 Vict. cap. 2). In the negotiation of that treaty Canada was represented by Sir John Macdonald; in the negotiations of the abortive treaties of 1874 and 1888, the representatives of Canada were respectively the Hon. George Brown and Sir Charles Tupper.

65 The Parliament of Canada subsequently authorized the use of both languages in the Legislature of Manitoba (33 Vict. cap. 3), and in the Legislative Council of the North-West Territories (43 Vict. cap. 25, sec. 94; Rev. Stat. of Canada, 1886, cap. 50, sec. 110). The Manitoba Legislature in 1890 abolished the use of the French language in its proceedings (53 Vict. cap. 14), and in the session of 1890 the Canadian House of Commons declared it "expedient and proper" that the Legislative Assembly of the North-West Territories should have, after next general election of the Assembly, the right to decide for itself the question of its continued use (Com. Journals, 1890, pp. 106-108).

66 The Ontario Legislature in 1872 authorized the increase of the Executive Council to six members (35 Vict. cap. 3, sec. 6), but did not add to the number of

executive departments till 1876, when the office of Minister of Education was created (39 Vict., cap. 16). In 1888 the limitation to six was removed, and the Department of Agriculture was placed in charge of a "Minister" (51 Vict. cap. 8). In Quebec the membership of the Executive Council is fixed by the Revised Statutes of 1888 (sec. 593), as follows: President of Council, Attorney-General, Provincial Secretary, Provincial Treasurer, Commissioner of Crown Lands, Commissioner of Agriculture, and Commissioner of Public Works.

67 The arbitrator chosen by the Government of Ontario was the Hon. (more recently Sir) David Lewis Macpherson, of Toronto; by the Government of Quebec, the Hon. Charles Dewey Day, of Quebec; and by the Government of Canada, the Hon. John Hamilton Gray, then of St. John, N.B., afterwards Chief Justice of British Columbia. See Ont. Sess. Papers, No. 27 of 1873, and No. 42 of 1878 for (1) a full account of all the proceedings of the arbitrators down to the time of their award on the 3rd of September, 1870; (2) the text of the award itself; (3) all the correspondence resulting from its repudiation by successive Executive Councils of Quebec; (4) the proceedings preliminary to the submission of a "special case" to the Imperial Privy Council; and (5) the final decision of that body on the 11th of March, 1878, declaring the award to be binding.

68 For proceedings of the House of Commons in connection with the adoption of the address for the admission of British Columbia, and for the text of the address itself see Com. Jour. for 1871, pp. 182-203. The Order of Her Majesty in Council declaring the union of Canada and British Columbia will be found on pp. lxxxiv-cvii of the Statutes of Canada for 1872. The proceedings of the House of Commons in connection with the admission of Prince Edward Island are given on pp. 401-405 of Com. Jour. for 1873, and the Imperial Order-in-Council on pp. ix-xxiii of the Statutes of Canada for the same year.

69 For the text of the Order of Her Majesty-in-Council annexing "Rupert's Land and the North-Western Territory" to the Dominion of Canada, see Can. Stat. of 1872, pp. lxiii-lxxxiii. The Order is dated, Windsor, June 23, 1870, and has appended to it the terms and conditions of the surrender of the territory by the Hudson's Bay Company.

70 See Note 14 above.

71 As to the nature of these "assets," and the manner in which they have been finally disposed of, as between Ontario and Quebec, see Ontario Sessional Papers of 1873, Nos. 27 and 37; and of 1878, No. 42.

72 This Act is 34-35 Vict. cap. 28. The text is reprinted from "The Public General Statutes" in the "Law Reports, Vol. VI., 1871," but it has been compared with the text in "The Public General Acts" published by the Queen's Printers, London, 1871. The Earl of Kimberley made in the House of Lords a brief statement of the reasons for introducing the bill (Hansard, Third Series, Vol. 206, p. 1171).

73 The "doubts" here mentioned were raised in the Canadian Parliament. According to Lord Kimberley (see vote 72 above) the Law Officers of the Crown believed the Acts specified in section 5 of this Act to be within the competency of the Dominion Parliament to pass.

74 The limits of Manitoba were enlarged by the joint action of the Dominion Parliament and the Manitoba Legislature in 1881. See Manitoba Statutes, 44 Vict., cc. I and VI.; Dom. Stat., 44 Vict. cap. 14 and Rev. Stat Can., 1886, cap. 47.

75 Such provision is made by Chapters 50-54 of the Rev. Stat. Can. 1886. Amongst previous enactments are the following: 38 Vict. cap. 49; 39 Vict. cap. 21; 41 Vict. cap. 15; 47 Vict. cap. 23; 48 & 49 Vict. cap. 51 ; 49 Vict. cap. 25.

76 This Act is 38 & 39 Vict. cap. 38. The text is reprinted from "The Public General Statutes," issued with "The Law Reports," London, 1875. The occasion of its passage was the opinion expressed by the Law Officers of the Crown in 1873 that the statute (36 Vict. cap. 1) passed by the Canadian Parliament in the first session of that year "to provide for the examination of witnesses on oath by Committees of either House" was beyond the competence of that Parliament, under sec. 18 of the British North American Act. The Statute was in consequence disallowed by Her Majesty, and the inquiry into certain charges respecting the Pacific Railway, to facilitate which the passage of the Act was deemed necessary, was entrusted to a Royal Commission. See Com. Jour., 1873, (first session) pp. 115. 137, 166, 267 ; and correspondence respecting the disallowance, Com. Jour., 1873, (second session) pp. 5—12 In the latter volume (pp. 12—119) will be found the narrative of the case sent by the Governor-General, Lord Dufferin, to the Colonial Secretary, Lord Kimberley. The Appendix to the same volume contains the Report of the Royal Commission above mentioned.

77 The "doubts" here mentioned seem to have arisen chiefly in the Senate (Com. Journals, 1873, second session, p. 6). See Ibid., pp. 7-10, for the opinions of Lord Dufferin, Sir John Macdonald, Alpheus Todd, and the Law Officers of the Crown.

78 This Act is entitled "An Act to provide for Oaths being administered in certain cases for the purposes of either House of Parliament." The first section is as follows : " Witnesses may be examined upon oath at the Bar of the Senate, and for that purpose the Clerk of the House may administer an oath to any such witness." The second and third sections empower committees of the two Houses, respectively, to take evidence on oath as to matters relating to Private Bills. The Colonial Secretary (Com. Journals of 1873, second session, pp. 10-11), points out that the first section, in view of the opinion of the Crown Law Officers on the Oaths Act of 1873, is "void" under section 2 of the " Colonial Laws Validity Act," 1865. See pp. 241-243 below.

79 This Act is 49 & 50 Vict., cap. 35. The text is reprinted from "The Public General Statutes," issued with "The Law Reports," London, 1886. As to the necessity of this statute see sections 2 and 5 of the "British North America Act, 1871,' pp. 225-226 above.

80 The Act passed by the Dominion Parliament giving representation therein to the North-West Territories (Can. Stat. 49 Vict., cap. 24), was assented to by the Governor-General on the 2nd of June, 1886. See date of assent to this Act above.

81 See Note 14 above.

COLONIAL HABEAS CORPUS ACT, 1862.

An Act[1] respecting the issue of Writs of Habeas Corpus out of England into Her Majesty's Possessions abroad.

[16th May, 1862.

WHEREAS it is expedient that writs of Habeas Corpus should not issue out of England into any colony or foreign dominion of the Crown, where Her Majesty has a lawfully established court or courts of justice having authority to grant and issue the said writ, and to ensure the due execution thereof throughout such colony or foreign dominion:

Be it therefore enacted by the Queen's Most Excellent Majesty, by and with the advice and consent of the Lords Spiritual and Temporal, and Commons, in this present Parliament assembled, and by the authority of the same, as follows :

Writ not to issue into Colony,&c., having Court authorized to grant same.
1. No writ of Habeas Corpus shall issue out of England, by authority of any judge or court of justice therein, into any colony or foreign dominion of the Crown, where Her Majesty has a lawfully established court or courts of justice having authority to grant and issue the said writ, and to ensure the due execution thereof throughout such colony or dominion.

Not to affect right of appeal.
2. Provided, that nothing in this Act contained shall affect or interfere with any right of appeal to Her Majesty in Council now by law existing.

---

[1] This Act is 25 & 26 Vict., cap. 2). The text is reprinted from the "Statutes at Large," vol. xxv, London, 1862.

COLONIAL LAWS VALIDITY ACT, 1865.

An Act[1] to remove Doubts as to the Validity of Colonial Laws.

[29TH JUNE, 1865.

WHEREAS doubts have been entertained respecting the validity of divers laws[2] enacted, or purporting to be enacted by the Legislatures of certain of Her Majesty's Colonies, and respecting the powers of such Legislatures; and it is expedient that such doubts should be removed:

Be it hereby enacted by the Queen's Most Excellent Majesty, by and with the advice and consent of the Lords Spiritual and Temporal, and Commons, in this present Parliament assembled, and by the authority of the same, as follows:—

1. The term "colony"[3] shall in this Act include all of Her Majesty's Possessions abroad, in which there shall exist a legislature as hereinafter defined, except the *Channel Islands*, the *Isle of Man*, and such territories as may for the time being be vested in Her Majesty, under or by virtue of any Act of Parliament for the government of *India*;

Definitions:
"Colony."

The terms "Legislature" and "Colonial Legislature" shall severally signify the authority (other than the Imperial Parliament or Her Majesty in Council), competent to make laws for any colony;

"Legislature."
"Colonial Legislature":

The term "Representative Legislature" shall signify any Colonial Legislature which shall comprise a legislative body of which one-half are elected by inhabitants of the colony;

"Representative Legislature;"

The term "Colonial Law" shall include laws made for any colony, either by such Legislature as aforesaid or by Her Majesty in Council;

"Colonial Law:"

An Act of Parliament, or any provision thereof, shall, in construing this Act, be said to extend to any colony when it

Act of Parliament, etc.,

when to extend to Colony: is made applicable to such colony by the express words or necessary intendment of any Act of Parliament;

"Governor:" The term "Governor" shall mean the officer lawfully administering the Government of any colony;

"Letters Patent" The term "Letters Patent" shall mean letters patent under the great seal of the United Kingdom of *Great Britain and Ireland*.

Colonial Law when void for repugnancy. 2. Any colonial law, which is or shall be repugnant to the provisions of any Act of Parliament extending to the colony to which such law may relate, or repugnant to any order or regulation made under authority of such Act of Parliament, or having in the colony the force or effect of such Act, shall be read subject to such Act, order, or regulation, and shall, to the extent of such repugnancy, but not otherwise, be and remain absolutely void and inoperative.[4]

Colonial Law when not void for repugnancy. 3. No colonial law shall be, or be deemed to have been, void or inoperative on the ground of repugnancy to the law of *England*, unless the same shall be repugnant to the provisions of some such Act of Parliament, order, or regulation, as aforesaid.

Colonial Law not void for inconsistency with instructions. 4. No colonial law, passed with the concurrence of or assented to by the Governor of any colony, or to be hereafter so passed or assented to, shall be, or be deemed to have been, void or inoperative by reason only of any instructions with reference to such law, or the subject thereof, which may have been given to such Governor, by or on behalf of Her Majesty, by any instrument other than the letters patent or instrument authorizing such Governor to concur in passing or to assent to laws for the peace, order, and good government of such colony, even though such instructions may be referred to in such letters patent, or last-mentioned instrument.

Colonial Legislatures may establish, &c., Courts of law. 5. Every colonial Legislature shall have, and be deemed at all times to have had, full power within its jurisdiction to establish courts of judicature, and to abolish and reconstitute the same, and to alter the constitution thereof, and to make provision for the administration of justice therein[5]; and every representative Legislature shall, in respect to the colony under its jurisdiction, have, and be deemed at all times to have had, full power to make laws respecting the constitution, powers, and procedure of such Legislature; provided that such laws shall have been passed in such manner and form as may from time to time be required, by any Act of Parliament, letters patent, Order in Council, or colonial law for the time being in force in the colony. *Representative Legislature may alter Constitution.*

6. The certificate of the clerk or other proper officer of a legislative body in any colony to the effect that the document to which it is attached is a true copy of any colonial law assented to by the Governor of such colony, or of any bill reserved for the signification of Her Majesty's pleasure by the said Governor, shall be *prima facie* evidence that the document so certified is a true copy of such law or bill, and, as the case may be, that such law has been duly and properly passed and assented to, or that such bill has been duly and properly passed and presented to the Governor; and any proclamation, purporting to be published by authority of the Governor, in any newspaper in the colony to which such law or bill shall relate, and signifying Her Majesty's disallowance of any such colonial law, or Her Majesty's assent to any such reserved bill as aforesaid, shall be *prima facie* evidence of such disallowance or assent. *Certified copies of laws to be evidence that they are properly passed. Proclamation to be evidence of assent and disallowance.*

And whereas doubts are entertained respecting the validity of certain Acts enacted, or reputed to be enacted, by the Legislature of South Australia: Be it further enacted as follows:

7. All laws or reputed laws enacted or purporting to have been enacted by the said Legislature, or by persons or bodies of persons for the time being acting as such Legislature, which have received the assent of Her Majesty in Council, or which have received the assent of the Governor of the said Colony in the name and on behalf of Her Majesty, shall be and be deemed to have been valid and effectual from the date of such assent for all purposes whatever; provided that nothing herein contained shall be deemed to give effect to any law or reputed law which has been disallowed by Her Majesty, or has expired, or has been lawfully repealed, or to prevent the lawful disallowance or repeal of any law.[6] *Certain Acts of Legislature of South Australia to be valid.*

H.C.C.

NOTES TO THE COLONIAL LAWS VALIDITY ACT, 1865.

1 This Act is 28 & 29 Vict. cap. 63. The text is reprinted from the "Statutes at Large," vol. xxvii. London, 1866. The English "Hansard" is silent as to the reasons given in the British Parliament for enacting it. In point of importance, as a charter of colonial liberties, it must be allowed a place alongside of Lord Mansfield's judgment in the Grenada Case. See pp. 79-89 above.

2 Amongst the "laws," the validity of which was questioned, were "divers Acts" passed by the Legislature of South Australia "for the purpose of altering the constitution of the Legislative Council and House of Assembly," of that colony (see section 7 below), and with a view to set at rest the doubts that had been raised the British Parliament passed an Act (26 & 27 Vict. cap. 84) "to confirm certain Acts of Colonial Legislatures," thus making it general in its operation. The text of this statute is obviously a prelude to the "Colonial Laws Validity Act." It is as follows:—

1 "In this Act of Parliament the term 'Colonial Legislature' shall mean the authority (other than Her Majesty-in-Council) competent to make laws for any of Her Majesty's possessions abroad, except India, the Channel Islands, and the Isle of Man. The term 'Governor' shall mean the officer lawfully administering the Government of any colony.

2 All laws heretofore passed or purporting to have been passed by any colonial Legislature with the object of declaring or altering the constitution of such Legislature, or of any branch thereof, or the mode of appointing or electing the members of the same, shall have, and be deemed to have had, from the date at which the same shall have received the assent of Her Majesty or of the Governor of the colony on behalf of Her Majesty, the same force and effect for all purposes whatever as if the said Legislature had possessed full powers of enacting laws for the objects aforesaid, and as if all formalities and conditions by Act of Parliament or otherwise prescribed in respect of the passing of such laws had been duly observed."

3 See Tarring's "Chapters on the Laws relating to the Colonies" (pp. 1-2) for a legal definition of the term "colony."

4 See Note 73, p. 239, for an illustration of the nullification of a Canadian Statute *pro tanto* on the ground of "repugnancy." The Acts passed for the regulation of copyright in Canada afford other illustrations of the operation of the same principle. The Imperial Copyright Act of 1842 (5 & 6 Vict. cap. 45) is made applicable to "all the colonies, settlements, and possessions of the Crown, which now are, or hereafter may be acquired." In 1872 the Canadian Parliament passed a Copyright Bill, to which, after it had been reserved for Her Majesty's pleasure, her assent was refused on the ground that some of its provisions conflicted with those of the Imperial Copyright Act. See Dom. Sess. Papers, 1875, No. 28. The Canadian Parliament in 1875 passed a Copyright Act which would also have been nullified on the ground of "repugnancy," had it been assented to in the usual way; but the Imperial Parliament in the same year passed an Act (38 & 39 Vict. cap. 53) authorizing Her Majesty to give assent by Order-in-Council, which was subsequently done. In the case of Smiles v. Belford. (Ont. Chancery Reports, vol. 23, pp. 590-605; Ont. Appeal Reports, 1876-77, pp. 136-145), it was decided that the Canadian Act of 1875 did not impair the British author's right under the Imperial Act of 1842.

5 Compare the action of the first Parliament of Upper Canada in repealing part of the Quebec Act of 1774, and passing an Act which made the "Laws of England" instead of the "Laws of Canada," "the rule of decision in all matters of controversy relative to property and civil rights."

6 See Note 2 above. Canada had in 1854 been expressly authorized to alter the constitution of her Legislative Council and had done so. (See pp. 177-179 above.)

GOVERNOR-GENERAL'S COMMISSIONS AND ROYAL INSTRUCTIONS.[1]

1. Commission and Instructions[2] of Viscount Monck, 1867.

Draft of a Commission to be passed under the Great Seal of the United Kingdom, appointing Viscount Monck to be Governor-General of Canada, on and after the first day of July, 1867.

VICTORIA, by the Grace of God, of the United Kingdom of Great Britain and Ireland, Queen, Defender of the Faith, to our Right Trusty and Well-beloved Cousin, Charles Stanley, Viscount Monck,—GREETING:

I. Whereas We did, by divers Letters Patent, under the Great Seal of Our United Kingdom of Great Britain and Ireland, bearing date severally at Westminster the second day of November, one thousand eight hundred and sixty-one, in the Twenty-fifth year of Our Reign, constitute and appoint you, Our Right Trusty and Well-beloved Cousin, Charles Stanley, Viscount Monck, to be, during Our pleasure, Our Captain General and Governor in Chief in and over Our Province of Canada, and in and over the Province of Nova Scotia and its Dependencies,[3] and in and over the Province of New Brunswick, and also Governor General of all Our Provinces in North America and of the Island of Prince Edward,[4] as by the said several recited Letters Patent, relation being thereunto had, may more fully and at large appear:

And whereas by an Act of Parliament passed in the Thirtieth year of Our Reign, intituled, "The British North America Act, 1867," it is, amongst other things, enacted that it shall be lawful for Us, by and with the advice of Our Privy Council, to declare, by Proclamation, that, on and after a day therein appointed, not being more than Six Months after the passing of the said Act, the Provinces of Canada, Nova Scotia and New Brunswick, shall form and be One Dominion, under the name of Canada; and on and after that day those three Provinces shall form and be One Dominion under that name, accordingly, and that Canada shall be divided into Four Provinces, named Ontario, Quebec, Nova Scotia, and New Brunswick:

And whereas We did, on the twenty-second day of May, one thousand eight hundred and sixty-seven, by and with the advice of Our Privy Council, declare by Proclamation[5] that, on and after the first day of July, one thousand eight hundred and sixty-seven, being within six months after the passing of the said Act, the Provinces of Canada, Nova Scotia, and New Brunswick, should form and be One Dominion, under the name of Canada :

Now know You, that We do by these Presents declare Our pleasure to be, that the said recited Letters Patent, and every clause, article and thing therein contained, shall be, and they are hereby declared to be Revoked and Determined, on the said first day of July, one thousand eight hundred and sixty-seven :

And further Know You, that We, reposing especial Trust and Confidence in the prudence, courage and loyalty of you, the said Charles Stanley, Viscount Monck, of Our special Grace, certain knowledge and mere motion, have thought fit to constitute and appoint, and do by these Presents constitute and appoint you to be, on and after the said first day of July, one thousand eight hundred and sixty-seven, during Our pleasure, Our Governor General of Canada ; and We do hereby authorize, empower, require and command you thereafter, in due manner to do and execute all things that shall belong to your said Command and the Trust We have reposed in you, according to the several powers, provisions, and directions granted or appointed you by virtue of this Our Commission, and of the said recited Act of Parliament, and according to such instructions as are herewith given to you,[6] or which may from time to time hereafter be given to you, in respect of the said Dominion of Canada, under Our Sign Manual and Signet, or by Our Order in Our Privy Council, or by Us, through one of Our principal Secretaries of State, and according to such laws as are or shall be in force within Our said Dominion.

II. And We do hereby authorize and empower you to keep and use the Great Seal of Canada, for the sealing of all things whatsoever that shall pass the said Seal.

III. And We do further authorize and empower you to exercise all such powers as We may be at any time entitled to exercise, in respect of the constitution and appointment of Judges ; and, in cases requisite, Commissioners of Oyer and Terminer, Justices of the Peace, and other necessary Officers and Ministers of Our said Dominion of Canada, for the better administration of Justice, and putting the Laws into execution.[7]

IV. And We do hereby give and grant unto you, so far as We lawfully may, full power and authority, upon sufficient cause to you appearing, to remove from his Office, or to suspend from the exercise of the same, any person exercising any office or place within Our said Dominion, under or by virtue of any Commission or Warrant granted, or which may be granted by Us, in Our name or under Our authority.

V. And We do hereby give and grant unto you full power and authority, when you shall see cause, in Our name and on Our behalf, to grant to any offender convicted of any crime in any Court, or before any Judge, Justice or Magistrate within Our said Dominion, a Pardon, either free or subject to lawful conditions, or any respite of the execution of the sentence of any such offender, for such period as to you may seem fit; and to remit any fines, penalties or forfeitures, which may become due and payable to Us.[8]

VI. And We do hereby authorize you to exercise, from time to time, as you may judge necessary, all powers belonging to Us, in respect of Assembling or Proroguing the Senate or the House of Commons of Our said Dominion, and of Dissolving the said House of Commons; and We do hereby give the like authority to the several Lieutenant Governors for the time being, of the Four Provinces in Our said Dominion, with respect to the Legislative Councils or the Legislative or General Assemblies of those Provinces respectively.

VII. And We do by these Presents authorize and empower you, within our said Dominion, to exercise all such powers as We may be entitled to exercise therein, in respect of granting Licenses for Marriages, Letters of Administration and Probates of Wills, and with respect to the custody and management of Idiots and Lunatics, and their Estates; and to Present any person or persons to any Churches, Chapels or other Ecclesiastical Benefices, within Our said Provinces of Nova Scotia and New Brunswick, to which We shall from time to time be entitled to Present.

VIII. And whereas, by the said recited Act, it is amongst other things enacted, that it shall be lawful for Us, if We think fit, to authorize the Governor General of Canada to appoint any person or persons jointly or severally to be his Deputy or Deputies within any part or parts of Canada, and in that capacity to exercise, during the pleasure of the Governor General, such of the powers, authorities and functions of the Governor General as he may deem it necessary or expedient to assign to him or them, subject to any limitations or directions from time to time expressed or given by Us; now We do hereby authorize and empower you, subject to such limitations and directions as aforesaid, to appoint any person or persons jointly or severally, to be your Deputy or Deputies within any part or parts of Our Dominion of Canada, and in that capacity to exercise, during your pleasure, such of your powers, functions and authorities as you may deem it necessary or expedient to assign to him or them: Provided always, that the appointment of such a Deputy or Deputies shall not affect the exercise of any such power, authority, or function by you, the said Charles Stanley, Viscount Monck, in person.

IX. And in case of your death, incapacity, or absence out of Our said Dominion of Canada, We do by these Presents give and grant, all and singular, the powers and authorities herein to you granted to Our Lieutenant Governor for the time being of Our said Dominion of Canada, or in the absence of any such Lieutenant Governor to such person as we may by Warrant under Our Sign Manual and Signet, appoint to be the Administrator of the Government of Our said Dominion, or in the absence of any such Lieutenant Governor or person as aforesaid, to the senior Military Officer for the time being in command of Our regular forces in our said Dominion, such powers and authorities to be by him executed and enjoyed during Our pleasure.

X. And We do hereby require and command all Our Officers and Ministers, civil and military, and all other the inhabitants of Our said Dominion of Canada, to be obedient, aiding, and assisting unto you in the execution of this Our Commission, and of the powers and authorities herein contained.

Draft of Instructions to be passed under the Royal Sign Manual and Signet to Viscount Monck, Governor-General of Canada.

INSTRUCTIONS to Our Right Trusty and Well-beloved Cousin, Charles Stanley, Viscount Monck, Our Governor-General of Canada, or, in his absence, to Our Lieutenant-Governor or the Officer Administering the Government of Our Dominion of Canada for the time being. Given at Our Court at Balmoral, this First day of June, 1867, in the Thirtieth Year of Our Reign.

1. Whereas, by Our Commission, under the Great Seal of Our United Kingdom of Great Britain and Ireland, bearing even date herewith, We have constituted and appointed you, the said Charles Stanley, Viscount Monck, to be, on and after the first day of July, 1867, during Our pleasure, Our Governor General of Canada: And have required you to do and execute all things that shall belong to your said command, according to the several powers, provisions, directions, and instructions therein mentioned, and particularly according to such instructions as should be therewith given to you:

Now, therefore, by these Our instructions, under Our Sign-Manual and Signet, being the said last-mentioned instructions, We do declare Our will and pleasure to be, that on or immediately after the said First day of July, 1867, you do publish Our said Commission in Our Dominion of Canada, and do take the Oath[9] appointed to be taken by an Act passed in the Twenty-first and Twenty-second Year of Our Reign, intituled, "An Act to substitute one Oath for the Oaths of Allegiance, Supremacy, and Abjuration, and for the relief of Her Majesty's subjects professing the Jewish religion"; and likewise that you take the usual Oath for the due execution and performance of the Office and Trust of Our Governor-General of Our said Dominion, and for the due and impartial Administration of Justice; which said Oaths the Judges of Our Supreme Courts of Record within our said Dominion, or any three or more of such Judges, have hereby full power and authority, and are required to tender and administer unto you.

II. And We do hereby give and grant unto you full power and authority from time to time, and at any time hereafter, by yourself or by any other person to be authorized by you in that behalf, to administer to all and every person or persons as you shall think fit, who shall hold any office or place of trust or profit, or who shall at any time or times pass into Our said Dominion of Canada, or who shall be resident or abiding therein, the Oath commonly called the Oath of Allegiance, together with such other Oath or Oaths as may from time to time be prescribed by any Laws or Statutes in that behalf made and provided.

III. And to the end that Our Privy Council[10] for Canada may be assisting to you in all affairs relating to Our Service, you are to communicate to them these Our Instructions, and any additional instructions which may be in like manner hereafter given to you by Us.

IV. And We do hereby declare, and it is Our Pleasure, that Our said Privy Council shall not proceed to the despatch of business unless duly summoned by your authority, nor unless four Members of the said Council be present and assisting at the meetings at which any such business shall be despatched. And We do further direct, that if, in any case you see sufficient cause to dissent from the opinion of the major part or of the whole of Our said Privy Council so present, it shall be competent to you to execute the powers and authorities vested in you by Our said Commission, and by these Our Instructions, in opposition to such their opinion[11]; it being, nevertheless, Our Pleasure, that in every case it shall be competent to any Member of Our said Privy Council to record at length, on the Minutes of Our said Council, the grounds and reasons of any advice or opinion he may give upon any question brought under the consideration of such Council.

V. And it is Our Pleasure and you are hereby authorized to appoint by an instrument under the Great Seal of Canada, one Member of our said Privy Council to preside in your absence, and to remove him and appoint another in his stead. And if, during your absence, the Member so appointed shall also be absent, then the senior Member of the Privy Council, actually present shall preside, the seniority of the Members of the said Council being regulated according to the date or order of their respective appointment thereto.

VI. And We do further direct and command that a full and exact Journal or Minute be kept of all the Deliberations, Acts, Proceedings, Votes, and Resolutions of Our said Privy Council; and that at each Meeting of the said Council the Minutes of the last preceding Meeting shall be read over, confirmed, or amended, as the case may require before proceeding to the despatch of any other business.

VII. And for the execution of so much of the Powers vested in you by virtue of the "British North America Act, 1867," as relates to the declaring either that you Assent in Our Name to Bills passed by the Houses of the Parliament, or that you withhold Our Assent therefrom, or that you Reserve such Bills for the signification of Our pleasure thereon, it is Our Will and Pleasure that when any Bill is presented to you for Our Assent of either of the classes hereinafter specified, you shall (unless you shall think proper to withhold Our Assent from the same) Reserve the same for the signification of Our pleasure thereon ; Subject, nevertheless, to your discretion, in case you should be of opinion that an Urgent Necessity exists, requiring that such Bill be brought into immediate operation ; in which case you are Authorized to Assent to such Bill in Our Name, transmitting to Us by the earliest opportunity the Bill so Assented to, together with your reasons for assenting thereto; that is to say :

1. Any Bill for the Divorce of Persons joined together in Holy Matrimony.

2. Any Bill whereby any Grant of Land or Money, or other Donation or Gratuity, may be made to yourself.

3. Any Bill whereby any Paper or other Currency may be made a Legal Tender, except the Coin of the Realm, or other Gold or Silver Coin.

4. Any Bill imposing Differential Duties.

5. Any Bill, the Provisions of which shall appear inconsistent with obligations imposed upon Us by Treaty.

6. Any Bill interfering with the discipline or control of Our Forces in Our said Dominion by land and sea.

7. Any Bill of an extraordinary nature and importance, whereby Our Prerogative, or the rights and property of Our subjects not residing in Our said Dominion, or the trade and shipping of the United Kingdom and its dependencies, may be prejudiced.

8. Any Bill containing provisions to which Our Assent has been once refused, or which has been disallowed by Us.

VIII. You shall take care that all laws assented to by you in Our name, or reserved for the signification of Our pleasure thereon, be duly transmitted to Us with such explanatory observations as the nature of each law may require. and you are also to transmit fair Copies of the Journals and Minutes of the Proceedings of the said Houses of the Parliament, which you are to require from the Clerks or other proper Officers in that behalf of the said Houses of the Parliament.

IX. And whereas We have by Our said Commission given and granted unto you full power and authority, when you shall see cause, to pardon offenders convicted of any crime, and to remit Fines, Penalties, and Forfeitures; Now We do hereby enjoin you to call upon the Judge presiding at the trial of any offenders to make to you a written report of the cases of all persons who may from time to time be condemned to suffer death by the sentence of any Court within Our said Dominion, and such reports of the said Judge shall by you be taken into consideration at the first meeting thereafter which may be conveniently held of Our said Privy Council for Canada; and you shall not pardon any such offender unless it shall appear to you expedient so to do, upon receiving the advice of Our said Privy Council therein, but in all such cases you are to decide whether to extend or withhold a pardon, according to your own deliberate judgment whether the Members of Our said Privy Council concur therein, or otherwise; Entering, nevertheless, on the Minutes of the said Council, a Minute of your reasons at length, in case you should decide any such question in opposition to the judgment of the majority of Members thereof.[1][2]

X. It is Our further will and pleasure that all commissions to be granted by you to any person or persons to be Judge, Justice of the Peace, or other necessary Officer, unless otherwise provided by law, be granted during Our pleasure only.

XI. And whereas by Our said Commission We have authorized you to present any person or persons to any Church, Chapel, or other Ecclesiastical Benefice, within our said Provinces of Nova Scotia and New Brunswick, to which We may from time to time be entitled to present, We do declare Our will and pleasure to be that you do not present any Minister of the United Church of England and Ireland to any Ecclesiastical Benefice without a Certificate from the Bishop for the time being of the Diocese in which such presentation is made, or his Commissary, of his being conformable to the doctrine and discipline of the said Church. And it is Our will and pleasure that the person so presented shall be instituted by the said Bishop, or his Commissary duly authorized by him.

XII. And whereas you will receive through one of Our principal Secretaries of State a Book of Tables in blank (commonly called the "Blue Book") to be annually filled up with certain Returns relative to the Revenue and Expenditure, Militia, Public Works, Legislation, Civil Establishment, Pensions, Populations, Schools, Course of Exchange, Imports and Exports, Agricultural Produce, Manufactures, and other matters in the said "Blue Book" more particularly specified, with reference to the state and condition of Our said Dominion of Canada; Now We do hereby signify Our pleasure that all such Returns be accurately prepared and punctually transmitted to Us through one of Our principal Secretaries of State.

XIII. And whereas great prejudice may happen to Our service and to the security of Our said Dominion by the absence of the Governor General, you shall not, upon any pretence whatever, quit the said Dominion without having first obtained leave from Us for so doing, under Our Sign-Manual and Signet, or through one of Our principal Secretaries of State.

2. Letters-Patent[13] and Instructions, 1878.

Draft of Letters-Patent passed under the Great Seal of the United Kingdom, constituting the Office of Governor-General of the Dominion of Canada.

Letters-Patent,
Dated 5th October, 1878.

VICTORIA, by the Grace of God, of the United Kingdom of Great Britain and Ireland, Queen, Defender of the Faith, Empress of India ; To all to whom these Presents shall come, Greeting :

WHEREAS We did, by certain Letters-Patent under the Great Seal of Our United Kingdom of Great Britain and Ireland, bearing date at Westminster the Twenty-second day of May, 1872, in the Thirty-fifth Year of Our Reign, constitute and appoint Our Right Trusty and Right Well-beloved Cousin and Councillor, Frederick Temple, Earl of Dufferin, Knight of Our Most Illustrious Order of Saint Patrick, Knight Commander of Our Most Honorable Order of the Bath (now Knight Grand Cross of Our Most Distinguished Order of Saint Michael and Saint George), to be Our Governor-General in and over Our Dominion of Canada for and during Our will and pleasure :

And whereas by the 12th section of "The British North America Act, 1867," certain powers, authorities, and functions were declared to be vested in the Governor-General :

And whereas We are desirous of making effectual and permanent provision for the office of Governor-General in and over Our said Dominion of Canada, without making new Letters-Patent on each demise of the said Office :

Now know ye that We have revoked and determined, and by these presents do revoke and determine, the said recited Letters-Patent of the Twenty-second day of May, 1872, and every clause, article and thing therein contained :

And further know ye that We, of our special grace, certain knowledge, and mere motion, have thought fit to constitute, order, and declare, and do by these presents constitute, order, and declare that there shall be a Governor-General (hereinafter called Our said Governor-General) in and over Our Dominion of Canada (hereinafter called Our said Dominion), and that the person who shall fill the said Office of the Governor-General shall be from time to time appointed by Commission under our Sign-Manual and Signet. And we do hereby authorize and command Our said Governor-General to do and execute, in due manner, all things that shall belong to his said command, and to the trust We have reposed in him, according to the several powers and authorities granted or appointed him by virtue of "The British North America Act, 1867," and of these present Letters-Patent, and of such Commission[14] as may be issued to him under Our Sign-Manual and Signet, and according to such Instructions as may from time to time be given to him, under Our Sign-Manual and Signet, or by Our Order in Our Privy Council, or by us through one of Our Principal Secretaries of State, and to such Laws as are or shall hereafter be in force in Our said Dominion.

II. And We do hereby authorize and empower Our said Governor-General to keep and use the Great Seal of Our said Dominion for sealing all things whatsoever that shall pass the said Great Seal.

III. And We do further authorize and empower Our said Governor-General to constitute and appoint, in Our name and on Our behalf, all such Judges, Commissioners, Justices of the Peace, and other necessary Officers and Ministers of Our said Dominion, as may be lawfully constituted or appointed by Us.[15]

IV. And We do further authorize and empower Our said Governor-General, so far as we lawfully may, upon sufficient cause to him appearing, to remove from his office, or to suspend from the exercise of the same, any person exercising any office within Our said Dominion, under or by virtue of any Commission or Warrant granted, or which may be granted, by Us in Our name or under Our authority.

V. And We do further authorize and empower Our said Governor-General to exercise all powers lawfully belonging to us in respect of the summoning, proroguing, or dissolving the Parliament of Our said Dominion.[16]

VI. And whereas by "The British North America Act, 1867," it is amongst other things enacted, that it shall be lawful for Us, if We think fit, to authorize the Governor-General of Our Dominion of Canada to appoint any person or persons, jointly or severally, to be his Deputy or Deputies within any part or parts of Our said Dominion, and in that capacity to exercise, during the pleasure of Our said Governor-General, such of the powers, authorities, and functions of Our said Governor-General as he may deem it necessary or expedient to assign to such Deputy or Deputies, subject to any limitations or directions from time to time expressed or given by Us: Now We do hereby authorize and empower Our said Governor-General, subject to such limitations and directions as aforesaid, to appoint any person or persons, jointly or severally, to be his Deputy or Deputies within any part or parts of Our said Dominion of Canada, and in that capacity to exercise, during his pleasure, such of his powers, functions, and authorities as he may deem it necessary or expedient to assign to him or them: Provided always, that the appointment of such a Deputy or Deputies shall not affect the exercise of any such power, authority or function by Our said Governor-General in person.

VII. And We do hereby declare Our pleasure to be that, in the event of the death, incapacity, removal, or absence of Our said Governor-General out of Our said Dominion, all and every the powers and authorities herein granted to him shall, until Our further pleasure is signified therein, be vested in such person as may be appointed by Us under Our Sign-Manual and Signet to be Our Lieutenant-Governor of Our said Dominion; or if there shall be no such Lieutenant-Governor in Our said Dominion, then in such person or persons as may be appointed by Us under Our Sign-Manual and Signet to administer the Government of the same; and in case there shall be no person or persons within Our said Dominion so appointed by Us, then in the Senior Officer for the time being in command of Our regular troops in Our said Dominion: Provided that no such powers or authorities shall vest in such Lieutenant-Governor, or such other person or persons, until he or they shall have taken the oaths appointed to be taken by the Governor-General of Our said Dominion, and in the manner provided by the Instructions accompanying these Our Letters-Patent.

VIII. And We do hereby require and command all Our Officers and Ministers, Civil and Military, and all other the inhabitants of Our said Dominion, to be obedient, aiding and assisting unto Our said Governor-General, or, in the event of his death, incapacity, or absence, to such person or persons as may, from time to time, under the provisions of these Our Letters-Patent, administer the Government of Our said Dominion.

IX. And We do hereby reserve to Ourselves, Our heirs and successors, full power and authority from time to time to revoke, alter or amend these Our Letters-Patent as to Us or them shall seem meet.

X. And We do further direct and enjoin that these Our Letters-Patent shall be read and proclaimed at such place or places as Our said Governor-General shall think fit within Our said Dominion of Canada.

In Witness whereof We have caused these Our Letters to be made Patent. Witness Ourself at Westminster, the Fifth day of October, in the Forty-second Year of Our Reign.

By Warrant under the Queen's Sign-Manual.

C. ROMILLY.

Draft of Instructions passed under the Royal Sign-Manual and Signet to the Governor-General of the Dominion of Canada.

Dated 5th October, 1878.
VICTORIA R.

Instructions to Our Governor-General in and over Our Dominion of Canada, or, in his absence, to Our Lieutenant-Governor or the Officer for the time being administering the Government of Our said Dominion.

Given at Our Court at Balmoral, this Fifth day of October, 1878, in he Forty-second year of Our Reign.

WHEREAS by certain Letters-Patent bearing even date herewith, We have constituted, ordered, and declared that there shall be a Governor-General (hereinafter called Our said Governor-General) in and over Our Dominion of Canada (hereinafter called Our said Dominion), and We have thereby authorized and commanded Our said Governor-General to do and execute in due manner all things that shall belong to his said command, and to the trust We have reposed in him, according to the several powers and authorities granted or appointed him by virtue of the said Letters-Patent and of such Commission as may be issued to him under Our Sign-Manual and Signet, and according to such Instructions as may from time to time be given to him, under Our Sign-Manual and Signet, or by Our Order in Our Privy Council, or by Us through One of Our Principal Secretaries of State, and to such Laws as are or shall hereafter be in force in Our said Dominion:

Now, therefore, We do, by these, Our Instructions under Our Sign-Manual and Signet, declare Our pleasure to be that Our said Governor-General for the time being shall, with all due solemnity, cause Our Commission, under Our Sign-Manual and Signet, appointing Our said Governor-General for the time being, to be read and published in the presence of the Chief Justice for the time being, or other Judge of the Supreme Court of Our said Dominion, and of the members of the Privy Council in Our said Dominion:

And We do further declare Our pleasure to be that Our said Governor-General, and every other officer appointed to administer the Government of Our said Dominion, shall take the Oath[17] of Allegiance in the form provided by an Act passed in the Session holden in the thirty-first and thirty-second years of Our Reign, intituled : "An Act to Amend the Law relating to Promissory Oaths ;" and likewise that he or they shall take the usual Oath for the due execution of the Office of Our Governor-General in and over Our said Dominion, and for the due and impartial administration of justice; which Oaths the said Chief Justice for the time being, of Our said Dominion, or, in his absence, or in the event of his being otherwise incapacitated, any Judge of the Supreme Court of Our said Dominion shall, and he is hereby required to tender and administer unto him or them.

II. And We do authorize and require Our said Governor-General from time to time, by himself or by any other person to be authorized by him in that behalf, to administer to all and to every persons or person as he shall think fit, who shall hold any office or place of trust or profit in Our said Dominion, the said Oath of Allegiance, together with such other Oath or Oaths as may from time to time, be prescribed by any Laws or Statutes in that behalf made and provided.

III. And We do require Our said Governor-General to communicate forthwith to the Privy Council for Our said Dominion these Our Instructions, and likewise all such others from time to time as he shall find convenient for Our service to be imparted to them.

IV. Our said Governor-General is to take care that all laws assented to by him in Our name, or reserved for the signification of Our pleasure thereon, shall, when transmitted by him, be fairly abstracted in the margins, and be accompanied, in such cases as may seem to him necessary, with such explanatory observations as may be required to exhibit the reasons and occasions for proposing such Laws; and he shall also transmit fair copies of the Journals and Minutes of the proceedings of the Parliament of Our said Dominion, which he is to require from the clerks, or other proper officers in that behalf, of the said Parliament.

V. And We do further authorize and empower Our said Governor-General, as he shall see occasion, in Our name and on Our behalf, when any crime has been committed for which the offender may be tried within Our said Dominion, to grant a pardon to any accomplice not being the actual perpetrator of such crime, who shall give such information as shall lead to the conviction of the principal offender; and further, to grant to any offender convicted of any crime in any Court, or before any Judge Justice, or Magistrate, within Our said Dominion, a pardon, either free or subject to lawful conditions, or any respite of the execution of the sentence of any such offender, for such period as to Our said Governor-General may seem fit, and to remit any fines, penalties, or forfeitures which may become due and payable to Us. Provided always, that Our said Governor-General shall not in any case, except where the offence has been of a political nature, make it a condition of any pardon or remission of sentence that the offender shall be banished from or shall absent himself from Our said Dominion. And We do hereby direct and enjoin that Our said Governor-General shall not pardon or reprieve any such offender without first receiving in capital cases the advice of the Privy Council for Our said Dominion, and in other cases the advice of one, at least, of his Ministers; and in any case in which such pardon or reprieve might directly affect the interests of Our Empire, or of any country or place beyond the jurisdiction of the Government of Our said Dominion, Our said Governor-General shall, before deciding as to either pardon or reprieve, take those interests specially into his own personal consideration in conjunction with such advice as aforesaid.[18]

VI. And whereas great prejudice may happen to Our service and to the security of Our said Dominion by the absence of Our said Governor-General, he shall not, upon any pretence whatever, quit Our said Dominion without having first obtained leave from Us for so doing under Our Sign-Manual and Signet, or through one of Our Principal Secretaries of State.

V.R.

3. Commission[19] of the Marquis of Lorne, 1878.

Draft of a Commission passed under the Royal Sign-Manual and Signet, appointing the Right Honourable the Marquis of Lorne, K.T., G.C.M.G., to be Governor-General of the Dominion of Canada.

Dated 7th October, 1878.
VICTORIA R.

VICTORIA, by the Grace of God, of the United Kingdom of Great Britain and Ireland, Queen, Defender of the Faith, Empress of India, To Our Right, Trusty, and Well-beloved Councillor Sir JOHN DOUGLAS SUTHERLAND CAMPBELL (commonly called the Marquis of Lorne), Knight of Our Most Ancient and Most Noble Order of the Thistle, Knight Grand Cross of Our Most Distinguished Order of St. Michael and St. George, Greeting:

WE do, by this Our Commission under Our Sign-Manual and Signet, appoint you, the said Sir JOHN DOUGLAS SUTHERLAND CAMPBELL (commonly called the Marquis of Lorne), until Our further pleasure shall be signified, to be Our Governor-General in and over Our Dominion of Canada during Our will and pleasure, with all and singular the powers and authorities granted to the Governor-General of Our said Dominion in Our Letters-Patent under the Great Seal of Our United Kingdom of Great Britain and Ireland, constituting the Office of Governor, bearing date at Westminster the Fifth day of October, 1878, in the Forty-second year of Our Reign, which said powers and authorities We do hereby authorize you to exercise and perform, according to such Orders and Instructions as Our said Governor-General for the time being hath already or may hereafter receive from Us. And for so doing this shall be your Warrant.

II. And We do hereby command all and singular Our officers, Ministers, and loving subjects in Our said Dominion, and all others whom it may concern, to take due notice hereof, and to give their ready obedience accordingly.

Given at Our Court at Balmoral, this Seventh day of October, 1878, in the Forty-second year of Our Reign.

By Her Majesty's Command,

M. E. HICKS-BEACH.

NOTES TO GOVERNOR'S COMMISSIONS.

1 The changes which took place in 1878 in the form of the Commission to the Governor-General of Canada, and also in the Instructions accompanying the Commission, made it necessary to introduce these documents from two different periods. Those issued to Lord Monck are selected because he was the first Governor-General of the Dominion of Canada, and those issued to Lord Lorne, because he was the first appointed after the changes above referred to were made. The changes themselves can easily be ascertained by a comparison of the texts, and a lucid account of the circumstances which led to them will be found in Todd's "Parliamentary Government in the British Colonies," pp. 77-90. These documents may be usefully compared with the Commission issued to Governor Cornwallis, of Nova Scotia, in 1749 (pp. 9-16 above), and the Commission issued to Governor Murray, of Quebec, in 1763 (pp. 74-77 above). Lord Monck's "Commission" and "Instructions," 1867, are reprinted from the Dom. Sess. Papers of 1867, No. 22.

2 The "Commission" and "Instructions" issued to Lord Monck in 1861 do not differ materially from those issued to Sir John Young (afterwards Lord Lisgar) in 1868, and to Lord Dufferin in 1872.

3 The most important was Cape Breton.

4 Lord Monck did not actually administer the Government in Nova Scotia, New Brunswick, and Prince Edward Island, each of which had its own Lieutenant-Governor, while the "Province of Canada" under the Union Act of 1840 had none. Lord Durham had come to Canada in 1838, after having been appointed "by five several Commissions" Governor of each of the Provinces of Lower Canada, Upper Canada, Nova Scotia, New Brunswick, and Prince Edward Island; by an additional Commission he had been created "Governor-General of all the Provinces on the Continent of North America and of the Islands of Prince Edward and Newfoundland," each of the Provinces except Lower Canada, which was administered by Lord Durham himself, having its own Lieutenant-Governor. For the text of his Commission as Governor-General see Christie's "History of Lower Canada," vol. v., pp. 149-152. Sir George Arthur, then Lieutenant-Governor of Upper Canada, was the last who held that office. The successors of Lord Durham, prior to Lord Monck's appointment, were (1) Charles Edward Poulett Thompson (afterwards Lord Sydenham), whose Commission appointed him in 1839 "Governor-General of British North America, and Captain-General and Governor-in-Chief in and over the Provinces of Lower Canada and Upper Canada, Nova Scotia, New Brunswick, and the Island of Prince Edward"; (2) Sir Charles Bagot, 1842; (3) Sir Charles (afterward Lord) Metcalfe, 1843; (4) Lord Elgin, 1846; and (5) Sir Edmund Walker Head, 1854.

5 See Note 5, p. 231 above.

6 See pp. 248-252 above.

7 This and the five following sections of the Commission must be read in the light of the discussions of a quarter of a century before on the subject of "Responsible Government." See Appendix E. A good account of the crisis precipitated by Lord Metcalfe's action in 1843 in appointing an officer connected with the administration of justice without consulting his Executive Council, the Lafontaine-Baldwin Ministry, will be found in Dent's "Canada since the Union of 1841," vol. I., pp. 320-351. See also Sir Francis Hincks' "Reminiscences."

⁸ The last exercise of this prerogative by a Canadian Governor, without the advice of his responsible Ministers, was by Lord Dufferin in the case of Ambrose Lepine, in 1875. The death sentence pronounced upon him for complicity in the murder of Thomas Scott during the Red River rebellion of 1869-70 was commuted to two years' imprisonment with permanent deprivation of political rights, and Lord Dufferin, in an official communication to the then Minister of Justice, stated that he acted "under the Royal Instructions, which authorize the Governor-General in certain capital cases, to dispense with the advice of his Ministers, and to exercise the prerogative of the Crown according to his independent judgment and on his own personal responsibility." As to the "Instructions" here cited, see p. 251 above. Lord Dufferin's official letter to the Minister of Justice will be found in the "Canada Gazette Extra" of June 19, 1875, and in Dom. Sess. Papers for 1875, No. 11. An accurate summary of the whole case, together with a discussion of the administration of the prerogative of mercy in other self-governing colonies is given in Todd's "Parliamentary Government in the British Colonies," pp. 251-274. Compare Section V. of the "Royal Instructions" of 1878 (pp. 257-258 above). The Lepine commutation case was discussed with approbation in the House of Lords (Hansard, Third Series, vol. 223, pp. 1065-1077).

⁹ Compare the "Royal Instructions" of 1878 (p. 256 above).

¹⁰ This term was introduced into Canada by the Confederation Act, 1867 (section 11).

¹¹ See Note 7 above. Compare on this point the "Royal Instructions" of 1878 (pp. 256-258, above). See also Todd's "Parliamentary Government in the British Colonies" (pp. 331-343); Dom. Sess. Papers for 1876, No. 116; *ibid* for 1877, No. 89; and *ibid* for 1879, No. 181. As to the effect of refusal of advice by a Governor, note the precedent set by the Lafontaine-Baldwin Ministry in 1843.

¹² See Note 8 above.

¹³ Prior to the issue of these "Letters-Patent" there was no permanently constituted office of "Governor-General" of Canada, each successive Governor having been appointed by a special "Commission" which defined his functions, and informed by special "Instructions" as to the manner in which he should discharge them. As to the course of events which led to the issue of these "Letters-Patent" making the office a permanent one, and to the issue of permanent "Royal Instructions" to accompany them, see Todd's "Parliamentary Government in the British Colonies" (pp. 77-90); Dom. Sess. Papers, 1877, No. 13; *ibid*, 1879, No. 181; and Hansard, Third Series, vol. 244, p. 1312. The documents are reprinted from the Dom. Sess. Papers of 1879, No. 14.

¹⁴ See "Commission" to Lord Lorne (pp. 258-259 above).

¹⁵ See Note 7 above.

¹⁶ For a useful discussion of the relation of a Governor to his responsible Ministers in regard to the matters here enumerated, see Todd's "Parliamentary Government in the British Colonies," pp. 460-575.

¹⁷ Compare the "Royal Instructions," p. 249 above.

¹⁸ See Note 8 above. The whole subject of the exercise of the prerogative of mercy is discussed in Todd's "Parliamentary Government in the British Colonies," pp. 251-274. See also Dom. Sess. Papers, 1876, No. 117; *ibid*, 1877, No. 13; and *ibid*, 1879, No. 181.

¹⁹ With the office of Governor-General permanently constituted under the "Letters-Patent" of 1878 nothing beyond a brief Commission referring to the "Letters-Patent" is necessary to the appointment of a new incumbent. The successors so far of Lord Lorne, have been (1) Lord Lansdowne, whose Com-

mission is dated August 18th, 1883, and (2) Lord Stanley of Preston, the date of whose Commission is May 1st, 1888.

20 Some changes have been made in the form of the Commission since 1878, and to show their nature the Commission to Lord Stanley of Preston is here given from the official printed copy:

"We do by this Our Commission under our Sign Manual and Signet appoint you, the said Frederick Arthur, Baron Stanley of Preston, to be during our pleasure our Governor-General in and over our Dominion of Canada, with all the powers, rights, privileges, and advantages to the said office belonging or appertaining.

II. And we do hereby authorize, empower, and command you to exercise and perform all and singular the powers and directions contained in our Letters-Patent under the Great Seal of our United Kingdom of Great Britain and Ireland, bearing date at Westminster, the fifth day of October, 1878, constituting the said office of Governor-General, or in any other Letters-Patent adding to, amending, or substituted for the same, according to such orders and instructions as our Governor-General for the time being hath already received from us, or as you shall hereafter receive from us.

III. And, further, we do hereby appoint that so soon as you shall have taken the prescribed oaths, and have entered upon the duties of your office, this our present Commission shall supersede our Commission under our Sign Manual and Signet bearing date the eighteenth day of August, 1883, in the forty-seventh year of our reign, appointing our right trusty and entirely beloved cousin, Henry Charles Keith, Marquis of Lansdowne, now Knight Grand Cross of our most distinguished Order of Saint Michael and St. George, to be our Governor-General of our Dominion of Canada.

IV. And we do hereby command all and singular our Officers, Ministers, and loving subjects in our said Dominion, and all others whom it may concern, to take due notice hereof, and to give their ready obedience accordingly.

Given at our Court at Windsor, this first day of May, 1888, in the fifty-first year of our reign.

By Her Majesty's command.

KNUTSFORD."

APPENDIXES.

APPENDIX A.

EXTRACTS FROM TREATIES[1] RELATING TO CANADA, PRIOR TO AND INCLUDING THE YEAR 1783.

1. The Treaty of Ryswick, 1697.

VII. The Most Christian King[2] shall restore to the said King[3] of Great Britain all countries, islands, forts, and colonies, wheresoever situated, which the English did possess before the declaration of this present war. And in like manner the King of Great Britain shall restore to the Most Christian King all countries, islands, forts, and colonies, wheresoever situated, which the French did possess before the said declaration of war; and this restitution shall be made on both sides within the space of six months, or sooner if it can be done. . . . .

VIII. Commissioners shall be appointed on both sides to examine and determine the rights and pretensions which either of the said kings hath to the places situated in Hudson's Bay[4]; but the possession of those places which were taken by the French, during the peace that preceded this present war, and were retaken by the English during this war, shall be left to the French, by virtue of the foregoing article. . . . . .

2. The Treaty of Utrecht[5], 1713.

3. The Treaty of Aix-la-Chapelle, 1748.

V. All the conquests that have been made since the commencement of the war, or which, since the conclusion of the preliminary articles, signed on the 30th of April last, may have been or shall be made, either in Europe, or the East or West Indies, or in any other part of the world whatsoever, being to be restored without exception, in conformity to what was stipulated by the said preliminary articles and by the declaration since signed; the high con-

---

[1] The text of these extracts is taken from Chalmer's "Collection of Treaties between Great Britain and other Powers," London, 1790.

[2] Lewis XIV.

[3] William III.

[4] See Note 4 to the Treaty of Utrecht (p. 6).

[5] For extracts from this Treaty relating to Canada see pp. 3-5 above.

tracting parties[1] engage to give orders immediately for proceeding to that restitution. . . . .

IX. . . Whereas it is not possible, considering the distance of the countries, that what relates to America should be effected within the same time,[2] or even to fix the time of its entire execution, His Britannic Majesty likewise engages on his part to send to His Most Christian Majesty, immediately after the exchange of the ratifications of the present treaty, two persons of rank and consideration, who shall remain there as hostages, till there shall be received a certain and authentic account of the restitution of Isle Royal, called Cape Breton, and of all the conquests which the arms or subjects of His Britannic Majesty may have made, before or after the signing of the preliminaries, in the East or West Indies. . . . . . . Provided, nevertheless, that Isle Royal, called Cape Breton, shall be restored, with all the artillery and warlike stores which shall have been found therein on the day of its surrender, conformably to the inventories which have been made thereof, and in the condition that the said place was in on the said day of its surrender.

4. The Treaty of Paris[3], 1763.

5. The Treaty of Versailles[4], 1783.

IV. His Majesty, the King of Great Britain, is maintained in his right to the Island of Newfoundland, and to the adjacent islands, as the whole were assured to him by the thirteenth article of the Treaty of Utrecht; excepting the Islands of St. Pierre and Miquelon, which are ceded in full right, by the present treaty, to His Most Christian Majesty.

V. His Majesty the Most Christian King, in order to prevent the quarrels which have hitherto arisen between the two nations of England and France, consents to renounce the right of fishing, which belongs to him in virtue of the aforesaid article of the Treaty of Utrecht, from Cape Bonavista to Cape St. John, situated on the eastern coast of Newfoundland, in fifty degrees north latitude; and His Majesty the King of Great Britain consents on his part that the fishery assigned to the subjects of His Most Christian Majesty, beginning at the said Cape St. John, passing to the north, and descending by the western coast of the Island of Newfoundland, shall extend to the place called Cape Raye, situated in forty-seven degrees fifty minutes latitude. The French fishermen shall enjoy the fishery which is assigned to them by the

[1] So far as Canada was concerned, George II. of Great Britain and Lewis XV. of France.

[2] Six weeks.

[3] For extracts from this Treaty relating to Canada, see pp. 61-65 above.

[4] This treaty was signed at Versailles on the 3rd of September, 1783, by the Duke of Manchester, representing George III. of Great Britain, and the Count de Vergennes, representing Lewis XVI. of France.

present article, as they had the right to enjoy that which was assigned to them by the Treaty of Utrecht.

VI. With regard to the fishery in the gulph of St. Lawrence, the French shall continue to exercise it conformably to the fifth article of the Treaty of Paris.[1]

XX. As it is necessary to appoint a certain period for the restitutions and evacuations to be made by each of the high contracting parties, it is agreed that the King of Great Britain shall cause to be evacuated the islands of St. Pierre and Miquelon, three months after the ratification of the present treaty, or sooner, if it can be done. . . . .

6. The Treaty of Paris,[2] 1783.

I. His Britannic Majesty acknowledges the said United States, viz., New Hampshire, Massachusetts Bay, Rhode Island and Providence Plantations, Connecticut, New York, New Jersey, Pennsylvania, Delaware, Maryland, Virginia, North Carolina, South Carolina, and Georgia, to be free, sovereign, and independent states; that he treats with them as such; and for himself, his heirs and successors, relinquishes all claims to the government, propriety, and territorial rights of the same, and every part thereof.

II. And that all disputes which might arise in future on the subject of the boundaries of the said United States may be prevented, it is hereby agreed and declared that the following are and shall be their boundaries, viz., from the north-west angle of Nova Scotia,[3] viz., that angle which is formed by a line drawn due north, from the source of Saint Croix river to the Highlands, along the said Highlands which divide those rivers that empty themselves into the river St. Lawrence, from those which fall into the Atlantic Ocean, to the northwesternmost head of Connecticut river; thence down along the middle of that river to the forty-fifth degree of north latitude; from thence by a line due west on said latitude until it strikes the river Iroquois or Cataraquy[4]; thence

---

[1] Of 1763. See p. 62 above.

[2] On the 30th of November, 1782, "provisional articles of peace and reconciliation" between Great Britain and the United States, were signed at Paris, but it was agreed that the formal treaty between the two powers should not be "concluded until terms of peace should be agreed upon between Great Britain and France." The treaty of Paris was therefore signed on the 3rd of September, 1783, immediately after the signing of the Treaty of Versailles. (See note 4, p. 266). The contracting powers were George III. of Great Britain, and "the United States of America"; the former being represented by David Hartley M.P., and the latter by John Adams of Massachusetts, Benjamin Franklin of Pennsylvania, and John Jay of New York.

[3] Nova Scotia at this time, and until 1784, included New Brunswick. See Commission to Gov. Carleton, pp. 22-23.

[4] Now the St. Lawrence.

along the middle of said river into Lake Ontario; through the middle of said lake, until it strikes the communication by water between that lake and Lake Erie; thence along the middle of said communication into Lake Erie; through the middle of said lake, until it arrives at the water-communication between that lake and lake Huron; thence along the middle of said water-communication into the lake Huron; thence through the middle of said lake to the water-communication between that lake and Lake Superior; thence through Lake Superior, northward of the isles Royal and Phelipeaux, to the Long Lake; thence through the middle of said Long Lake, and the water-communication between it and the Lake of the Woods, to the said Lake of the Woods; thence through the said lake to the most northwestern point thereof, and from thence on a due west course to the river Mississippi; thence by a line to be drawn along the middle of the said river Mississippi, until it shall intersect the northernmost part of the thirty-first degree of north latitude:—South, by a line to be drawn due east from the determination of the line last-mentioned, in the latitude of thirty-one degrees north of the equator, to the middle of the river Apalachicola or Catahouche; thence along the middle thereof to its junction with the Flint river; thence strait to the head of St. Mary's river, and thence down along the middle of St. Mary's river to the Atlantic Ocean:—East, by a line to be drawn along the middle of the river St. Croix, from its mouth in the Bay of Fundy to its source; and from its source directly north to the aforesaid Highlands, which divide the rivers that fall into the Atlantic Ocean from those which fall into the river St. Lawrence: comprehending all islands within twenty leagues of any part of the shores of the United States, and lying between lines to be drawn due east from the points where the aforesaid boundaries between Nova Scotia on the one part, and East Florida on the other, shall respectively touch the Bay of Fundy, and the Atlantic Ocean; excepting such islands as now are, or heretofore have been, within the limits of the said Province of Nova Scotia.

III. It is agreed, that the people of the United States shall continue to enjoy unmolested the right to take fish of every kind on the Grand Bank and on all the other banks of Newfoundland: also in the gulph of St. Lawrence, and at all other places in the sea, where the inhabitants of both countries used at any time heretofore to fish. And also that the inhabitants of the United States shall have liberty to take fish of every kind on such part of the coast of Newfoundland, as British fishermen shall use (but not to dry or cure the same on that island) and also on the coasts, bays, and creeks of all other of his Britannic Majesty's dominions in America; and that the American fishermen shall have liberty to dry and cure fish in any of the unsettled bays, harbours, and creeks of Nova Scotia, Magdalen islands, and Labrador, so long as the same shall remain unsettled; but so soon as the same, or either of them, shall be settled, it shall not be lawful for the said fishermen to dry or cure fish at such settlement, without a previous agreement for that purpose with the inhabitants, proprietors, or possessors of the ground.

IV. It is agreed, that creditors on either side shall meet with no lawful impediment to the recovery of the full value in sterling money of all *bona fide* debts heretofore contracted.

V. It is agreed, that the Congress shall earnestly recommend it to the legislatures of the respective states, to provide for the restitution of all estates, rights, and properties which have been confiscated, belonging to real British subjects; and also of the estates, rights, and properties of persons resident in districts in the possession of His Majesty's arms, and who have not borne arms against the said United States; and that persons of any other description shall have free liberty to go to any part or parts of any of the Thirteen United States, and therein to remain twelve months unmolested in their endeavours to obtain the restitution of such of their estates, rights, and properties as may have been confiscated; and that Congress shall also earnestly recommend to the several states a re-consideration and revision of all acts or laws regarding the premises, so as to render the said laws or acts perfectly consistent, not only with justice and equity, but with that spirit of conciliation, which, on the return of the blessings of peace, should universally prevail. And that Congress shall also earnestly recommend to the several states, that the estates, rights, and properties of such last mentioned persons shall be restored to them, they refunding to any persons who may be now in possession the *bona fide* price (where any has been given) which such persons may have paid on purchasing any of the said lands, rights, or properties since the confiscation. And it is agreed, that all persons who have any interest in confiscated lands, either by debts, marriage settlements, or otherwise, shall meet with no lawful impediment in the prosecution of their just rights.[1]

VI. That there shall be no future confiscations made, nor any prosecutions commenced against any person or persons, for or by reason of the part which he or they may have taken in the present war; and that no person shall on that account suffer any future loss or damage, either in his person, liberty or property; and that those who may be in confinement on such charges at the time of the ratification of the treaty in America, shall be immediately set at liberty, and the prosecutions so commenced be discontinued.

VII. There shall be a firm and perpetual peace between His Britannic Majesty and the said states, and between the subjects of the one and the citizens of the other, wherefore all hostilities, both by sea and land, shall

---

[1] Some idea of the character of the laws passed by State Legislatures dealing with the estates of persons who had adhered to the Royalist cause during the Revolutionary war may be formed by reading the titles of Acts passed by the Legislature of New York. In 1779 there was passed " An Act for the forfeiture and sale of the estates of persons who have adhered to the enemies of this State, and for declaring the sovereignty of the people of this State, in respect to all property within the same." In 1780 an Act was passed approving of the Act of Congress of the same year relative to the finances of the United States, and providing that the lands "forfeited by the attainder of Sir John Johnson" and others should be " mortgaged and bound for the redemption and security" of New York's proportion of the new national " bills of credit." Several Acts, dealing further with forfeited estates, were passed between 1780 and 1785. In 1782 an Act was passed enabling debtors to discharge in depreciated currency debts due to creditors who had taken refuge within the British lines. In 1778 an Act was passed authorizing " Commissioners for Conspiracies " to require neutral or suspected persons to acknowledge on oath the independence of the State of New York, and declaring those who refused to be guilty of " misprision of treason."

from henceforth cease; all prisoners on both sides shall be set at liberty; and His Britannic Majesty shall with all convenient speed, and without causing any destruction or the carrying away any negroes, or other property of the American inhabitants, withdraw all his armies, garrisons,[1] and fleets from the said United States, and from every port, place, and harbour within the same; leaving in all fortifications the American artillery that may be therein; and shall also order and cause all archives, records, deeds, and papers belonging to any of the said states, or their citizens, which in the course of the war may have fallen into the hands of his officers, to be forthwith restored and delivered to the proper states and persons to whom they belong.

VIII. The navigation of the river Mississippi, from its source to the ocean, shall for ever remain free and open to the subjects of Great Britain and the citizens of the United States.

IX. In case it should so happen that any place or territory belonging to Great Britain, or to the United States, should have been conquered by the arms of either, from the other, before the arrival of the said provisional articles in America, it is agreed that the same shall be restored without difficulty, and without requiring any compensation.

X. The solemn ratifications of the present treaty, expedited in good and due form, shall be exchanged between the contracting parties in the space of six months, or sooner if possible, to be computed from the day of the signature of the present treaty.

[1] British garrisons continued to occupy the forts within the United States at Niagara, Detroit, Mackinac, and other frontier posts, until the Jay Treaty was concluded in 1794.

APPENDIX B.

BOUNDARIES OF CANADA, AND OF THE CANADIAN PROVINCES.

1. The Province of Nova Scotia.

This Province, with the exception of Cape Breton, was surrendered to Great Britain by France under the Treaty of Utrecht, 1713,[1] but its boundaries were left to be determined by "Commissioners" appointed by each Government within a year.[2] The provision respecting delimitation was not carried out, and in 1720 Major (afterwards Governor) Mascarene prepared for the information of the Lords of Trade and Plantations a description[3] of Nova Scotia from which the following extract is taken:

> The boundaries having as yet not been agreed on between the British and French Governments in these parts as stipulated in the 10th article of the Treaty of Utrecht, no just ones can be settled in this description. The extent of the Province of Nova Scotia or Acadie, according to the notion the Britains have of it, is from the limits of the Government of Massachusetts Bay in New England, or Kennebeck River, about the 44th degree north latitude, to Cape de Roziers on the south side of the entrance of the River of St. Lawrence in the 44th degree of the same latitude, and its breadth extends from the eastermost part of the Island of Cape Breton to the south side of the River St. Lawrence. Out of this large tract the French had yielded to them at the above treaty the islands situated at the mouth of the River St. Lawrence and in the Gulph of the same, with the Island of Cape Breton.[4]

An unsuccessful attempt was made by the appointment of "Commissaries" under the Treaty of Aix-la-Chapelle, 1748, to settle the question of the Acadian boundaries, Governor Shirly, of Massachusetts, representing the British Government.[5] The western and northern boundaries of Nova Scotia

---

[1] See p. 4 above.
[2] See p. 3 above.
[3] "Nova Scotia Archives," pp. 39-40.
[4] See pp. 4-5 above.
[5] Haliburton's History of Nova Scotia, vol. I., pp. 142-149.

remained undetermined until the British conquest of Canada, and the surrender of the whole country under the Treaty of Paris, 1763. According to Haliburton[1] they were then fixed " by the Crown " as follows :

" To the northward, our said Province shall be bounded by the southern boundary of our Province of Quebec,[2] as far as the western extremity of the Bay des Chaleurs. To the eastward by the said bay, and the Gulf of St. Lawrence, to the cape or promontory called Cape Breton in the island of that name, including that island, the island of St. Johns,[3] and all other islands[4] within six leagues of the coast, to the southward by the Atlantic Ocean from the said cape to Cape Sable, including the island of that name, and all other islands within 40 leagues of the coast, with all the rights, members and appurtenances, whatsoever, thereto belonging. And to the westward, although our said Province hath anciently extended, and doth of right extend, as far as the River Pentagoet or Penobscot, it shall be bounded by a line drawn from Cape Sable across the entrance of the Bay of Fundy, to the mouth of the River St. Croix ; by the said river to its source, and by a line drawn due north, from thence to the southern boundary of our colony of Quebec."[5]

In 1769 Prince Edward Island was created a separate Province, and the boundaries of Nova Scotia, as described in the Commission issued[6] to the first Governor, correspond with those cited by Haliburton.

In 1784 the part of Nova Scotia lying north of a line drawn across the isthmus from the head of the Bay of Fundy up the Musquash River to its source, and thence direct to Baie Verte was erected into the separate Province of New Brunswick,[7] and the line then fixed is still the boundary between that Province and Nova Scotia. In the same year Cape Breton was erected into a quasi-independent Province under a Lieutenant-Governor and Council, but it was re-annexed to Nova Scotia in 1820.

2. The Province of New Brunswick.

The early boundaries of New Brunswick are given above in connection with those of Nova Scotia. The area of the Province has remained unchanged, but the western and northern boundaries were more minutely defined by Imperial Statute in 1851 (14-15 Vict. cap. 63), which recites and ratifies an award made by arbitrators[8] appointed to settle disputes between Canada and New Brunswick, which award is in the following terms :

" That New Brunswick shall be bounded on the west by the boundary of the United States, as traced by the Commissioners of Boundary under the treaty

---

[1] History of Nova Scotia, vol. II., pp. 1-2.
[2] Royal Proclamation, 1763 (p. 67 above).
[3] Now Prince Edward Island.
[4] Royal Proclamation, 1763 (p. 68 above).
[5] Haliburton quotes this description but does not state where he gets it.
[6] See pp. 21-22 above.
[7] Commission to Governor Carleton (pp. 22-23 above).
[8] The arbitrators were: On behalf of Canada, Thomas Falconer ; on behalf of New Brunswick, Travers Twiss ; chosen by those two, Stephen Lushington, Judge of the Admiralty Court. The award was made by the latter two only.

of Washington[1] dated August, 1842, from the source of the St. Croix to a point near the outlet of Pech-la-wee-kaa-co-nies or Lake Beau, marked A in the accompanying copy of a part of plan 17 of the survey of the boundary under the above treaty ; thence by a straight line connecting that point with another point to be determined at the distance of one mile due south from the southernmost point of Long Lake ; thence by a straight line drawn to the southernmost point of the fiefs Madawaska and Temiscouata, and along the south-eastern boundary of those fiefs to the south-east angle of the same ; thence by a meridional line northwards till it meets a line running east and west, and tangent to the height of land dividing the waters flowing into the River Rimouski from those tributary to the St. John ; thence along this tangent line eastward until it meets another meridional line tangent to the height of land dividing waters flowing into the River Rimouski from those flowing into the Restigouche River ; thence along this meridional line to the 48th parallel of latitude ; thence along that parallel to the Mistouche[2] River ; and thence down the centre of the stream of that river to the Restigouche ; thence down the centre of the stream of the Restigouche to its mouth in the Bay of Chaleurs ; and thence through the middle of that bay to the Gulf of the Saint Lawrence ; the islands in the said rivers Mistouche[2] and Restigouche to the mouth of the latter river at Dalhousie being given to New Brunswick."

3. The Provinces of Quebec and Ontario.

It is impossible to state definitely how much territory was covered by the Articles of Capitulation, 1760, and the Treaty of Paris, 1763 (pp. 31-57 and 61-65 above). During the negotiations which preceded the treaty the French Government consented " to cede Canada in the most extensive manner," and disclaimed having affirmed " that all that does not belong to Canada belongs to Louisiana."[3] An offer was subsequently made on behalf of France "to guaranty Canada to England in the utmost extent she required."[4] The Marquis de Vaudreuil, who by this time had returned to France, stated in a published letter[5] that he had " traced out no limits whatever," and that to an

---

[1] Better known as the Ashburton Treaty. Repeated attempts to secure a satisfactory settlement of the boundary between the United States and New Brunswick were made before the treaty of 1842. The following is a list of the treaties, conventions, and awards which deal with it:
    1. Provisional articles of peace agreed on at Paris, 1782, Article II.
    2. Treaty of Paris, 1783, Article II. (see pp. 267-268 above).
    3. The Jay Treaty, London, 1794, Article V.
    4. Explanatory article added to the Jay Treaty at London, in 1798.
    5. The Treaty of Ghent, 1814, Articles I., IV., V.
    6. Decision of the Commissioners under Article IV. of the Treaty of Ghent 1817.
    7. Convention of London, 1827, in connection with Article V. of the Treaty of Ghent.
    8. The Ashburton Treaty, Washington, 1842, Articles I., VI. The last named treaty put a stop to the local trouble between New Brunswick and Maine, called the " Aroostook War," though there never was any fighting.

[2] Explained by a subsequent Imperial Statute (20-21 Vict. cap. 34) to be the stream " otherwise called the Patapedia."

[3] Annual Register for 1761, p. 263.

[4] See ibid p. 266.

[5] See ibid pp. 267-268.

officer sent to him for maps he had given the information that Louisiana extended on one side "to the carrying place of the Miamis, which is the height of the lands, whose rivers run into the Ouabache; and on the other to the head of the river of the Illinois." Gen. Haldimand, the officer above referred to, in a letter to Gen. Amherst, commenting on the letter of the Marquis de Vaudreuil, states that in the presence of the latter before he left Montreal and without any protest from him, he drew a pencil line on a map which carried the limits of Canada from the source of the Illinois River to the Mississippi and thence northward to Red Lake, and up the Ohio and Wabache from the junction of the former with the Mississippi.[1] This would seem to include in the ceded territory the States of Michigan, Wisconsin, Illinois, and parts of Indiana and Minnesota, as well as the territory east of the Wabash and north of the Ohio.

By the Royal Proclamation of 1763 the eastern part of Canada was included in the new Province of Quebec,[2] and by the Quebec Act of 1774 this Province was enlarged so as to be quite as extensive as Canada was in the conception of Gen. Haldimand.[3]

A new southern boundary was given to Quebec by the Treaty of Paris of 1783, the most important change being the severance from the Province of all the region south of Lakes Erie and Ontario as far as the Ohio, and of all west of Lakes Huron and St. Clair as far west as the Mississippi.[4] In 1791, by Order-in-Council,[5] in connection with the passing of the Constitutional Act, Quebec was divided into Upper and Lower Canada, the dividing line being thus defined:

"To commence at a stone boundary on the north bank of the Lake St. Francis, at the cove west of Pointe au Boudet, in the limit between the Township of Lancaster and the Seigneurie of New Longueuil, running along the said limit in the direction of north thirty-four degrees west to the westernmost angle of the said Seigneurie of New Longueuil, thence along the north-western boundary of the Seigneurie of Vaudreuil, running north twenty-five degrees east until it strikes the Ottawa river, to ascend the said river into the Lake Tomiscaming, and from the head of the said lake, by a line drawn due north until it strikes the boundary line of Hudson's Bay, including all the territory to the westward and southward of the said line, to the utmost extent of the country commonly called or known by the name of Canada."

In the Jay treaty of 1794 an effort was made to define the boundary between British America and the United States more accurately than had been done by the second article of the Treaty of Paris, 1783.[6] Article IV. of the Jay treaty provided a method of locating the boundary west from the Lake of

[1] An English translation of this letter is published in full in the "Documents" which made part of the Ontario boundary case before the Privy Council in 1884 (pp. 519-520). The original French text is given in Ramsay's Report on the boundaries of Ontario (Appendix to Commons Journals of 1880, pp. 233-234).
[2] See p. 67 above.
[3] See pp. 90-91 above, and Gov. Carleton's Commission (Ontario Boundary case 1884, pp. 375-376).
[4] Treaty of Paris, 1783 (pp. 267-268 above).
[5] "Documents" in Ontario Boundary case, 1884 (p. 400).
[6] See Note 4 above.

the Woods in the event of its being ascertained that the Mississippi did not extend so far north as a due west line from its north-west angle. Article V. provided for the appointment of three Commissioners to decide what river was meant by the "St. Croix," mentioned in the Treaty of 1783.

The Treaty of Ghent, 1814, contained further provisions for the accurate definition of the same boundary. Article V. provided for the appointment of two Commissioners to "ascertain and determine" the points mentioned in the Treaty of 1783 between the mouth of the St. Croix and the intersection of the St. Lawrence by the 45th parallel of latitude. Article VI. provided a similar method for ascertaining the precise location of the boundary through the River St. Lawrence and the great lakes to the "water communication" between Lake Huron and Lake Superior; and Article VII. made similar provision for ascertaining the boundary between the same "water communication" and "the most north-western part of the Lake of the Woods."

In 1822 the Commissioners[1] under Article VI. of the Treaty of Ghent gave a decision, the text of which minutely describes the international boundary from a "stone monument,[2] 1840 yards distant from the stone church in the Indian village of St. Regis," on the south bank of the St. Lawrence, to "the foot of the Neebish rapids," in the River St. Mary, which is the outlet of Lake Superior. This boundary line is described with reference mainly to the islands amongst which it passes, and which are especially numerous in the "Thousand Islands" archipelago. The utmost care is taken to name or number all the islands adjacent to it in the St. Lawrence River proper, in the Niagara River, at the west end of Lake Erie, in the Detroit and St. Clair Rivers, and in the River St. Mary as far as the Neebish Rapids, which the Commissioners made the terminus of their survey.

The Convention of London, 1827,[3] provided for a reference of the matter dealt with by Article V. of the Treaty of Ghent "to some friendly sovereign or state," but no precise and detailed definition of the boundary between the head waters of the St. Croix and the intersection of the St. Lawrence by the 45th parallel of latitude was given until it was embodied in the first article of the Ashburton Treaty of 1842. The second article of the same treaty gave a detailed description of the boundary from the Neebish Rapids up the River St. Mary, amongst the islands of Lake Superior to the mouth of Pigeon River, and thence to the "northwestern point" of the Lake of the Woods."[4]

By these various conventions and awards the southern boundary of Quebec and Ontario was permanently determined from the "northwest angle of Nova Scotia" (now New Brunswick) westward to the "northwest angle" of the

[1] Peter B. Porter and Anthony Barclay.
[2] Erected in 1817.
[3] October 20. There was another convention agreed to on the 6th of August of the same year, dealing with the disputed territory west of the Rocky Mountains. For a good account of the state of the boundary controversy at this time see Bouchette's "British Dominions in North America," London, 1832.
[4] The Commissioners who had been appointed to settle this part of the boundary under Article VII. of the Treaty of Ghent differed hopelessly on some parts of the route. Their report is given in full in Hertslet's "Treaties," vol. XIII., pp. 892-913.

Lake of the Woods. By the unanimous award of three arbitrators[1] in 1878 the western and northern boundaries of Ontario were given in detail from the last mentioned angle by way of the English and Albany rivers to Hudson's Bay where its shore is intersected by a line drawn due north from Lake Temiscaming.[2] The Imperial Privy Council in 1884 made an independent award[3] under a joint reference by the Governments of Ontario and Manitoba, virtually confirming the award of 1878 *pro tanto*. Both of these decisions were superseded by the passage of an Imperial Act[4] in 1889, in response to the subjoined address from both Houses of the Dominion Parliament. The preamble to the Act states that the Government of Ontario have assented[5] to the boundaries specified in the address, that the boundary between Ontario and Quebec is identical with the one fixed by the proclamation[6] of the Governor-General in November, 1791, and that the boundary between Ontario and Manitoba is identical with the one found correct by the Privy Council in 1884. The address above referred to contains the details of the westerly, northerly, and easterly boundaries of Ontario, which are thus made legally valid, as follows :

We, your Majesty's most dutiful and loyal subjects, the Senate and Commons of Canada, in Parliament assembled, humbly approach your Majesty with the request that your Majesty may be graciously pleased to cause a measure to be submitted to the Parliament of the United Kingdom, declaring and providing the following to be the westerly, northerly, and easterly boundaries of the Province of Ontario, that is to say :—

Commencing at the point where the international boundary between the United States of America and Canada strikes the western shore of Lake Superior, thence westerly along the said boundary to the northwest angle of the Lake of the Woods, thence along a line drawn due north until it strikes the middle line of the course of the river discharging the waters of the lake called Lake Seul or the Lonely Lake, whether above or below its confluence with the stream flowing from the Lake of the Woods towards Lake Winnipeg, and thence proceeding eastward from the point at which the before-mentioned line strikes the middle line of the course of the river last aforesaid, along the middle line of the course of the same river (whether called by the name of the English River or, as to the part below the confluence, by the name of the River Winnipeg) up to Lake Seul or the Lonely Lake, and thence along the middle line of Lake Seul or Lonely Lake to the head of that lake, and thence by a straight line to the nearest point of the middle line of the waters of Lake St.

[1] Sir Francis Hincks acting for the Dominion of Canada, Chief Justice Harrison for the Province of Ontario, and Sir Edward Thornton as referee. See Ontario Sessional Papers of 1879, No. 22.

[2] See Order-in-Council of 1791, dividing Quebec into Upper and Lower Canada, p. 274 above.

[3] Ontario Sessional Papers for 1885, No. 8, and Dom. Sess. Papers for 1885, No. 123 *b*.

[4] Known as "The Canada (Ontario Boundary) Act," 52 and 53 Vict. cap. 28.

[5] See Revised Statutes of Ontario, 1887, cap. 4; and Ont. Stat. 42 Vict. cap. 2.

[6] The proclamation fixes the boundary in a general way from Lake Temiscaming to Hudson's Bay. In 1874 the Ontario Legislature passed an Act (38 Vict. cap. 5), which makes provision for a determination of the boundary in detail. A similar Act was passed in the same year by the Quebec Legislature (38 Vict. cap. 6), but though each of these statutes has been re-enacted (R. S. O., 1877, cap. 3; R. S. O., 1887, cap. 3; and R. S. Q., 1888, Title I., cap. I.) the Dominion Parliament has not taken any steps to establish the line of boundary agreed upon by the Provinces.

Joseph, and thence along that middle line until it reaches the foot or outlet of that lake, and thence along the middle line of the river by which the waters of Lake St. Joseph discharge themselves to the shore of the part of Hudson's Bay commonly known as James' Bay, and thence south-easterly following upon the said shore to a point where a line drawn due north from the head of Lake Temiscamingue would strike it, and thence due south along the said line to the head of the said lake, and thence through the middle channel of the said lake into the Ottawa River, and thence descending along the middle of the main channel of the said river to the intersection by the prolongation of the western limits of the Seigneurie of Rigaud, such main channel being as indicated on a map of the Ottawa Ship Canal Survey made by Walter Shanly, C.E., and approved of by an Order of the Governor-General-in-Council, dated the twenty-first July, one thousand eight hundred and eighty-six ; and thence southerly following the said westerly boundary of the Seigneurie of Rigaud to the southwest angle of the said Seigneurie, and then southerly along the western boundary of the augmentation of the township of Newton to the northwest angle of the Seigneurie of Longueuil, and thence south-easterly along the south-western boundary of the said Seigneurie of New Longueuil to a stone boundary on the north bank of the Lake St. Francis at the cove west of Point au Baudet, such line from the Ottawa River to Lake St. Francis being as indicated on a plan of the line of boundary between Upper and Lower Canada, made in accordance with the Act 23 Victoria, chaper 21, and approved by Order of the Governor-General-in-Council, dated the 16th of March, 1861.

The easterly boundary of Ontario is the westerly boundary of Quebec, and the southerly boundary of that Province is fixed by the Ashburton Treaty, 1842, on the side of the United States, and by Imperial Statute[1] on the side of New Brunswick. On the east Quebec is bounded by the Gulf of St. Lawrence and Labrador and its northerly boundary is still undetermined as a whole, but is fixed as to its western extremity at the point where the due north line from Lake Temiscaming intersects the south shore of Hudson's Bay.[2]

4. The Province of Manitoba.

The boundary between the then Province of Quebec and the United States, as fixed by the Treaty of Paris of 1783, stopped at the Mississippi.[3] Article

---

[1] See pp. 272-273 above.

[2] By the Royal Proclamation of 1763 the River St. John was made the easterly limit of the Province of Quebec on the north shore of the St. Lawrence, all the rest of that shore and of the Atlantic coast of Labrador to Hudson's Straits being, with Anticosti and the other islands in the Gulf of St. Lawrence, annexed to Newfoundland. Labrador, the north shore of the river and Gulf of St. Lawrence, and the islands in the gulf, were all transferred to Quebec by the Quebec Act of 1774. They remained part of Quebec till 1791 and part of Lower Canada till 1809, in which year the Imperial Parliament passed an Act (49 George III. cap. 27), which re-annexed to Newfoundland, with the exception of the "Madelaine" islands, all that had been added to it by the Proclamation of 1763. The Imperial Parliament passed an Act in 1825 (6 George IV. cap. 59), restoring to Lower Canada part of what had been thus taken from it in 1807, including the Island of Anticosti and so much of the north shore of the river and Gulf of St Lawrence as "lies to the westward of a line to be drawn due north and south from the bay or harbour of Ance Sablon, inclusive, as far as the fifty-second degree of north latitude." Though the northern boundary of Quebec has never been defined it is worthy of remark that the fifty-second parallel is further north than the intersection of the south shore of Hudson's Bay by the due north line from Lake Temiscaming.

[3] See p. 268 above.

IV. of the Jay Treaty of 1794 provided for a survey of that river from below the falls of St. Anthony (Minneapolis) for the purpose of ascertaining whether it extended far enough north to intercept a due west line from the northwest angle of the Lake of the Woods. By the London Convention of 1818:

"It is agreed that a line drawn from the most northwestern point of the Lake of the Woods along the 49th parallel of north latitude, or if the said point shall not be in the 49th parallel of north latitude then that a line drawn from the said point due north or south, as the case may be, until the said line shall intersect the said parallel of north latitude, and from the point of such intersection due west along and with the said parallel, shall be the line of demarcation between the territories of the United States and those of his Britannic Majesty, and that the said line shall form the northern boundary of the said territories of the United States and the southern boundary of the territories of his Britannic Majesty, from the Lake of the Woods to the Stony[1] Mountains.

The western, northern, and eastern boundaries of Manitoba have been twice defined by the Parliament of Canada, (1) by the Act[2] which created the Province in 1870, and (2) by the Act[3] which enlarged its area and extended its boundaries in 1881. By the definition in the latter statute Manitoba extends from the United States boundary on the south to "the twelfth base line in the system of Dominion Land Surveys" on the north, and from the line between the twenty-ninth and thirtieth ranges of townships west of the first principal meridian on the west, to a line drawn due north from the point where the Ontario boundary intersects that of the United States on the east.

5. The Province of British Columbia.

When by the London Convention of 1818 the 49th parallel of north latitude was fixed as the international boundary the region west of the Rocky Mountains was comparatively unknown, and neither Great Britain nor the United States was in undisputed possession of it. By the same convention (Article III.) it was arranged that the commerce and navigation of the whole Pacific slope should be "free and open" to the citizens of both countries for ten years.

In 1825, by Articles III. and IV. of the Treaty of St. Petersburgh, it was agreed between Great Britain and Russia that the boundary of Alaska should begin at Prince of Wales Island in 54 degrees 40 minutes north latitude, run up the Portland Channel to the 56th degree, thence pass along the summit of the mountain chain till it intersected the 141st meridian, and then follow that meridian to the "Frozen Ocean."

---

[1] Now "Rocky" Mountains.
[2] Dom. Stat. 33 Vict. cap. 3.
[3] Dom. Stat. 44 Vict. cap. 14; R. S. C., 1886, cap 47.

In 1827 (Aug. 6) a convention was adopted at London between Great Britain and the United States by which the agreement of the third article of the Convention of 1818 was "indefinitely extended and continued in force," and it continued in force until superseded by the Treaty of Washington, 1846, which provided that the 49th parallel should be the international boundary from the Rocky Mountains " to the middle of the channel which separates the continent from Vancouver's Island, and thence southerly through the middle of the said channel, and of Fuca's straits to the Pacific Ocean."

Further knowledge of this "channel" brought to light the fact that there are two channels, the Rosario Strait on the United States side of the San Juan archipelago, and the Canal de Haro on the British side of it. The dispute as to which was the one meant in the treaty of 1846 was settled by an award of the Emperor of Germany under a provision of the Treaty of Washington, 1871, and in favour of the United States contention. The Canal de Haro is now, therefore, a part of the boundary.

By Imperial Statute [1] Vancouver's Island was in 1849 made virtually a self-governing colony. A similar status was in 1858 [2] conferred on British Columbia, the Act of the British Parliament giving it boundaries as follows: On the south "the frontier of the United States "; on the east the " main chain of the Rocky Mountains "; on the north "Simpson's river and the Finlay branch of the Peace "; on the west the Pacific Ocean, Queen Charlotte's Island being included. In 1863, by Imperial Statute, [3] the boundaries at present in existence were thus fixed :

" British Columbia shall * * * * be held to comprise all such territories within the dominions of Her Majesty as are bounded to the south by the territories of the United States of America, to the west by the Pacific Ocean and the frontier of the Russian territories in North America, to the north by the sixtieth parallel of north latitude, and to the east, from the boundary of the United States northwards by the Rocky Mountains and the one hundred and twentieth meridian of west longitude, and shall include Queen Charlotte's Island and all other islands adjacent to the said territories, except Vancouver's Island and the islands adjacent thereto."

Vancouver's Island became part of British Columbia in 1866,[4] and five years later the united colony became a Province of the Dominion of Canada.

6. The North-West Territories.

This title[5] is applied to the whole region formerly known as "Rupert's Land " and the " North-West Territory," except the Province of Manitoba

---

[1] 12 & 13 Vict. cap. 48.
[2] By 21 & 22 Vict. cap. 99.
[3] 26 & 27 Vict. cap. 83.
[4] See Note 30, p. 233 above.
[5] See Dom. Stat. 43 Vict. cap. 25 ; R. S. C. 1886, cap. 50.

and the District of Keewatin.[1] It is bounded on the south by the 49th parallel of north latitude; on the west by the Rocky Mountains, the 120th meridian, the 60th parallel of north latitude west to Alaska, and the 141st meridian to the Arctic Ocean; and on the east by the western boundaries of Manitoba[2] and the District of Keewatin.[3] Politically the "Northwest Territories" is a unit, there being but one Lieutenant-Governor and one Legislative Assembly for the whole territory; but the southern portion of it has been divided[4] into four "provisional districts"—Assiniboia, Alberta, Saskatchewan, and Athabasca.

7. The Dominion of Canada.

A synthesis of the boundaries of the various Provinces, as given above, furnishes the data for a description of the boundary of the Dominion as a whole. Beginning at the intersection of the shore of the Arctic Ocean by the 141st meridian, the Arctic and Atlantic Oceans form the boundary as far as Hudson's Straits. Labrador,[5] the Gulf of St. Lawrence and the Atlantic Ocean, continue it as far as Cape Sable, including the Magdelene Islands, Anticosti, Prince Edward Island, Cape Breton, Sable Island and all other islands within six leagues[6] of the coast in the Gulf of St. Lawrence, and within forty leagues of the Atlantic coast of Nova Scotia.[7] From Cape Sable to the mouth of the St. Croix River the boundary is a line drawn across the entrance of the Bay of Fundy,[8] so as to give the Grand Manan group of islands and most of those in Passamoquoddy Bay to Canada.[9] It follows the St. Croix to its source,[10] runs due north to the St. John, and then passes by a very irregular route to the intersection of the south bank of the St. Lawrence

---

[1] For the boundaries of Keewatin, see Dom. Stat. 39 Vict. cap. 21; R.S.C. 1886, cap. 53.

[2] See p. 278 above.

[3] This is a line due north to the Arctic ocean from "Cedar Portage," at the head of Lake Winnipegosis.

[4] By order of the Governor-General in Council, on the 8th of May, 1882. See Dom. Sess. Paper of 1882, No. 172.

[5] See Note 2, p. 277. On the 31st of July, 1880, an Imperial Order-in-Council was passed in the following terms: "From and after the first day of September, 1880, all British territories and possessions in North America, not already included within the Dominion of Canada, and all islands adjacent to any of such territories or possessions, shall (with the exception of the Colony of Newfoundland and its dependencies) become, and be annexed to, and form part of, the said Dominion of Canada, and become and be subject to the laws for the time being in force in the said Dominion, in so far as such laws may be applicable thereto." This affected part of the Labrador peninsula, but how much of it cannot be precisely specified.

[6] Commission to Gov. Paterson, pp. 21-22 above.

[7] Article 11 of the Treaty of Paris, 1783, pp. 267-268 above.

[8] Gov. Paterson's commission, pp. 21-22 above.

[9] Article IV. of the Treaty of Ghent, 1814; and Decision of the Commission under that article, Nov. 24th, 1817.

[10] Article II. of the Treaty of Paris, 1783; Article V. of the Jay Treaty of 1794; explanatory article added to the Jay Treaty in 1798; the Convention of London, September 29th, 1827.

by the 45th parallel.[1] From that point it follows the navigable channel of the St. Lawrence to Lake Ontario, passes through that lake, the Niagara River, Lake Erie, Detroit River, Lake St. Clair, River St. Clair, Lake Huron and the lower part of the St. Mary River to the foot of the Neebish Rapids.[2]

From the Neebish Rapids the boundary is continued up the St. Mary River to and through Lake Superior to the mouth of Pigeon River, thence by way of Rainy Lake and Rainy River to the northwest angle of the Lake of the Woods.[3]

From the northwest angle of the Lake of the Woods the boundary runs due south to the 49th parallel and along that parallel to the Strait of San Juan de Fuca, and through it to the Pacific Ocean.[4]

The western boundary of the Dominion is the Pacific Ocean and the Portland Channel to the inland terminus of the latter, the Rocky Mountains to their intersection by the 141st meridian, and that meridian to the Arctic Ocean.[5]

---

[1] Article I. of the Ashburton Treaty, 1842.

[2] Article II. of the Treaty of Paris, 1783; Article VI. of the Treaty of Ghent, 1814; Decision of the Commissioners under the last mentioned Article, made at Utica, June 18th, 1822.

[3] Article II. of the Treaty of Paris, 1783; Article IV. of the Jay Treaty of 1794; Article VII. of the Treaty of Ghent, 1814; Article II. of the Ashburton Treaty, 1842.

[4] Article II. of the Convention of London, October 20th, 1818; Article I. of the Treaty of Washington, 1846; Article XXXV. of the Treaty of Washington, 1871; Award of the Emperor of Germany, October 21st, 1872.

[5] Articles II. and III. of the Treaty of St. Petersburg, 1825.

APPENDIX C.

I. EXTRADITION OF FUGITIVE CRIMINALS.

Fugitive criminals may be surrendered by one country at the request of another, in accordance with international comity;[1] they must be surrendered by one country at the demand of another, if both countries have agreed by treaty to make such surrenders. Extradition is now for the most part a matter of treaty arrangement among civilized nations. As between Great Britain and the United States, the only treaty provisions heretofore adopted are the following :

1. The Jay Treaty,[2] London, 1794.

Article XXVII. It is further agreed that His Majesty and the United States, on mutual requisitions by them respectively, or by their respective ministers or officers authorized to make the same, will deliver up to justice all persons, who, being charged with murder or forgery,[3] committed within the jurisdiction of either, shall seek an asylum within any of the countries of the other, provided that this shall only be done on such evidence of criminality, as, according to the laws of the place where the fugitive or person so charged shall be found, would justify his apprehension and commitment for trial, if the offence had there been committed. The expense of such apprehension and delivery shall be borne and defrayed by those who make the requisition and receive the fugitive.[4]

---

[1] For a lucid discussion of this ground of surrender, see Spears " Law of Extradition," Chapter I ; Clarke's " Law of Extradition," Third Edition, Chapter I.

[2] See Clarke's "Law of Extradition," Chapter III.

[3] Compare the list of crimes in the Ashburton Treaty of 1842.

[4] By Article XXVIII. of the same Treaty, it was provided that Article XXVII. should remain in force for only twelve years. The strained relations between the two powers prevented its renewal. Each of the treatises mentioned in Note 1, gives some account of the difficulty thrown in the way of its operation by the want of legislation to give it effect.

2. The Ashburton Treaty,[1] Washington, 1842.

Article X. It is agreed that the United States and Her Britannic Majesty shall, upon mutual requisition by them, or their ministers, officers, or authorities, respectively made, deliver up to justice all persons who, being charged with the crime[2] of murder, or assault with intent to commit murder, or piracy, or arson, or robbery, or forgery, or the utterance of forged paper, committed within the jurisdiction of either, shall seek an asylum, or shall be found within the territories of the other; provided that this shall only be done upon such evidence of criminality as, according to the laws of the place where the fugitive or person so charged shall be found, would justify his apprehension and commitment for trial, if the crime or offence had there been committed; and the respective judges and other magistrates of the two governments shall have power, jurisdiction, and authority,[3] upon complaint made under oath, to issue a warrant for the apprehension of the fugitive or person so charged, that he may be brought before such judges or other magistrates, respectively, to the end that the evidence of criminality may be heard and considered; and if, on such hearing, the evidence be deemed sufficient to sustain the charge, it shall be the duty of the examining judge or magistrate to certify the same to the proper executive authority, that a warrant may issue for the surrender of such fugitive. The expense of such apprehension and delivery shall be borne and defrayed by the party who makes the requisition, and receives the fugitive.

XI. * * * * The tenth article shall continue in force until one or the other of the parties shall signify its wish to terminate it, and no longer.[4]

---

[1] For an account of the Holmes case, which was the occasion of Article X. of the Ashburton Treaty, see Spears' "Law of Extradition," Chapter II., and Clarke's "Law of Extradition," Chapter III.

[2] Compare this list of extradition crimes with the list in the Jay Treaty above. The two treatises specified in Note 1 contain ample data for arriving at a definition of these terms.

[3] Two alleged criminals were extradited under this treaty by the United States authorities at the request of the British Government, before any statute was enacted by Congress to give it effect. This was done in 1848 (9 U. S. Statutes at Large, 302), This Act was supplemented by another in 1860 (U. S. Statutes at Large, 84), and by subsequent enactments of less importance. In 1843 an Act (6 & 7 Vict. cap. 76) was passed by the British Parliament to give effect to the tenth Article of the Ashburton Treaty, and this was supplemented by two later Acts (8 & 9 Vict. cap. 120, and 29 & 30 Vict. cap 121). These three Statutes were all repealed by "The Extradition Act, 1870" which is still in force. The Canadian Statutes dealing with this subject are "The Extradition Act, 1877" (40 Vict. cap. 25); an Act passed in 1882 (45 Vict. cap. 21) to amend the Act of 1877; the consolidation of these two Acts in the Revised Statutes of Canada, 1886 (cap. 142); and an Act (52 Vict. cap. 36) passed in 1889 to provide for the extradition of criminals to countries between which and Great Britain no extradition treaty exists.

[4] The Ashburton Treaty was virtually suspended for a short time in 1876 as the result of a difference of opinion between the British and United States Governments over its working. (Spear's "Law of Extradition," cases of Caldwell, Lawrence, and Winslow.)

II. STIPULATIONS WITH FRANCE RESPECTING FISHERIES.

1. The Treaty of Utrecht, 1713.[1]
2. The Treaty of Paris, 1763.[2]
3. The Treaty of Versailles, 1783.[3]

British Declaration,[4] *Versailles, 1783.*

* * * In order that the fishermen of the two nations may not give cause for daily quarrels, His Britannic Majesty will take the most positive measures for preventing his subjects from interrupting, in any manner, by their competition, the fishery of the French, during the temporary exercise of it which is granted to them, upon the coasts of the Island of Newfoundland; and he will, for this purpose, cause the fixed settlements which shall be formed there to be removed. His Britannic Majesty will give orders, that the French fishermen be not incommoded, in cutting the wood necessary for the repair of their scaffolds, huts, and fishing vessels.

The thirteenth article of the Treaty of Utrecht, and the method of carrying on the fishery, which has at all times been acknowledged, shall be the plan upon which the fishery shall be carried on there; it shall not be deviated from by either party; the French fishermen building only their scaffolds, confining themselves to the repair of their fishing vessels, and not wintering there; the subjects of His Britannic Majesty, on their part, not molesting in any manner the French fishermen during their fishing, nor injuring their scaffolds during their absence.

The King of Great Britain, in ceding the islands of St. Pierre and Miquelon to France, regards them as ceded for the purpose of serving as a real shelter to the French fishermen, and in full confidence that these possessions will not become an object of jealousy between the two nations; and that the fishery between the said islands and that of Newfoundland shall be limited to the middle of the channel.

French Counter-Declaration,[4] *Versailles 1783.*

* * * The King of Great Britain undoubtedly places too much confidence in the uprightness of His Majesty's intentions, not to rely upon his constant attention to prevent the islands of St. Pierre and Miquelon from becoming an object of jealousy between the two nations.

As to the fishery on the coasts of Newfoundland, which has been the object of the new arrangements settled by the two sovereigns upon this matter, it is sufficiently ascertained by the fifth article of the treaty of peace signed this

---

[1] See Articles XII.-XIII., pp. 4-5 above.
[2] See Articles V.-VI., pp. 62-63, above.
[3] See Articles IV.-VI., pp. 266-267 above.
[4] Signed on the same day with the Treaty of Versailles, 1783. Both the treaty and the declarations were annulled by the outbreak of the war in 1793.

day, and by the declaration likewise delivered to-day by His Britannic Majesty's Ambassador Extraordinary and Plenipotentiary; and His Majesty declares that he is fully satisfied on this head.

In regard to the fishery between the island of Newfoundland and those of St. Pierre and Miquelon, it is not to be carried on by either party but to the middle of the channel; and His Majesty will give the most positive orders that the French fishermen shall not go beyond this line. His Majesty is firmly persuaded that the King of Great Britain will give like orders to the English fishermen.[1]

4. Treaty of Paris, 1814.

XIII. The French right of fishery upon the Great Banks of Newfoundland, upon the coasts of the island of that name, and of the adjacent islands in the Gulph of St. Lawrence, shall be replaced[2] upon the footing[3] in which it stood in 1792.

III. TREATY STIPULATIONS WITH THE UNITED STATES RESPECTING FISHERIES.

1. Treaty of Paris, 1783.[4]
2. Convention of London, 1818.

I. Whereas differences have arisen respecting the liberty claimed by the United States, for the inhabitants thereof, to take, dry, and cure fish, on certain coasts, bays, harbours, and creeks, of his Britannic Majesty's dominions in America, it is agreed between the high contracting parties, that the inhabitants of the said United States shall have forever, in common with the subjects of his Britannic Majesty, the liberty to take fish of every kind on that part of the southern coast of Newfoundland which extends from Cape Ray to the Rameau Islands, on the western and northern coast of Newfoundland, from

---

[1] In 1788 the British Parliament passed an Act (28 George III. cap. 35) "to carry into effect the Treaty of Peace with France of 1783, and the declaration annexed thereto, relative to the Newfoundland fishery." The preamble to this Statute recites Article XIII. of the Treaty of Utrecht (1713), Article V. of the Treaty of Versailles (1783), and the above declaration of the same date, and authorize the King in Council to give from time to time such "orders and instructions" as may seem necessary to fulfil the purposes of these various conventions.

[2] See Note 4, p 284.

[3] What that footing was, in the opinion of the British Government, may be seen from a note sent by Lord Palmerston in 1838 to Count Sebastiani, the French Ambassador. See Pedley's "History of Newfoundland," Appendix VI. In 1857, a Convention between Great Britain and France, "relative to the rights of fishery on the Coast of Newfoundland and the neighbouring coasts," was concluded at London in 1857 (Hertslet's Treaties, vol. X., pp. 749-755), subject to ratification by the "Imperial Parliament of Great Britain and by the Provincial Legislature of Newfoundland, Her Britannic Majesty engaging to use her best endeavours to procure the passing of such laws." The additional concessions made to France by this convention aroused such opposition in the Newfoundland Legislature that the convention itself became a dead letter (See Pedley's "History of Newfoundland," p. 432, for the despatch withdrawing the proposals.)

[4] See p. 268 above.

the said Cape Ray to the Quirpon Islands, on the shores of the Magdalen Islands, and also on the coasts, bays, harbours, and creeks, from Mount Joly on the southern coast of Labrador to and through the Streights of Belleisle, and thence northwardly indefinitely along the coast, without prejudice, however, to any of the exclusive rights of the Hudson Bay Company: And that the American fishermen shall also have liberty forever to dry and cure fish in any of the unsettled bays, harbours, and creeks of the southern part of the coast of Newfoundland hereabove described, and of the coast of Labrador; but so soon as the same, or any portion thereof shall be settled, it shall not be lawful for the said fishermen to dry or cure fish at such portion so settled, without previous agreement for such purpose with the inhabitants, proprietors, or possessors of the ground. And the United States hereby renounce forever any liberty heretofore enjoyed or claimed by the inhabitants thereof to take, dry, or cure fish, on or within three marine miles of any of the coasts, bay, creeks, or harbours, of his Britannic Majesty's dominions in America, not included within the above mentioned limits: Provided, however, that the American fishermen shall be admitted to enter such bays or harbours for the purpose of shelter and of repairing damages therein, of purchasing wood, and of obtaining water, and for no other purpose whatever. But they shall be under such restrictions as may be necessary to prevent their taking, drying, or curing fish therein, or in any other manner whatever abusing the privileges hereby reserved to them.[1]

3. The Treaty[2] of Washington, 1854.

I. It is agreed by the high contracting parties, that in addition to the liberty secured to the United States fishermen by the Convention of October 20, 1818, of taking, curing, and drying fish on certain coasts of the British North American colonies therein defined, the inhabitants of the United States shall have, in common with the subjects of her Britannic Majesty, the liberty to take fish of every kind, except shell-fish, on the sea coasts and shores, and in the bays, harbours, and creeks of Canada, New Brunswick, Nova Scotia, Prince Edward Island, and of the several islands thereunto adjacent, without being restricted to any distance from the shore; with permission to land upon the coasts and shores of those colonies and the islands thereof, and also upon the Magdalen Islands, for the purpose of drying their nets and curing their fish; provided that in so doing they do not interfere with the rights of private property, or with British fishermen in the peaceable use of any part of the said coast in their occupancy for the same purpose. It is understood that the above

---

[1] The convention of 1818 was supplemented in 1819 by an Act of the British Parliament (59 George III. cap 38), to enable the British Government to make regulations for its effective enforcement. Under the authority of this Act an Imperial Order-in-Council was passed in the same year prohibiting all molestation of United States fishermen so long as they kept within the limits assigned to them by treaty (Hertslet's Treaties, Vol. X., pp. 635-636). In 1844, an Imperial Order-in-Council was passed confirming an Act passed in 1843 by the Prince Edward Island Legislature (6 Vict. cap. 14) to regulate fishing by United States citizens in the vicinity of that Province (Hertslet's "Treaties," Vol. X., pp. 636-638)

[2] Better known as the "Reciprocity" Treaty.

mentioned liberty applies solely to the sea fishery, and that the salmon and shad fisheries, and all fisheries in rivers and the mouths of rivers, are hereby reserved exclusively for British fishermen. * * *

II. It is agreed by the high contracting parties that British subjects shall have, in common with the citizens of the United States, the liberty to take fish of every kind, except shell-fish, on the eastern sea-coasts and shores of the United States north of the 36th parallel of north latitude, and on the shores of the several islands thereunto adjacent, and in the bays, harbours, and creeks of the said sea-coasts and shores of the United States and of the said islands, without being restricted to any distance from the shore : with permission to land upon the said coasts of the United States and of the islands aforesaid for the purpose of drying their nets and curing their fish, provided that in so doing they do not interfere with the rights of private property, or with the fishermen of the United States in the peaceable use of any part of the said coasts in their occupancy for the same purpose. It is understood that the above-mentioned liberty applies solely to the sea fishery, and that salmon and shad fisheries and all fisheries in rivers and mouths of rivers, are hereby reserved exclusively for fishermen of the United States.[1]

4. The Treaty of Washington, 1871.[2]

[1] Article V. provided that the treaty should remain in force ten years from the date when it came into operation, and further until the expiration of twelve months after either of the high contracting parties should give notice to the other of its wish to terminate it; each party being at liberty to give such notice to the other at the end of the said term of ten years, or at any time afterwards. The United States gave notice under this Article on the 17th of March, 1865, and the treaty lapsed on the 17th of March, 1866. For the Act of Congress of the United States, and the Acts of the Parliaments of Canada, Nova Scotia, New Brunswick, Prince Edward Island, Newfoundland, and Great Britain, giving effect to the Treaty of 1854, see Hertslet's "Treaties," Vol. X. pp. 647-655.

[2] The fishing privileges extended to the fishermen of each country under Articles XVIII-XX of this treaty were co-extensive, geographically and otherwise, with those embodied in the treaty of 1854 above. Article XVI. secured the admission of fish-oil and fish (except fresh water fish and fish preserved in oil) into the United States, and Articles XXII.-XXV. provided for the settlement by arbitration of the amount that should be paid by the United States to compensate for the greater value of the British concession. The articles dealing with the fisheries were to continue in force for ten years, after which either party might give two years' notice of its wish to terminate them. The treaty took effect from the first of July, 1873, and the United States Government having given notice as provided, the fisheries articles lapsed in 1885. A treaty dealing with the fisheries question was negotiated at Washington in 1888 (Dom. Sess. Papers for 1888, No. 36), but it was not approved of by the United States Senate. An arrangement was proffered by the British plenipotentiaries as a *modus vivendi* pending the ratification of the treaty, and this arrangement was in 1890 embodied in an Act of the Canadian Parliament (53 Vict. cap. 19).

IV. TREATY STIPULATIONS WITH RUSSIA RESPECTING FISHERIES.

1. Convention of St. Petersburg,[1] 1824.

I. It is agreed that in any part of the Great Ocean, commonly called the Pacific Ocean, or South Sea, the respective citizens or subjects of the high contracting powers shall be neither disturbed nor restrained, either in navigation or in fishing, or in the power of resorting to the coasts, upon points which may not already have been occupied, for the purpose of trading with the natives, saving always the restrictions and conditions determined by the following articles.

IV. It is nevertheless understood that during a term of ten years, counting from the signature of the present convention, the ships of both Powers, or which belong to their citizens or subjects, respectively, may reciprocally frequent, without any hindrance whatever, the interior seas, gulfs, harbours, and creeks, upon the coasts[2] mentioned in the preceding article, for the purpose of fishing and trading with the natives of the country.

2. Convention of St. Petersburg,[3] 1825.

I. It is agreed that the respective subjects of the high contracting parties shall not be troubled or molested, in any part of the ocean, commonly called the Pacific Ocean, either in navigating the same, in fishing therein, or in landing at such parts of the coast as shall not have been already occupied, in order to trade with the natives, under the restrictions and conditions specified in the following articles.

---

[1] Between Russia and the United States. As to its effect, Wharton (International Law Digest, vol. I., p. 111) says: "Russia having asserted, in 1822-24, an exclusive jurisdiction over the northwest coast and waters of America from Behring strait to the fifty-first degree of north latitude, this claim was resisted by the United States and Great Britain, and was surrendered in a convention between Russia and the United States, in April, 1824, for ten years (not technically renewed) and in a convention between Great Britain and Russia, in February, 1825, for ten years, re established by the treaty of June, 1743. The Russian claim was disputed by J. Q. Adams, in his note to the Russian Minister of March 30, 1822."

[2] The "Northwest coast of America" and the islands adjacent to it.

[3] Between Great Britain and Russia.

VI. It is understood that the subjects of His Britannic Majesty, from whatever quarter they may arrive, whether from the ocean, or from the interior of the continent, shall forever enjoy the right of navigating freely, and without any hindrance whatever, all the rivers and streams which in their course towards the Pacific Ocean may cross the line of demarcation upon the line of coast described in Article III. of the present convention.[1]

VII. It is also understood that, for the space of ten[2] years from the signature of the present convention, the vessels of the two powers, or those belonging to their respective subjects, shall mutually be at liberty to frequent, without any hindrance whatever, all the inland seas, the gulfs, havens, and creeks, on the coast[3] mentioned in Article III., for the purpose, of fishing and of trading with the natives.

---

[1] From the southern point of Prince of Wales island up the Portland Channel to the 56th degree of north latitude and thence along the summit of the Rocky Mountains to their intersection by the 141st meridian.
[2] As to this limit see Note 1, p. 288.
[3] See Note 1 above.

APPENDIX D.

1. The Introduction of English Law into Upper Canada.

An Act[1] to repeal certain parts of an Act passed in the fourteenth year of His Majesty's Reign, entitled "An Act[2] for making more effectual provision for the Government of the Province of Quebec in North America," and to introduce the English Law as the Rule of Decision in all matters of controversy relating to Property and Civil Rights.

[15TH OCTOBER, 1792.

WHEREAS by an Act passed in the fourteenth year of his present Majesty, intituled "An Act for making more effectual Provision for the Government of the Province of Quebec in North America," it was amongst other things provided, "that in all matters of controversy relative to property and civil rights resort should be had to the laws of Canada[3] as the rule for the decision of the same," such provision being manifestly and avowedly intended for the accommodation of His Majesty's Canadian subjects : AND WHEREAS, since the passing of the Act aforesaid, that part of the late Province of Quebec, now comprehended within the Province of Upper Canada, having become inhabited principally by British subjects born and educated in countries where the English laws were established, and who are unaccustomed to the laws of Canada, it is inexpedient that the provision aforesaid, contained in the said Act of the fourteenth year of his present Majesty, should be continued in this Province :

Be it enacted by the King's Most Excellent Majesty, by and with the advice and consent of the Legislative Council and Assembly of the Province of Upper Canada, constituted and assembled by virtue of and under the authority of an Act[4] passed in the Parliament of Great Britain, intituled "An Act to repeal

---

[1] Passed by the first Parliament of Upper Canada as the first Act of its first session, and known as 32 George III. cap. 1.
[2] The Quebec Act, 1774.
[3] These were the laws of French Canada. See the Quebec Act, 1774, section VIII.
[4] The Constitutional Act, 1791.

certain parts of an Act passed in the fourteenth year of His Majesty's Reign, intituled 'An Act for making more effectual provision for the Government of the Province of Quebec in North America,' and to make further provision for the Government of the said Province," and by the authority of the same, that from and after the passing of this Act the said provision, contained in the said Act of the fourteenth year of his present Majesty, be, and the same is hereby repealed; and the authority of the said laws of Canada, and every part thereof, as forming a rule of decision in all matters of controversy relative to property and civil rights, shall be annulled, made void, and abolished throughout this Province, and that the said laws, nor any part thereof as such, shall be of any force or authority within the said Province, nor binding on any of the inhabitants thereof.

II. Provided always, and be it enacted by the authority aforesaid, that nothing in this Act shall extend to extinguish, release or discharge, or otherwise affect any existing right, lawful claim or incumbrance, to and upon any lands, tenements or hereditaments within the said Province, or to rescind or vacate, or otherwise affect any contract or security already made and executed conformably to the usages prescribed by the said Laws of Canada.

III. And be it further enacted by the authority aforesaid, that from and after the passing of this Act, in all matters of controversy relative to property and civil rights, resort shall be had to the laws of England, as the rule for the decision of the same.

IV. Provided always, and be it enacted by the authority aforesaid, that nothing in this Act shall extend, or be construed to extend, to repeal or vary any of the Ordinances made and passed by the Governor and Legislative Council of the Province of Quebec previous to the division of the same into the Provinces of Upper and Lower Canada, otherwise than as they are necessarily varied by the provisions herein mentioned.

V. And be it further enacted by the authority aforesaid, that all matters relative to testimony and legal proof in the investigation of fact, and the forms thereof, in the several Courts of Law and Equity within this Province, be regulated by the rules of evidence established in England.

VI. Provided always, and be it enacted by the authority aforesaid, that nothing in this Act contained shall vary or interfere, or be construed to vary or interfere with any of the subsisting provisions respecting Ecclesiastical rights or dues within this Province, or with the forms of proceeding in civil actions, or the jurisdiction of Courts already established, or to introduce any of the laws of England respecting the maintenance of the poor, or respecting bankrupts.

2. The Introduction of Trial by Jury into Upper Canada.

An Act[1] to Establish Trials by Jury.

WHEREAS the trial by jury has been long established and approved in our Mother Country, and is one of the chief benefits to be attained by a free Constitution;

Be it therefore enacted by the King's Most Excellent Majesty, by and with the advice and consent of the Legislative Council and Assembly of the Province of Upper Canada, constituted and assembled by virtue of and under the authority of an Act passed in the Parliament of Great Britain, intituled, "An Act to repeal certain parts of an Act passed in the fourteenth year of His Majesty's reign, intituled, ' An Act for making more effectual provision for the Government of the Province of Quebec in North America,' and to make further provision for the government of the said Province," and by the authority of the same, that from and after the first day of December in this present year of Our Lord, one thousand seven hundred and ninety-two, all and every issue and issues of fact, which shall be joined in any action, real, personal, or mixed, and brought in any of His Majesty's courts of justice within the Province aforesaid, shall be tried and determined by the manimous verdict of twelve jurors, duly sworn for the trial of such issue or issues, which jurors shall be summoned and taken conformably to the law and custom of England.

II. Provided always, and be it further enacted by the authority aforesaid, that nothing herein contained shall prevent, or be construed to prevent, the said jurors from bringing in a special verdict.

[1] The second Act passed by the first Parliament of Upper Canada at its first session, and known as 32 George III. cap. 2.

APPENDIX E.

THE INTRODUCTION OF RESPONSIBLE GOVERNMENT INTO CANADA.

1. Lord Durham's Report.[1]

* * * * * * *

Such are the lamentable results of the political and social evils[2] which have so long agitated the Canadas ; and such is their condition that at the present moment we are called on to take immediate precautions against dangers so alarming as those of rebellion, foreign invasion, and utter exhaustion and depopulation.[3] When I look on the various and deep-rooted causes of mischief which the past inquiry has pointed out as existing in every institution, in the constitutions, and in the very composition of society throughout a great part of these Provinces, I almost shrink from the apparent presumption of grappling with these gigantic difficulties. Nor shall I attempt to do so in detail. I rely on the efficacy of reform in the constitutional system by which these colonies are governed, for the removal of every abuse in their administration which defective institutions have engendered. If a system can be devised which shall lay in these countries the foundation of an efficient and popular government, ensure harmony in place of collision between the various powers of the State, and bring the influence of a vigorous public opinion to

---

[1] These extracts are reprinted from the British Parliamentary paper, printed by order of the House of Commons. The Report is dated "London, 31st January, 1839," and the order for printing was made on the 11th of February of the same year.

[2] The "results" and "evils" here mentioned are described in the previous part of the report. Amongst them are the struggle between the French and English races in Lower Canada, collisions between the Executive and the Legislative Assembly in different Provinces, collisions between the Legislative Councils and the Legislative Assemblies, abuse of the system of Provincial grants for local public works, want of vigorous administration of the royal prerogative, interference of the Colonial Department in the details of Colonial Government, irresponsibility of the Executive Council, the absence of any division of the public service into regular ministerial departments, the want of municipal institutions, the inefficient administration of justice in Lower Canada, defective means of education, the clergy reserves and the establishment of rectories, the want of means of communication between different parts of each Province, wasteful misappropriation of Crown lands, and lack of proper arrangements for the reception and disposition of immigrants. Some of these matters are dealt with at great length in the Appendixes to the Report.

[3] Lord Durham felt and expressed the fear that an emigration of English speaking settlers from Upper Canada to the United states was likely to take place. He cites, in support of his position a number of cases which had come to his knowledge, and avows his belief that these emigrants were not all politically disaffected towards the Government.

bear on every detail of public affairs, we may rely on sufficient remedies being found for the present vices of the administrative system.

The preceding pages have sufficiently pointed out the nature of those evils, to the extensive operation of which I attribute the various practical grievances, and the present unsatisfactory condition of the North American colonies. It is not by weakening, but strengthening the influence of the people on its government; by confining within much narrower bounds than those hitherto allotted to it, and not by extending the interference of the imperial authorities in the details of colonial affairs, that I believe that harmony is to be restored, where dissension has so long prevailed; and regularity and vigour, hitherto unknown, introduced into the administration of these Provinces. It needs no change in the principles of government, no invention of a new constitutional theory, to supply the remedy which would, in my opinion, completely remove the existing political disorders. It needs but to follow out consistently the principles of the British constitution, and introduce into the government of these great colonies those wise provisions, by which alone the working of the representative system can in any country be rendered harmonious and efficient. We are not now to consider the policy of establishing representative government in the North American colonies. That has been irrevocably done;[1] and the experiment of depriving the people of their present constitutional power is not to be thought of. To conduct their government harmoniously, in accordance with its established principles, is now the business of its rulers; and I know not how it is possible to secure that harmony in any other way than by administering the government on those principles which have been found perfectly efficacious in Great Britain.[2] I would not impair a single prerogative of the Crown; on the contrary I believe that the interests of the people of these colonies require the protection of prerogatives which have not hitherto been exercised.[3] But the Crown must on the other hand, submit to the necessary consequences of representative institutions; and if it has to carry on the government in unison with a representative body, it must consent to carry it on by means of those in whom that representative body has confidence.

[1] See pp. 7-25, and 112-118.

[2] Elsewhere in his Report (p. 29 of the British Parliamentary paper) Lord Durham, speaking of the freedom of the administration from the influence of the Legislative Assembly, says "This entire separation of the legislative and executive powers of a State is the natural error of governments desirous of being free from the check of representative institutions. Since the Revolution of 1688, the stability of the English Constitution has been secured by that wise principle of our government which has vested the direction of the national policy, and the distribution of patronage, in the leaders of the parliamentary majority."

[3] On p. 37 of the Report he says: "The defective system of administration in Lower Canada commences at the very source of power; and the efficiency of the public service is impaired throughout by the entire want in the Colony of any vigorous administration of the prerogative of the Crown. The fact is that, according to the present system, there is no real representative of the Crown in in the Province; there is in it, literally no power which originates and conducts the Executive government. The Governor, it is true, is said to represent the Sovereign, and the authority of the Crown is, to a certain extent, delegated to him; but he is, in fact, a mere subordinate officer, receiving his orders from the Secretary of State, responsible to him for his conduct, and guided by his instructions."

In England this principle has been so long considered an indisputable and essential part of our constitution, that it has really hardly ever been found necessary to inquire into the means by which its observance is enforced. When a ministry ceases to command a majority in Parliament on great questions of policy, its doom is immediately sealed; and it would appear to us as strange to attempt for any time, to carry on a government by means of ministers perpetually in a minority, as it would be to pass laws with a majority of votes against them. The ancient constitutional remedies, by impeachment and stoppage of the supplies, have never since the reign of William III. been brought into operation for the purpose of removing a ministry. They have never been called for, because in fact it has been the habit of ministers rather to anticipate the occurrence of an absolutely hostile vote, and to retire when supported only by a bare and uncertain majority. If colonial legislatures have frequently stopped the supplies, if they have harassed public servants by unjust or harsh impeachments, it was because the removal of an unpopular administration could not be effected in the colonies by those milder indications of a want of confidence, which have always sufficed to attain the end in the Mother Country.

The means which have occasionally been proposed in the Colonies themselves appear to me by no means calculated to attain the desired end in the best way. These proposals indicate such a want of reliance on the willingness of the Imperial Government to acquiesce in the adoption of a better system, as, if warranted, would render an harmonious adjustment of the different powers of the State utterly hopeless. An elective Executive Council would not only be utterly inconsistent with monarchical government, but would really, under the nominal authority of the Crown, deprive the community of one of the great advantages of an hereditary monarchy. Every purpose of popular control might be combined with every advantage of vesting the immediate choice of advisers in the Crown, were the Colonial Governor to be instructed to secure the co-operation of the Assembly in his policy, by intrusting its administration to such men as could command a majority; and if he were given to understand that he need count on no aid from home in any difference with the Assembly, that should not directly involve the relations between the Mother Country and the colony. This change might be effected by a single despatch[1] containing such instructions; or if any legal enactment were requisite, it would only be one that would render it necessary that the official acts of the Governor should be countersigned by some public functionary. This would induce responsibility for every act of the Government, and, as a natural consequence, it would necessitate the substitution of a system of administration, by means of competent heads of departments, for the present rude machinery of an Executive Council.[2] The Governor, if he wished to retain advisers not possessing

---

[1] See despatches of Lord John Russell to Lord Sydenham (pp. 299-302 below).

[2] In a previous part of his report, Lord Durham gives this description of the Executive Council (p. 39): "It is a body of which the constitution somewhat resembles that of the Privy Council; it is bound by a similar oath of secresy; it discharges in the same manner certain anomalous judicial functions; and its 'consent and advice' are required in some cases in which the observance of that form has been thought a requisite check on the exercise of particular prerogatives

the confidence of the existing Assembly, might rely on the effect of an appeal to the people,[1] and, if unsuccessful, he might be coerced by a refusal of supplies, or his advisers might be terrified by the prospect of impeachment. But there can be no reason for apprehending that either party would enter on a contest, when each would find its interests in the maintenance of harmony; and the abuse of the powers which each would constitutionally possess, would cease when the struggle for larger powers became unnecessary. Nor can I conceive that it would be found impossible or difficult to conduct a Colonial Government with precisely that limitation of the respective powers which has been so long and so easily maintained in Great Britain.

I know that it has been urged that the principles which are productive of harmony and good government in the Mother Country, are by no means applicable to a colonial dependency. It is said that it is necessary that the administration of a colony should be carried on by persons nominated without any reference to the wishes of its people; that they have to carry into effect the policy, not of that people, but of the authorities at home; and that a colony which should name all its own administrative functionaries would in fact cease to be dependent. I admit that the system which I propose would in fact place the internal government of the colony in the hands of the colonists themselves; and that we should thus leave to them the execution of the laws, of which we have long entrusted the making solely to them. Perfectly aware of the value of our colonial possessions, and strongly impressed with the necessity of maintaining our connexion with them, I know not in what respect it can be desirable that we should interfere with their internal legislation in matters which do not affect their relations with the Mother Country. The matters which so concern us are very few.[2] The constitution of the form of government,—the regulation of foreign relations, and of trade with the Mother Country, the other British colonies and foreign nations,—and the disposal of the public lands, are the only points on which the Mother Country requires a control.[3] This control is now sufficiently

---

of the Crown. But in other respects it bears a greater resemblance to a Cabinet, the Governor being in the habit of taking its advice on most of the important questions of his policy. But as there is no division into departments in the Council there is no individual responsibility and no individual superintendence. Each member of the Council takes an equal part in all the business brought before it. The power of removing members being very rarely exercised, the Council is in fact for the most part composed of persons placed in it long ago; and the Governor is obliged either to take the advice of persons in whom he has no confidence, or to consult only a portion of the Council. The secrecy of the proceedings adds to the irresponsibility of the body; and when the Governor takes an important step, it is not known, or not authentically known, whether he has taken the advice of this Council or not, what members he has consulted, or by the advice of which of the body he has been finally guided."

[1] Todd's "Parliamentary Government in the British Colonies," pp. 525-573.

[2] Lord Durham (Report, p. 30) says "it has never been very clearly explained what are the imperial interests" which make it necessary that "officers of Government should be nominated by the Crown, without any reference to the community, whose interests are entrusted to their keeping."

[3] Compare the British North America Act, 1867, with respect to the first and third of these subjects; Canada is apparently completely autonomous in the matter of trade—that is to say, she can impose any conditions she pleases on the import and export of goods of all kinds.

secured by the authority of the Imperial Legislature ; by the protection which the colony derives from us against foreign enemies ; by the beneficial terms which our laws secure to its trade ; and by its share of the reciprocal benefits which would be conferred by a wise system of colonization. A perfect subordination, on the part of the colony, on these points is secured by the advantages which it finds in the continuance of its connexion with the Empire. It certainly is not strengthened, but greatly weakened, by a vexatious interference on the part of the Home Government, with the enactment of laws for regulating the internal concerns of the colony, or in the selection of the persons entrusted with their execution. The colonists may not always know what laws are best for them, or which of their countrymen are the fittest for conducting their affairs ; but at least they have a greater interest in coming to a right judgment on these points, and will take greater pains to do so than those whose welfare is very remotely and slightly affected by the good or bad legislation of these portions of the Empire. If the colonists make bad laws, and select improper persons to conduct their affairs, they will generally be the only, always the greatest sufferers ; and, like the people of other countries, they must bear the ills which they bring on themselves, until they choose to apply the remedy. But it surely cannot be the duty or the interest of Great Britain to keep a most expensive military possession of these colonies, in order that a Governor or Secretary of State may be able to confer colonial appointments on one rather than another set of persons in the colonies. For this is really the only question at issue. The slightest acquaintance with these colonies proves the fallacy of the common notion, that any considerable amount of patronage in them is distributed among strangers from the Mother Country. Whatever inconvenience a consequent frequency of changes among the holders of office may produce is a necessary disadvantage of free government, which will be amply compensated by the perpetual harmony which the system must produce between the people and its rulers. Nor do I fear that the character of the public servants will, in any respect, suffer from a more popular tenure of office. For I can conceive no system so calculated to fill important posts with inefficient persons as the present, in which public opinion is too little consulted in the original appointment, and in which it is almost impossible to remove those who disappoint the expectations of their usefulness, without inflicting a kind of brand on their capacity or integrity.

* * * * * * * *

The important alteration in the policy of the Colonial Government which I recommend, might be wholly or in part effected for the present by the unaided authority of the Crown ; and I believe that the great mass of discontent in Upper Canada, which is not directly connected with personal irritation arising out of the incidents of the late troubles,[1] might be dispelled by an assurance that the government of the colony should henceforth be carried on in conformity with the views of the majority in the Assembly. But I think that for the well-being of the colonies and the security of the Mother Country,

[1] The Rebellion of 1837-38.

it is necessary that such a change should be rendered more permanent[1] than a momentary sense of the existing difficulties can ensure its being. I cannot believe that persons in power in this country will be restrained from the injudicious interference with the internal management of these colonies which I deprecate, while they remain the petty and divided communities which they now are. The public attention at home is distracted by the various and sometimes contrary complaints of these different contiguous Provinces. Each now urges its demands at different times, and in somewhat different forms, and the interests which each individual complainant represents as in peril are too petty to attract the due attention of the Empire. But if these important and extensive colonies should speak with one voice, if it were felt that every error of our colonial policy must cause a common suffering and a common discontent throughout the whole wide extent of British America, those complaints would never be provoked ; because no authority would venture to run counter to the wishes of such a community, except on points absolutely involving the few imperial interests which it is necessary to remove from the jurisdiction of colonial legislation.[2]

It is necessary that I should also recommend what appears to me an essential limitation on the present powers of the representative bodies in these colonies. I consider good government not to be attainable while the present unrestricted powers of voting public money, and of managing the local expenditure of the community are lodged in the hands of an Assembly. As long as revenue is raised, which leaves a large surplus after the payment of the necessary expenses of the civil government, and as long as any member of the Assembly may, without restriction, propose a vote of public money, so long will the Assembly retain in its hands the powers which it everywhere abuses, of misapplying that money. The prerogative of the Crown which is constantly exercised in Great Britain for the real protection of the people, ought never to have been waived in the colonies ; and if the rule of the Imperial Parliament, that no money vote should be proposed without the previous consent of the Crown,[3] were introduced into these colonies, it might be wisely employed in protecting the public interests, now frequently sacrificed in that scramble for local appropriations, which chiefly serves to give an undue influence to particular individuals or parties.

[1] Among the specific proposals formulated by Lord Durham as the basis of an Act to repeal the Constitutional Act, 1791, was the following one: "The responsibility to the United Legislature of all the officers of the Government, except the Governor and his Secretary, should be secured by every means known to the British Constitution. The Governor, as the representative of the Crown, should be instructed that he must carry on his Government by heads of departments, in whom the United Legislature shall repose confidence ; and that he must look for no support from home in any contest with the Legislature, except on points involving strictly Imperial interests" (Report, p. 117).

[2] A Special Committee of the Legislative Council of Upper Canada, of which the Hon. J. S. Macaulay was chairman, prepared a reply to Lord Durham's plea for responsible government. It is dated, May 11, 1839, and appears, with other comments on the Report, as Appendix G.G. to the Council's Journals for the session of that year.

[3] This recommendation is repeated (Report, p. 117) as one of the proposals to be embodied in the Act of Parliament. See the Union Act, 1840, section 57 ; and the Confederation Act, section 54.

2. Lord John Russell's Despatches.[1]

(*a*) *Instructions*[2] *to Lord Sydenham (Sept. 7th, 1839).*

* * * * * * * *

The intelligence which has reached me from Upper Canada makes it probable that you may be called upon for some explanation of the views of the Ministers of the Crown, on a question respecting which the Bill[3] to which I have referred, is necessarily silent. I allude to the nature and extent of the control, which the popular branch of the United Legislature will be admitted to exercise over the conduct of the Executive Government ; and the continuance in the public service of its principal officers. But it is evidently impossible to reduce into the form of a positive enactment, a constitutional principle of this nature. The importance of maintaining the utmost possible harmony between the policy of the Legislature and of the Executive Government, admits of no question ; and it will of course be your anxious endeavour to call to your Counsels and to employ in the public service those persons who, by their position and character, have obtained the general confidence and esteem of the inhabitants of the Province.

* * * * * * * *

---

[1] The text of these despatches is reprinted from a return to an address from the Legislative Assembly of Canada to the Governor-General, Lord Sydenham. The return is dated, August 17, 1841, and the address was adopted by the Assembly on the 5th of the same month. The latter was moved by Mr. Baldwin, seconded by Mr. Viger, and carried without a division. The return is printed as Appendix B.B. to the Assembly Journals of 1841, the first session of the first Parliament of the Province of Canada. It is worthy of note that when Lord Sydenham was asked by address of the Legislative Assembly of Upper Canada in the session of 1839 for copies of despatches from the Imperial Government relating to responsible Government, he evaded the request, though those here printed were then in his possession. That address was adopted by the Assembly on the 13th of December, 1839; on that day a despatch of the 16th of October from Lord John Russell to Lieut.-Governor Sir George Arthur, dealing with the tenure on which public offices were held, was brought down to the Assembly. No reply was made to the address of the 13th of December until the 14th of January, 1840, on which day Lord Sydenham sent a message regretting that it was "not in his power to communicate to the House of Assembly any despatches on the subject referred to," and adding : " The Governor-General has received Her Majesty's commands to administer the Government of these Provinces in accordance with the well understood wishes and interests of the people, and to pay to their feelings, as expressed through their representatives, the deference that is justly due to them. These are the commands of Her Majesty, and these are the views with which Her Majesty's Government desire that the administration of these Provinces should be conducted ; and it will be the earnest and anxious desire of the Governor-General to discharge the trust committed to him, in accordance with these principles." The address to which this message was a reply had been moved by Mr. Sherwood and seconded by Mr. Rykert.

[2] The despatch containing the " instructions" from which the above extract is taken, will be found printed in full in the Assembly Journals of 1841, pp. 390-396. It was brought down in response to an address moved by Sir Allan McNab and seconded by Mr. Cartwright. Lord Sydenham arrived in Quebec on the 18th of October, 1839.

[3] Based on Lord Durham's Report.

(b) *Despatch to Lord Sydenham (October 14th, 1839).*

DOWNING STREET, 14th October, 1839.

Sir, It appears from Sir George Arthur's Despatches, that you may encounter much difficulty in subduing the excitement which prevails on the question of what is called " Responsible Government." I have to instruct you, however, to refuse any explanation which may be construed to imply an acquiescence in the Petitions and Addresses upon this subject. I cannot better commence this Despatch than by a reference to the Resolutions of both Houses of Parliament[1] of the 28th April and 9th May in the year 1837.

The Assembly of Lower Canada having repeatedly pressed this point, Her Majesty's Confidential Advisers at that period thought it necessary not only to explain their views in the communications of the Secretary of State, but expressly called for the opinion of Parliament on the subject. The Crown and the two Houses of Lords and Commons have thus decisively pronounced a judgment upon the question ; you will consider yourself precluded from entertaining any proposition on the subject. It does not appear indeed, that any very definite meaning is generally agreed upon by those who call themselves the advocates of this principle, but its very vagueness is a source of delusion, and if at all encouraged, would prove the cause of embarrassment and danger.

The Constitution of England after long struggles and alternate success, has settled into a form of Government in which the prerogative of the Crown is undisputed, but is never exercised without advice. Hence the exercise only is questioned, and however the use of the authority may be condemned, the authority itself remains untouched.

This is the practical solution of a great problem—the result of a contest which from 1640 to 1690 shook the Monarchy and disturbed the peace of the Country.

But if we seek to apply such a practice to a Colony, we shall at once find ourselves at fault. The power for which a Minister is responsible in England, is not his own power, but the power of the Crown, of which he is for the time the organ. It is obvious that the Executive Councillor of the Colony is in a situation totally different. The Governor under whom he serves receives his orders from the Crown of England. But can the Colonial Council be the Advisers of the Crown of England? Evidently not, for the Crown has other Advisers for the same functions, and with superior authority.

It may happen, therefore, that the Governor receives at one and the same time instructions from the Queen and advice from his Executive Council, totally at variance with each other. If he is to obey his instructions from England, the parallel of constitutional responsibility entirely fails ; if on the

---

[1] The Imperial Parliament. Amendments looking to the recognition of responsible government were moved in the House of Commons, but voted down, and Lord Brougham entered his dissent, with reasons, on the Journals of the House of Lords. The resolution dealing with responsible government is as follows: " That while it is expedient to improve the composition of the Executive Council in Lower Canada, it is unadvisable to subject it to the responsibility demanded by the House of Assembly of that Province."

other hand, he is to follow the advice of his Council, he is no longer a subordinate Officer, but an independent Sovereign.

There are some cases in which the force of these objections is so manifest, that those who at first made no distinction between the Constitution of the United Kingdom and that of the Colonies, admit their strength. I allude to the questions of foreign war and international relations whether of trade or diplomacy. It is now said that internal Government is alone intended.

But there are some cases of internal Government in which the honor of the Crown or the faith of Parliament, or the safety of the State are so seriously involved, that it would not be possible for Her Majesty to delegate the authority to a Minister in a Colony. I will put for illustration some of the cases which have occurred in that very Province, where the Petition for a responsible Executive first arose—I mean Lower Canada.

During the time when a large majority of the Assembly of Lower Canada followed Mr. Papineau as their leader, it was obviously the aim of that gentleman to discourage all who did their duty to the Crown within the Province, and to deter all those who should resort to Canada with British habits and feelings from without. I need not say that it would have been impossible for any Minister to support in the Parliament of the United Kingdom the measures which a Ministry, headed by Mr. Papineau, would have imposed upon the Governor of Lower Canada. British Officers punished for doing their duty,—British Emigrants defrauded of their property,—British Merchants discouraged in their lawful pursuits, would have loudly appealed to Parliament against Canadian Ministry, and would have demanded protection.[1]

Let us suppose the Assembly, as then constituted, to have been sitting when Sir John Colborne suspended two of the Judges. Would any Councillor, possessing the confidence of the Assembly, have made himself responsible for such an act? And yet the very safety of the Province depended upon its adoption,—nay, the very orders of which Your Excellency is yourself the bearer respecting Messrs. Bedard and Panet, would never be adopted or put in execution by a Ministry depending for existence on a majority led by Mr. Papineau.

Nor can any one take upon himself to say that such cases will not again occur. The principle once sanctioned, no one can say how soon its application might be dangerous or even dishonorable, while all will agree that to recall the power thus conceded, would be impossible.

While I thus see insuperable objections to the adoption of the principle as it has been stated, I see little or none to the practical views of Colonial Government recommended by Lord Durham, as I understand them. The Queen's Government have no desire to thwart the Representative Assemblies of British North America in their measures of reform and improvement. They have no

---

[1] Lord John Russell's information was derived from many despatches from Governors, and especially from (1) the report presented in 1837 by Lord Gosford, and his fellow commissioners, Sir Charles Grey, and Sir George Gipps, and (2) the report submitted by Lord Durham early in 1839.

wish to make those Provinces the resource for patronage at home. They are earnestly intent on giving to the talent and character of leading persons in the Colonies advantages similar to those which talent and character employed in the public service, obtain in the United Kingdom. Her Majesty has no desire to maintain any system of policy among Her North American subjects which opinion condemns. In receiving the Queen's commands, therefore, to protest against any declaration at variance with the honour of the Crown and the unity of the Empire, I am at the same time instructed to announce Her Majesty's gracious intention to look to the affectionate attachment of Her people in North America as the best security for permanent dominion.

It is necessary for this purpose, that no official misconduct should be screened by Her Majesty's Representative in the Provinces, and that no private interests should be allowed to compete with the general good.

Your Excellency is fully in possession of the principles which have guided Her Majesty's advisers on this subject, and you must be aware that there is no surer way of earning the approbation of the Queen than by maintaining the harmony of the Executive with the Legislative authorities.

While I have thus cautioned you against any declaration from which dangerous consequences might hereafter flow, and instructed you as to the general line of your conduct, it may be said that I have not drawn any specific line beyond which the power of the Governor on one hand and the privilege of the Assembly on the other, ought not to extend. But this must be the case in any mixed Government. Every political Constitution in which different bodies share the supreme power, is only enabled to exist by the forbearance of those among whom this power is distributed. In this respect the example of England may well be imitated. The Sovereign using the Prerogative of the Crown to the utmost extent, and the House of Commons exerting its power of the purse to carry all its resolutions into immediate effect, would produce confusion in the country in less than a twelve month. So in a Colony, the Governor thwarting every legitimate proposition of the Assembly, and the Assembly continually recurring to its power of refusing supplies can but disturb all political relations, embarrass trade, and retard the prosperity of the people. Each must exercise a wise moderation. The Governor must only oppose the wishes of the Assembly where the honour of the Crown or the interests of the Empire are deeply concerned; and the Assembly must be ready to modify some of its measures for the sake of harmony and from a reverent attachment to the authority of Great Britain.

I have, etc.,

(Signed,)   J. RUSSELL.

The Right Honorable C. POULETT THOMSON, etc.

3. Legislative Assembly Resolutions, 1841.[1]

(a) *Proposed by Hon. Robert Baldwin.*

1. That the most important as well as the most undoubted of the political rights of the people of this Province is that of having a Provincial Parliament for the protection of their liberties, for the exercise of their constitutional influence over the Executive Departments of their Government, and for legislation upon all matters which do not, on the grounds of absolute necessity, constitutionally belong to the jurisdiction of the Imperial Parliament, as the paramount authority of the Empire.

2. That the head of the Provincial Executive Government of the Province being within the limits of his Government, the representative of the Sovereign, is not constitutionally responsible to any other than the authorities of the Empire.

3. That the representative of the Sovereign for the proper conduct and efficient disposal of the public business is necessarily obliged to make use of the advice and assistance of subordinate officers in the administration of his Government.

4. That in order to preserve that harmony between the different branches of the Provincial Parliament which is essential to the happy conduct of public affairs the principal of such subordinate officers, advisers of the representative of the Sovereign, and constituting as such the Provincial administration under him as the head of the Provincial Government, ought always to be men possessed of the public confidence, whose opinions and policy harmonizing with those of the representatives of the people, would afford a guarantee that the well understood wishes and interests of the people, which Our Gracious Sovereign has declared shall be the rule of the Provincial Government, will at all times be faithfully represented to the head of that Government, and through him to the Sovereign and Imperial Parliament.

---

[1] The text of these resolutions is reprinted from the Assembly Journals of the first session of the first Parliament of Canada, pp. 480-482. The procedure leading to their adoption indicates a well-marked purpose. Lord Sydenham's first Executive Council was composed of Messrs. Sullivan, Dunn, Daly, Harrison, Ogden, Draper, Baldwin and Day. Mr. Baldwin withdrew from it, and on the 5th of August moved for the production of copies of Lord John Russell's despatches on responsible government, and of other papers on the same subject. The order was made and the return containing these documents was on the 20th of August laid on the table of the Assembly by Mr. Harrison. On the 3rd of September Mr. Baldwin moved the first series of resolutions here given, and the second series were moved by Mr. Harrison as amendments and adopted. It is generally admitted that Mr. Harrison's resolutions were drawn up by Lord Sydenham himself. A melancholy interest is added to these facts by the tragic end of his term of office. He was fatally injured on the 5th September by a fall from his horse. Parliament was prorogued by his substitute, Gen. Clitherow, at noon on the 18th, and he died early on the morning of the following day.

5. That as it is practically always optional with such advisers to continue in or retire from office at pleasure, this House has the constitutional right of holding such advisers politically responsible for every act of the Provincial Government of a local character, sanctioned by such Government while such advisers continue in office.

6. That for the like reason this House has the constitutional right of holding such advisers in like manner responsible for using, while they continue in office, their best exertions to procure from the Imperial authorities the exercise of their right of dealing with such matters affecting the interests of the Province as constitutionally belong to those authorities, in the manner most consistent with the well understood wishes and interests of the people of this Province.

(b) *Proposed in amendment by Hon. S. B. Harrison.*

1. That the most important, as well as the most undoubted, of the political rights of the people of this Province is that of having a Provincial Parliament for the protection of their liberties, for the exercise of a constitutional influence over the Executive Departments of their Government, and for legislation upon all matters of internal Government.

2. That the head of the Executive Government of the Province being, within the limits of his Government, the representative of the Sovereign is responsible to the Imperial authority alone; but that, nevertheless the management of our local affairs can only be conducted by him, by and with the assistance, counsel and information, of subordinate officers in the Province.

3. That in order to preserve between the different branches of the Provincial Parliament that harmony which is essential to the peace, welfare and good Government of the Province the chief advisers of the representative of the Sovereign, constituting a Provincial administration under him, ought to be men possessed of the confidence of the representatives of the people, thus affording a guarantee that the well understood wishes and interests of the people, which our Gracious Sovereign has declared shall be the rule of the Provincial Government, will, on all occasions, be faithfully represented and advocated.

4. That the people of this Province have, moreover, a right to expect from such Provincial administration, the exertion of their best endeavours that the Imperial authority, within its constitutional limits shall be exercised in the manner most consistent with their well understood wishes and interests.[1]

[1] The text of these resolutions is often quoted inaccurately, through following the version given in Scrope's "Life of Lord Sydenham." The biographer omits the first resolution altogether, and states that they were "carried unanimously." On the third resolution a division was taken and the yeas and nays were recorded. The vote stood 56 to 7, the members of the minority being Messrs. Burnett, Cartwright, MacNab (Sir A. N.), McLean, Moffatt (Hon. G.), Sherwood, Watts. For the subsequent history of responsible Government till its final recognition by Lord Elgin, see Kaye's "Life of Metcalfe," and Dent's "Forty Years," and Hinck's "Reminiscences." Lord Metcalfe in one of his papers, entitled "The System of Government," formulated an argument against the system, and in another, "Resignation of the Executive Council," he gave his version of the rupture between him and the first Baldwin-Lafontaine administration. See also Ryerson's and Sullivan's letters on the same subject, coupled with the pen-names respectively of "Leonidas" and "Legion."

APPENDIX F.

QUEBEC CONFERENCE RESOLUTIONS,[1] 1864.

1. The best interests and present and future prosperity of British North America will be promoted by a federal[2] union, under the Crown of Great Britain, provided such union can be effected on principles just to the several Provinces.

2. In the federation of the British North American Provinces, the system of Government best adapted under existing circumstances to protect the diversified interests in the several Provinces, and secure efficiency, harmony and permanency in the working of the union, would be a general Government, charged with matters of common interest to the whole country; and Local Governments for each of the Canadas, and for the Provinces of Nova Scotia, New Brunswick, and Prince Edward Island, charged with the control of local matters in their respective sections; provision being made for the admission into the union, on equitable terms, of Newfoundland, the North-West Territory, British Columbia, and Vancouver.[3]

3. In framing a constitution for the general Government, the Conference, with a view to the perpetuation of our connection with the mother country,

---

[1] The text of these resolutions is reprinted from the Journals of the Legislative Assembly of Canada, 1865 (pp. 202-209). They were adopted as part of an address to the Queen, praying for the submission to the Imperial Parliament of a measure to unite into one Government the "Colonies of Canada, Nova Scotia, New Brunswick, Newfoundland, and Prince Edward Island." The ordinary histories of Canada give ample information as to the events which brought about the Quebec Conference. The best special narrative of the whole period is contained in Gray's "Confederation; or the Political and Parliamentary History of Canada from the Conference at Quebec to the admission of British Columbia" (vol. I,). The author, Hon. John Hamilton Gray, was one of the delegates to the Conference from New Brunswick. The resolutions were adopted by the Conference on the 10th of October, 1864, and by the Legislative Assembly of Canada, after a long discussion and many unsuccessful attempts to secure modifications, on the 11th of March, 1865. A full report of the debates was in 1865 published "by order of the Legislature," under the title "Parliamentary Debates on the subject of the Confederation of the British North American Provinces." The text has been carefully compared with the versions of the resolutions given in Gray's "Confederation" and the "Debates on Confederation," the points of difference being noted where they occur.

[2] For a definition of the term "Federal," see Freeman's "History of Federal Government," vol. I, first two chapters. See also the essays of Hamilton and Madison in the "Federalist"; Story's "Commentaries on the Constitution of the United States"; Cooley's "Constitutional Law in the United States"; and numerous decisions of the United States Supreme Court, the Canadian Supreme Court, and the Judicial Committee of the Privy Council.

[3] Prince Edward Island as well as Newfoundland afterwards declined to come into the union. British Columbia and Vancouver were then separate Provinces. See Note 30, pp. 233-234 above.

and to the promotion of the best interests of the people of these Provinces, desire to follow the model of the British constitution so far as our circumstances will permit.

4. The Executive authority or government shall be vested in the Sovereign of the United Kingdom of Great Britain and Ireland, and be administered according to the well-understood principles of the British constitution, by the Sovereign personally, or by the representative of the Sovereign duly authorized.

5. The Sovereign or Representative of the Sovereign[1] shall be Commander in Chief of the land and naval militia forces.

6. There shall be a General Legislature or Parliament for the federated Provinces, composed of[2] a Legislative Council and a House of Commons.

7. For the purpose of forming the Legislative Council, the federated Provinces shall be considered as consisting of three divisions: 1st, Upper Canada, 2nd, Lower Canada, 3rd, Nova Scotia, New Brunswick, and Prince Edward Island: each division with an equal representation in the Legislative Council.

8. Upper Canada shall be represented in the Legislative Council by 24 members, Lower Canada by 24 members, and the three maritime Provinces by 24 members, of which Nova Scotia shall have 10, New Brunswick 10, and Prince Edward Island 4 members.[3]

9. The Colony of Newfoundland shall be entitled to enter the proposed union, with a representation in the Legislative Council of 4 members.

10. The North-West Territory, British Columbia and Vancouver shall be admitted into the union on such terms and conditions as the Parliament of the federated Provinces shall deem equitable, and as shall receive the assent of Her Majesty; and, in the case of the Province of British Columbia or Vancouver, as shall be agreed to by the Legislature of such Province.[4]

11. The members of the Legislative Council shall be appointed by the Crown under the great seal of the general government, and shall hold office during life; if any Legislative Councillor shall, for two consecutive sessions of Parliament, fail to give his attendance in the said Council, his seat shall thereby become vacant.

---

[1] In November, 1866, representatives from Canada, New Brunswick, and Nova Scotia met in London to aid in the preparation of a confederation measure for submission to the Imperial Parliament. As a result of their conferences several changes were made in the text of the resolutions, amongst them the omission of these words "or representative of the Sovereign." See Gray's "Confederation," p. 385.

[2] The words "the Sovereign," were here inserted at the London Conference. See Note 1 above.

[3] On account of the refusal of Prince Edward Island to join the Union this resolution was altered at the London Conference so as to give Nova Scotia and New Brunswick 12 members each, until the third Province should come in.

[4] See Notes 68 and 69, p. 238 above.

12. The members of the Legislative Council shall be British subjects by birth or naturalization, of the full age of thirty years, shall possess a continuous real property qualification of four thousand dollars over and above all incumbrances, and shall be and continue worth that sum over and above their debts and liabilities, but in the case of Newfoundland and Prince Edward Island the property may be either real or personal.[1]

13. If any question shall arise as to the qualification of a Legislative Councillor, the same shall be determined by the Council.

14. The first selection of the members of the Legislative Council shall be made, except as regards Prince Edward Island, from the Legislative Councils of the various Provinces, so far as a sufficient number be found qualified and willing to serve ; such members shall be appointed by the Crown at the recommendation of the general executive Government, upon the nomination of the respective local Governments, and in such nomination due regard shall be had to the claims of the members of the Legislative Council of the opposition in each Province, so that all political parties may as nearly as possible be fairly represented.

15. The Speaker of the Legislative Council (unless otherwise provided by Parliament) shall be appointed by the Crown from among the members of the Legislative Council, and shall hold office during pleasure, and shall only be entitled to a casting vote on an equality of votes.

16. Each of the twenty-four Legislative Councillors representing Lower Canada in the Legislative Council of the general Legislature, shall be appointed to represent one of the twenty-four electoral divisions mentioned in Schedule A of chapter first of the Consolidated Statutes[2] of Canada, and such Councillor shall reside or possess his qualification in the division he is appointed to represent.

17. The basis of representation in the House of Commons shall be population, as determined by the official census every ten years ; and the number of members at first shall be 194, distributed as follows :—

    Upper Canada... 82
    Lower Canada... 65
    Nova Scotia............................... 19
    New Brunswick.. 15
    Newfoundland 8
    Prince Edward Island..................................... 5

18. Until the official census of 1871 has been made up, there shall be no change in the number of representatives from the several sections.

---

[1] In the conference of delegates at London (Note 1, p. 306) the twelfth resolution was changed so as to make the necessary qualifications of a senator embrace both a continuous property possession and continuous residence in the Province for which he was appointed, except in case of an official residence at the Capital (Gray's "Confederation," p. 385).

[2] Of 1859.

19. Immediately after the completion of the census of 1871, and immediately after every decennial census thereafter, the representation from each section in the House of Commons shall be readjusted on the basis of population.

20. For the purpose of such re-adjustments, Lower Canada shall always be assigned sixty-five members, and each of the other sections shall at each readjustment receive, for the ten years then next succeeding, the number of members to which it will be entitled on the same ratio of representation to population as Lower Canada will enjoy according to the census last taken by having sixty-five members.

21. No reduction shall be made in the number of members returned by any section, unless its population shall have decreased, relatively to the population of the whole union, to the extent of five per centum.

22. In computing at each decennial period the number of members to which each section is entitled, no fractional parts shall be considered, unless when exceeding one-half the number entitling to a member, in which case a member shall be given for each such fractional part.

23. The Legislature of each Province shall divide such Province into the proper number of constituencies, and define the boundaries of each of them.

24. The local Legislature of each Province may, from time to time, alter the electoral districts for the purposes of representation in such local Legislature, and distribute the representatives to which the Province is entitled in such local Legislature, in any manner such Legislature may see fit.[1]

25. The number of members may at any time be increased by the general Parliament,—regard being had to the proportionate rights then existing.

26. Until provisions are made by the General Parliament, all the laws which, at the date of the proclamation constituting the union, are in force in the Provinces respectively, relating to the qualification and disqualification of any person to be elected, or to sit or vote as a member of the Assembly in the said Provinces respectively; and relating to the qualification or disqualification of voters and to the oaths to be taken by voters, and to returning officers and their powers and duties,—and relating to the proceedings at elections, and to the period during which such elections may be continued,—and relating to the trial of controverted elections, and the proceedings incident thereto,—and relating to the vacating of seats of members, and to the issuing and execution of new writs, in case of any seat being vacated otherwise than by a dissolution, —shall respectively apply to elections of members to serve in the House of Commons, for places situate in those Provinces respectively.

---

[1] The twenty-third and twenty-fourth resolutions were omitted at the London Conference. (See Note 1, p. 306.) The text of the twenty-fourth as given in Gray's "Confederation," p. 69, differs materially from the one given above; it is as follows: "The local Legislature of each Province may from time to time alter the electoral districts for the purposes of representation in the House of Commons, and distribute the representatives to which the Province is entitled in any manner such Legislature may think fit."

27. Every House of Commons shall continue for five years from the day of the return of the writs choosing the same, and no longer ; subject, nevertheless, to be sooner prorogued or dissolved by the Governor.

28. There shall be a session of the general Parliament once, at least, in every year, so that a period of twelve calendar months shall not intervene between the last sitting of the general Parliament in one session, and the first sitting thereof in the next session.

29. The general Parliament shall have power to make laws for the peace, welfare, and good government of the federated provinces (saving the sovereignty of England), and especially laws respecting the following subjects :—

(1) The public debt and property.
(2) The regulation of trade and commerce.
(3) The imposition or regulation of duties of customs on imports and exports,—except on exports of timber, logs, masts, spars, deals and sawn lumber from New Brunswick, and of coal and other minerals from Nova Scotia.[1]
(4) The imposition or regulation of excise duties.
(5) The raising of money by all or any other modes or systems of taxation.
(6) The borrowing of money on the public credit.
(7) Postal service.
(8) Lines of steam or other ships, railways, canals and other works, connecting any two or more of the Provinces together or extending beyond the limits of any Province.
(9) Lines of steamships between the federated provinces and other countries.
(10) Telegraphic communication and the incorporation of telegraphic companies.
(11) All such works as shall, although lying wholly within any Province be specially declared by the Acts authorizing them to be for the general advantage.
(12) The census.
(13) Militia—military and naval service and defence.
(14) Beacons, buoys and light houses.
(15) Navigation and shipping.
(16) Quarantine.
(17) Sea-coast and inland fisheries.
(18) Ferries between any province and a foreign country, or between any two provinces.

[1] The words "from New Brunswick," and "from Nova Scotia." are omitted in Gray's text.

(19) Currency and coinage.
(20) Banking—incorporation of banks, and the issue of paper money.
(21) Savings banks.
(22) Weights and measures.
(23) Bills of exchange and promissory notes.
(24) Interest.
(25) Legal tender.
(26) Bankruptcy and insolvency.
(27) Patents of invention and discovery.
(28) Copyrights.
(29) Indians and lands reserved for the Indians.
(30) Naturalization and aliens.
(31) Marriage and divorce.[1]
(32) The criminal law, excepting the constitution of courts of criminal jurisdiction, but including the procedure in criminal matters.
(33) Rendering uniform all or any of the laws relative to property and civil rights in Upper Canada, Nova Scotia, New Brunswick, Newfoundland, and Prince Edward Island, and rendering uniform the procedure of all or any of the courts in these Provinces; but any statute for this purpose shall have no force or authority in any Province until sanctioned by the Legislature thereof.[2]
(34) The establishment of a general Court of Appeal for the federated Provinces.
(35) Immigration.
(36) Agriculture.
(37) And generally respecting all matters of a general character, not specially and exclusively reserved for the local Governments and Legislatures.

30. The general Government and Parliament shall have all powers necessary or proper for performing the obligations of the federated Provinces, as part of the British Empire, to foreign countries arising under treaties between Great Britain and such countries.

31. The general Parliament may also, from time to time, establish additional courts, and the general Government may appoint judges and officers thereof, when the same shall appear necessary or for the public advantage, in order to the due execution of the laws of Parliament.

32. All courts, judges and officers of the several Provinces shall aid, assist and obey the general Government in the exercise of its rights and powers, and

---

[1] At the London Conference it was resolved to place "solemnization of marriage" under the jurisdiction of the local Legislatures. See Note 1, p. 306.

[2] To this sub-section was added at the London Conference a clause providing that the power of altering, repealing, or amending laws so legislated upon "should thereafter remain with the general Government only."

for such purposes shall be held to be courts, judges and officers of the general Government.

33. The general Government shall appoint and pay the judges of the Superior Courts in each Province, and of the County Courts in Upper Canada, and Parliament shall fix their salaries.

34. Until the consolidation of the laws of Upper Canada, New Brunswick, Nova Scotia, Newfoundland and Prince Edward Island, the judges of these Provinces appointed by the general Government shall be selected from their respective bars.

35. The judges of the courts of Lower Canada shall be selected from the bar of Lower Canada.

36. The judges of the Court of Admiralty now receiving salaries shall be paid by the general Government.

37. The judges of the Superior Courts shall hold their offices during good behaviour, and shall be removable only on the address of both Houses of Parliament.

LOCAL GOVERNMENT.

38. For each of the Provinces there shall be an executive officer, styled the Lieutenant Governor, who shall be appointed by the Governor General in Council, under the Great Seal of the federated Provinces, during pleasure; such pleasure not to be exercised before the expiration of the first five years, except for cause; such cause to be communicated in writing to the Lieutenant Governor immediately after the exercise of the pleasure as aforesaid, and also by message to both Houses of Parliament, within the first week of the first session afterwards.

39. The Lieutenant Governor of each Province shall be paid by the general Government.

40. In undertaking to pay the salaries of the Lieutenant Governors, the Conference does not desire to prejudice the claim of Prince Edward Island upon the Imperial Government for the amount now paid for the salary of the Lieutenant Governor thereof.

41. The local Government and Legislature of each Province shall be constructed in such manner as the existing Legislature of such Province shall provide.

42. The local Legislatures shall have power to alter or amend their constitution from time to time.

43. The local Legislatures shall have power to make laws respecting the following subjects :—

(1) Direct taxation, and in New Brunswick the imposition of duties on the export of timber, logs, masts, spars, deals and sawn lumber; and in Nova Scotia, on coals and other minerals.[1]

(2) Borrowing money on the credit of the Province.

(3) The establishment and tenure of local offices, and the appointment and payment of local officers.

(4) Agriculture.

(5) Immigration.

(6) Education; saving the rights and privileges which the Protestant or Catholic minority in both Canadas may possess as to their denominational schools, at the time when the union goes into operation.[2]

(7) The sale and management of public lands excepting lands belonging to the general Government.

(8) Sea-coast and inland fisheries.[3]

(9) The establishment, maintenance and management of penitentiaries,[4] and of public and reformatory prisons.

(10) The establishment, maintenance and management of hospitals, asylums, charities, and eleemosynary institutions.

(11) Municipal institutions.

(12) Shop, saloon, tavern, auctioneer and other licenses.

(13) Local works.

(14) The incorporation of private or local companies, except such as relate to matters assigned to the general Parliament.

(15) Property and civil rights, excepting those portions thereof assigned to the general Parliament.

(16) Inflicting punishment by fine, penalties, imprisonment or otherwise, for the breach of laws passed in relation to any subject within their jurisdiction.

(17) The administration of justice, including the constitution, maintenance and organization of the courts,—both of civil and criminal jurisdiction, and including also the procedure in civil matters.

(18) And generally all matters of a private or local nature, not assigned to the general Parliament.

[1] In Gray's text this sub-section reads: "Direct taxation, and the imposition of duties on export of timber, logs, masts, spars, deals, and sawn lumber, and of coals and other minerals."

[2] The saving provision here applied to "both Canadas" was at the London Conference extended to minorities having in any Province, when the Union went into operation, legal rights or privileges as to denominational schools. It was at the same time further provided that "in any Province where a system of separate or dissentient schools by law obtains, or where the local Legislature may hereafter adopt a system of separate or dissentient schools, an appeal shall be to the Governor-General-in-Council of the general government from the acts and decisions of the local authorities, which may affect the rights or privileges of the Protestant or Catholic minority in the matter of education, and the general Parliament shall have power in the last resort to legislate on the subject."

[3] This sub-section was omitted at the London Conference. See Note 1, p. 306.

[4] "Penitentiaries" were at the London Conference transferred by resolution to the jurisdiction of the general Parliament.

44. The power of respiting, reprieving, and pardoning prisoners convicted of crimes, and of commuting and remitting of sentences in whole or in part which belongs of right to the Crown, shall be administered by the Lieutenant Governor of each Province in Council,[1] subject to any instructions he may, from time to time, receive from the general Government, and subject to any provisions that may be made in this behalf by the general Parliament.

MISCELLANEOUS.

45. In regard to all subjects over which jurisdiction belongs to both the general and local Legislatures, the laws of the general Parliament shall control and supersede those made by the local Legislature, and the latter shall be void so far as they are repugnant to, or inconsistent with, the former.

46. Both the English and French languages may be employed in the general Parliament and in its proceedings, and in the local Legislature of Lower Canada, and also in the Federal courts and in the courts of Lower Canada.

47. No lands or property belonging to the general or local Governments shall be liable to taxation.

48. All bills for appropriating any part of the public revenue, or for imposing any new tax or impost, shall originate in the House of Commons or House of Assembly, as the case may be.

49. The House of Commons or House of Assembly shall not originate or pass any vote, resolution, address or bill for the appropriation of any part of the public revenue, or of any tax or impost to any purpose, not first recommended by message of the Governor General or the Lieutenant Governor, as the case may be, during the session in which such vote, resolution, address or bill is passed.

50. Any bill of the general Parliament may be reserved in the usual manner for Her Majesty's assent, and any bill of the local Legislatures may, in like manner, be reserved for the consideration of the Governor General.

51. Any bill passed by the general Parliament shall be subject to disallowance by Her Majesty within two years, as in the case of bills passed by the Legislatures of the said provinces hitherto; and, in like manner, any bill passed by a local Legislature shall be subject to disallowance by the Governor general within one year after the passing thereof.

52. The seat of Government of the federated Provinces shall be Ottawa, subject to the Royal Prerogative.

---

[1] By resolution of the London Conference this prerogative of pardon was restricted to cases not "capital." See Note 1, p. 306.

53. Subject to any future action of the respective local Governments, the seat of the local Government in Upper Canada shall be Toronto; of Lower Canada, Quebec; and the seats of the local Governments in the other Provinces shall be as at present.

PROPERTY AND LIABILITIES.

54. All stocks, cash, bankers' balances and securities for money belonging to each Province at the time of the Union, except as hereinafter mentioned, shall belong to the general Government.

55. The following public works and property of each Province shall belong to the general Government, to wit :—

   (1) Canals.
   (2) Public harbours.
   (3) Light houses and piers.
   (4) Steamboats, dredges and public vessels.
   (5) River and lake improvements.
   (6) Railway and railway stocks, mortgages and other debts due by railway companies.
   (7) Military roads.
   (8) Custom houses, post offices and other public buildings, except such as may be set aside by the general Government for the use of the local Legislatures and Governments.
   (9) Property transferred by the Imperial Government and known as ordnance property.
   (10) Armories, drill sheds, military clothing and munitions of war; and
   (11) Lands set apart for public purposes.

56. All lands, mines, minerals and royalties vested in Her Majesty in the Provinces of Upper Canada, Lower Canada, Nova Scotia, New Brunswick and Prince Edward Island, for the use of such Provinces, shall belong to the local Government of the territory in which the same are so situate; subject to any trusts that may exist in respect to any of such lands or to any interest of other persons in respect of the same.

57. All sums due from purchasers or lessees of such lands, mines or minerals at the time of the union, shall also belong to the local Governments.

58. All assets connected with such portions of the public debt of any Province as are assumed by the local Governments shall also belong to those Governments respectively.

59. The several Provinces shall retain all other public property therein, subject to the right of the general Government to assume any lands or public property required for fortifications or the defence of the country.

60. The general government shall assume all the debts and liabilities of each Province.

61. The debt of Canada, not specially assumed by Upper and Lower Canada respectively, shall not exceed, at the time of the union, $62,500,000 ; Nova Scotia shall enter the union with a debt not exceeding $8,000,000 ; and New Brunswick with a debt not exceeding $7,000,000.

62. In case Nova Scotia or New Brunswick do not incur liabilities beyond those for which their Governments are now bound, and which shall make their debts at the date of union less than $8,000,000 and $7,000,000 respectively, they shall be entitled to interest at five per cent. on the amount not so incurred, in like manner as is hereinafter provided for Newfoundland and Prince Edward Island ; the foregoing resolution being in no respect intended to limit the powers given to the respective Governments of those Provinces, by Legislative authority, but only to limit the maximum amount of charge to be assumed by the general Government ; provided always, that the powers so conferred by the respective Legislatures shall be exercised within five years from this date, or the same shall then lapse.

63. Newfoundland and Prince Edward Island, not having incurred debts equal to those of the other Provinces, shall be entitled to receive, by half-yearly payments, in advance, from the general Government, the interest at five per cent. on the difference between the actual amount of their respective debts at the time of the union, and the average amount of indebtedness per head of the population of Canada, Nova Scotia and New Brunswick.

64. In consideration of the transfer to the general Parliament of the powers of taxation, an annual grant in aid of each Province shall be made, equal to eighty cents per head of the population, as established by the census of 1861 ; the population of Newfoundland being estimated at 130,000. Such aid shall be in full settlement of all future demands upon the general Government for local purposes, and shall be paid half-yearly in advance to each Province.[1]

65. The position of New Brunswick being such as to entail large immediate charges upon her local revenues, it is agreed that for the period of ten years, from the time when the Union takes effect, an additional allowance of $63,000 per annum shall be made to that Province. But that so long as the liability of that Province remains under $7,000,000, a deduction equal to the interest on such deficiency shall be made from the $63,000.

66. In consideration of the surrender to the general Government, by Newfoundland, of all its rights in mines and minerals, and of all the ungranted and unoccupied lands of the Crown, it is agreed that the sum of $150,000 shall each year be paid to that Province, by semi-annual payments ; provided that

---

[1] At the London Conference (See Note 1, p. 306) "an increased subsidy, in addition to the 80 cents per head, of $80,000, $70,000, $60,000 and $50,000 was made severally to Upper Canada, Lower Canada, Nova Scotia, and New Brunswick, and the capitation subsidy of 80 cents in both New Brunswick and Nova Scotia extended until the population reached 400,000." (Gray's "Confederation," p. 386)

that Colony shall retain the right of opening, constructing and controlling roads and bridges through any of the said lands, subject to any laws which the general Parliament may pass in respect of the same.[1]

67. All engagements that may, before the union, be entered into with the Imperial Government for the defence of the country, shall be assumed by the general Government.

68. The general Government shall secure, without delay, the completion of the Intercolonial Railway from Riviere du Loup, through New Brunswick, to Truro in Nova Scotia.[2]

69. The communications with the North-Western Territory, and the improvements required for the development of the trade of the great west with the seaboard, are regarded by this conference as subjects of the highest importance to the federated Provinces, and shall be prosecuted at the earliest possible period that the state of the finances will permit.

70. The sanction of the Imperial and local Parliaments shall be sought for the union of the Provinces, on the principles adopted by the Conference.

71. That Her Majesty the Queen be solicited to determine the rank and name of the federated Provinces.

72. The proceedings of the Conference shall be authenticated by the signatures of the delegates, and submitted by each delegation to its own Government; and the Chairman is authorized to submit a copy to the Governor General for transmission to the Secretary of State for the Colonies.

---

[1] For the "statement and figures" used in the Quebec Conference as a means of arriving at the financial settlement contained in resolutions 54 to 66 inclusive, see Appendix to Gray's "Confederation," pp. 398-405.

[2] The delegates to the London Conference agreed with the Imperial Government as to the terms on which a loan to the United Provinces of £3,000,000 stg. for the construction of the Intercolonial Railway should be guaranteed. In 1867, these terms were embodied in an Act of the Imperial Parliament (30 & 31 Vict. cap. 16).

APPENDIX G.

CONSTITUTION[1] OF THE UNITED STATES OF AMERICA.

WE the people of the United States, in order to form a more perfect union, establish justice, insure domestic tranquillity, provide for the common defence, promote the general welfare, and secure the blessings of liberty to ourselves and our posterity, do ordain and establish this Constitution for the United States of America.

ARTICLE I.

Section 1. All legislative powers herein granted shall be vested in a Congress of the United States, which shall consist of a Senate and House of Representatives.

Section 2. The House of Representatives shall be composed of members chosen every second year by the people of the several States, and the electors in each State shall have the qualifications requisite for electors of the most numerous branch of the State Legislature.

No person shall be a Representative who shall not have attained to the age of twenty-five years, and been seven years a citizen of the United States, and who shall not, when elected, be an inhabitant of that State in which he shall be chosen.

---

[1] This document is re-printed from the text in the "History of the origin, formation, and adoption of the Constitution of the United States," by George Ticknor Curtis; but it has been carefully compared with several other texts, and especially with the official one contained in Poore's "Federal and State constitutions, colonial charters, and other organic laws of the United States." Curtis states that his text " has been compared with the Rolls in the Department of State." It is the third great national document in the evolution of the United States, the first being the " Declaration of Independence " of July 4, 1776, and the second the " Articles of Confederation " of July 9, 1778. All three documents were prepared and promulgated at Philadelphia, the date of the Constitution being September 17, 1787. The history by Curtis above mentioned is still one of the best sources of information on the subject, and another is Bancroft's "History of the Constitution," which has been re-printed as vol vi. of the edition of his " History of the United States," published in 1886. A useful re-print of the Constitution will be found appended to Von Holst's " Constitutional Law of the United States," with references to the pages of the treatise on which the various topics are discussed, and to the author's great work on the history of the Constitution. Story's " Commentaries on the Constitution," Cooley's " Principles of Constitutional Law " and his " Constitutional Limitations," and Kent's " Constitutional Jurisprudence " (re-printed in 1889 as part of the " Blackstone " edition of his " Commentaries on American Law") are classical expositions of the law of the Constitution. Its practical operation has been described in Wilson's " Congressional Government," Von Holst's "Constitutional History," and Bryce's " American Commonwealth."

Representatives and direct taxes shall be apportioned among the several States which may be included within this Union, according to their respective numbers, which shall be determined by adding to the whole number of free persons, including those bound to service for a term of years, and excluding Indians not taxed, three-fifths of all other persons.[1] The actual enumeration shall be made within three years after the first meeting of the Congress of the United States, and within every subsequent term of ten years, in such manner as they shall by law direct. The number of Representatives shall not exceed one for every thirty thousand, but each State shall have at least one Representative; and until such enumeration shall be made, the State of New Hampshire shall be entitled to chuse three, Massachusetts eight, Rhode Island and Providence Plantations one, Connecticut five, New York six, New Jersey four, Pennsylvania eight, Delaware one, Maryland six, Virginia ten, North Carolina five, South Carolina five, and Georgia three.[2]

When vacancies happen in the representation from any State, the Executive authority thereof shall issue writs of election to fill such vacancies.

The House of Representatives shall chuse their Speaker[3] and other officers; and shall have the sole power of impeachment.

Section 3. The Senate of the United States shall be composed of two Senators from each State, chosen by the Legislature thereof, for six years; and each Senator shall have one vote.

Immediately after they shall be assembled in consequence of the first election, they shall be divided as equally as may be into three classes. The seats of the Senators of the first class shall be vacated at the expiration of the second year, of the second class at the expiration of the fourth year, and of the third class at the expiration of the sixth year, so that one-third may be chosen every second year; and if vacancies happen by resignation, or otherwise, during the recess of the Legislature of any State, the Executive thereof may make temporary appointments until the next meeting of the Legislature, which shall then fill such vacancies.

No person shall be a Senator who shall not have attained to the age of thirty years, and been nine years a citizen of the United States, and who shall not, when elected, be an inhabitant of that State for which he shall be chosen.

The Vice-President of the United States shall be President of the Senate, but shall have no vote, unless they be equally divided.

---

[1] The "other persons" here implied were the slaves. Compare the fourteenth amendment (p. 331 below) with this part of the above sentence: "Which shall be determined by adding to the whole number of free persons, including those bound to service for a term of years, and excluding Indians not taxed, three-fifths of all other persons."

[2] The 65 members allowed to the first Congress became 105 after the first census was taken, while the unit of representation rose from 30,000 to 33,000 at the same time.

[3] The law of the Constitution is silent as to the powers of the Speaker of the House of Representatives. As to the functions assigned to him in practice see Cushing's "Law and Practice of Legislative Assemblies," Wilson's "Congressional Government" (chapter ii.), and several articles in the *North American Review* for 1890.

The Senate shall chuse their other officers, and also a President pro tempore, in the absence of the Vice-President, or when he shall exercise the office of President of the United States.[1]

The Senate shall have the sole power to try all impeachments. When sitting for that purpose, they shall be on oath or affirmation. When the President of the United States is tried, the Chief Justice shall preside : And no person shall be convicted without the concurrence of two-thirds of the members present.[2]

Judgment in cases of impeachment shall not extend further than to removal from office, and disqualification to hold and enjoy any office of honour, trust or profit under the United States ; but the party convicted shall nevertheless be liable and subject to indictment, trial, judgment and punishment, according to law.

Section 4. The times, places and manner of holding elections for Senators and Representatives, shall be prescribed in each State by the Legislature thereof ; but the Congress may at any time by law make or alter such regulations, except as to the places of chusing Senators.

The Congress shall assemble at least once in every year, and such meeting shall be on the first Monday in December, unless they shall by law appoint a different day.

Section 5. Each House shall be the judge of the elections, returns, and qualifications of its own members, and a majority of each shall constitute a quorum to do business ; but a smaller number may adjourn from day to day, and may be authorized to compel the attendance of absent members, in such manner, and under such penalties, as each House may provide.

Each House may determine the rules of its proceedings, punish its members for disorderly behavior, and with the concurrence of two-thirds, expel a member.

Each House shall keep a journal of its proceedings, and from time to time publish the same, excepting such parts as may in their judgment require secrecy, and the yeas and nays of the members of either House on any question shall, at the desire of one-fifth of those present, be entered on the journal.

Neither House, during the session of Congress, shall, without the consent of the other, adjourn for more than three days, nor to any other place than that in which the two Houses shall be sitting.

---

[1] It has become the custom for the Vice-President to allow the Senate before the close of each session to appoint a president *pro tempore*, so that the organization of that body may not be affected during the recess by the death of either the President or the Vice-President.

[2] There have been five impeachments under the joint authority of this sub-section and the last sub-section of section 2, namely : (1) Of Senator William Blount, in 1799 ; (2) of Judge John Pickering, in 1803 ; (3) of Judge Samuel Chase, in 1804 ; (4) of Judge James H. Peck, in 1830 ; and (5) of President Andrew Johnson, in 1868. In the last case, the only one of impeachment of a President, Chief Justice Chase presided. A good account of the proceedings is to be found in Blaine's "Twenty Years of Congress," vol. II, chapter XIV., and in McCulloch's "Men and Measures of Half a Century," chapter XXVI. The vote stood 35 for conviction, and 19 for acquittal.

Section 6. The Senators and Representatives shall receive a compensation for their services, to be ascertained by law, and paid out of the treasury of the United States.[1] They shall in all cases except treason, felony, and breach of the peace, be privileged from arrest during their attendance at the session of their respective Houses, and in going and returning from the same; and for any speech or debate in either House, they shall not be questioned in any other place.

No Senator or Representative shall, during the time for which he was elected, be appointed to any civil office under the authority of the United States, which shall have been created, or the emoluments whereof shall have been increased during such time; and no person holding any office under the United States, shall be a member of either house during his continuance in office.[2]

Section 7. All bills for raising revenue shall originate in the House of Representatives; but the Senate may propose or concur with amendments as on other bills.[3]

Every bill which shall have passed the House of Representatives and the Senate, shall, before it becomes law, be presented to the President of the United States; if he approve he shall sign it, but if not he shall return[4] it, with his objections to that House in which it shall have originated, who shall enter the objections at large on their journal, and proceed to reconsider it. If after such reconsideration two-thirds of that House shall agree to pass the bill, it shall be sent, together with the objections, to the other House, by which it shall likewise be reconsidered, and if approved by two-thirds of that House, it shall become a law. But in all cases the votes of both Houses shall be determined by yeas and nays, and the names of the persons voting for and against the bill shall be entered on the journal of each House respectively. If any bill shall not be returned by the President within ten days (Sundays excepted) after it shall have been presented to him, the same shall be a law, in like manner as if he had signed it, unless the Congress by their adjournment prevent its return, in which case it shall not be a law.

Every order, resolution, or vote to which the concurrence of the Senate and House of Representatives may be necessary (except on a question of adjournment) shall be presented to the President of the United States; and before the same shall take effect, shall be approved by him, or being disapproved by him, shall be repassed by two-thirds of the Senate and House of Representatives, according to the rules and limitations prescribed in the case of a bill.

---

[1] Since July, 1866, the salary of a member of Congress has been $5,000 a year, except for a few months in 1873-74 when it was raised to $7,500. Public indignation caused a return almost immediately to the former amount. Each member is allowed 20 cents a mile for the journey to and from Washington.

[2] Compare this provision with sections 11, 41, 63, 64, 81, and 88 of the Confederation Act, 1867, and the documents in Appendix E, relating to responsible government (pp. 293-304 above).

[3] Under cover of the term "raising revenue," the House of Representatives has successfully asserted its exclusive right to initiate proposals to spend money.

[4] The word "veto," popularly used in connection with the President's action here specified, nowhere occurs in the constitution, and does not correctly describe his functions in the matter.

UNITED STATES CONSTITUTION. 321

Section 8. The Congress shall have power[1] to lay and collect taxes, duties, imposts and excises, to pay the debts and provide for the common defence and general welfare of the United States; but all duties, imposts and excises shall be uniform throughout the United States;

To borrow money on the credit of the United States;

To regulate commerce with foreign nations, and among the several States, and with the Indian tribes;

To establish an uniform rule of naturalization,[2] and uniform laws on the subject of bankruptcies throughout the United States;

To coin money, regulate the value thereof, and of foreign coin, and fix the standard of weights and measures;

To provide for the punishment of counterfeiting the securities and current coin of the United States;

To establish post offices and post roads;

To promote the progress of science and useful arts, by securing for limited times to authors and inventors the exclusive right to their respective writings[3] and discoveries[4];

To constitute tribunals inferior to the Supreme Court;

To define and punish piracies and felonies committed on the high seas, and offences against the laws of nations;

To declare war, grant letters of marque and reprisal, and make rules concerning captures on land and water;

To raise and support armies, but no appropriation of money to that use shall be for a longer term than two years[5];

To provide and maintain a navy;

To make rules for the government and regulation of the land and naval forces;

To provide for calling forth the militia to execute the laws of the Union, suppress insurrections and repel invasions;

To provide for organizing, arming, and disciplining the militia, and for governing such part of them as may be employed in the service of the United States, reserving to the States respectively, the appointment of the officers, and the authority of training the militia according to the discipline prescribed by Congress;

To exercise exclusive legislation in all cases whatsoever, over such district[6] (not exceeding ten miles square) as may, by cession of particular States, and the acceptance of Congress, become the seat of government of the United

---

[1] For an account of the manner in which this power has been exercised see Bolles' "Financial History of the United States" and Sumner's "History of American Currency."

[2] See Morse's "Treatise on Citizenship," and Sir Alexander Cockburn's "Nationality."

[3] See Morgan's "Law of Literature."

[4] See Walker's "Patent Laws of the United States," edition of 1889.

[5] Compare the statute passed annually by the British Parliament under the title of "An Act to provide, during twelve months for the discipline and regulation of the army."

[6] The District of Columbia, chosen for this purpose in June, 1790, belonged to Maryland and Virginia, 64 square miles having been ceded by the former and 36 by the latter.

States, and to exercise like authority over all places purchased by the consent of the legislature of the State in which the same shall be, for the erection of forts, magazines, arsenals, dock-yards, and other needful buildings ;—and

To make all laws which shall be necessary and proper for carrying into execution the foregoing powers, and all other powers vested by this Constitution in the Government of the United States, or in any department or officer thereof.

Section 9. The migration or importation of such persons as any of the States now existing shall think proper to admit, shall not be prohibited by the Congress prior to the year one thousand eight hundred and eight, but a tax or duty may be imposed on such importation, not exceeding ten dollars for each person.[1]

The privilege of the writ of habeas corpus shall not be suspended, unless when in cases of rebellion or invasion the public safety may require it.

No bill of attainder or ex post facto law shall be passed.

No capitation, or other direct tax shall be laid, unless in proportion to the census or enumeration hereinbefore directed to be taken.

No tax or duty shall be laid on articles exported from any State.[2]

No preference shall be given by any regulation of commerce or revenue to the ports of one State over those of another: nor shall vessels bound to, or from, one State, be obliged to enter, clear, or pay duties in another.

No money shall be drawn from the Treasury, but in consequence of appropriations made by law ; and a regular statement and account of the receipts and expenditures of all public money shall be published from time to time.

No title of nobility shall be granted by the United States : and no person holding any office of profit or trust under them, shall, without the consent of the Congress, accept of any present, emolument, office, or title, of any kind whatever, from any king, prince, or foreign State.

Section 10. No State shall enter into any treaty, alliance, or confederation ; grant letters of marque and reprisal ; coin money ; emit bills of credit ; make anything but gold and silver coin a tender in payment of debts ; pass any bill of attainder, ex post facto law, or law impairing the obligation of contracts, or grant any title of nobility.

No State shall, without the consent of the Congress, lay any imposts or duties on imports or exports, except what may be absolutely necessary for executing its inspection laws : and the net produce of all duties and imposts, laid by any State on imports or exports, shall be for the use of the Treasury of the United States ; and all such laws shall be subject to the revision and control of the Congress.

No State shall, without the consent of Congress, lay any duty of tonnage, keep troops, or ships of war in time of peace, enter into any agreement or compact with another State, or with a foreign power, or engage in war, unless actually invaded, or in such imminent danger as will not admit of delay.

[1] In the Convention which framed the Constitution a keen discussion took place on this sub-section, the first of many discussions on the question of slavery.

[2] Inserted in compliance with the demand of the delegates from the South as a measure of protection against adverse fiscal legislation.

ARTICLE II.

Section 1. The executive power shall be vested in a President of the United States of America. He shall hold his office during the term[1] of four years, and, together with the Vice-President, chosen for the same term, be elected, as follows :—

Each State shall appoint, in such manner as the Legislature thereof may direct, a number of Electors, equal to the whole number of Senators and Representatives to which the State may be entitled in the Congress : but no Senator or Representative, or Person holding an office of trust or profit under the United States, shall be appointed an Elector.

The Electors shall meet in their respective States, and vote by ballot for two persons, of whom one at least shall not be an inhabitant of the same State with themselves. And they shall make a list of all the persons voted for, and of the number of votes for each ; which list they shall sign and certify, and transmit sealed to the seat of the Government of the United States, directed to the President of the Senate. The President of the Senate shall, in the presence of the Senate and House of Representatives, open all certificates, and the votes shall then be counted. The person having the greatest number of votes shall be the President, if such number be a majority of the whole number of Electors appointed ; and if there be more than one who have such majority and have an equal number of votes, then the House of Representatives shall immediately chuse by ballot one of them for President ; and if no person have a majority, then from the five highest on the list the said house shall in like manner chuse the President. But in chusing the President, the votes shall be taken by States, the representation from each State having one vote ; a quorum for this purpose shall consist of a member or members from two-thirds of the States, and a majority of all the States shall be necessary to a choice. In every case, after the choice of the President, the person having the greatest number of votes of the Electors shall be the Vice-President. But if there should remain two or more who have equal votes, the Senate shall chuse from them by ballot the Vice-President.[2]

The Congress may determine the time of chusing the Electors, and the day on which they shall give their votes ; which day shall be the same throughout the United States.

No person except a natural born citizen, or a citizen of the United States at the time of the adoption of this Constitution, shall be eligible to the office of President ; neither shall any person be eligible to that office who shall not have attained to the age of thirty-five years, and been fourteen years a resident within the United States.

In case of the removal of the President from office, or of his death, resignation, or inability to discharge the powers and duties of the said office, the same

---

[1] For legislation fixing the beginning and end of the presidential term, the salaries of President and Vice-President, the time for the choice of electors, their number, the manner of filling vacancies, etc., see the Revised Statutes of the United States.

[2] This sub-section was subsequently repealed and replaced by Article XII. of the amendments to the Constitution (p. 329 below).

shall devolve on the Vice-President, and the Congress may by law provide for the case of removal, death, resignation, or inability, both of the President and Vice-President, declaring what officer shall then act as President, and such officer shall act accordingly, until the disability be removed, or a President shall be elected.[1]

The President shall, at stated times, receive for his services, a compensation, which shall neither be increased nor diminished during the period for which he shall have been elected, and he shall not receive within that period any other emolument from the United States, or any of them.

Before he enter on the execution of his office, he shall take the following oath or affirmation :—

" I do solemnly swear (or affirm) that I will faithfully execute the office of " President of the United States, and will to the best of my ability, preserve, " protect and defend the Constitution of the United States."

Section 2. The President shall be Commander in chief of the army and navy of the United States, and of the militia of the several States, when called into the actual service of the United States ; he may require the opinion, in writing, of the principal officer in each of the executive Departments, upon any subject relating to the duties of their respective offices, and he shall have power to grant reprieves and pardons for offences against the United States, except in cases of impeachment.

He shall have power, by and with the advice and consent of the Senate, to make treaties, provided two-thirds of the Senators present concur ; and he shall nominate, and by and with the advice and consent of the Senate, shall appoint, Ambassadors, other public Ministers and Consuls, Judges of the Supreme Court, and all other officers of the United States, whose appointments are not herein otherwise provided for, and which shall be established by law : but the Congress may by law vest the appointment of such inferior officers, as they think proper, in the President alone, in the courts of law, or in the heads of Departments.

The President shall have power to fill up all vacancies that may happen during the recess of the senate, by granting commissions which shall expire at the end of their next session.

Section 3. He shall from time to time give to the Congress information of the state of the Union, and recommend to their consideration such measures as he shall judge necessary and expedient ; he may, on extraordinary occasions, convene both Houses, or either of them, and in case of disagreement between them, with respect to the time of adjournment, he may adjourn them to such time as he shall think proper ; he shall receive Ambassadors and other public Ministers ; he shall take care that the laws be faithfully executed, and shall commission all the officers of the United States.

---

[1] It has been provided by Act of Congress that in the last resort the Speaker of the House of Representatives shall assume the duties of President, until a new President is elected.

Section 4. The President, Vice-President and all civil officers of the United States, shall be removed from office on impeachment for, and conviction of, treason, bribery, or other high crimes and misdemeanors.[1]

ARTICLE III.

Section 1. The judicial power of the United States shall be vested in one Supreme Court, and in such inferior courts as the Congress may from time to time ordain and establish. The judges, both of the Supreme and inferior courts, shall hold their offices during good behavior, and shall, at stated times, receive for their services a compensation which shall not be diminished during their continuance in office.[2]

Section 2. The judicial power shall extend to all cases, in law and equity, made, arising under this Constitution, the laws of the United States, and treaties or which shall be made, under their authority; to all cases affecting ambassadors, other public ministers, and consuls; to all cases of admiralty and maritime jurisdiction; to controversies to which the United States shall be a party; to controversies between two or more States, between a State and citizens of another State, between citizens of different States, between citizens of the same State claiming lands under grants of different States, and between a State, or the citizens thereof, and foreign States, citizens or subjects.

In all cases affecting ambassadors, other public ministers and consuls, and those in which a State shall be party, the Supreme Court shall have original jurisdiction. In all the other cases before mentioned, the Supreme Court shall have appellate jurisdiction, both as to law and fact; with such exceptions, and under such regulations as the Congress shall make.

The trial of all crimes, except in cases of impeachment, shall be by jury; and such trial shall be held in the State where the said crimes shall have been committed; but when not committed within any State, the trial shall be at such place or places as the Congress may by law have directed.

Section 3. Treason against the United States shall consist only in levying war against them, or in adhering to their enemies, giving them aid and comfort. No person shall be convicted of treason unless on the testimony of two witnesses to the same overt act, or on confession in open court.

The Congress shall have power to declare the punishment of treason, but no attainder of treason shall work corruption of blood or forfeiture except during the life of the person attainted.

---

[1] See Note 2, p. 319 above.

[2] In addition to the works enumerated in Note 1, p. 317 above, the student may usefully consult a monograph on "The Supreme Court of the United States," one of the John Hopkins historical studies, by W. W. Willoughby; and also "Constitutional History as seen in American Law," a course of lectures delivered by Judge Cooley and others before the Political Science Association of the University of Michigan, 1889. See also Curtis' "Jurisdiction, Practice, and Peculiar Jurisprudence of the Courts of the United States."

ARTICLE IV.

Section 1. Full faith and credit shall be given in each State to the public acts, records, and judicial proceedings of every other State. And the Congress may by general laws prescribe the manner in which such acts, records and proceedings shall be proved, and the effect thereof.

Section 2. The citizens of each State shall be entitled to all privileges and immunities of citizens in the several States.

A person charged in any State with treason, felony, or other crime, who shall flee from justice, and be found in another State, shall, on demand of the executive authority of the State from which he fled, be delivered up, to be removed to the State having jurisdiction of the crime.

No person held to service[1] or labor in one State, under the laws thereof, escaping into another, shall, in consequence of any law or regulation therein be discharged from such service or labor, but shall be delivered up on claim of the party to whom such service or labor may be due.

Section 3. New States may be admitted by the Congress into this Union; but no new State shall be formed or erected within the jurisdiction of any other State; nor any State be formed by the junction of two or more States, or parts of States, without the consent of the Legislatures of the States concerned as well as of the Congress.

The Congress shall have power to dispose of and make all needful rules and regulations respecting the territory or other property belonging to the United States; and nothing in this Constitution shall be so construed as to prejudice any claims of the United States, or of any particular State.

Section 4. The United States shall guarantee to every State in this Union a republican form of government, and shall protect each of them against invasion, and on application of the Legislature, or of the Executive, (when the Legislature cannot be convened,) against domestic violence.

ARTICLE V.

The Congress, whenever two-thirds of both Houses shall deem it necessary, shall propose amendments to this Constitution, or, on the application of the Legislatures of two-thirds of the several States, shall call a Convention for proposing amendments, which in either case, shall be valid to all intents and purposes, as part of this Constitution, when ratified by the Legislatures of three-fourths of the several States, or by Conventions in three-fourths thereof, as the one or the other mode of ratification may be proposed by the Congress; provided that no amendment which may be made prior to the year one thousand eight hundred and eight, shall in any manner affect the first and

---

[1] The term "service" in this sub-section was, according to Madison, substituted for "servitude" in the original draft.

fourth clauses in the ninth section of the first article; and that no State, without its consent, shall be deprived of its equal suffrage in the Senate.[1]

ARTICLE VI.

All debts contracted and engagements entered into, before the adoption of this Constitution, shall be as valid against the United States under this Constitution, as under the Confederation.

This Constitution, and the laws of the United States which shall be made in pursuance thereof, and all treaties made, or which shall be made, under the authority of the United States, shall be the supreme law of the land; and the judges in every State shall be bound thereby, anything in the Constitution or laws of any State to the contrary notwithstanding.

The Senators and Representatives before mentioned, and the members of the several State Legislatures, and all executive and judicial officers, both of the United States and of the several States, shall be bound by oath or affirmation, to support this Constitution; but no religious test shall ever be required as a qualification to any office or public trust under the United States.

ARTICLE VII.

The ratification of the conventions of nine States shall be sufficient for the establishment of this Constitution between the States so ratifying the same.[2]

Done in Convention by the unanimous consent of the States present the seventeenth day of September in the year of our Lord one thousand seven hundred and eighty-seven[3] and of the independence of the United States of America the twelfth. In witness whereof we have hereunto subscribed our names.[4]

GO. WASHINGTON—
Presidt and deputy from Virginia.

[1] Randolph and Mason, of Virginia, and Gerry of Massachusetts, refused to sign the Constitution because no provision was made for allowing State Conventions to offer amendments which should be submitted to and finally decided by another general Convention, before the Constitution was adopted. Under this article as it stands the first Congress, on the 25th of September, 1789, proposed to the Legislatures of the several states the first ten of the "Amendments" given below, which were ratified by more than the necessary three-fouths of the States. The other five amendments were adopted at later dates. See Notes on pp. 329-332 below.

[2] The date fixed for the beginning of the operations of Government under the new Constitution was March 4, 1789, and by that day it had been ratified by Conventions chosen for that purpose in Delaware, Pennsylvania, New Jersey, Georgia, Connecticut, Massachusetts, Maryland, South Carolina, New Hampshire, Virginia, and New York. This was two states more than the necessary number, and North Carolina and Rhode Island, all that were left of the original 13, ratified it a few months afterwards. Vermont, after having in Convention ratified the Constitution, was in 1791, by Act of Congress, admitted into the Union "as a new and entire member of the United States." The old Congress in September, 1788, declared that the Constitution had been duly ratified, and set dates for the election of President and the assembling of the first Constitutional Congress.

[3] The Convention on the same date drew up resolutions intimating to Congress the mode in which the new constitutional machinery should be put in operation.

[4] The Constitution was signed by 38 "deputies" besides Washington, and by the Secretary as a witness. At Franklin's suggestion the formula of subscription adopted was that the Constitution had received "the unanimous consent of the States present." Hamilton wrote the names of the States in geographical order on the parchment, but his own signature was inserted in a peculiar way. Curtis in his "History of the Constitution" says that "New York was not regarded as officially present; but in order that the proceedings might have all the weight that a name of so much importance could give to them, in the place that should have been filled by this State was recited the name of 'Mr. Hamilton of New York.'"

AMENDMENTS[1] OF THE CONSTITUTION.

ARTICLE I.

Congress shall make no law respecting an establishment of religion, or prohibiting the free exercise thereof; or abridging the freedom of speech, or of the press; or the right of the people peaceably to assemble, and to petition the Government for a redress of grievances.[2]

ARTICLE II.

A well regulated militia being necessary to the security of a free State, the right of the people to keep and bear arms shall not be infringed.

ARTICLE III.

No soldier shall, in time of peace, be quartered in any house, without the consent of the owner, nor in time of war, but in a manner to be prescribed by law.

ARTICLE IV.

The right of the people to be secure in their persons, houses, papers, and effects, against unreasonable searches and seizures, shall not be violated, and no warrants shall issue, but upon probable cause, supported by oath or affirmation, and particularly describing the place to be searched, and the persons or things to be seized.

ARTICLE V.

No person shall be held to answer for a capital, or otherwise infamous crime, unless on a presentment or indictment of a grand jury, except in cases arising in the land or naval forces, or in the militia, when in actual service in time of war or public danger; nor shall any person be subject for the same offence to be twice put in jeopardy of life or limb; nor shall be compelled in any criminal case to be a witness against himself, nor be deprived of life, liberty, or property, without due process of law; nor shall private property be taken for public use, without just compensation.

---

[1] The official title of this document is "Articles in addition to, and amendment of, the Constitution of the United States of America, proposed by Congress, and ratified by the Legislatures of the several states, pursuant to the fifth Article of the original Constitution."

[2] The first ten of these Articles were "proposed" by the first Congress in 1789, and were between that year and 1791 ratified by the following States: New Jersey, Maryland, North Carolina, South Carolina, New Hampshire, Delaware, Pennsylvania, New York, Rhode Island, Vermont, and Virginia. Poore ("Federal and States Constitutions") states that "there is no evidence on the journals of Congress that the Legislatures of Connecticut, Georgia, and Massachusetts ratified them." Some of the amendments were suggested by States which would have preferred to modify parts of the original Constitution had it been open to them to do so.

UNITED STATES CONSTITUTION.

ARTICLE VI.

In all criminal prosecutions, the accused shall enjoy the right to a speedy and public trial, by an impartial jury of the State and district wherein the crime shall have been committed, which district shall have been previously ascertained by law, and to be informed of the nature and cause of the accusation ; to be confronted with the witnesses against him ; to have compulsory process for obtaining witnesses in his favor, and to have the assistance of counsel for his defence.

ARTICLE VII.

In suits at common law, where the value in controversy shall exceed twenty dollars, the right of trial by jury shall be preserved, and no fact tried by a jury shall be otherwise re-examined in any court of the United States, than according to the rules of the common law.

ARTICLE VIII.

Excessive bail shall not be required, nor excessive fines imposed, nor cruel and unusual punishments inflicted.

ARTICLE IX.

The enumeration in the Constitution, of certain rights, shall not be construed to deny or disparage others retained by the people.

ARTICLE X.

The powers not delegated to the United States by the Constitution, nor prohibited by it to the States, are reserved to the States respectively, or to the people.

ARTICLE XI.

The judicial power of the United States shall not be construed to extend to any suit in law or equity, commenced or prosecuted against one of the United States by citizens of another State, or by citizens or subjects of any foreign State.[1]

ARTICLE XII.

The electors shall meet in their respective States and vote by ballot for President and Vice President, one of whom, at least, shall not be an inhabitant of the same State with themselves ; they shall name in their ballots the person voted for as President, and in distinct ballots the person voted for as Vice President, and they shall make distinct lists of all persons voted for as President, and of all persons voted for as Vice President, and of the number of votes for each ; which lists they shall sign and certify, and transmit sealed to the seat of government of the United States, directed to the President of the Senate. The President of the Senate shall, in the presence of the Senate and House of Representatives, open all the certificates and the votes shall then be counted ; the person having the greatest number of votes for President, shall be the President, if such number be a majority of the whole number of electors appointed ; and if no person have such majority, then

---

[1] The eleventh amendment was "proposed" by the third Congress to the State Legislatures in 1794. Three-fourths of the states ratified it between that year and 1798.

from the persons having the highest numbers not exceeding three on the list of those voted for as President, the House of Representatives shall choose immediately, by ballot, the President. But in choosing the President, the votes shall be taken by States, the representation from each State having one vote ; a quorum for this purpose shall consist of a member or members from two-thirds of the States, and a majority of all the States shall be necessary to a choice. And if the House of Representatives shall not choose a President whenever the right of choice shall devolve upon them, before the fourth day of March, next following, then the Vice-President shall act as President, as in the case of the death or other constitutional disability of the President.

The person having the greatest number of votes as Vice-President shall be the Vice-President, if such number be a majority of the whole number of electors appointed ; and if no person have a majority, then from the two highest numbers on the list the Senate shall choose the Vice-President; a quorum for the purpose shall consist of two-thirds of the whole number of Senators, and a majority of the whole number shall be necessary to a choice. But no person constitutionally ineligible to the office of President shall be eligible to that of Vice-President of the United States.[1]

ARTICLE XIII.

Section 1. Neither slavery nor involuntary servitude, except as a punishment for crime whereof the party shall have been duly convicted, shall exist within the United States, or any place subject to their jurisdiction.

Section 2. Congress shall have power to enforce this article by appropriate legislation.[2]

[1] The twelfth amendment was proposed by the eighth Congress in 1803, and in 1804 was declared to have been ratified by all the states except New Hampshire, Massachusetts, Connecticut, and Delaware. It took the place of the original third sub-section of the first section of Article II. (p. 323 above). Under that sub-section each "elector" was required to vote for two persons without designating them as "President" and "Vice-President" respectively, the candidate receiving the largest number of votes, if that were a majority of the whole, to be President, and the candidate receiving the next largest to be Vice-President. In 1800 Thomas Jefferson and Aaron Burr, the candidates of what was then called the "Republican" party, received 73 electoral votes each, and John Adams 65. Jefferson had been his party's candidate for the Presidency, but his political opponents endeavoured to defeat him by voting for Burr in the House of Representatives, which had the election in its hands. Thirty-six ballots were taken before this scheme was finally defeated and Jefferson elected, and the twelfth amendment was adopted to prevent the recurrence of so dangerous a crisis. The Hayes-Tilden contest in 1876 developed a crisis of a different kind, which was met by a temporary device instead of a constitutional amendment (see McCulloch's "Men and Measures of Half a Century," chap. xxvi.; and Blaine's "Twenty Years of Congress," chap. xxv).

[2] The thirteenth amendment was "proposed" early in 1865 by the thirty-eighth Congress, and before the end of that year was officially declared to have been ratified by 27 of the then 36 states, namely: Illinois, Rhode Island, Michigan, Maryland, New York, West Virginia, Maine, Kansas, Massachusetts, Pensylvania, Virginia, Ohio, Missouri, Nevada, Indiana, Louisiana, Minnesota, Wisconsin, Vermont, Tennessee, Arkansas, Connecticut, New Hampshire, South Carolina, Alabama, North Carolina, and Georgia. The States of New Jersey, Oregon, California, Iowa, and Florida ratified the amendment after the official declaration of its adoption. Mississippi, Kentucky, Delaware, and Texas took no action. This amendment was the natural sequel to President Lincoln's "Emancipation Proclamation," which was issued on the 22nd of September, 1862, to take effect a hundred days later, on the first of January, 1863. For a full account of the Congressional proceedings connected with the amendment see Blaine's "Twenty Years of Congress" (vol. I., chapters xxiv.-xxv.).

ARTICLE XIV.

Section 1. All persons born or naturalized in the United States, and subject to the jurisdiction thereof, are citizens of the United States and of the State wherein they reside. No State shall make or enforce any law which shall abridge the privileges or immunities of citizens of the United States; nor shall any State deprive any person of life, liberty, or property, without due process of law; nor deny to any person within its jurisdiction the equal protection of the laws.

Section 2. Representatives shall be apportioned among the several States according to their respective numbers, counting the whole number of persons in each State, excluding Indians not taxed. But when the right to vote at any election for the choice of electors for President and Vice-President of the United States, Representatives in Congress, the executive and judicial officers of a State, or the members of the legislature thereof, is denied to any of the male inhabitants of such State, being twenty-one years of age, and citizens of the United States, or in any way abridged, except for participation in rebellion, or other crime, the basis of representation therein shall be reduced in the proportion which the number of such male citizens shall bear to the whole number of male citizens twenty-one years of age in such State.[1]

Section 3. No person shall be a Senator or Representative in Congress, or elector of President and Vice-President, or hold any office, civil or military, under the United States, or under any State, who, having previously taken an oath, as a member of Congress, or as an officer of the United States, or as a member of any State legislature, or as an executive or judicial officer of any State, to support the Constitution of the United States, shall have engaged in insurrection or rebellion against the same, or given aid or comfort to the enemies thereof. But Congress may, by a vote of two-thirds of each house, remove such disability.

Section 4. The validity of the public debt of the United States, authorized by law, including debts incurred for payment of pensions and bounties for services in suppressing insurrection or rebellion, shall not be questioned. But neither the United States nor any State shall assume or pay any debt or obligation incurred in aid of insurrection or rebellion against the United States, or any claim for the loss or emancipation of any slave; but all such debts, obligations and claims shall be held illegal and void.

Section 5. The Congress shall have power to enforce, by appropriate legislation, the provisions of this article.[2]

---

[1] Compare this sub-section with the third sub-section of the second section of Article I. of the Constitution (p. 318 above).

[2] The fourteenth amendment was "proposed" by the thirty-ninth Congress in June, 1866. In July, 1868, it was formally declared to have been ratified by 30 of the 37 states, namely: Connecticut, New Hampshire, Tennessee, New Jersey, Oregon, Vermont, Georgia, North Carolina, South Carolina, New York, Ohio, Illinois, West Virginia, Kansas, Maine Nevada, Missouri, Indiana, Minnesota, Rhode Island, Wisconsin, Pennsylvania, Michigan, Massachusetts, Nebraska, Iowa, Arkansas, Florida, Louisiana, Alabama. Of these states New Jersey and Ohio withdrew their consent before the declaration of 1868. Georgia, North Carolina, and South Carolina rejected the amendment and afterwards ratified it. Delaware, Kentucky, California, and Maryland rejected it conclusively. Mississippi,

ARTICLE XV.

Section 1. The right of citizens of the United States to vote shall not be denied or abridged by the United States or by any State on account of race, color, or previous condition of servitude.

Section 2. The Congress shall have power to enforce this article by appropriate legislation.[1]

Texas, and Virginia do not appear to have taken any action. Secretary Seward in his certificate, on which the President's proclamation of the amendment is based, declines to recognize the right of Ohio and New Jersey to withdraw consent once regularly given. The text of these documents is given in Macpherson's "History of the Reconstruction," pp. 379-380. The object of the amendment was to secure for the recently emancipated slaves the exercise of the political franchise, and the states then recently in rebellion were constrained to accept the amendment as the price of their own representation in Congress. See Blaine's "Twenty Years of Congress," vol. II., chapter ix.

[1] The fifteenth amendment was "proposed" in February, 1869, by the fortieth Congress to the State Legislatures, and was formally declared in March, 1870, to have been ratified by 29 of the 37 states. The assenting states were: West Virginia, North Carolina, Massachusetts, Wisconsin, Maine, Louisiana, Michigan, South Carolina, Pennsylvania, Arkansas, Connecticut, Florida, Illinois, Indiana, New York, New Hampshire, Nevada, Vermont, Virginia, Alabama, Missouri, Mississppi, Ohio, Iowa, Kansas, Minnesota, Rhode Island, Nebraska, Texas. The dissenting states were: Delaware, Kentucky, California Maryland, New Jersey, all of which rejected the amendment, Tennessee, in which one House rejected the amendment and the other shelved it and Oregon, from which no action was reported. New York withdrew her assent, but the withdrawal, as before (see note 2, p. 331 above), was not recognized. Ohio first rejected and afterwards ratified the amendment and was counted affirmatively. Georgia ratified it, but too late to be counted in the proclamation. For proceedings in Congress and the various State Legislatures see Macpherson's "History of the Reconstruction" (pp. 399-406, 488-498, 557-562, 545-72). See also Blaine's "Twenty Years of Congress," vol. II., chapter xvi.

www.ingramcontent.com/pod-product-compliance
Lightning Source LLC
Chambersburg PA
CBHW032353230426
43672CB00007B/685